OVERCOMING THE ODDS

OVERCOMING THE ODDS

THE BENEFITS OF COMPLETING COLLEGE FOR UNLIKELY GRADUATES

Jennie E. Brand

Russell Sage Foundation • New York

Library of Congress Cataloging-in-Publication Data

Names: Brand, Jennie E., author.
Title: Overcoming the odds : the benefits of completing college for unlikely graduates / Jennie E. Brand.
Description: New York : Russell Sage Foundation, [2023] | Series: The American sociological association's rose series in sociology | Includes bibliographical references and index. | Summary: "Debates about college access often do not carefully consider what is required to speak knowledgeably about the benefits of college degrees. First, we want to know what an individual's life would look like without a college education. Second, we need to consider unequal access to higher education. Who attends and completes college, and who does not? Third, we need to determine which benefits of college we consider and how diverse benefits differ across diverse graduates. Too often, the rewards valued in public and academic debate begin and end with wages. The traditional focus on wages does not capture all the life-enhancing effects of higher education. In this book, Jennie Brand assesses how a range of long-term benefits of four-year college degree completion differs across the population. Considering socioeconomic, family-level, social assistance, and civic outcomes measures, she concludes that colleges are far from failing disadvantaged students. Their returns to degrees are substantial: a college degree not only enables underprivileged students to circumvent unemployment, low-wage work, job instability, poverty, and social assistance but also increases their likelihood of engaging in civic society"—Provided by publisher.
Identifiers: LCCN 2023011119 (print) | LCCN 2023011120 (ebook) | ISBN 9780871540089 (paperback) | ISBN 9781610448932 (ebook)
Subjects: LCSH: Education, Higher—Social aspects. | College choice—Economic aspects. | Universities and colleges—Admission. | Youth with social disabilities—Education, Higher. | Educational equalization.
Classification: LCC LC191.9 .B75 2023 (print) | LCC LC191.9 (ebook) | DDC 378--dc23/eng/20230426
LC record available at https://lccn.loc.gov/2023011119
LC ebook record available at https://lccn.loc.gov/2023011120

The paper used in this publication meets the minimum requirements of American National Standard for Information Sciences—Permanence of Paper for Printed Library Materials. ANSI Z39.48-1992.

Text design by Suzanne Nichols.

RUSSELL SAGE FOUNDATION
112 East 64th Street, New York, New York 10065
10 9 8 7 6 5 4 3 2 1

The Russell Sage Foundation

The Russell Sage Foundation, one of the oldest of America's general purpose foundations, was established in 1907 by Mrs. Margaret Olivia Sage for "the improvement of social and living conditions in the United States." The foundation seeks to fulfill this mandate by fostering the development and dissemination of knowledge about the country's political, social, and economic problems. While the foundation endeavors to assure the accuracy and objectivity of each book it publishes, the conclusions and interpretations in Russell Sage Foundation publications are those of the authors and not of the foundation, its trustees, or its staff. Publication by Russell Sage, therefore, does not imply foundation endorsement.

Previous Volumes in the Series

American Memories: Atrocities and the Law
Joachim J. Savelsberg and Ryan D. King

America's Newcomers and the Dynamics of Diversity
Frank D. Bean and Gillian Stevens

Beyond the Boycott: Labor Rights, Human Rights, and Transnational Activism
Gay W. Seidman

Beyond College for All: Career Paths for the Forgotten Half
James E. Rosenbaum

Changing Rhythms of the American Family
Suzanne M. Bianchi, John Robinson, and Melissa Milkie

Collateral Damages: Landlords and the Urban Housing Crisis
Meredith J. Greif

The Company We Keep: Interracial Friendships and Romantic Relationships from Adolescence to Adulthood
Grace Kao, Kara Joyner, and Kelly Stamper Balistreri

Counted Out: Same-Sex Relations and Americans' Definitions of Family
Brian Powell, Lala Carr Steelman, Catherine Bolzendahl, and Claudi Giest

Divergent Social Worlds: Neighborhood Crime and the Racial-Spatial Divide
Ruth D. Peterson and Lauren J. Krivo

Egalitarian Capitalism: Jobs, Incomes, and Growth in Affluent Countries
Lane Kenworthy

Ethnic Origins: History, Politics, Culture, and the Adaptation of Cambodian and Hmong Refugees in Four American Cities
Jeremy Hein

Family Consequences of Children's Disabilities
Denis Hogan

Golden Years? Social Inequality in Later Life
Deborah Carr

Good Jobs, Bad Jobs: The Rise of Polarized and Precarious Employment Systems in the United States, 1970s to 2000s
Arne L. Kalleberg

The Long Shadow: Family Background, Disadvantaged Urban Youth, and the Transition to Adulthood
Karl Alexander, Doris Entwisle, and Linda Olson

Making Hate a Crime: From Social Movement to Law Enforcement
Valerie Jenness and Ryken Grattet

Market Friendly or Family Friendly? The State and Gender Inequality in Old Age
Madonna Harrington Meyer and Pamela Herd

Nurturing Dads: Social Initiatives for Contemporary Fatherhood
William Marsiglio and Kevin Roy

Passing the Torch: Does Higher Education for the Disadvantaged Pay Off across the Generations?
Paul Attewell and David Lavin

Pension Puzzles: Social Security and the Great Debate
Melissa Hardy and Lawrence Hazelrigg

A Pound of Flesh: Monetary Sanctions as Punishment for the Poor
Alexes Harris

Sites Unseen: Uncovering Hidden Hazards in American Cities
Scott Frickel and James R. Elliott

Social Movements in the World-System: The Politics of Crisis and Transformation
Dawn Wiest and Jackie Smith

They Say Cut Back, We Say Fight Back! Welfare Activism in an Era of Retrenchment
Ellen Reese

Trust in Schools: A Core Resource for Improvement
Anthony S. Bryk and Barbara Schneider

Forthcoming Titles

Chains of Discrimination
Reginald A. Byron and Vincent. J. Roscigno

The Great Dispersion: Geography, Diversity, and Opportunity among Hispanics in the United States
Emilio A. Parrado and Chenoa A. Flippen

Horatio Alger Lives in Brooklyn, but Check His Papers
Robert C. Smith

Immigrant Growth Machines: Urban Growth Politics in Koreatown and Monterey Park
Angie Y. Chung and Jan Lin

The Journey to Adulthood in Uncertain Times
Robert Crosnoe and Shannon E. Cavanagh

Learning to Lead: The Intersectional Politics of the Second Generation
Veronica Terriquez

The Rose Series in Sociology

The American Sociological Association's Rose Series in Sociology publishes books that integrate knowledge and address controversies from a sociological perspective. Books in the Rose Series are at the forefront of sociological knowledge. They are lively and often involve timely and fundamental issues on significant social concerns. The series is intended for broad dissemination throughout sociology, across social science and other professional communities, and to policy audiences. The series was established in 1967 by a bequest to ASA from Arnold and Caroline Rose to support innovations in scholarly publishing.

Contents

	List of Illustrations	xiii
	About the Author	xxi
	Acknowledgments	xxiii
Chapter 1	Expanding Access to Higher Education	1
Chapter 2	Diverse Benefits for Diverse Graduates	22
Chapter 3	College Counterfactuals and Estimating Effects	41
Chapter 4	Unequal College Chances	70
Chapter 5	Cultivating Privilege and Circumventing Precarity	98
Chapter 6	Forming Families and Preventing Poverty	130
Chapter 7	Reducing Social Assistance	157
Chapter 8	Engaging in Civic Society	174
Chapter 9	Inequality and Investment	191
	Notes	213
	References	255
	Index	291

Illustrations

Figures

Figure 1.1 High School and Four-Year College Completion Rates, 1940–2020 7
Figure 1.2 Diverse Benefits of College Completion 20
Figure 2.1 College Completion as an Equalizer and Variation in College Completion Effects 31
Figure 3.1 How Counterfactuals Differ across Social Origins: Chantelle and Nancy 53
Figure 3.2 Four-Year College Completion Effects 56
Figure 3.3 Common Support in Matching 59
Figure 4.1 The O-E-D Triangle: The Effects of Socioeconomic Origins (O) and Education (E) on Socioeconomic Destinations (D) 71
Figure 4.2 College Attendance and Completion by Selected Characteristics: NLSY79 76
Figure 4.3 College Attendance and Completion by Selected Characteristics: NLSY97 77
Figure 4.4 Parental Income Distribution by Four-Year College Completion Likelihood: NLSY79 89
Figure 4.5 Parental Income Distribution by Four-Year College Completion Likelihood: NLSY97 90
Figure 4.6 Mother's Education Distribution by Four-Year College Completion Likelihood: NLSY79 91
Figure 4.7 Mother's Education Distribution by Four-Year College Completion Likelihood: NLSY97 92
Figure 4.8 Racial and Ethnic Distribution by Four-Year College Completion Likelihood: NLSY79 93
Figure 4.9 Racial and Ethnic Distribution by Four-Year College Completion Likelihood: NLSY97 94
Figure 4.10 Test Score Distribution by Four-Year College Completion Likelihood: NLSY79 95

Figure 4.11 Test Score Distribution by Four-Year College Completion Likelihood: NLSY97 96
Figure 5.1 Effects of Four-Year College Completion on (Log) Wages by College Completion Likelihood: NLSY79 107
Figure 5.2 Effects of Four-Year College Completion on (Log) Wages by College Completion Likelihood: NLSY97 108
Figure 5.3(a) Effects of Four-Year College Completion on Unemployment and Not in the Labor Force (NILF) by College Completion Likelihood (y-Axis Reversed): NLSY79 111
Figure 5.3(b) Effects of Four-Year College Completion on Low-Wage and Low-Skilled Work by College Completion Likelihood (y-Axis Reversed): NLSY79 112
Figure 5.3(c) Effects of Four-Year College Completion on Job Instability by College Completion Likelihood: NLSY79 112
Figure 5.4(a) Effects of Four-Year College Completion on Unemployment and Not in the Labor Force (NILF) by College Completion Likelihood (y-Axis Reversed): NLSY97 113
Figure 5.4(b) Effects of Four-Year College Completion on Low-Wage and Low-Skilled Work by College Completion Likelihood (y-Axis Reversed): NLSY97 114
Figure 5.4(c) Effects of Four-Year College Completion on Job Loss during the COVID-19 Pandemic by College Completion Likelihood: NLSY97 115
Figure 5.5(a) Levels of Wages and Effects of Four-Year College Completion on Wages by College Completion Likelihood: NLSY79 119
Figure 5.5(b) Levels of Unemployment and Effects of Four-Year College Completion on Unemployment by College Completion Likelihood (y-Axis Reversed): NLSY79 121
Figure 5.5(c) Levels of Not in the Labor Force (NILF) and Effects of Four-Year College Completion on NILF by College Completion Likelihood (y-Axis Reversed): NLSY79 122
Figure 5.5(d) Levels of Low-Wage Work and Effects of Four-Year College Completion on Low-Wage Work by College Completion Likelihood (y-Axis Reversed): NLSY79 122

Figure 5.5(e)	Levels of Low-Skilled Work and Effects of Four-Year College Completion on Low-Skilled Work by College Completion Likelihood (y-Axis Reversed): NLSY79	123
Figure 5.5(f)	Levels of Job Instability and Effects of Four-Year College Completion on Job Instability by College Completion Likelihood (y-Axis Reversed): NLSY79	124
Figure 5.6(a)	Levels of (Log) Wages and Effects of Four-Year College Completion on (Log) Wages by College Completion Likelihood: NLSY97	125
Figure 5.6(b)	Levels of Unemployment and Effects of Four-Year College Completion on Unemployment by College Completion Likelihood (y-Axis Reversed): NLSY97	125
Figure 5.6(c)	Levels of Not in the Labor Force (NILF) and Effects of Four-Year College Completion on NILF by College Completion Likelihood (y-Axis Reversed): NLSY97	126
Figure 5.6(d)	Levels of Low-Wage Work and Effects of Four-Year College Completion on Low-Wage Work by College Completion Likelihood (y-Axis Reversed): NLSY97	126
Figure 5.6(e)	Levels of Low-Skilled Work and Effects of Four-Year College Completion on Low-Skilled Work by College Completion Likelihood (y-Axis Reversed): NLSY97	127
Figure 5.6(f)	Levels of Job Loss during the COVID-19 Pandemic and Effects of Four-Year College Completion on Job Loss during the Pandemic by College Completion Likelihood (y-Axis Reversed): NLSY97	127
Figure 6.1	Effects of Four-Year College Completion on (Log) Household Income and Family Poverty by College Completion Likelihood: NLSY79	139
Figure 6.2	Effects of Four-Year College Completion on (Log) Household Income and Family Poverty by College Completion Likelihood: NLSY97	141
Figure 6.3	Effects of Four-Year College Completion on Family Formation by College Completion Likelihood: NLSY79	145
Figure 6.4	Effects of Four-Year College Completion on Family Formation by College Completion Likelihood: NLSY97	146

Figure 6.5(a) Levels of (Log) Household Income and Effects of Four-Year College Completion on (Log) Household Income by College Completion Likelihood: NLSY79 148

Figure 6.5(b) Levels of Family Poverty and Effects of Four-Year College Completion on Family Poverty by College Completion Likelihood (y-Axis Reversed): NLSY79 148

Figure 6.5(c) Levels of Family Poverty and Effects of Four-Year College Completion on Family Poverty by College Completion Likelihood (y-Axis Reversed): NLSY79 149

Figure 6.5(d) Levels of Marriage and Effects of Four-Year College Completion on Marriage by College Completion Likelihood: NLSY79 151

Figure 6.5(e) Levels of Spouse with High-Skilled Work and Effects of Four-Year College Completion on Spouse with High-Skilled Work by College Completion Likelihood: NLSY79 151

Figure 6.5(f) Levels of Single Parenthood and Effects of Four-Year College Completion on Single Parenthood by College Completion Likelihood (y-Axis Reversed): NLSY79 152

Figure 6.6(a) Levels of (Log) Household Income and Effects of Four-Year College Completion on (Log) Household Income by College Completion Likelihood: NLSY97 153

Figure 6.6(b) Levels of Poverty and Effects of Four-Year College Completion on Poverty by College Completion Likelihood (y-Axis Reversed): NLSY97 153

Figure 6.6(c) Levels of Poverty and Effects of Four-Year College Completion on Poverty by College Completion Likelihood (y-Axis Reversed): NLSY97 154

Figure 6.6(d) Levels of Marriage and Effects of Four-Year College Completion on Marriage by College Completion Likelihood: NLSY97 154

Figure 6.6(e) Levels of Single Parenthood and Effects of Four-Year College Completion on Single Parenthood by College Completion Likelihood (y-Axis Reversed): NLSY97 155

Figure 7.1(a)	Effects of Four-Year College Completion on Social Assistance by College Completion Likelihood (y-Axis Reversed): NLSY79	162
Figure 7.1(b)	Effects of Four-Year College Completion on Social Assistance by College Completion Likelihood (y-Axis Reversed): NLSY79	163
Figure 7.2	Effects of Four-Year College Completion on Social Assistance by College Completion Likelihood (y-Axis Reversed): NLSY97	164
Figure 7.3(a)	Levels of Social Assistance and Effects of Four-Year College Completion on Social Assistance by College Completion Likelihood (y-Axis Reversed): NLSY79	167
Figure 7.3(b)	Levels of AFDC/TANF Receipt and Effects of Four-Year College Completion on AFDC/TANF Receipt by College Completion Likelihood (y-Axis Reversed): NLSY79	167
Figure 7.3(c)	Levels of SNAP Receipt and Effects of Four-Year College Completion on SNAP Receipt by College Completion Likelihood (y-Axis Reversed): NLSY79	168
Figure 7.3(d)	Levels of SSI Receipt and Effects of Four-Year College Completion on SSI Receipt by College Completion Likelihood (y-Axis Reversed): NLSY79	169
Figure 7.3(e)	Levels of UI Receipt and Effects of Four-Year College Completion on UI Receipt by College Completion Likelihood (y-Axis Reversed): NLSY79	169
Figure 7.3(f)	Levels of Social Assistance and Effects of Four-Year College Completion on Social Assistance by College Completion Likelihood (y-Axis Reversed): NLSY79	170
Figure 7.4(a)	Levels of Social Assistance and Effects of Four-Year College Completion on Social Assistance by College Completion Likelihood (y-Axis Reversed): NLSY97	171
Figure 7.4(b)	Levels of TANF Receipt and Effects of Four-Year College Completion on TANF Receipt by College Completion Likelihood (y-Axis Reversed): NLSY97	171

Figure 7.4(c) Levels of SNAP/WIC Receipt and Effects of Four-Year College Completion on SNAP/WIC Receipt by College Completion Likelihood (y-Axis Reversed): NLSY97 172
Figure 7.4(d) Levels of SSI Receipt and Effects of Four-Year College Completion on SSI Receipt by College Completion Likelihood (y-Axis Reversed): NLSY97 172
Figure 8.1(a) Effects of Four-Year College Completion on Volunteering by College Completion Likelihood: NLSY79 181
Figure 8.1(b) Effects of Four-Year College Completion on Voting and Trust in Government by College Completion Likelihood: NLSY79 182
Figure 8.2 Effects of Four-Year College Completion on Volunteering and Voting by College Completion Likelihood (y-Axis Reversed): NLSY97 183
Figure 8.3(a) Levels of Volunteering and Effects of Four-Year College Completion on Volunteering by College Completion Likelihood: NLSY79 185
Figure 8.3(b) Levels of Civic Volunteering and Effects of Four-Year College Completion on Civic Volunteering by College Completion Likelihood: NLSY79 186
Figure 8.3(c) Levels of Educational Volunteering and Effects of Four-Year College Completion on Educational Volunteering by College Completion Likelihood: NLSY79 187
Figure 8.3(d) Levels of Charitable Volunteering and Effects of Four-Year College Completion on Charitable Volunteering by College Completion Likelihood: NLSY79 187
Figure 8.3(e) Levels of Voting and Effects of Four-Year College Completion on Voting by College Completion Likelihood: NLSY79 188
Figure 8.3(f) Levels of Trust in Government and Effects of Four-Year College Completion on Trust in Government by College Completion Likelihood: NLSY79 188
Figure 8.4(a) Levels of Volunteering and Effects of Four-Year College Completion on Volunteering by College Completion Likelihood: NLSY97 189

Figure 8.4(b) Levels of Voting and Effects of Four-Year College Completion on Voting by College Completion Likelihood: NLSY97 189

Tables

Table 1.1 Educational Trajectories by Four-Year College Attendance and Completion 17

Table 3.1 Potential and Observed Outcomes for Selected Individuals 44

Table 3.2 Matched Vignettes 69

Table 4.1 Factors Predicting Four-Year College Attendance and Completion in the NLSY 74

Table 4.2 Educational Trajectories by Four-Year College Completion Likelihood 88

Table 9.1 Summary of Results from Chapters 5 to 8 196

About the Author

Jennie E. Brand is professor of sociology and statistics, director of the California Center for Population Research, and co-director of the Center for Social Statistics, all at the University of California, Los Angeles.

Acknowledgments

My interest in educational inequality and unlikely college graduates goes back to my undergraduate days, when I worked in San Diego classrooms on a research team with the sociologist Hugh "Bud" Mehan. I studied a detracking program called Advancement via Individual Determination (AVID), which supported the achievement of disadvantaged students in high school and their efforts to attend college. When I went to the University of Wisconsin for graduate studies, I continued to be interested in educational inequality and developed methodological interests in causal inference. I completed my master's thesis at Wisconsin using propensity score matching techniques to study the effects of elite college attendance on occupational attainment, with Charles Halaby as my adviser. For the master's thesis, I matched cases by hand, one by one, sorting students according to their propensity for elite college attendance and looking for the "nearest neighbor" (the case with the most similar propensity). Later published with Halaby, that paper eventually used a matching program. Guido Imbens, one of the authors of the program, was very supportive and helped us with extensions to the program. Our estimates of average treatment effects for the treated and average treatment effects for the controls suggested an interesting pattern of variation in effects: the impact of elite college attendance on those students who attended elite schools was small compared to the potential impacts on students who instead had attended non-elite colleges. In other words, students with a low propensity to attend an elite college experienced larger returns to attending a selective college than did those with a high propensity.

My dissertation explored a different application—the effects of job displacement on workers' careers—but I used a similar approach. I returned to studying college effects as a Robert Wood Johnson Scholar at the University of Michigan. I began collaborating with Yu Xie, and we have now continuously collaborated on propensity-related projects for almost twenty years. Yu Xie and I began a project on college completion effects on earnings, using three data sources to represent three cohorts of workers. We aimed to test positive selection, but the results consistently suggested a negative selection pattern—students unlikely to complete college reaped the largest rewards. I later explored other outcomes, including family formation and civic participation, using a similar approach. Yu Xie and I went on to develop the method and several alternative related approaches. This book is an effort to compile and advance the work that I have been doing on heterogeneity in the effects of college for more than twenty years.

I am indebted to many people on this journey. Charles Halaby and Robert Hauser were instrumental in my early work at the University of Wisconsin. As my primary collaborator over the years on the effects of college and propensity score methods, Yu Xie has been highly influential and inspirational. He is a brilliant scholar, and I have learned a great deal from our ongoing collaboration. Robert Mare, with whom I cotaught "Social Stratification, Inequality, and Mobility" for almost a decade at UCLA, informed my thinking on college effects and stratification processes more broadly, among many other topics. Often in my studies and writing, I hear Rob's voice in my head, questioning a key issue. Rob passed away in February 2021, and I miss his presence dearly. But his voice remains clear. Mike Hout provided intellectual inspiration and support as this work progressed. I greatly admire his work and drew upon it extensively as I wrote the book. I recently worked with Siwei Cheng, Xiang Zhou, Yu Xie, and Mike Hout on a project on the heterogeneous effects of college completion on wage trajectories. They are all exceptional scholars who have furthered my understanding of selection processes and long-term wage trajectories. Ben Jann produced the statistical program for our early heterogeneous treatment effects approach and collaborated with Yu Xie and me on developing that methodology. I am grateful for these collaborations and friendships.

My collaborators Dwight Davis and Kelly Musick furthered the work related to family formation patterns. Several discussions with Paula England likewise informed this set of findings. Juli Simon Thomas, my student at UCLA, and I wrote a heterogeneity chapter for Steve Morgan's volume on causal inference. Sara Goldrick-Rab, Fabian Pfeffer, and I wrote a paper on heterogeneity in community college effects. David Grusky asked Yu Xie and me to write a condensed version of our *American Sociological Review* paper for his *Social Stratification* reader, and I wrote a piece on college completion effects on reducing poverty for *The Inequality Reader*, which helped us focus on essential details. A meeting with Sandra Smith when I was dropping my daughter off at her dorm at Berkeley was consequential to the chapter on college counterfactuals. John Goldthorpe and Tom DiPrete have offered valuable comments on this work. Caitlin Ahearn and Amber Villalobos, both my UCLA PhD students, collaborated on projects on college effects on various outcomes. I am also grateful to Ian Lundberg, my postdoc at UCLA, who provided detailed feedback on several chapters of the manuscript.

Developing the methodology for this project has been an ongoing process. My work with Yu Xie evolved over the years as we forged new ways of thinking about heterogeneity. Xiang Zhou's work with Yu Xie on observed and unobserved selection has been incredibly insightful. My work with Xiang and other collaborators on various projects has been instrumental in developing this book. In addition, several UCLA students, Pablo Geraldo, Bernard Koch, and Jiahui Xu, worked with me to produce new methods for causal effects based on machine learning over the last several years. I presented these new methods, applying them to heterogeneous college effects on low-wage work, and received helpful feedback from participants at seminars at the University of California at Los Angeles, the University of North Carolina at Chapel Hill, Harvard University, Duke University, the Max Planck Institute for Demographic Research, the University of Chicago, the University of California at Berkeley, the University of Texas at Austin, the Ohio State University, Syracuse University, Cornell University, the State University of New York at Albany, Northwestern University, Pennsylvania State University, and the Leibniz Institute for the Social Sciences. I likewise received feedback on the heterogeneous treatment effects approach in presentations at seminars at the University of California at Irvine, Harvard, Princeton University, the University of Pennsylvania, Stanford University, the University of Michigan, Yale University, and the University of Oxford. Participants at each seminar were constructive in clarifying key components of evaluating treatment effect heterogeneity.

My UCLA colleagues have informed my thinking on most of these issues: Moshe Buchinsky, Jacob Foster, Jeff Guhin, Mark Handcock, Erin Hartman, Chad Hazlett, Patrick Heuveline, Adriana Lleras-Muney, Robert Mare, Judea Pearl, Anne Pebley, Meredith Phillips, Natasha Quadlin, Mike Rose, Judith Seltzer, Megan Sweeney, Donald Treiman, Till von Wachter, and many others. Many UCLA doctoral students whom I have not yet mentioned have provided input, including Taylor Aquino, Ryan Cho, Matthew Curry, Bowei Hu, Ben Jarvis, Nanum Jeon, Kristin Liao, Ravaris Moore, Shiva Rouhani, and John Sullivan; most of them are researchers in the Social Inequality Data Science (SIDS) Lab (https://www.sidatasciencelab.org). My undergraduate "Sociology of Education" students and graduate "Social Stratification" students impacted my thinking over many years of class sessions. Several collaborators I have not yet mentioned have influenced my work as well, including Ken Bollen, Sarah Burgard, Jim House, Ted Mouw, Florencia Torche, and Rob Warren.

The National Institutes of Health (NIH) grant R01 HD07460301A1 provided financial support for my work on heterogeneous treatment effects in demographic research. I also benefited from facilities and resources provided by the California Center for Population Research at UCLA (CCPR), which receives core support (P2C-HD041022) from the Eunice Kennedy Shriver National Institute of Child Health and Human Development (NICHD). The excellent staff at the California Center for Population Research (CCPR), especially Lucy Shao, facilitated that funding. In addition, I serve on the Technical Review Committee of the Bureau of Labor Statistics for the National Longitudinal Surveys program. Involvement on this committee aided my understanding of the data, and I am grateful to other committee members, staff, and the principal investigators of the surveys for their assistance.

I am very much indebted to the Rose Series editors and Russell Sage Foundation. Suzanne Nichols at Russell Sage has been incredible to work with. I thank her for her patience and continual guidance and encouragement. Lauren Krivio approached me about a book for the series and then worked carefully with me throughout the proposal-writing stage. Richard Alba was wonderfully supportive in seeing the manuscript come to fruition and provided detailed comments on manuscript drafts. He is a perfect book editor. He gave constructive comments that improved the manuscript and, at the same time, offered truly encouraging remarks. Amy Adamczyk, Lynn Chancer, Nancy Foner, Philip Kasinitz, and Gregory Smithsimon were a supportive editorial team. I am also grateful to Sheldon Danziger, Jennifer Glass, Pilar Gonalons-Pons, and Jennifer Van Hook at Russell Sage and Jennifer Rappaport and the Russell Sage editorial staff. The Rose Series Seminar held in October 2021 was tremendously helpful in generating feedback for editing the book. I am grateful to everyone who attended, including Deirdre Bloome, Siwei Cheng, Christina Ciocca Eller, Michael Hout, Grace Kao, Samuel Lucas, Fabian Pfeffer, Florencia Torche, Yu Xie, and Xiang Zhou. I appreciate the input of three anonymous reviewers, who gave detailed and constructive feedback on the draft manuscript.

Finally, I am grateful for my family. My parents cultivated a context in which I valued college. They always expected high academic achievement, and I, in turn, expected that of myself. My father wanted to know when I began this project when my book would be ready for him to read; he passed away before it was complete. I thank my mother- and father-in-law for their support over the years, including childcare. I am grateful to my children and husband, who are the foundation of my life. To my daughter Sarah, who was born during my first semester of graduate school, who recently completed a BA in sociology at UC-Berkeley and an MA in sociology at the University of Oxford, and who helped make the text more accessible to a broad audience. To my son Joshua, who continually inspires us and strives for excellence. To my husband Stephen, my high school sweetheart, whose love is my constant.

Each year I attend the UCLA commencement ceremony and volunteer to distribute students' college diplomas. As I study the sea of smiling faces, I cannot help but believe that college for these students has been a life-altering experience. One would have difficulty finding an undergraduate in the crowd who would disagree with that assessment. Yet I also have noticed over the years that it is my students of color, first-generation students, and students who overcame the odds to attain higher levels of education who invariably are the ones to tell me that their college education changed the course of their lives. This book is dedicated to them and to all students who wonder whether higher education is the right path for them.

Chapter 1

Expanding Access to Higher Education

Nick had a high likelihood of getting a four-year college degree. Both of his parents attended college. His father worked as a general manager, and his mother worked as a nurse. Their family income was higher than about 80 percent of families (equivalent to about $110,000 in 2020). Nick attended high school in a large metropolitan area with mostly high-income, high-achieving students. He firmly believed in his capabilities and took pride in his achievements. He felt in control of his life. He expected to go to college, as did his friends, and his parents supported his aim to attend college. Nick enrolled in college prep courses and performed well in high school. As planned, he went to college after high school and completed his bachelor's degree in four years. Nick benefited from structural conditions and resources that facilitated educational success and made his chances of completing college high.

Each year, millions of students consider whether to continue their schooling by attending college and completing a degree. For some, like Nick, the path is relatively straightforward. Their parents went to college and have the income to help finance their children's education. They expect to complete college, as do their peers. They achieve high grades and test scores in high school and anticipate high-status careers. They perhaps never even questioned whether they would attend college and complete their degree, only which college and major they would choose.

For others, the path is less clear. They are students whose parents did not attend college. Their family income is low. Many face disadvantages associated with segregated neighborhoods, poorly resourced schools, and racial discrimination. Their academic performance may have suffered from their school's lack of resources. They may wonder whether they can succeed in college and whether the benefits will exceed the costs. Those who do attend college often face persistent socioeconomic obstacles, including economic insecurity, to completing a four-year degree. Many of these students are on the margin of school continuation. Some factor might induce them to attend college—such as close proximity to a college, or access to one where costs are minimized.

Differential access to higher education is consequential for life chances. Four-year college graduates are more likely to be employed and to have higher earnings and household income than high school graduates.[1] The unemployment rate is very low among college graduates, roughly half that of high school graduates.[2] They fare better than less-educated workers in times of economic downturn. College graduates hold higher-status and higher-quality jobs that offer a greater sense of accomplishment, independence, recognition, and support, and they report higher job satisfaction than high school graduates.[3] College graduates are also less likely than the less-educated to live in poverty and receive social assistance.[4] Higher education increases health and emotional well-being, family stability, and social and political participation.[5] The benefits of completing college have also substantially increased over the last quarter-century.[6]

Despite extensive research that four-year college degrees offer many benefits to life outcomes, the United States has fallen behind other developed nations in the share of its younger population with postsecondary degrees.[7] And despite general academic agreement about the value of college degrees, some discourse insinuates that the benefits are limited, particularly for individuals deemed unqualified or ill suited for higher education. "College does not pay off" is often casually expressed in news outlets. We may hear family and friends, journalists, public figures, educators, and researchers asserting that "too many students are going to college" or that "college is not for everyone."[8] Some of these constituencies question the value of college degrees, stating that many graduates are unemployed or employed at low-wage jobs and facing student loan debt.[9] Some Americans question whether college prepares students for jobs in today's economy.[10] Those questioning broad college attendance and, by extension, college completion may argue that the potential benefits do not offset the costs for some students. Many policies that broadened access to higher education for more disadvantaged students—including affirmative action, open admissions, and need-based financial aid—have been criticized by those alleging that institutions admit unqualified students unlikely to benefit from a college education. Some critics are concerned that too many students are enrolling and not completing a degree. Others, however, question the value of a college education more broadly, including the importance of four-year degrees.[11] Some also contend that access to higher education has gone too far, and that colleges confer devalued degrees upon unworthy students.[12]

When critics of educational expansion assert that some students do not stand to benefit from attending and completing college, what evidence do they use to defend such statements? What would those students have done had they not attained a college degree? Who are the college-unworthy youth, and who are the college-worthy youth? In other words, who is excluded and who is not from claims that college does not pay off? Generally, contentions like "college does not pay off" or "too many students are going to college" are aimed at disadvantaged students who are unlikely to attend and complete college. The whole enterprise of higher education is seldom questioned, and the appropriateness of college attendance is seldom questioned for subsets of advantaged or high-achieving students. That is, the voices arguing against college rarely question the value of college for all students; they question the value of college for *some* students.[13] Discussions largely focus on whether it is worth the investment for *particular* students to attend college and obtain a degree. The veiled rhetoric about "low-achieving" students often suggests limiting enrollment for students from low-income families and students of color—students who have historically been denied access to higher education by various state and institutional policies and practices and who have made some strides in college attendance. If the primary concern of these critics is that many students who attend college do not complete a degree, they should not say that too many students are going to college. They should instead state that *not enough students* are completing a four-year degree. This would represent a key shift in the narrative: the former implies that fewer people should attend college, while the latter suggests that more people would benefit from attending college and persisting to completion. As a nation, we should not want young people who stand to benefit from attending and completing college to receive a message that college is not the right path for them. We should want them to be sufficiently supported to succeed in college and complete their degree.

Debates about college often do not carefully consider what is required to speak knowledgeably about the benefits of college degrees. First, we want to know what an individual's life would look like without a college education. In the language of causal inference, what is the *college counterfactual*? When people question the benefits of college degrees for particular groups of students, what is the basis for that question? How do these commentators determine that the effect of attending and completing college for some students is negligible or detrimental? Often in public and academic discussions of the value of college, people compare the outcomes of low-income and high-income students. Or they compare the outcomes of college graduates with high test scores and those who do not have high test scores. Or they compare the outcomes of current college graduates to those of a past generation. Despite their ubiquity in everyday discourse, such comparisons are invalid for assessing the benefits of a college degree. Only when we appropriately identify college counterfactuals—life outcomes in the presence and absence of a four-year degree—can we describe the benefits or detriments of completing a college education. Once we do so, we must further consider how the counterfactuals, and ultimately the effects, differ across the college-educated population. The presumed counterfactual pathways that individuals without a college degree may have followed vary considerably depending on where their lives began and on how likely they were to complete a four-year degree. Identifying differential counterfactuals is key to understanding how the benefits vary across the population. And knowing how the benefits vary is key to having an informed discussion of the value of college degrees for diverse students.

Second, we need to consider unequal access to higher education. Who attends and completes college, and who does not? Scholars know from extensive research in the social sciences, beginning with Peter Blau and Otis Dudley Duncan's seminal work on status attainment, that there is a strong link between social origins and youths' educational prospects.[14] Sociodemographic and social background factors such as family income, parents' education, parents' occupation, race and ethnicity, immigration status, family structure, and neighborhood- and school-level resources influence educational attainment. We can use this information to describe the typical characteristics of individuals who are more or less likely to attend and complete college. While I draw on family, individual, and school-level characteristics to estimate college completion likelihood, the likelihood also reflects broader structural conditions that generate differential college completion chances, such as unequal access to resources and racial discrimination. Students from different socioeconomic backgrounds differ in their likelihood of attending and completing college, or their *propensity* to do so. The propensity for college is a summary measure of the many factors influencing who does and does not complete college. It is an imprecise estimate of college chances. For some students with a low estimated propensity, some factor might tilt their schooling decision toward either continuing or discontinuing. Once we estimate the propensity for college completion, we can assess how the benefits of a college degree vary across those with different likelihoods of completing.

Third, we need to determine which benefits of college we are considering and how diverse benefits differ across diverse graduates. Too often the rewards valued in public and academic debate begin and end with wages. The traditional focus on jobs and wages does not capture all the life-enhancing effects of higher education. Attending to a broader array of conditions influenced by higher education gives us a more holistic view of the impact of college on life chances. Although many benefits are difficult to quantify, we can certainly do a far better accounting by extending our analysis beyond wages. Americans are firmly committed to the vision that young people can escape poverty by attending and completing college. Yet economists and sociologists studying the effects of college degrees seldom empirically assess how attaining a college degree enables an individual to circumvent poverty, as well as outcomes such as unemployment, low-wage work, and job instability. Our conception of college degree benefits should evolve as a more diverse population attends and completes college. Do students unlikely to complete college benefit more or less than students with a high likelihood of completing college in terms of time spent out of the labor force, work in low-skilled jobs, experiences of job displacement, poverty, and social assistance? Moreover, how do the benefits differ if we consider outcomes beyond individual well-being by examining family and community well-being measures? Finally, the benefits of a college degree accrue over many decades. We need to consider how benefits accumulate over the life course rather than over a short period following the college-going years.

In this book, I assess how the long-term benefits of completing a four-year college degree differ across the population. I consider socioeconomic, family-level, social assistance, and civic outcome measures. I draw on nationally representative data from the Bureau of Labor Statistics (BLS) National Longitudinal Surveys (NLS) program, specifically the National Longitudinal Survey of Youth 1979 (NLSY79) and 1997 (NLSY97) cohorts. The NLSY79 and NLSY97 cohorts were born in the early 1960s and early 1980s, respectively. College-goers in the NLSY79 cohort largely entered college in the early 1980s, and those in the NLSY97 cohort entered in the early 2000s. The Bureau of Labor Statistics is a unit of the U.S. Department of Labor and the principal federal agency focused on labor economics and statistics. For more than fifty years, the NLS program, one of the most important and widely used nationally representative longitudinal data source in the social sciences, has followed nationally representative samples of men and women and gathered extensive information about their lives. NLS data inform social science researchers, government agencies, think tanks, policymakers, and the public about vital social and economic issues.[15]

I draw on data from the NLSY79 cohort to assess the effects of college completion on long-term life outcomes and provide evidence of the similarity of patterns in the more recent NLSY97 cohort. For most analyses, I compare those who completed a four-year college degree by age twenty-five to those who did not (but who did complete high school). In some analyses, I also compare those who attended a four-year college by age twenty to those who did not (but who completed high school). I use thirty-five years of NLSY79 data collection—from 1979, when respondents were in their adolescence, through 2014, when they were in their early fifties. I use NLSY97 data from 1997, when respondents were in their adolescence, through 2019, when they were in their mid to late thirties.

In this chapter, I provide a brief overview of expanding access to higher education and the economic effects of attending and completing college. Educational expansion indicates an increasing share of people completing high school and attending and completing college.[16] If considerable benefits accrue to those who are unlikely college graduates, expanding education benefits individuals and society. Moreover, when education expands and socioeconomic effects are large, intergenerational persistence of social class decreases. The United States is more open if a smaller share of the population ends up in the same social class as their parents and poverty is not reproduced across generations. Yet disinvestment in educational capacity has coincided with a more diverse student population attending and completing four-year colleges. I conclude the chapter with an overview of the rest of the book.

A Brief History of Educational Expansion and Access to College

Expanding access to higher levels of education was a key feature of U.S. society over the twentieth century. In 1900, most Americans had only a primary school education. Only 6 percent graduated from high school, and 3 percent graduated from college. Years of educational attainment soared in the mid-twentieth century as the United States led the world in mass secondary school.[17] Median years of schooling increased from seven to fourteen years; in other words, the average American's schooling almost doubled.[18] Figure 1.1 charts high school and college completion rates from 1940 to 2020. In 1940, about 25 percent of people aged twenty-five and older had completed high school, and only about 5 percent had completed college. The transition to mass secondary schooling, accompanied by relatively high rates of postsecondary education, was remarkably rapid. By 2020, over 90 percent of the U.S. population had completed high school, and 38 percent had completed college.

Employer and student demand, as well as an investment of public resources to meet that demand, were key drivers of educational expansion throughout the latter part of the twentieth century.[19] The founding of many state colleges following World War II paved the way for the

Figure 1.1 High School and Four-Year College Completion Rates, 1940–2020

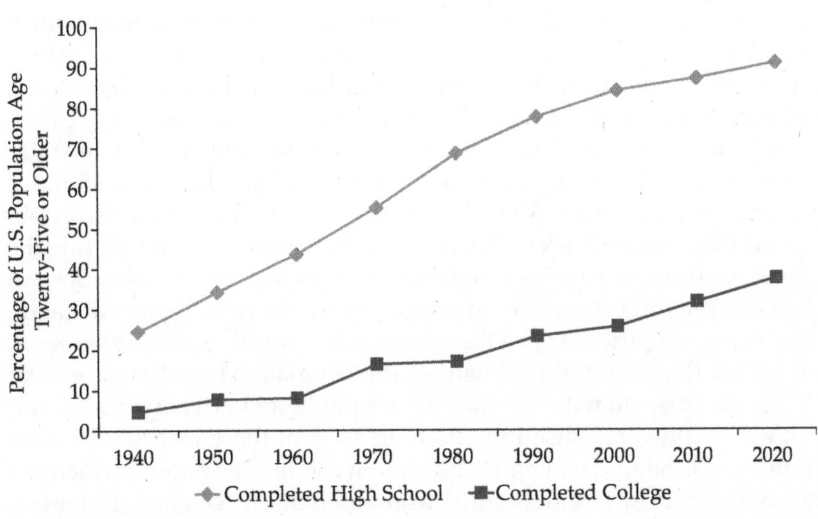

Source: U.S. Census Bureau, March Current Population Survey and Annual Social and Economic Supplement to the Current Population Survey.

rapid growth of higher education, and enrollment at public colleges increased dramatically.[20] America also saw a rapid growth of two-year community colleges during that period.[21] Community colleges and open-access institutions gave students who had not been well served by elementary and secondary school paths to reenter education. College completion by age twenty-five among cohorts born between 1915 and the early 1980s more than quadrupled.[22] Between the two NLSY cohorts, however, college completion rates increased modestly, from about 22 percent to 27 percent.[23] The six-year completion rate for students who began college in 2011 was 57 percent. That rate varies across colleges, with a 76 percent completion rate for students at private nonprofit institutions, 65 percent for those at public institutions, 35 percent for those at private for-profit institutions, and 38 percent for students who began at two-year public institutions.[24] About two-thirds of students starting at four-year institutions earned degrees within six years.[25] Less-advantaged students who continue their schooling beyond high school are more likely than advantaged students to attend vocational schools, community colleges, nonselective colleges, and, increasingly, for-profit colleges, which are institutions with low completion rates. In contrast, advantaged students attend more selective four-year colleges and have higher completion rates.[26] Only a small share of students attending elite public and private universities are low-income.[27]

Historically, expanding educational access to a broader and more diverse population of students often involved state intervention, both in founding new institutions and in establishing and enforcing antidiscrimination policies.[28] The Morrill Act of 1862 let states sell land to establish colleges, and the Second Morrill Act of 1890 included a key provision that colleges could not discriminate based on race. Some states responded, however, by opening separate colleges, barring students of color from traditionally White institutions. Some states then also established Historically Black Colleges and Universities (HBCUs). During the 1960s, civil rights activists fought for more inclusive campuses. Several laws played important roles in promoting diversity in higher education by forcing campuses to open their doors to historically excluded students. The Civil Rights Act of 1964 banned discrimination based on race, Title VI banned discrimination in the nation's public and private colleges, and Title IX banned sex discrimination. In spite of these measures, access remained limited. The Higher Education Act of 1965 aimed to increase accessibility to low- and middle-income students by creating the federal student aid program. Need-blind admissions and need-based financial aid furthered the aims of admitting and supporting students from low-income backgrounds. Affirmative action had a measurable impact on diversity in higher education, but legal challenges to affirmative action reduced that diversity. For example, California's ban on affirmative action significantly impacted underrepresented students seeking admission to the state's public universities.

Although progress has often met with resistance, shifts in the composition of the student population to include more previously underserved groups have shifted our collective understanding of who is served by college.[29] The economists Claudia Goldin and Lawrence Katz argue that after World War II, as college became the mass institution that high school had become a century earlier, America entered a third great educational transformation.[30] That educational transformation stalled, however, in the latter part of the twentieth century.[31] By the 1970s, high school completion rates had reached a plateau.[32] Over the last several decades, the United States has seen increasing college enrollment and stagnating four-year completion rates.[33] Only about half of students who enroll in college earn a four-year degree, and college completion rates are disproportionately low among students from disadvantaged backgrounds.[34] Although rates increased across the two NLSY cohorts, attainment gains were larger for high-income youth than for low-income youth. Four-year college completion rates increased by only four percentage points for low-income NLSY97 youth (born around 1980) over rates for NLSY79 youth (born in the early 1960s); by contrast, there was an eighteen-percentage-point gain across cohorts for high-income youth.[35] Moreover, what looked at first like a pandemic-induced recent decline in college enrollment has persisted. In fact, the decrease in the college enrollment rate since 2018 is the steepest on record, with the largest declines occurring among Black, Hispanic, and low-income students.[36]

A generation ago, America led the world in the college attainment of young adults, yet today it no longer ranks in the top ten among OECD nations.[37] Americans generally want more schooling than they receive, and employer demand for college graduates exceeds supply.[38] A significant hurdle is public disinvestment and the limited expansion of educational capacity. Roughly three-quarters of college students attend public colleges, which are partly funded by state and local subsidies and federal aid. In previous generations, states built new public colleges and universities and expanded existing ones. These investments ensured a rising educational tide.[39] Yet states have progressively invested less in higher education. In the 1970s in California, for example, a series of tax revolts led to disinvestment in higher education. Such disinvestment spread beyond California and has persisted. The share of funding that states provide to postsecondary institutions has declined across the college enrollment period for the two NLSY cohorts I studied, from about 44 percent in 1980 to 22 percent in the early 2000s.[40] Today many flagship public universities receive only a small proportion of their funding from state dollars.[41] Tuition has risen rapidly, and state universities admit an increasing number of out-of-state students, who pay higher fees, in order to address shortfalls in state funding. Tuition at public four-year colleges has more than doubled over the last three decades (adjusted for inflation).[42] For low-income and many middle-income families, college is unaffordable without financial aid. The levels of student debt acquired over recent decades are inconsistent with the idea that higher education should be accessible to all. A college degree has never been more critical, and it has never been more expensive.

Many Americans believe that individuals and families bear responsibility for paying college costs and that public colleges and universities should find ways to compensate for reduced state funding.[43] Despite a widespread public perception that tuition rises resulted from rising institutional costs of educating students, per-student expenditures at public institutions have not increased much more than inflation in recent years.[44] Instead, rising tuition is associated with the decline in the percentage of state funds in public college and university budgets.[45] Accordingly, despite their public missions, flagship state universities have come to operate more like elite private universities, increasingly relying on endowments, grants, and donations rather than state dollars. The 2008 recession reduced those sources of revenue as well. To make up for funding shortfalls, public state colleges shifted a share of costs to students, further restricting access and encouraging student debt.[46]

Disinvestment in higher education has happened at the federal level as well. With the Higher Education Act of 1965, the federal government funded students rather than institutions, with repercussions for today's student debt crisis. Basic Educational Opportunity Grants, or Pell grants, were created via the Higher Education Act, and the federal government expanded credit by offering student loans. States also developed need-based aid (and merit aid) awarded directly to students, supplementing state operating subsidies to public colleges.[47] The reasoning was that if students had access to loans, they had access to education, thus negating the need to create the public-sector edifices that characterized earlier eras. As a result, the quintessentially American education model changed from free, high-quality public education to private or privatized institutions with costs borne by students and families, aid, and debt.[48] The percentage of college costs covered by Pell grants fell dramatically from nearly 90 percent of the cost of public education and 40 percent of the cost of private education in the 1970s (near the time the NLSY79 cohort attended college) to 25 percent and 10 percent, respectively, in the early 2000s (when the NLSY97 cohort attended college).

The expansion of higher education and the high cost of college are matters of economics and politics.[49] The economist David Deming notes that college resource inequality results from intentional policy choices by U.S. policymakers over the last fifty years.[50] Educational expansion enabled broader segments of the population—including a larger proportion of racially minoritized and poor students—to be educated at a low cost. Although causality is difficult to establish here, disinvestment in higher education has occurred alongside growing diversity on college campuses.[51] The public support once received when the student population was predominantly White declined at state universities.[52] The economist Sandy Baum and her colleagues write: "Perhaps no demographic shift has been as visible or as consequential for the colleges and for society as the movement of the college population from being largely White to having substantial representation of students of color."[53] In a recent editorial, Richard Greenwald describes the racism underlying resistance to expansion. He argues that as people of color attended colleges and universities in historic numbers, U.S. policy cut funds to the institutions that they were most likely to attend.[54]

The opening of colleges to previously excluded groups has undergone ebb and flow.[55] Resistance to progress repeats itself, as various constituencies charge different groups with invading campuses at different times.[56] As more diverse students attend college, some members of the public and policymakers question the value of college for broader segments of the population. Some students, they contend, such as those who perform poorly in high school or those with limited economic resources, would be better served by entering the labor market or being sorted to community colleges or vocational training rather than attending and completing four-year colleges. As I argue throughout this book, however, the reasoning underlying these assertions largely disregards the logic necessary to evaluate the value of college and the substantial long-term and varied benefits of college for disadvantaged graduates.

Educational Expansion and Economic Rewards

As higher education expanded in the United States, the economic rewards associated with a college degree also increased.[57] The wage return for college-educated U.S. workers relative to high school–educated workers grew from about 40 percent in 1980, when the NLSY79 cohort entered college and the labor market, to about 70 percent in the early 2000s, when the NLSY97 cohort entered college and the labor market.[58] In the 1980s, the demand for college-educated workers started to outpace supply. That gap between supply and demand has widened.[59] As worker supply lagged demand, the premium on higher-order skills grew and schooling became an increasingly key determinant of economic rewards.[60] The economic benefits of a college degree have consequently also increased since the early 2000s.

The Bureau of Labor Statistics reported that median earnings in 2022 for college graduates were $78,000 compared to $43,000 among those with no more than a high school degree, for an almost 80 percent advantage. Since these are estimates for the full population in 2022, they include members from both NLSY cohorts, who would be in their early sixties and in their forties.[61] Economists have confirmed a roughly 80 to 90 percent earnings advantage for college graduates over high school graduates in recent years.[62] The average lifetime income and wealth accumulation of college graduates also exceed the incomes and wealth of those with a high school degree and those with some college. However, estimates of the precise economic value vary across studies.[63] Some scholars estimate that the college payoff for a working career of forty years translates to roughly $1 million; yet, after accounting for costs, discount rates, and selection into obtaining a college degree, returns are smaller.[64]

College graduates receive economic rewards beyond wages. The unemployment rate is also low among college graduates, roughly one-third to one-half that of high school graduates. College graduates also fare better than high school graduates during economic downturns.[65] In the 2007–2009 recession, less-educated workers were almost four times more likely than college graduates to be unemployed.[66] Roughly four times as many high school graduates as college graduates live in poverty and rely on social assistance programs.[67] A more-educated population pays higher taxes. A Pew Research Center brief reports: "On virtually every measure of economic wellbeing and career attainment—from personal earnings to job satisfaction to the share employed full time—young college graduates are outperforming their peers with less education." The brief also notes that "when we compare today's young adults with previous generations, the disparity in economic outcomes between college graduates and those with a high school diploma or less formal schooling has never been greater."[68]

Many of these reported figures are levels of economic outcomes by education, that is, differences in outcomes between high school and college graduates. Yet differences in economic levels may not represent the causal effect of attaining a four-year college degree. To estimate the causal effect of college completion—that is, the economic return to a four-year college degree—we need to compare the outcomes of college graduates to their potential outcomes had they not completed college. A widely shared view in economics and sociology is that schooling not only is associated with earnings and employment outcomes but also causally affects economic outcomes. Even adjusting for factors that influence college completion status and subtracting costs, the evidence is overwhelming that pursuing a college degree is worth the investment.[69] In the words of the economist David Deming: "One of the most robust findings in social science is that education pays off."[70] Sandy Baum describes the scientific evidence (rather than anecdotal accounts) of the benefits of higher education:

> The evidence for the individual economic benefits of college is overwhelming. . . . Obviously, there is considerable variation in earnings among those with similar levels of education, and it is not difficult to find individuals who never went to college but earn more than some of those who graduated. Those exceptions neither prove anything about the payoff of education nor provide sound examples for young people.[71]

College causally affects economic outcomes because it increases human and social capital, both of which raise workers' skills, productivity, and networks. The increase in human and social capital leads to higher wages and improved life chances over and above the characteristics that individuals bring to college.[72] The sociologist Michael Hout writes:

> Education pays off because, in addition to sorting and certifying America's young people, it adds value. In the nation's colleges and universities, students acquire new skills and new perspectives that make them better workers, life partners, and citizens. The universities do not merely identify the young people who fit the desired profile, they disseminate skills and foster values. Higher education causes good things to happen.[73]

Some social scientists have argued that employers use education to select new employees for elite positions who share the elite culture rather than those with the best job skills.[74] For example, according to Randall Collins, educational degrees signify a type of social respectability, and educational requirements for jobs reflect credential inflation as more people attain higher levels of schooling. Collins contends that few skills acquired in higher education translate to skills used on the job and that college graduates have more education than they need to perform their jobs.[75] Whether college increases socioeconomic well-being because of signaling or skill enhancement does not undermine the causal effect of education. Nevertheless, Michael Hout incisively argues, Collins's work assumes that the American economy somehow got the share of high school– and college-educated workers right in the 1950s or 1960s and that subsequent increases in the college-educated population, such as those represented by the two NLSY cohorts, represent irrationality on the part of employers, students, or both.[76]

Technological advancement and reorganization of how firms produce goods and services have increased demand for employees with the more abstract, multilevel, and cognitive and noncognitive skills characteristic of more-educated workers. Colleges disseminate needed skills, from specific skills like coding to broader skills like constructing reasoned empirical arguments.[77] Hout states: "An educated person invents things, works around tough problems, understands directions, documents tasks, misses less work, and puts in a more nearly full day on the job—in short, educated workers possess the cognitive and noncognitive skills that employers value." He further states that "an educational credential is substance and acquired abilities, not just status."[78] The skills and knowledge most valued in today's economy include leadership, communication and coordination, and analysis.[79] The economist David Autor has shown that occupations that have grown over the past two decades require more nonroutinized skills—that is, skills associated with higher education.[80] The labor market also rewards social skills that reduce coordination costs and allow workers to collaborate more efficiently.[81] The college return results from the demand for critical thinking, problem-solving, originality, and strategizing in a knowledge-based society.[82] Most such job training now occurs in colleges.[83]

Demand for college-educated workers has steadily increased. The economists Peter Blair and David Deming contend that increasing demand for educated workers is probably a persistent feature of the U.S. economy and that "many more job candidates will have to obtain a four-year college degree to compete in the labor market of the twenty-first century."[84] In 2020, about two-thirds of jobs required a college degree compared to less than one-third in the mid-1970s.[85] The U.S. Department of Education recently reported that three-quarters of the fastest-growing occupations require a college education.[86] Employers pay a premium for college-educated workers across occupational sectors.[87] For example, over the last several decades the manufacturing and mining industries have been automated and consolidated. As a result, many jobs that once did not "require" a college degree have declined in number; manufacturers are now on track to employ more college graduates than high school graduates.[88] Employment in new manufacturing jobs—such as industrial engineers and technological workers who can code commands for machines making complex components—requires that applicants have more high-level skills and knowledge in programming, mathematics, and engineering than in the past.[89] Likewise, some of the fastest-growing occupations in health care require postsecondary education. Administrative assistant and customer service representative jobs have increasingly complex organizational and communications responsibilities that require advanced skills.[90] The U.S. Department of Education reports that higher education is "a necessity for individual economic opportunity" in today's economy and that "a college education remains the best investment a student can make in his or her future."[91]

Returns to four-year college degrees have increased as a result of both high wages for college graduates and the precarious economic position of less-educated workers.[92] As the share of the less-educated population has declined, they have become increasingly marginalized. From the 1970s to the early 2000s, when both NLSY cohorts were making college choices, college graduates' inflation-adjusted wages grew by 25 percent. In comparison, high school graduates' wages increased by only 1 percent.[93] Real wages have thus largely remained flat for workers without a college education. The percentage of young male workers without a college degree making poverty wages rose from one-quarter to one-half from 1979 to 2017.[94] The sociologist Arne Kalleberg notes a forty-year decline in the quality in the jobs filled by less-educated workers.[95] The skill demands described earlier, as well as the declining value of the minimum wage, declines in unionization, and changes in corporate governance, have limited high school–educated workers' economic prospects.[96] Youth from low-income families without college degrees have especially bleak labor market trajectories. These workers are deeply committed to work and careers, yet they frequently hold low-wage, part-time, unstable jobs with limited or no career advancement and endure spells of unemployment and poverty.[97] These trends reflect the labor market conditions for the two NLSY cohorts, and trends appear similar for recent cohorts. The sociologists Florencia Torche and Amy Johnson show that while college-educated millennials are doing as well as comparable college-educated young adults in the past, less-educated workers are doing worse than their counterparts in the past. They state: "The story that emerges is one of diverging destinies: A growing gap in economic well-being between those with high and low levels of education, and a particularly precarious situation for millennials with no more than a high school diploma."[98]

Representative Data on Two Cohorts from the National Longitudinal Surveys

Throughout this book I draw on data from the National Longitudinal Survey of Youth 1979 and 1997—two nationally representative cohorts who entered college and completed degrees in the early 1980s and the early 2000s, respectively. The data enable me to consider the benefits of a college degree across the population and over the life course during a period of increasing returns to college. I observe life outcomes to the early fifties and late thirties for the NLSY79 and NLSY97 cohorts, respectively. NLS data are unusually broad for longitudinal surveys. The data contain extensive measures of demographic characteristics, family background, cognitive ability, academic achievement, psychosocial well-being, school-level factors, and educational attainment. They also have extensive information on employment status, job separation, wages, income, and poverty. In addition, they include information on family formation, social assistance, and civic participation. The data thus enable researchers to study a sample representative of the U.S. population over time and across multiple domains. The data also have high response rates for longitudinal, nationally representative social surveys.[99] I also merge NLSY geocode data with data from the Bureau of Labor Statistics, U.S. Bureau of Economic Analysis (BEA), American Community Survey (ACS), Higher Education General Information Survey (HEGIS), and *Barron's Profiles of American Colleges* to construct various measures throughout the analyses.

The NLSY79 sample consists of 12,686 men and women born from 1957 to 1964. They were first interviewed in 1979 when they were fourteen to twenty-two years old. I restrict analyses throughout the book to NLSY79 respondents who were ages fourteen to seventeen at the baseline survey in 1979 ($n = 5,582$) and who had completed at least the twelfth grade (or a GED) ($n = 4,548$), as well as those with common support, which I describe in chapter 3 ($n = 4,085$). The NLSY97 sample consists of 8,984 men and women born from 1979 to 1985. I restrict the sample to individuals who had completed at least the twelfth grade (or a GED) ($n = 7,753$) and those who had common support ($n = 7,626$). I assess the impact of four-year college attendance by age twenty and of four-year college completion by age twenty-five. For analyses of four-year college completion, I compare college graduates to those who did not complete a four-year degree but may have attended some college.

Students' experiences in college differ. Many students attend a two-year or four-year college but do not complete a four-year degree. Some students begin at a two-year college and transfer to a four-year college, while others stay at the same college. Some have discontinuous enrollment patterns. Table 1.1 describes the educational trajectories of the two NLSY samples of high school graduates. In the NLSY79, about two-fifths of high school graduates attended a four-year college by age twenty, and about one-fourth completed a four-year college by age twenty-five. About one-third of those who did not complete college by age twenty-five attended some college. Fewer than 5 percent who did not complete a degree by age twenty-five went on to complete college within the next five years. Among those who attended a four-year college by age twenty, about two-thirds completed a degree by age twenty-five. Among those who completed college, about 12 percent attended a highly selective school (according to the 1980 *Barron's Profiles*).[100] About one-third obtained a graduate degree by age forty. As expected, a larger percentage of students who did not complete a degree by age twenty-five in the more recent NLSY97 cohort attended two- and four-year schools in their twenties. Additionally, a slightly larger percentage of those who did not complete a degree by age twenty-five did so by age thirty in the more recent cohort. Nevertheless, the numbers are small for both cohorts (6.5 percent in the NLSY97 and 4.4 percent in the NLSY79).

Throughout the book I focus on the effects of four-year degree completion across broad life outcomes and how they vary across students of diverse backgrounds. I attend to various dimensions of individual characteristics that govern heterogeneous responses to college completion and estimate the heterogeneous effects across about two dozen outcomes for each of the two cohorts. I descriptively consider the diversity of college experiences in the vignettes of selected individuals but do not consider how results vary across different college experiences. I thus attend to effect heterogeneity by individual characteristics that impact the likeli-

Table 1.1 Educational Trajectories by Four-Year College Attendance and Completion

	Analytic Sample (High School Graduates)	No College Attendance (Four-Year by Age Twenty)	College Attendance (Four-Year by Age Twenty)	No College Completion (Four-Year by Age Twenty-five)	College Completion (Four-Year by Age Twenty-five)
NLSY 1979 cohort					
Attended any college by age twenty	42.6%	8.4%	100.0%	23.8%	96.3%
Attended any college by age twenty-five	51.4	22.4	100.0	34.4	100.0
Attended 4-year college by age twenty	37.4	0.0	100.0	17.1	95.3
Completed 4-year college by age twenty-five	25.9	1.9	66.1	0.0	100.0
Completed 4-year college by age thirty	29.2	3.3	72.6	4.4	100.0
Completed graduate degree by age fourty	10.3	1.1	25.7	2.1	33.9
Weighted percent	100.0	62.6	37.4	74.1	25.9
Sample size	4,085	2,732	1,353	3,237	848
NLSY 1997 cohort					
Attended any college by age twenty	51.9%	15.4%	100.0%	34.8%	97.1%
Attended any college by age twenty-five	60.5	30.8	100.0	45.6	100.0
Attended 4-year college by age twenty	43.1	0.0	100.0	22.9	96.8
Completed 4-year college by age twenty-five	27.5	1.6	61.6	0.0	100.0
Completed 4-year college by age thirty	32.2	4.0	69.3	6.5	100.0
Weighted percent	100.0	56.9	43.1	72.6	27.5
Sample size	7,626	4,591	3,035	5,781	1,845

Source: Author's calculations using data from the U.S. Bureau of Labor Statistics National Longitudinal Surveys.
Notes: NLSY sample weights used to adjust percentages. NLSY79 sample is restricted to individuals who were fourteen to seventeen years old at the baseline survey in 1979 (n = 5,582), who have completed at least the 12th grade ($n = 4{,}548$), and who have common support ($n = 4{,}085$). NLSY97 sample is restricted to individuals who had completed at least the twelfth grade ($n = 7{,}753$) and who had common support ($n = 7{,}626$).

hood of completing a four-year college degree rather than effect heterogeneity by college characteristics. The literature on the effects of two-year college attendance and completion and the policy implications of those effects is in many ways distinct from the literature on four-year attendance and completion. The sociology and economics literature on college effect heterogeneity and the equalizing role of college that I am addressing focuses on four-year attendance and completion.[101]

I report the average effects of both four-year college attendance and completion but do not consider heterogeneity in the effects of college attendance by subgroups. Although it would be informative to assess variation in the effects of four-year college attendance and highly selective college attendance, space constraints limit my ability to consider these dimensions of college-going in addition to the dimensions of student characteristics and the large range of life outcomes I do explore. I am also principally interested in how completing a four-year degree shapes life outcomes, especially for disadvantaged students, rather than how attending for one or two years and not completing a degree impacts outcomes. Analyses of the effects of attendance encounter a greater divergence in college experiences across the likelihood of attending than analyses of completion. Far more advantaged college-goers complete degrees than do disadvantaged college-goers, and thus heterogeneity in attendance effects may reflect heterogeneity in degree completion. Analyses of highly selective four-year college attendance encounter less divergence in college experiences across students with varying likelihoods than focusing on any four-year college attendance but comprise a more selective population. Since most students attending highly selective colleges complete a degree, they are generally also a more selective group than the graduates of any four-year college on whom I focus. The research in this area suggests that the patterns I observe that point to large benefits for four-year college graduates would extend to, or in fact be stronger for, those attending selective four-year colleges. Attending to the effects of any four-year completion is, in some sense, a middle ground with respect to the diversity of college experiences and selectivity of the student population between focusing on attendance at a four-year college and attendance at or completion of a selective four-year college.

A great deal of academic literature and public debate attends to the effects of four-year degree completion on life outcomes, and I speak to that literature. Although more students are attending colleges, four-year completion rates have stalled; moreover, they are disproportionately low among students from disadvantaged backgrounds. By considering the benefits of completing a four-year degree for unlikely graduates, I add to the literature on and policy implications of getting more students to complete a degree.

An Overview of the Book

In the remainder of this book, I consider selection into college and variation in the effects of completing college across various life outcomes. In chapter 2, I first review theories of and existing evidence on variation in the economic returns to college attendance and completion. I summarize the research suggesting that considerable economic benefits accrue to disadvantaged students as well as the literature on the equalizing effect of college attendance and completion. I offer a brief history of the progression of the expressed rewards of higher education and discuss which benefits we attend to as we evaluate the effects of completing college. Moving beyond a narrow focus on wage returns is a key, yet frequently unacknowledged, consideration for constructing a more accurate and holistic narrative of how the value of college degrees varies across the population.

In chapter 3, I describe the importance of considering counterfactuals to assess college completion benefits. I discuss the omission in public discourse and in some social research to draw on counterfactuals. The reader familiar with causal inference can safely omit the beginning of this chapter. For others, the beginning of this chapter offers a conceptual apparatus for considering the benefits of completing college. I then provide an overview of the analytic methods I use throughout the book to assess the effects of college completion on life outcomes. The latter part of chapter 3 requires more technical knowledge. Those who are either less interested in those technical details or are intimately familiar with statistical matching, effect heterogeneity, and machine learning methods can skip this part.

I describe factors that influence selection into college attendance and completion in chapter 4. Beginning with a review of theories of how social origins affect selection into college, I explain how we estimate the likelihood of college attendance and completion. I provide descriptive statistics on social origins across the likelihood of college completion in the two NLSY cohorts. Throughout the chapter, I describe the experiences of respondents with varying college chances, using their trajectories to provide narratives that contextualize the quantitative results.

In chapters 5 through 8, I assess the effects of four-year college degree completion on life outcomes. Figure 1.2 depicts the conceptual diagram and range of outcomes I consider in these chapters. I consider outcomes across the working career (from about ages twenty-five to fifty for the NLSY79 cohort and ages twenty-five to thirty-five for the NLSY97 cohort). For each outcome, I apply various approaches to identifying unlikely college graduates versus more traditional graduates, as described in chapter 3. In chapter 5, I consider the differential effects of college on

Figure 1.2 Diverse Benefits of College Completion

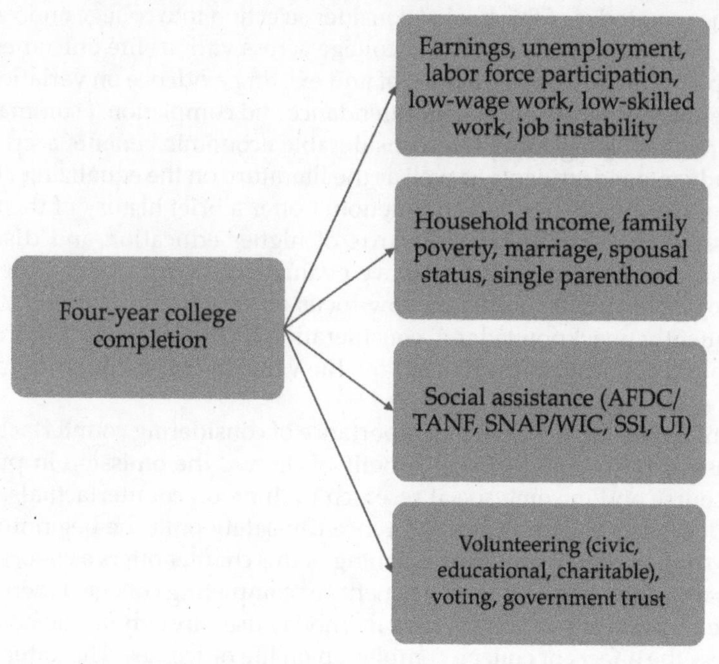

Source: Author's conceptual diagram.

socioeconomic outcomes, using a broader range of socioeconomic outcomes to give a more balanced assessment of the effects of college and how they vary across the population. I consider earnings, unemployment, labor force participation, low-wage work, low-skilled work, and job instability.

Chapter 6 parallels the analytic approach of chapter 5, but here I consider family-level outcomes, including household income, family-level poverty, marriage, spousal status, and single parenthood. Chapters 7 and 8 parallel the analytic approach of chapters 5 and 6, but I consider measures of social assistance (chapter 7) and civic engagement (chapter 8). Estimates of the returns to education often overlook reductions in social assistance and increases in civic involvement. When we consider these benefits, we substantially increase the expected rate of return to college.[102] If college completion decreases public assistance and increases civic participation more among disadvantaged students than among advantaged students, this is a vital and generally omitted consideration relevant to debates about college degree returns for unlikely graduates and the societal benefits to expanding access to schooling.

In chapter 9, I consider how we interpret the large benefits for students who complete a college degree against the odds. I comment on the generality of patterns of individuals unlikely to secure scarce educational resources reaping large benefits and the implications of such patterns for social inequality. Chapter 9 also revisits the central question of this book: Do disadvantaged students benefit from completing college? The answer is clear. Viewing college attendance and degree completion with a counterfactual lens and considering a wide range of long-term benefits, I find that colleges are far from failing disadvantaged students. The returns to degrees for this population are substantial. A college degree enables underprivileged students to circumvent unemployment, low-wage work, job instability, poverty, and social assistance. It increases their likelihood of engaging in civic society. Arguments that college has limited benefits either purposely or unintentionally reinforce existing inequalities and harm the lives of students from disadvantaged backgrounds. We should invest in educating those students who have low odds of completing a degree.

Chapter 2

Diverse Benefits for Diverse Graduates

In light of all the improvement in life chances associated with higher education, presumably young people should believe that they would do well to stay in school. Then again, maybe young people and colleges make well-informed decisions about who stands to gain from college and behave accordingly. While others opt out of higher education, perhaps the people who go on to get more education are well positioned to benefit from more schooling. If so, there is "positive selection" into schooling. The theory of positive selection in economics is that individuals invest in their human capital—for example, by acquiring more schooling—because of expected returns on that investment in the form of lifetime earnings minus economic costs.[1] Individuals make near-term financial sacrifices in exchange for long-term economic rewards. They choose to attend and complete college if the expected rewards exceed the anticipated costs, which include tuition, fees, books and supplies, forgone earnings, and possibly psychic expenses. The rewards that economists study are primarily economic.[2]

Sociologists, in contrast, have long emphasized a view of educational attainment in which multiple structural conditions constrain choices and sort youth into unequal educational pathways.[3] The costs and benefits involved when considering whether to attend college are neither purely economic nor always utility-maximizing, at least not in the classic economic sense. Decision-makers systematically violate basic principles of utility maximization.[4] In most sociological literature that examines the factors governing college-going behavior, family and institutional characteristics dominate and the utility-maximizing self-selection component is given the secondary role or sometimes ignored.[5] In other words, socially structured and unequally distributed opportunities limit educational "choice." While the exclusive focus on economic self-selection determinants of college education leads to the positive selection hypothesis, social inequality research provides a compelling theoretical and empirical basis for postulating a pattern of "negative selection." The theory of negative selection predicts that individuals who are least likely to attend and complete college based on observed characteristics benefit most from college.

In this chapter, I first describe the theories of positive and negative selection in greater detail. I then consider evidence suggesting that there are large returns to completing four-year college for unlikely graduates. I interpret patterns of large returns for unlikely graduates by drawing on two explanations: that a college degree acts as an equalizer; and that unlikely graduates are more strongly self-selected and more economically motivated than more traditional graduates. I conclude the chapter by expanding the theoretical discussion to benefits beyond wages.

Theories of Positive and Negative Selection

The economist Gary Becker's influential work on human capital underscores the rational calculation of educational decisions.[6] Becker assumes that individuals are utility maximizers, that is, that they seek to maximize their economic interests, subject to constraints. He further assumes that students take a lifetime monetary perspective when making choices, that they can reasonably predict future earnings, and that the economic system fairly rewards differences in human capital.[7] Many labor economists take this theory to imply that the most "college-worthy" individuals are, rationally, the most likely to select into college, to persist until they attain a degree, and to have the highest economic returns. Those most likely to choose college are largely those with the most advantaged family backgrounds. In contrast, individuals who anticipate that they will not improve their economic standing by obtaining a college degree are less likely to attend and complete college. Such a pattern yields a system of comparative advantage, whereby the college-educated earn more than the less-educated would have earned if they had chosen college and the less-educated earn more than the college-educated would have earned if they had not chosen college.[8]

In an influential paper published in the late 1970s, the economists Robert Willis and Sherwin Rosen empirically test the comparative advantage claim, using data on male World War II veterans who applied for the Army Air Corps.[9] While they find support for comparative advantage, their sample is not nationally representative. The economist James Heckman and his colleagues also find support for the theory of comparative advantage and positive selection using a sample of White males. They state that "marginal expansions in college attendance attract students with lower returns than those enjoyed by persons currently attending college" and go so far as to conclude that "too many people go to college."[10] Not only does this sample, of course, not generalize to the full population of college-goers, but they consider returns to college attendance rather than college completion.

The theory of comparative advantage is not without critique. Are students utility maximizers in their educational decisions? Do individuals have perfect information about the costs and benefits of continuing their schooling and consequently attend college because of the expected long-term economic returns? Are costs and benefits differentially distributed across potential college students? What factors constrain choices? As I noted earlier, family factors and unequal structural conditions influence educational attainment. Children grow up in different kinds of families, live in different neighborhoods, and attend schools with differing levels of access to resources. The social theorist Pierre Bourdieu, for one, resisted the notion that individuals behave according to economic criteria and highlighted cultural and social criteria instead.[11] Privileged youth are likely to attend college even without a financial cost-benefit analysis, as attending college is largely a foregone conclusion for them.[12] Disadvantaged youth are presented with a different choice set—that is, they face a different set of options they deem reasonable given their socioeconomic constraints. College is associated with financial burden and with family pressure to adhere to class-based cultural norms. Racial and ethnic minoritized students face discriminatory messages about their prospects for educational attainment. Thus, some students must overcome considerable odds to attend college and complete a degree, and many may perceive that the immediate costs overwhelm the prospect of long-term benefits.[13] Variations in perceived costs and benefits across individuals with different social class backgrounds can yield different college trajectories.[14]

In my earlier work with the sociologist Yu Xie, we developed a behavioral model that allows economic self-selection and non-economic social and structural factors to influence college attainment.[15] By economic self-selection, I refer to students' anticipated economic returns to college, which are generally unobserved in survey data. By non-economic social and structural factors, I refer to observed sociodemographic and social class indicators and school characteristics. We assume that the weight given to the self-selection component decreases as the social and structural determinants increase. The economic self-selection component drives the education continuation decision in the rational behavioral model described earlier. Considering an expanded model, social and structural factors play a primary role, and the self-selection component plays a secondary role.

Although a pattern in which students with a high likelihood of college attainment receive lower returns than those with a low likelihood seems economically irrational, it is nevertheless consistent with Daniel Kahneman and Amos Tversky's prospect theory, which suggests that individuals make decisions based on potential gains or losses relative to their situation and references.[16] They make decisions by evaluating outcomes, comparing them to the reference point and considering the gains greater than the reference and the losses less than the reference. Individuals seek a class position at least as advantageous as that from which they originated. High-income parents thus find high intergenerational persistence desirable and hope that their children will avoid falling down the economic ladder, whereas low-income parents, hoping that their children will climb the rungs, find low persistence desirable.

Prospect theory further suggests that individuals seek to avoid losses more than they seek gains. High-income parents strongly encourage their children to obtain higher education and support them in doing so as a rational strategy to maintain class boundaries. High-income youth minimize potential economic and social losses by attending and completing college, as they would otherwise face a risk of downward mobility. Low-income youth face economic and social risks in pursuing higher education and may assume that their prospects for high-wage growth are uncertain. Disadvantaged students lack knowledge about higher education, are far more resource- and credit-constrained, and may be debt-averse.[17] Some youth may attach lower utility to education because they question their likelihood of success in college and their chance of access to high-status jobs.[18] The sociologists John Goldthorpe and Michelle Jackson write: "For disadvantaged students, enrolling in college is a risky investment with an uncertain payoff."[19] Despite the risks of pursuing higher education perceived by low-propensity youth, there is also a considerable risk of long-term disadvantage associated with the counterfactual of *not* pursuing higher education. Still, some disadvantaged youth overlook known risks and focus on "rationally optimistic" anticipated gains.[20]

Evidence on Economic Returns for Unlikely College Graduates

Let us now consider the evidence suggesting the considerable economic benefits of completing a four-year college for unlikely graduates. My work with Yu Xie assessed how the effects of four-year college completion on wages differed for students who differed in their estimated likelihood of completing college. We found no evidence for positive selection and descriptive evidence suggesting negative selection for several life-course stages and two cohorts.[21] That is, the predicted effect of college completion on wages was greatest for those who were least likely to complete college, and the effect decreased as the observed likelihood of completing college increased.

The pattern we observed is consistent with a large literature on educational stratification. Scholars have found that racially minoritized students and students with low-income parents—students who generally have a low likelihood of college attendance and completion—experience larger returns to education than White students and those with high-income parents. For example, Heckman stated in the late 1990s that "the return to college education for Blacks was higher than the return for Whites by the mid-1970s, and continues to be higher today."[22] This finding has strong support.[23] The economists Daniel Henderson, Solomon Polachek, and Le Wang examine the rate of return to education (years of schooling) from 1940 to 2005 using U.S. census data and find larger returns for Black than White students.[24] They contend that individuals from disadvantaged groups tend to have larger returns to education. Similarly, Benjamin Backes, Harry Holzer, and Erin Dunlop Velez note that, "for young people growing up in disadvantaged families, obtaining a college degree is the surest way to achieve upward mobility."[25] Other work in economics suggests that education increases men's earnings more at the bottom of the earnings distribution than at the top.[26] Recent work by sociologists corroborates these results.[27] The sociologist Paul Attewell argues that access to four years of higher education for underprivileged students facilitates upward mobility. Recent research has also shown that students of color and those from low-income families experience the greatest improvements in labor market outcomes from college attendance, even without degree completion.[28]

As described earlier, some early work in economics suggests evidence for positive selection, such that more-advantaged youth benefit more from college attendance than less-advantaged youth or average college-goers.[29] Yet overwhelmingly, studies in economics over the last four decades using instrumental variable models have found that students on the margin of college attendance have larger benefits than average students.[30] Let us consider how comparing instrumental variables and ordinary least squares regression estimates of college effects on wages leads to this conclusion. Suppose we want to know the relationship between college and wages, and we have a third variable, the "instrument." An instrumental variable is a source of natural variation that approximates random experimental assignment. Scholars often use compulsory schooling laws, secondary and university reforms, and distance to the nearest college or university as instruments for college access. Assume, for example, that a local college affects college-going, but there is no direct relationship between a local college and wages. Then we can use the instrument to estimate the effect of college attendance on wages. Economists have used instrumental variables owing to concerns that selection bias has made the typical estimates of the returns to schooling too large—that is, that the estimated effects of college attendance resulted from the nonrandom selection of individuals into college. Instead, the instrumental variable estimates in many influential studies have produced the opposite result: they were larger than the least squares regression estimates. Yet if the effects of attending college vary across the population, the results of instrumental variable models do not correspond to the full college-going population. Instead, they represent the effect of college on those individuals induced into attending college by the instrument, such as students who attend college only if there is one nearby. Instrumental variable estimates that exceed ordinary least squares regression estimates thus suggest that the effect of college on marginal students' wages exceeds the effects for the larger student population.

The economist David Card states that a consistent finding based on instrumental variable models across many studies is that the estimated returns to schooling are roughly 20 to 30 percent larger than the corresponding estimates for average college-goers based on ordinary least squares regression models.[31] Card contends that the standard instrumental variables used in college return analyses, like college proximity, matter more for disadvantaged youth. This is consistent with the idea that accessibility matters more for individuals on the margin of continuing their schooling. He notes that the findings suggest that returns to schooling for relatively disadvantaged groups are higher than the average returns to education in the population.[32] Michael Hout contends that marginal students gain the most from educational opportunities, more than do traditional college students.[33] Although "it runs counter to intuition, this result accords well with experience," he notes. "Reforms that opened universities to nontraditional students produced graduates who gained a return to the college degree as large as or larger than that of traditional college students."[34] Claudia Goldin and Lawrence Katz note that the marginal college entrant who does not attend college is forgoing large returns to attending college.[35]

In several recent studies, economists continue to find a large wage return for students on the margin of college attendance.[36] For example, when Seth Zimmerman tracked large samples of students over the early 2000s in Florida and Georgia, he found that students just above the college admissions eligibility cutoff earned substantially more early to midcareer than those just below it.[37] Noting that the largest effects accrue to "groups of students who are relatively unlikely to attend college," he adds, "If you give these students a shot, they're ready to succeed."

Zimmerman "was surprised by the strength of the findings."[38] Other economists note that significant returns for students on the margin hold across various data and instrumental variable sets.[39] Lisa Barrow and Ofer Malamud comment on the similarity across different studies, stating that the results suggest that individuals on the margin of attending college will have higher returns than those already attending college.[40] David Leonhardt reports that "studies have come to remarkably similar conclusions: Enrolling in a four-year college brings large benefits to marginal students."[41] Carl Bialik reports that "prospective students who are on the fence about college are the most likely to benefit, according to several studies."[42]

While instrumental variable results suggest larger returns for college-goers who are more disadvantaged than average college-goers, it could still be true that very advantaged college-goers have returns that exceed those of average college-goers or disadvantaged college-goers. Although both positive and negative selection connote a linear pattern—either increasing returns as the likelihood of attending or completing college increases or decreases, respectively—some recent work suggests a more complex pattern. For example, in my work on long-term wage returns to completing college with the sociologists Siwei Cheng, Xiang Zhou, Yu Xie, and Michael Hout, we find a curvilinear pattern that suggests significant returns for both low- *and* high-propensity college graduates.[43] Similarly, Tim Bartik and Brad Hershbein observe the largest returns to a college degree among students with the lowest and the highest parental income and moderate returns among students with middle parental income. In particular, they find a 179 percent return to a four-year college degree for those below 100 percent of the poverty line, a 48 percent return among the near-poor (between 100 and 200 percent of the poverty line), and a 129 percent return among upper-income students (over 400 percent of the poverty line).[44] These findings present a more complex picture than negative or positive selection for wage outcomes, but they still suggest significant effects for unlikely college graduates.

The human capital theory implies that college is associated with higher initial wages and faster wage growth. However, the growth rates may vary across the population completing college. If unlikely college graduates require economic justification to attend college, they may be more strongly motivated to generate an immediate monetary payoff. Conversely, suppose that those with a high likelihood of completing college can afford to take a long-term perspective and be less driven by an immediate monetary return, given their privileged positions. In that case, they may choose a career with long-term wage growth and accumulate economic returns to college more slowly, resulting in a lower initial return but long-term wage growth.[45] The work by Cheng's team suggests that high-propensity college graduates have large increasing returns over the life course. Bartik and Hershbein also note that large gains for college graduates from upper-income backgrounds are partially driven by those who obtain a graduate degree and by the highest earners, who have high career wage growth.[46] Given the influence of the highest earners, focusing on median rather than average effects suggests larger returns for disadvantaged than advantaged college graduates.

While most of the work described here does not differentiate the type of college, other research considers the differential effects of attending and graduating from highly selective or "elite" colleges. For example, my earlier work with the sociologist Charles Halaby suggests larger returns to attending an elite college for students who were unlikely to attend such an institution.[47] Likewise, the economists Stacy Dale and Alan Krueger find that while elite college attendance effects are insignificant for average students, they are significant for racial and ethnic minorities and students whose parents have low levels of education. These subgroups' estimates remain large even in models that adjust for unobserved student characteristics.[48] More recent work in sociology documents similar patterns.[49] Economics research also suggests large socioeconomic returns to attendance at a selective college for racially minoritized students admitted through affirmative action programs and for students who attended a disadvantaged high school and were admitted through policy levers to expand access.[50] The work of Raj Chetty and his colleagues describes the importance of selective colleges for economic mobility. They find that students from less-privileged backgrounds benefit significantly from selective colleges.[51] Derek Thompson summarizes this research: "The simplest answer to the question 'Do elite colleges matter?' is: It depends on who you are. In the big picture, elite colleges don't seem to do much extra for rich white guys. But if you're not rich, not white, or not a guy, the elite-college effect is huge. It increases earnings for minorities and low-income students."[52]

Understanding Large Economic Returns for Unlikely College Graduates

College as an Equalizer

Research on social mobility offers potential insight into the processes that lead to differential college attendance and completion effects for students with different college chances. Influential work by Michael Hout suggesting that the relationship between social origins and occupational destinations is nil for college graduates and strong for high school graduates points to the equalizing power of a college degree.

Hout writes: "This finding provides a new answer to the old question about education's overcoming disadvantaged origins. A college degree can do it."[53] He notes that disadvantaged youth's limited access to higher education remains a key factor limiting social mobility, but "labor-market inequities do not compound those advantages for college graduates in the way that they do for workers with less education."[54] Family background constrains the occupational achievements of people without a college degree but not the achievements of those with a degree.[55] Consequently, education affects the socioeconomic attainment of workers with a disadvantaged family background more than the attainment of those from an advantaged family background. The American Council on Education reports that "young people from low-income backgrounds who complete a bachelor's degree have income and employment characteristics after graduation equivalent to their peers from more affluent backgrounds. Education truly can be 'the great equalizer.'"[56]

Figure 2.1 depicts this mobility pattern. The economic destinations of less-educated individuals are strongly associated with their social origins, while college-educated individuals' attainment does not depend upon their origins. Now let us consider how this pattern results in higher returns to college degrees for those with more-disadvantaged social origins. Suppose we change the perspective in figure 2.1 and examine the effects of education—that is, the difference in destinations between less-educated and college-educated workers. The figure reveals a smaller college degree difference in economic destinations for workers with more-advantaged social origins than for those with less-advantaged origins. Education affects the economic success of disadvantaged workers more than advantaged workers.

Sociologists and economists have replicated Hout's finding over the last several decades in the U.S. and in other advanced industrial countries.[57] The sociologists Fabian Pfeffer and Florian Hertel showed that substantial class mobility among college graduates in the 1970s was not a historical anomaly but pertained to all cohorts born between the 1920s and 1970s.[58] Torche replicates the pattern that Hout found in data from the 1960s, 1970s, and 1980s with five more recent data sources and four measures of economic well-being. Her findings indicate that the intergenerational association is strong among those with low educational attainment and disappears or substantially weakens among bachelor's degree holders.[59] Torche writes: "A college degree fulfills the promise of meritocracy—it offers equal opportunity for economic success regardless of the advantages of origins."[60] Hout also replicates the pattern for recent data from the General Social Survey: for high school graduates, the association between origins and destinations is strong; for college graduates, it is not.[61] Chetty and his colleagues, drawing on 30 million college

Figure 2.1 College Completion as an Equalizer and Variation in College Completion Effects

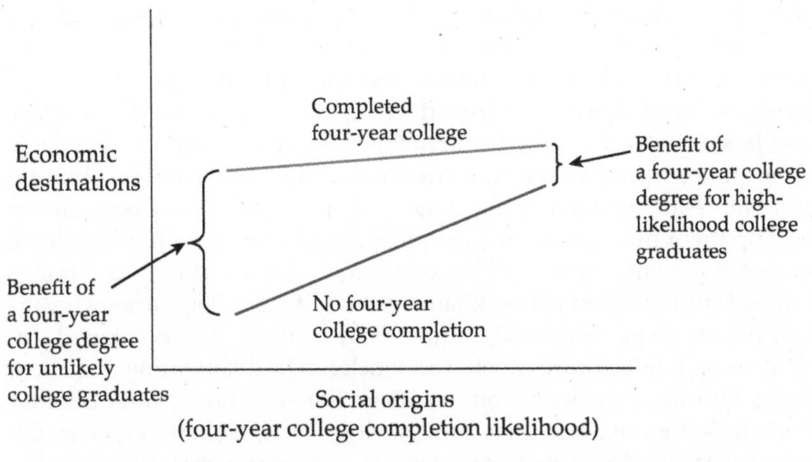

Source: Adapted from Brand and Xie 2010. Reprinted by permission of Sage Publications.

students from 1990 to 2013, find that intergenerational income persistence is relatively weak among college graduates. Children from low- and high-income families have very similar earnings, conditional on the college they attend. They conclude that colleges "successfully level the playing field" across enrolled students with different socioeconomic backgrounds and can be engines of upward mobility.[62] This finding is strong for students who attend highly selective colleges, suggesting that students whose parents are low-income are not "mismatched" at elite institutions. In fact, evidence suggests that Black students are more likely than White students to "undermatch," that is, to enroll in a less selective college than their academic record warrants.[63]

Scholars emphasize that for colleges to serve an equalizing role, low-propensity students must gain access to higher education. John Friedman notes: "This paints a very positive picture of the potential of higher education—if we can get those students in the door."[64] As David Deming states, "Education really can be an economic equalizer, but right now it only is so for a chosen few, and I think that really needs to change."[65] Recent work by the sociologists Deidre Bloome, Shauna Dyer, and Xiang Zhou suggests that educational expansion among low-income families enables social mobility and can offset broader declines in social mobility.[66] Educational expansion can reduce social reproduction because more people benefit from low intergenerational income persistence.[67]

Let us consider three factors that may contribute to the equalizing influence of a college degree relative to a high school degree across social origins. First, schooling provides students from low-income backgrounds with the productivity-enhancing skills, network connections, and economically rewarded cultural orientations that students from high-income backgrounds receive in the family and through other privileged networks.[68] "For children from less-advantaged backgrounds," Goldthorpe and Jackson observe, "whether or not they do well educationally is likely to be quite crucial for their chances of upward mobility, but for children from more-advantaged backgrounds, other resources may be available to help them maintain their parents' position even if their educational attainment is only modest."[69] The education scholar Anthony Jack points out that students from affluent families find life in college largely unsurprising; for them, "it feels like home."[70] By contrast, disadvantaged students experience culture shock. The shock can be disorienting and alienating, limiting their inclusion in college life. Yet shocks can also alter one's trajectory in a way that familiar experiences do not. A college degree has large effects precisely because of the significant difference between what students would be doing instead of going to college. Jack describes a low-income student who called her college attendance a "defining moment"; for more privileged students it was "just expected." One low-income student saw her attendance at college as a privilege, not a right, and another stated that colleges transform disadvantaged students.[71]

Unlikely college graduates may have higher returns than traditional students because a college degree increases their job networks. The economist Doug Webber contends that the wealthy already have access to job networks, while those from low-income backgrounds are gaining something they did not have before.[72] Richard Wright writes in *Black Boy*: "I went to school, feeling that my life depended not so much upon learning as upon getting into another world of people."[73] Dale and Krueger similarly reason that an explanation for highly selective college equalization patterns is that while more privileged students rely on their families and friends to provide job-networking opportunities, "networking opportunities that become available from attending a selective college may be particularly valuable for Black and Hispanic students, and students from less educated families."[74] Finally, a college degree can lessen employer racial discrimination because it gives employers more achievement indicators to augment their hiring decisions among more-educated workers.[75]

Second, the particularly poor labor market prospects for workers with low levels of education combined with low levels of other forms of labor market capital generate notably low earnings levels. Less-educated workers without the resources and attributes of privileged youth have limited labor market leverage. "With the disappearance of virtually all highly paid, low-skill jobs," Daniel Yankelovich notes, "the only way most Americans can fulfill their aspirations for middle-class status is through acquiring a higher-education credential."[76] Average incomes have stagnated or declined in real terms for people with a high school education in recent decades, when the two NLSY cohorts entered the labor market. These declines are particularly high for more-disadvantaged high school-educated workers.[77] The resources to support other success strategies abound among less-educated advantaged individuals, as described earlier. Children from high-income families benefit from class-biased hiring practices that help them become high-income adults regardless of their education.[78] High-income parents may secure jobs for their adult children within their own professional or business networks, or they may help them pursue entrepreneurial activities through either direct financial support or a safety net to fall back on in case of failure.[79] These factors produce a steep slope in economic outcomes among less-educated workers, as depicted in figure 2.1. Throughout the book, I will revisit how less-educated disadvantaged individuals' poor labor market prospects shape the benefits of completing degrees for unlikely graduates.

Third, disadvantaged students may exhibit positive selection into college. In other words, positive selection may operate *within* groups of students and most strongly for underprivileged students who are unlikely to complete a degree. Figure 2.1 depicts a descriptive result that does not fully account for how students select into varying educational attainment levels. Xiang Zhou as well as the sociologists Dirk Witteveen and Paul Attewell have questioned the implicit assumption of causality in research on social mobility and equalization. They ask whether equalization or selection explains the pattern of results found by Hout, Torche, and others.[80] They find that parent-child income correlations are not zero among college graduates. Thus, they contend, there is a stronger association between origins and destinations (a steeper slope) among the college graduates in figure 2.1. Other recent work, however, shows that selectivity does not explain the high levels of mobility among college graduates, lending further support to the college equalization finding.[81]

Many factors can limit the equalizing role of a college degree. The social origins of college graduates may continue to be influential because of their unequal college experiences. Students from low-income backgrounds are less likely to attend selective colleges and pursue advanced degrees than their high-income peers.[82] Some scholars note that selective college completion, rather than any college completion, may be needed to equalize wage outcomes across social origins.[83] College degrees can be a great equalizer, but only when students attend similar postsecondary institutions. Even when college selectivity is the same, class and race distinctions can shape college experiences, professional perspectives, internships, social connections, advanced degrees, job search, employment options, and socioeconomic attainment.[84] The sociologist Lauren Rivera suggests that employers prefer college graduates from privileged backgrounds to those with disadvantaged origins.[85] Racism and discrimination limit the job prospects of Black job applicants relative to White applicants with a college degree.[86] Nevertheless, even with a steeper slope for college graduates (imperfect equalization) in figure 2.1, we can still observe larger returns for more-disadvantaged college graduates. Moreover, as I argue throughout the book, we may not equalize some outcomes while equalizing others.

Self-Selection and Economic Motivation among Unlikely College Graduates

Youth who had a low likelihood of completing college but who pursue higher education and complete a degree are likely to be positively selected on potentially unobserved attributes that also affect labor market returns, including economic motivation. The influential work of the sociologist Robert Mare emphasizes educational selection patterns.[87] When a person unexpected to attend and complete college based on observed characteristics (low propensity) attends and completes college, strong self-selection factors may be involved. By contrast, the decision of children from advantaged families with high educational expectations (high propensity) to go to college is likely to be dictated less by self-selection. For these students, college is the norm. The economic motivation to attend and complete college is thus negatively correlated with the observed propensity for college attendance and completion. Thus, the extent of misspecification caused by omitting unobserved factors, like economic motivation, declines with the observed propensity score. In my earlier work with Yu Xie, we write:

> The very pattern of heterogeneous treatment effects of college education on earnings by the propensity to complete college suggests an unobserved selection mechanism at work: individuals from disadvantaged social backgrounds, for whom college is not a culturally expected outcome, overcome considerable odds to attend college and may be uniquely driven by the economic rationale. . . . For students from disadvantaged groups, college is a novelty that demands economic justification. . . . By contrast, for students from advantaged backgrounds, college is a culturally expected norm. Economic gain is less of a motivation.[88]

Positive selection based on economic drive among students with a low propensity for completing college can generate an observed pattern of negative selection across the larger population.

Unlikely college graduates not only may require economic justification to attend college but may be more motivated to generate an immediate economic payoff. Attending college is a significant financial burden for many disadvantaged students, so the economic payoff is key. The sociologist Stefanie DeLuca and her colleagues describe the "expedited path to adulthood" on which many low-income youth find themselves. Unlike their more-advantaged peers, low-income youth do not have the luxury of emerging slowly into adulthood by spending their twenties exploring who they want to be. Instead, they absorb the risk and responsibility of adulthood early and seek expediently to find a means to financial security to escape poverty.[89] While advantaged students explore their passions during college and possibly for some years after, disadvantaged students are more likely to focus on the surest paths to entry into the labor market.[90]

Research in psychology and economics also suggests variation in future orientation by social background. Irving Fisher noted in 1930 that low-income youth, given pressing needs and an uncertain future, tended toward a belief in providing for immediate economic necessities.[91] Disadvantaged youth perceive themselves as having less certainty and control over future events, and they develop less future orientation. More-advantaged youth place greater weight on the future and focus on investments with long-term returns.[92] College graduates with privileged social origins may thus choose careers where economic returns to college accumulate relatively slowly, resulting in a lower initial return but long-term wage growth. Therefore, college graduates from low-income families are more likely to choose fields with more immediate labor market rewards, such as business, education, and health care.[93] Meanwhile, more-advantaged college graduates are more likely to pursue the social sciences and humanities in college and subsequently to obtain advanced degrees.[94] Liberal arts majors, especially those who attain graduate degrees, may earn more over the long term. Still, the path to professional success is more of a marathon than a sprint.[95]

Self-selection and strong economic motivation among unlikely college graduates may reduce the causal portion of the observed effects of a college degree on wages for these students. Nevertheless, studies have used various data and statistical modeling strategies to address selection into college and reached remarkably similar conclusions: completing a four-year degree brings significant economic returns to unlikely graduates.

Beyond Narrow Economic Returns

The discussion here reflects the overwhelming emphasis on wage returns to college. Public and policy debates about the role of schooling in U.S. society and educational expansion primarily focus on how college affects individuals' job prospects and wages, resting on the assumption that the central purpose of attending college and completing a degree is to get a good-paying job. The coalition supporting the focus on wage returns includes politicians and policymakers, businesses, economic and social reformers, educators and academics, and parents and college-goers.[96] The conventional narrative is that we educate youth to enhance their position in the economic order and secure the nation's economic future. Andrew Delbanco writes that for many students, particularly disadvantaged ones, "college means the anxious pursuit of marketable skills in overcrowded, under-resourced institutions, where little attention is paid to that elusive entity sometimes called the 'whole person.'"[97] The message that higher education matters only for jobs and wages, or *should* only matter for jobs and wages, especially for disadvantaged students, limits our understanding of the value of college. It also limits our recognition of the richness of individuals' lives. Ultimately, this message limits the society in which we live.

How did this narrative come to be so dominant? According to early reformers, philosophers, and social theorists, the original goals of education included philosophical, moral, and civic benefits rather than individual economic rewards. Thomas Jefferson would not even prescribe a particular course of study for vocational purposes at the University of Virginia, embracing a broader view of the purpose of higher learning for the individual and society. For Jefferson, an educated citizenry was necessary to protect freedom and maintain democracy. In describing self-government, he wrote: "If we think [the people] not enlightened enough to exercise their control with a wholesome discretion, the remedy is not to take it from them, but to inform their discretion by education."[98] For Ralph Waldo Emerson, rote education was a form of corruption; education, in his view, should set souls aflame.[99] W.E.B. Du Bois embraced the Jeffersonian-Emerson tradition, asserting that education aims to "train a self whose balanced assertion will mean as much as possible for the great ends of civilization."[100] Du Bois insisted that the "function of the university is not simply to teach bread-winning . . . it is, above all, to be the organ of that fine adjustment between real life and the growing knowledge of life."[101] Jane Addams emphasized education as central to deepening empathy, acting in concert with others, and recognizing and overcoming our social distance from one another. She asserted that we should value an ethic of mutual relationships and responsibilities above individual striving in higher education.[102] John Dewey believed that education should enhance our capacities for human significance and not reduce us to mere tools of an industrial system.[103]

In the early years of American higher education, educators and policymakers expected colleges to inform the "whole person." Students studied religion, history, and philosophy in order to contribute to civic life without being narrowly utilitarian. In 1867, John Stuart Mill told students at the University of St. Andrews: "Universities are not intended to teach the knowledge required to fit men for some special mode of gaining their livelihood. Their object is not to make skillful lawyers, or physicians, or engineers, but capable and cultivated human beings."[104] "The object of the university," according to the first president of Johns Hopkins, Daniel Gilman, "is to develop character. . . . It should prepare for the service of society a class of students who will be wise, thoughtful, progressive guides."[105] Hunter Rawlings, president of the Association of American Universities, writes that most current commentary on the value of college—whether college costs too much, creates too much debt, or is not worth the investment—is "naïve, or worse, misleading." He continues: "Most everyone now evaluates college in purely economic terms, thus reducing it to a commodity," and tries to determine its worth by some formula. "Genuine education is not a commodity, it is the awakening of a human being."[106]

For more than two hundred years, there has been public doubt and derision over the relevance of a broad "whole person" curriculum, particularly for nontraditional students. Public debate has long questioned whether students unlikely to complete a degree, whose composition shifts over time, should educate themselves beyond narrow vocational training. Many people have viewed higher education as a "luxury that rich families gifted to their sons as a sign of their breeding," as Michael Roth states, a luxury that did not easily extend to the broader population.[107] Finding oneself and developing intellectual capacity are acceptable aims for the privileged college-goer, so the implicit argument goes, but those struggling to bear college costs should concern themselves with practical economic returns. Roth contends that the opportunity to "find oneself" and explore the world has been "seen as a luxury for the entitled, one that is scarcely affordable."[108]

Given this historical milieu, we should be mindful of an overriding focus on economic gain. First, a narrow focus on economic returns to college limits our understanding of education and social inequality. The theories of positive and negative selection described earlier focus on earnings returns. The college equalization hypothesis is a pattern based on earnings or occupational standing. There are good reasons to recognize the economic returns to college, as college markedly increases economic standing and social mobility. Yet what if there are larger returns for disadvantaged than advantaged students with respect to other consequential socioeconomic outcomes? Would we then say that there is negative selection? What if college equalizes poverty but not earnings? Is college then a "great equalizer"? Earnings represent just one outcome that college may equalize. As I noted earlier, there is a deeply held American notion that young people can escape poverty by attaining higher education.[109] There are reasons to expect that completing college more significantly reduces unemployment, low-wage work, job instability, poverty, and social assistance for disadvantaged than for advantaged youth. Yet research on how college differentially affects these socioeconomic outcomes is limited.

Research should also attend to non-economic outcomes. Scholars have suggested that nonmarket effects substantially increase the estimated returns to college.[110] College may differentially affect varied life conditions, and the patterns may diverge from the differential effect on economic outcomes. James Heckman, John Eric Humphries, and Gregory Veramendi, for example, find that, in contrast with their work on wage returns, the benefits to education for many nonmarket outcomes are greater for individuals of low measured aptitude than for individuals of high measured aptitude—"a feature of the returns to education that is missed if only market returns are analyzed."[111] Goldin and Katz note that the social returns for marginal entrants exceed labor market returns.[112] Some of my earlier work shows that college has the largest effect on low-propensity college graduates in their volunteering in civic and community activities, youth groups, charitable organizations, and social welfare groups.[113] Without considering a broad array of benefits, we overlook the many consequential and nonpecuniary effects of college for disadvantaged students.

Second, a narrow focus on wage returns to college limits our conception of the value of education for a diverse population and for our policy perspective. Henry Giroux argues that we need to rethink what kind of education matters to democracy and "restate our commitment to public and higher education in terms of its value for political culture and democratic public life in addition to its contributions to economic prosperity."[114] The sociologist Prudence Carter writes: "A fundamental and philosophical purpose of public education is to grow generations of literate, critically thinking, creative, civically engaged students who work to edify and build a cohesive nation and democracy."[115] Higher learning minimizes our dependence on authority structures and encourages independent thought. For Thomas Jefferson and John Adams, education was the best protection against indoctrination. Only an informed citizenry can see through political deception and judge who will best represent their interests.[116] To maintain a functioning democracy, we need a citizenry that participates in the democratic process and can distinguish between demagoguery and logical arguments, between misleading information and responsible reporting. We need citizens to be capable of identifying when someone is spewing rot. Expanding education to more students expands that collective capacity.

If we focus exclusively on individual wage returns rather than these civic benefits, we obscure the societal value of educating the broader population. We cannot determine the appropriate level of public investment in higher education without a concrete sense of the broad societal benefits. Jefferson, Du Bois, and Dewey emphasized the importance of liberal education for increasing the proportion of students attending institutions of higher learning beyond just the privileged few. In 1787, Jefferson wrote: "Above all things I hope the education of the common people will be attended to, convinced that on their good sense we may rely with the most security for the preservation of a due degree of liberty." John Adams said that the "people must take upon themselves the education of the whole people and must be willing to bear the expense of it."[117] Du Bois also stated that the "ideal would be to train every man in [liberal learning]."[118] In stark contrast, the vocational narrative perpetuates policies that limit college access to reduce competition over scarce economic rewards. The characterization of college as serving a narrow utilitarian economic purpose, especially for nontraditional students, rather than a broader public purpose has paralleled disinvestment in higher education.[119] We need to invest in educating the population for the common good.

Third, as implied earlier, a narrow focus on wage returns to college is often differentially applied. Given the substantial economic costs of college, various factions inundate disadvantaged students with the message that college must pay off for them or it is not worth their time and investment. The message is conveyed at an early age, when narrow academic goals lead to a stripping of the curriculum for working-class youth that Jonathan Kozol, in a recent interview, describes as an "apartheid of the intellect."[120] Schooling for disadvantaged students has often taken a functional approach that is heavy on vocational training and thin on the broader intellectual, aesthetic, and civic dimensions of education.[121] An overwhelming emphasis on wage returns impoverishes our conception of the varied factors that motivate students from low-income families to go to college and what they take from it. The education scholar Mike Rose underscores that a narrow economic focus reflects an unfortunate tendency in American education policy to misconstrue the varied factors motivating the working class to continue schooling.[122]

Du Bois defended liberal learning against the arguments of those who deemed it impractical, specifically for Black Americans. He contended that while the objective of technical training is to enable the student to master the present methods of earning a living, we must provide youth with "a training designed above all to make them men of power, of thought, of trained and cultivated taste; men who know where civilization is tending and what it means."[123] He warned against confusing the means of living for the object of life. Technical competence was important but should not be allowed to overshadow education's purpose of enabling citizens to discover their humanity.[124] If we collectively treat individuals—and specifically disadvantaged individuals—as if they are singularly focused capitalistic tools that perform narrow tasks, we limit human development and human freedom. Ultimately, our society is defined by the education we promote and foster and by whom we include in it.

In this book, I consider a more comprehensive array of outcomes than are typically studied, including socioeconomic, family-level, social assistance, and civic outcomes. Given space and data limitations, I cannot consider the full breadth of the life chances, indicators of well-being, and awareness and attitudes that college influences. Nonetheless, I hope that expanding the focus to a broader set of outcomes and indicating how these diverse benefits vary for diverse students will motivate continued assessment of the multifarious value of a college education across the population.

Chapter 3

College Counterfactuals and Estimating Effects

Henry did not attend college. In moments of frustration, when his work is especially unfulfilling or when he has difficulty making ends meet, he might say to himself, "I should have gotten a college degree!" What does he mean by that?

Henry may believe that *if* he had obtained a four-year degree, he would not hold a low-wage job or struggle to make ends meet. As social scientists, we aim to say that our estimate of the time Henry would have spent in a low-wage job had he completed college, at that same time and under identical circumstances, would have been less than the time he has spent in a low-wage job over his career without completing college. That crucial, hypothetical *if* statement is the counterfactual. The counterfactual for Henry is his life trajectory had he completed college. The potential outcomes are the wages Henry would have earned by not completing college and the wages he would have earned by completing college. College is our intervention, exposure, or treatment condition, in the causal vocabulary of statisticians and social scientists. We are pointing to a causal effect of college on wages when we say that Henry's wages, had he completed college, would differ from what he actually receives without having completed college. The causal effect for Henry is unidentified because it depends on a counterfactual. We cannot go back in time and change Henry's educational path. Statisticians describe this missing data problem as the fundamental problem of causal inference.[1] This issue lies at the core of modern social science and policy analysis.

In this chapter, I first describe the logic of counterfactuals and potential outcomes. I consider the difference between counterfactuals and simple comparisons that do not draw on counterfactuals and discuss how such comparisons can lead to misleading conclusions. This clarification is critical for understanding how the effect of college completion varies across the population. I then describe the difference between levels and effects. For example, I distinguish between the poverty level among college graduates and the effect of college completion on poverty, where the latter requires invoking a counterfactual comparison between poverty in the presence and absence of a college degree. Finally, I describe the methods I use throughout the book to estimate the differential effects of college completion. The reader initiated in causal inference can skip the first half of this chapter, while the reader less interested in technical methodological details can skip the second half of this chapter.

Counterfactuals and Potential Outcomes

A large proportion of questions of interest in the social sciences, as well as in everyday life, are causal questions. We may want to know the causal effect of getting married, having a child, or migrating to a new country. We want to know the causal effect of parents divorcing, experiencing a health shock, or losing a job. We want to know the effect of completing college. Causal questions are ubiquitous. And we make regular causal attributions about the decisions we make. For example, we might say: "If I had a college degree, I would not have lost my job." Statements such as these draw on counterfactual reasoning to make causal attributions. David Lewis contends that we "think of a cause as something that makes a difference, and the difference it makes must be different from what would have happened without it."[2] In other words, we attempt to understand what could have happened in an alternative state where we chose to act differently.

One unsatisfactory characterization of causal effects is that the cause produces an outcome in every case.[3] Applying this definition to the effects of college completion, we would need to contend that a college degree does not cause high wages unless every college graduate has a high-wage job. Although we expect variation in how people respond to life circumstances, those unsophisticated in causality frequently draw on this underlying logic and use single cases to make causal claims. For example, consider how often we hear statements like, "My cousin Fred graduated from college and works at Starbucks. College doesn't pay off." Alternatively, consider how often we hear that college is inconsequential because some highly successful individuals did not complete a degree. For example, Elon Musk recently stated: "There is no need to even have a college degree. . . . Look at people like Bill Gates or Larry Ellison, Steve Jobs; they did not graduate from college."[4]

The counterfactual framework provides a conceptual apparatus to consider causal effects and counter these types of reasoning. In a series of papers published in the early 1970s, the statistician Donald Rubin advanced the counterfactual model, or potential outcome model.[5] Using potential outcomes allows us to define causal effects by explicitly considering alternative counterfactual realities based on manipulations of the treatment condition—in this case, a college degree. As the economist Guido Imbens notes, Rubin expanded the insights of the potential outcomes notation to settings outside of randomized experiments.[6] The approach gained widespread popularity in economics and sociology in the 1990s and early 2000s.[7] Social scientists widely accepted the potential outcome model as the basis for understanding causal effects near the end of the twentieth century.[8] Over the last several decades, conceptual and statistical advances, data access, technological innovation, and computing have fueled increased confidence in our ability to draw causal conclusions. The computer scientist Judea Pearl and the political scientist Gary King contend that we have entered a causal revolution.[9]

To assess the effect of college completion, we draw on potential outcomes: the outcome when an individual completed college, and the outcome when that same individual did not complete college. We begin with this conceptual stage that precisely formulates the causal questions in the potential outcome framework.[10] In theory, we could observe each outcome had the individual completed or not completed college. However, only the potential outcome corresponding to the treatment received (a college degree) is realized and observed. Causal effects involve comparing the potential outcome observed with the potential outcome that could have been observed had that individual received a different treatment condition. We need to impute the missing potential outcome.

Consider Henry and his time in a low-wage job over his career. Attributing Henry's wages to his not completing college assumes that he would have had different wages had he completed college. Potential outcomes help us conceptualize our comparison of Henry's wage outcome under the same conditions, which differ only by whether he completed college. Henry spent almost three-quarters of his career in a low-wage job. If we could somehow know that had Henry completed college he would have spent less than three-quarters of his time in a low-wage job, we could then assess the causal effect of college on his wages. That is, to get some leverage on the effect of college on low-wage work for those who did not complete college, we compare (1) actual time spent in a low-wage job in the absence of a college degree and (2) time spent in a low-wage job in the presence of a college degree (the counterfactual). Likewise, to get leverage on the effect of college on low-wage work for those who completed college, we aim to compare (1) actual time spent in a low-wage job in the presence of a college degree and (2) time spent in a low-wage job in the absence of a college degree (the counterfactual).

Table 3.1 displays potential outcomes for selected individuals, includ-

Table 3.1 Potential and Observed Outcomes for Selected Individuals

Individual	Potential Outcomes Y_{i0}	Potential Outcomes Y_{i1}	Four-Year College Degree	Observed Outcome
Henry	73%	(0%)	0	73%
Brian	(73%)	0%	1	0%
Javier	80%	(7%)	0	80%
Diego	(80%)	7%	1	7%

Source: Author's calculations using data from the U.S. Bureau of Labor Statistics National Longitudinal Surveys.
Notes: Outcomes for each individual indicate the proportion of time in a low-wage job from about age twenty-five to age fifty. Potential outcomes without parentheses are observed and those in parentheses are unobserved and estimated from a matched comparison.

ing Henry. Henry did not complete a four-year college degree, and we observe his wage in the non-college graduate state (Y_{i0}), where Y_i is the outcome for an individual i, and 0 indicates that he did not complete college. To determine whether Henry would be correct in his assessment that he spent much of his working life in a low-wage job because he did not complete college, we need to know what position he would have had had he instead completed college. Potential outcomes exist as possibilities, but only one remains once an individual decides on a life course. We must estimate the counterfactual.

Let us consider the wage outcome of Brian, a college graduate. Both Henry and Brian are U.S.-born White males. They both grew up with both parents, and their parents earned about the same income, higher than average (equivalent to about $90,000 in 2020). Neither Henry's nor Brian's parents completed college. Henry and Brian attended high schools in urban areas in the northeast United States. They both had test scores in the top quartile of the distribution, and they both performed reasonably well in high school. They enrolled in college preparatory courses and expected to attend college, even though many of their friends did not. Suppose that Brian provides information that we believe may approximate what Henry would have earned had he completed a four-year degree. While Henry spent three-quarters of his career in a low-wage job, Brian spent none of his time in a low-wage job. We need to believe that Henry's wages would have looked like Brian's had he completed college—or put another way, that Brian's wages can substitute for Henry's counterfactual wages had he not completed college. For causal inference and estimation of unobserved potential outcomes, we want to compare college and noncollege graduates who were as similar as possible before college. We could do the same for Diego and Javier, a matched comparison also described in table 3.1. Diego completed a college degree, and Javier did not. Diego spent 7 percent of his time in a low-wage job, while Javier spent 80 percent of his life earning low wages.

Although the contrast between Henry and Brian, or between Diego and Javier, is instructive, we must make many such contrasts and define causal effects for populations rather than individuals. We estimate average effects by taking many contrasts, like Henry and Brian, and averaging the difference in their outcomes. I nevertheless draw on "counterfactual" narratives throughout the book to illustrate possible alternative pathways. College counterfactual vignettes illustrate the matched comparisons that form the basis of the estimated effects of college completion and orient the reader to consider life conditions in the presence and absence of a college degree.

Comparisons versus Counterfactuals

People routinely make causal statements without referring to any counterfactual. Naive causal attributions ("He's rich because he's smart," "She's unemployed because she's lazy") are ubiquitous. Likewise, many people routinely make causal attributions like "college does not pay off" without carefully considering counterfactuals. Indeed, much of the rhetoric on the value of college and how it varies across the population neglects the counterfactual framework necessary to assess causal effects. Let us consider three common forms of faulty reasoning related to the value of a college degree. First, some compare the outcomes of low-achieving to high-achieving college students or graduates, or low-income to high-income college students or graduates, or Black and Hispanic to White college students or graduates. Second, others compare low-income college-goers or graduates to middle- or high-income high school graduates, yielding even more confounded contrasts than the first set of comparisons. Third, some compare outcomes for current college graduates to outcomes for past college graduates. In each case, the comparisons obscure the logic of causal effects. Moreover, the "outcomes" described are often not long-term life chances but experiences in college itself. And when postcollege outcomes are considered, they seldom encapsulate the broad long-term benefits of college.

Consider an article from the *Chronicle of Higher Education*, which also appeared in the *New York Times*.[11] The article "Are Too Many Students Going to College?" states that "there is a growing sentiment that college may not be the best option for all students." Charles Murray is quoted as stating: "It has been empirically demonstrated that doing well (B average or better) in a traditional college major in the arts and sciences requires levels of linguistic and logical/mathematical ability that only 10 to 15 percent of the nation's youth possess." Murray concludes that "the four-year residential program leading to a B.A. is the wrong model for a large majority of young people."[12] His implicit conclusion is that 85 to 90 percent of the population—those who, in his opinion, lack high measured ability as adolescents—should not attend a four-year college and complete a degree. Murray's basis for concluding that the many young people who do not score high by some threshold on measured ability tests should not pursue a college degree is how they compare to students with high measured ability. His assessment does not draw on the counterfactual of how they would do without a college degree. Murray is also not invoking outcomes associated with a degree; instead, he simply states that "low ability" students should not even attempt a college degree because of their test scores.[13]

Murray is known for making controversial statements with demonstrably faulty reasoning.[14] Yet others use similar logic in assessing the value of college for low-achieving and disadvantaged students. For example, Richard Sander and Stuart Taylor argue that low-income students are mismatched on college campuses relative to high-income students and would be better served elsewhere.[15] They claim that affirmative action policies hurt minority students by placing them in academic situations where they cannot compete. They compare low- and high-income students and do not invoke potential outcomes. They also do not consider life outcomes after college—only experiences within college. Similarly, Richard Vedder states: "A large proportion of our population should not go to college, or at least not at public expense. . . . More and more graduates are filling jobs for which they are academically overqualified."[16] He suggests that the students who do not currently complete college—who are overwhelmingly low-income and disadvantaged—should not pursue a college degree. Vedder asks, "Is it really advantageous to the economic aspirations of low-income Americans with mediocre secondary education backgrounds to push them into four-year degree programs when, for a large proportion of them, the result will be dropping out of college, a sizable student loan debt, and the psychological scars arising from being considered something of an academic failure?"[17] He compares advantaged and disadvantaged students and does not consider counterfactuals. Indeed, in many debates around academic "mismatch" and affirmative action, the same comparisons are habitually invoked—that is, between the achievements of college students of different social backgrounds or race. Vedder does not consider the evidence suggesting high achievement among low-income first-generation college students.[18] Although he could have concluded that we should do more to support students who enroll in college to complete a degree, he instead suggests that they should not attend at all. Finally, the outcomes he considers are the college experience and financial debt rather than the long-term life outcomes.

In 2014, the *Daily Princetonian* published "Many People Shouldn't Go to College."[19] Concluding that "the reality is that a large number of college students have no business being at four-year universities"—the implication being that students who cannot afford to pay tuition without acquiring debt should not be attending college—this author makes no mention of returns to college. Writing in *The New Republic* that many college graduates are filling low-wage, low-skilled, and part-time jobs, Nader Habibi states: "A large portion of the money spent on college education of a student that ends up in a non-college job is wasted. The student has also wasted four years of his/her life on acquiring skills that he/she does not utilize to earn a living."[20] There is no reasonable basis for Habibi to assume that these skills are unneeded; moreover, Habibi makes no reference to the counterfactual socioeconomic trajectory and gives no assessment of outcomes beyond jobs and wages.

Contending that many students find "academics daunting and dull," the economist Bryan Caplan states, "College graduation—not to mention elite careers—is unrealistic for such students. Hence, they're better off training to be plumbers, electricians, and mechanics." Caplan continues: "We should steer academically uninclined kids toward vocational education when they're 12."[21] The "uninclined," low-achieving students to whom Caplan refers are disproportionately low-income and racially minoritized students. How does he conclude that they are "better off"? He contends that the "American underclass" should initially pursue vocational training rather than college, as they will be too bitter to do so after "failing." Caplan also notes that these "students don't seem to be getting much out of higher education," by which he means learning useful skills.[22] Caplan's statements that certain students find academics daunting and dull or are better off with different types of training are full of assumptions about disadvantaged students' interests and capabilities. Moreover, in none of these arguments does Caplan compare students' outcomes to counterfactual outcomes without college. He also often considers only vague outcomes (for example, that certain positions are "unrealistic," or that these students would be "better off" without college) and does not evaluate broad life outcomes beyond labor market rewards.[23]

A *CBS News* segment reporting on Tim Bartik and Brad Hershbein's findings concludes: "College graduates who come from poorer families largely miss out on the same type of earnings boost that their cohorts from wealthier backgrounds earn across their lifetimes."[24] Drawing on Bartik and Hershbein's findings, the segment suggests that those who grew up in poverty and completed college certainly rise above poverty and have high incomes, just not as high as those from high-income backgrounds.[25] Again, these commentaries make comparisons between college graduates from low-income and high-income backgrounds rather than drawing on counterfactuals and estimating college effects. In a *New York Times* article, "College May Not Be Worth It Anymore: For the Poor, Higher Education May Hurt More than It Helps," the author draws on Bartik and Hershbein's research and concludes that a college degree is worth less to poor and Black students because Black college graduates and those from poor backgrounds on average earn only slightly more than White holders of a high school degree and those from middle-class backgrounds.[26] The article does not draw on counterfactuals and falls into the second confounded comparisons approach. To assess college completion effects, we need to consider what college graduates would have earned had they not completed college, not what unmatched students earn when they do not complete college. Nevertheless, the author takes this as evidence that college is not worth it for poor and Black students. Interestingly, she concludes that "none of this is to suggest that higher education is not desirable: I've encouraged my own children to take that path." Indeed, commentators who discourage college as inappropriate for some students—typically more-disadvantaged students—seldom include their own children in the mix of those who should not attend.

A quick read of Bartik and Hershbein's results could lead to conclusions like those just cited. Upon closer inspection, however, their results are more nuanced and suggest significant gains for low-income and Black college graduates, as I note in chapter 2.[27] In response to the *New York Times* editorial, Bartik and Hershbein state in "College Worth It for Persons from Low-Income Backgrounds" that they "strongly disagree with the op-ed's implicit conclusion, that college is not worth it for various disadvantaged groups. Our research does not support that conclusion. College has good returns for groups from lower-income backgrounds and has particularly high returns for those from poverty backgrounds and for African-Americans."[28] They also note that college graduates, particularly White males, who end up in the upper tail of the income distribution drive much of the high return for advantaged individuals.

The media are not alone in drawing on comparisons rather than counterfactuals. Some social science research does not invoke counterfactual reasoning. For example, scholars often compare Black and White college graduates' wages and note a sizable gap—over 20 percent by some estimates.[29] It is important to note that White graduates earn more than Black graduates. Scholars often use this evidence to enforce antidiscrimination laws in hiring and promotion. But we should not use such evidence to make a comparison that would beget a false conclusion—that college does not pay off for Black students. We should instead compare Black college graduates' wages to their counterfactual wages (the wages they would have earned had they not completed college) and compare White college graduates' wages against their counterfactual wages. Once we do that, we can then compare college *returns* by race. Here we tend to reach a different conclusion: the returns are more significant for Black college graduates than for White graduates.[30]

To highlight inequality in the college experience among disadvantaged students, work in sociology and education has drawn on comparisons between students of different backgrounds on college campuses. For example, in a widely cited study, the sociologists Elizabeth Armstrong and Laura Hamilton argue that family resources enable upper-class and upper-middle-class college-going women to be more successful in college than the working-class women they observe in their study. They note that, "if the experiences we document are common rather than atypical, the chorus questioning the value of a four-year degree may grow louder."[31] We should not underestimate the importance of unequal college experiences. The college setting should better accommodate students from disadvantaged backgrounds, but that is different from saying that college is the wrong path for students from underprivileged backgrounds or that it has no value for them. These latter claims invoke causal effects of college, for which we need to consider relevant counterfactuals. If we are going to evaluate the value of college for different students, we need to consider what these women would be doing without a college degree throughout their careers, not how they compare to one another in their experiences during college. The risk lies in concluding that college degrees are not of value for disadvantaged women because their college experiences and perhaps early labor market wages are unequal to those of more-advantaged women. This is not the right evidence to marshal regarding the value of college degrees for the disadvantaged.

Likewise, Anthony Jack's book describes sources of often-overlooked inequality underlying the experiences of students from differing class backgrounds on elite college campuses.[32] Students enter college unequally, with varying higher education knowledge and resources to navigate the experience. Low-income, racially minoritized students often feel intimidated, inadequate, and excluded on elite college campuses, with implications for their academic and social experiences.[33] Jack highlights that elite higher education privileges a narrow set of experiences that are more likely to be those of upper-income students. This work fits into the extensive literature that documents how poor and racially minoritized students face unfamiliar and conflictual sociocultural environments that are insufficiently supportive of diverse backgrounds.[34]

Yet Jack's book, even in its title, suggests that colleges are "failing disadvantaged students." What is the counterfactual? The suggestion is that colleges fail disadvantaged students because they do not have the same experience on elite campuses that advantaged students do, and because they do not sufficiently support diverse students. However, what are the experiences and outcomes of similar individuals who do not attend and obtain a degree from an elite college? These assertions do not establish the benefit or harm of college with counterfactual reasoning. A *Chronicle of Higher Education* article describing Jack's work states that, in many cases, "elite colleges widen rather than narrow the gulf between the wealthy and the poor."[35] This is a strong claim. To say that elite colleges widen the gap between the wealthy and the poor suggests that the differences between wealthy and poor elite college students, on some outcome, are greater than the differences between wealthy and poor high school graduates or graduates of non-elite colleges. In other words, for this to be a valid claim, we need to compare the outcomes of the wealthy and the poor who attend and complete a degree at an elite college to the outcomes of the wealthy and the poor who do not. The sociologists Mario Small and Christopher Winship show that, "contrary to common belief," attending a selective college increases the probability that Black students will graduate from college and "helps Blacks more than it helps whites."[36]

Scholars studying racial inequality have long emphasized the gap between Black and White economic outcomes at every level of schooling. Some recent work, for example, shows that Black households with college-educated heads have less wealth than White families whose heads did not complete high school.[37] This work makes an important contribution: raising the educational level of Blacks will not eradicate the racial wealth gap. Yet we should also emphasize evidence that the median net worth of college-educated Black households is ten times higher than the median net worth of high school–educated Black households; the same ratio for White households is two times.[38] Similarly, education scholars focusing on economic insecurity among college students in the face of rising costs suggest that college is creating poverty.[39] This work rightly focuses on students who experience food and housing insecurity on college campuses and on the need for college affordability. Colleges can and should do better to promote students' success, especially the success of disadvantaged college-goers. Yet statements that college is creating poverty or failing students could be interpreted to mean that college negatively affects students' lives. To make this claim, we should consider what these students' lives would look like in the absence of college and consider outcomes throughout their lives.

I do not mean to detract from the importance of this research. We must acknowledge and seek to rectify the disadvantages experienced by underprivileged and racially minoritized students on college campuses.

We need to move toward a society in which higher education is a more effective equalizer. This work fills a critical space in the sociology of education literature and social policy discussions. Yet the narrative we present to achieve these goals is important. A narrative suggesting that disadvantaged students are not well served by their presence on college campuses can be taken to mean by some constituencies that a college degree has less value for them than it does for advantaged students when in fact it may hold greater value for them. Such narratives may be used to justify claims that disadvantaged students are "mismatched" and should not attend college rather than taken as evidence that the context in which they are received should be improved.

We should be mindful of conflating college heterogeneity and college *completion effect* heterogeneity. College heterogeneity reflects differences in college experiences. Armstrong and Hamilton and Jack point to variation in college experiences—that is, to college heterogeneity. By contrast, variation in the effects of college completion on life outcomes reflects college completion effect heterogeneity. Studying college completion effect heterogeneity involves taking the difference between college graduates and matched non-college graduates and comparing effects across subgroups.

Finally, it is also commonly asserted that college degree returns are decreasing and graduates no longer benefit from college. Some people claim that many college graduates hold jobs that previously did not require a college degree.[40] The implication is that if a college degree was unnecessary for a particular job yesterday, it is also unnecessary today.[41] Yet, once again, these commentators make no reference to counterfactuals. We know that the labor market prospects for high school graduates have been deteriorating, so failing to describe the alternative pathways for college graduates crucially obscures conclusions as to the value of higher education. Whether the wage level for college graduates in 2020 was less than that in 1990 does not invalidate the return in 2020. From an individual perspective, what matters is what the graduate earns by completing college relative to not completing it. It makes little difference to that calculus whether the wage was greater in the past. As I discuss at length in chapter 2, there is considerable evidence for rising returns to college. Moreover, wages are only one outcome of interest.

Distinguishing Levels from Effects

A related, yet at times overlooked, distinction necessary to understand college degree returns is the difference between *levels* and *effects*. As mentioned earlier, some scholars suggest that college degrees equalize occupational status and wages across students from different social origins.[42] Others describe differences across social origins among college graduates.[43] Both sides of this debate focus on occupational status and wage levels among college graduates. For example, in the NLSY79 cohort, college graduates who grew up in the top quartile of the income distribution earned on average about $32 per hour over their career, and college graduates who grew up in the bottom quartile earned on average about $24 per hour (a factor of about 1.3). College does not fully equalize this measure of wages by parental income. Nevertheless, high school graduates who grew up in the top quartile earned, on average, about $21 per hour over their career, and high school graduates who grew up in the bottom quartile earned about $14 per hour (a factor of 1.5). In the NLSY79 cohort, a college degree, while not fully equalizing, equalized average wages relative to those with no more than a high school degree.

A comparison of wage levels by college degree status and parental income differs from a comparison of college degree effects on wages by parental income. We calculate college degree effects not by comparing the wages of a low-income college graduate to those of a high-income college graduate. Instead, we compare the wages of a low-income college graduate to the wages they would have earned without a college degree, and likewise for a high-income college graduate. Then we compare these relative effects. College does not need to equalize wages to benefit low-income students. Even if underprivileged students' wages are lower, college can still be *more* valuable for these students than it is for advantaged students.

In figure 2.1, I noted the distinction between levels and effects. The outcome levels—in this case, wages—are the lines. This stylized diagram shows that college-educated workers have higher wages than high school–educated workers. Their wages are similar regardless of their social origins (although I have included some slope to the line). This pattern corresponds to the "college as an equalizer" argument. However, suppose we increase the slope of the line for college-educated workers such that those from more-disadvantaged social origins have lower wages than those from advantaged social origins. Such a pattern may cause some to correctly note the unequal distribution of wages but to incorrectly minimize the value of college for those with disadvantaged social origins. To assess the latter, we consider college effects. If the slope for less-educated workers remains steeper than the slope for college-educated workers, we observe a larger benefit of college for those with underprivileged social origins. College does not need to be the great equalizer to affect the wages of low-income youth more than the wages of high-income youth.[44] Moreover, we may have varied patterns across life outcomes. A college degree may not equalize wages, but it may equalize poverty or social assistance or civic engagement. We should consider an array of life outcomes when assessing the equalizing role of higher education.

Figure 3.1 is a revision of figure 2.1 in which I focus on two cases, Chantelle and Nancy, and the outcome is poverty (rather than wages). I reverse the y-axis in order to focus on the effect of college on reducing poverty. Chantelle had a low propensity to complete college, and Nancy had a high propensity. Chantelle is a Black woman who grew up with her uncle in the South. She attended a disadvantaged high school, where both her test scores and achievement were low. Chantelle did not expect to attend college. Nancy is a White woman who grew up with both parents. Her father had an advanced degree, and her mother had a college degree. Her mother stayed home while her father worked and earned a high income. Nancy had high test scores and expected to go to college. These two women had very different backgrounds, yet they both graduated from a four-year college.

Now let us consider Chantelle's and Nancy's outcomes after college. To focus the discussion, I consider one life outcome: time spent in poverty. Neither Chantelle nor Nancy spent time in poverty from about age twenty-five through fifty. They experienced an equal level of poverty over most of their lives. Would we have expected Chantelle or Nancy to spend time in poverty without a college degree? Here we turn to our best estimate of their counterfactual trajectories. Given her social background, Nancy's family might have provided a safety net to prevent her from spending time in poverty. By contrast, given Chantelle's more-disadvantaged social background, we may expect college to have had a

Figure 3.1 How Counterfactuals Differ across Social Origins: Chantelle and Nancy

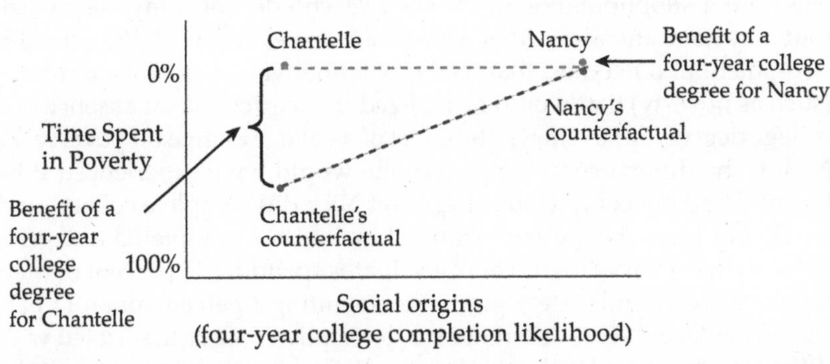

Source: Author's calculations using data from the U.S. Bureau of Labor Statistics National Longitudinal Surveys.

more meaningful effect on her poverty status. The matched comparisons lead to this conclusion, as depicted in figure 3.1. Although college equalized poverty for Chantelle and Nancy, their matched comparisons in the absence of a college degree have very different outcomes. This counterfactual heterogeneity yields a considerable estimated college benefit for Chantelle.

Identifying Effects of College Completion

To infer causality, we need to know what would have happened if the social process, event, or intervention we are studying, such as a college degree, had not occurred. Generally, individuals who complete college have other characteristics, abilities, and skills that predispose them to complete college and render them likely to do well even without a degree. The fundamental problem of causal inference is that we cannot observe counterfactual outcomes.[45] For example, we cannot know that Nick would be making less money if he had not gone on to college, or that Rich would be making more if he had earned a degree. The credibility of our causal claim rests on the plausibility of identification assumptions we make to infer counterfactual outcomes. In the remainder of this chapter, I give a broad overview of methods for identifying and estimating average and heterogeneous college effects. I refer the reader to the online methodological appendix for more details (https://www.russellsage.org/publications/overcoming-odds).

How would life outcomes differ for a high school graduate who did or did not complete a four-year college degree? Let college completion status be a binary variable, that is, one that takes on a value of 1 for four-year degree completion and 0 otherwise. We divide the high school–educated population into a subpopulation of the *treated,* who complete college, and a subpopulation of the *control,* who do not complete college (but may have attended either a two- or four-year college). We consider two potential outcomes, that is, the potential values of some outcome (such as poverty) that would be realized in the presence or absence of a college degree. For example, the effect of a college degree on poverty for Nick is the difference in the poverty he would have experienced if he had and had not completed college. Yet Nick did complete college, and we do not know his poverty status if he had not completed a degree. Let's say we observe high school graduates spending 13 percent of their time in poverty and college graduates spending 2 percent, or an 11 percent lower level.[46] This difference is a descriptive pattern associated with different education levels. While informative, it does not represent the causal effect of college on poverty. As college graduates tend to be more-advantaged and high-achieving individuals, we anticipate that their time in poverty without college might have been lower than for those who were not college graduates. If so, the effect of college on poverty would be biased, making the observed average difference in levels appear to reduce poverty more than it does.[47]

How can we impute unobserved potential outcomes and identify the causal effect of college on life outcomes? Suppose we could randomly assign college degrees to some individuals but not to others and then measure their poverty status. We could then estimate the average college completion effect as the difference in mean poverty levels between these two groups. With randomization, observed and unobserved precollege characteristics would be identical on average between college and non-college graduates. The only systematic difference between the two groups would be college degree status. Although we cannot estimate the effect of a treatment for any individual, randomization enables us to estimate an average treatment effect over a group of people. Randomization yields estimates with high internal validity, that is, estimates that minimize bias due to confounding (or selection into college). Confounding variables are precollege variables associated with college completion and, for example, poverty that create an association for reasons other than the causal effect of college completion on poverty. Some plausible confounding variables in estimating college effects include measures of sociodemographic characteristics, family background, psychosocial factors, secondary school achievement, and secondary school characteristics. Differences in these variables between college and non-college graduates that influence college attainment and subsequent life outcomes bias our inference of the college degree effect.

Random assignment of individuals to complete college can address the selection bias issue. Yet randomized trials are never perfect, and they are often impractical or unethical as well, especially in social research. Moreover, the strong internal validity of effect estimates in randomized trials often comes at the expense of external validity, that is, whether the conclusions generalize beyond the population under study.[48] The sample of individuals selected and willing to have a researcher randomly assign them to treatment status is generally unrepresentative of the broader population. Much social scientific research draws instead on nonexperimental observational data, which does not allow an investigator to control the assignment of treatments to the individuals under study.[49] Rather than manipulate the social process, researchers observe naturally occurring events or interventions in such studies. Using such observational data increases the external validity of effect estimates, yielding results that are generalizable to the population from which the sample was drawn. Internal validity, however, is less credible, owing to lingering selection bias.[50]

Donald Rubin's potential outcome model extends the conceptual apparatus of randomized experiments to observational studies. We aim to identify a treated group of college graduates and a control group of non-college graduates whose precollege characteristics are statistically identical on average in the absence of college. Suppose that we observe that completing college reduces poverty. Completing college may reduce poverty, or individuals who grow up in more-advantaged families may be more likely to complete college and less likely to fall below the poverty line regardless of whether they complete college. Or both factors may be at work. To evaluate college completion effects, we must thus first posit an assignment mechanism.[51] The assignment mechanism determines which individuals receive treatment (those with a college degree) and which receive control (those with no college degree). After adjusting for precollege characteristics, we assume that college and non-college graduates differ in terms of observed characteristics, but not unobserved characteristics.[52] This is the assumption of unconfoundedness.[53] If it does not fully hold, our estimated college completion effects will be biased by confounding (selection into college degree status).

Consider figure 3.2, a directed acyclic graph (DAG) of the effect of college completion on an outcome (such as poverty) adjusting for precollege characteristics. A DAG is a way of formalizing our causal assumptions. There are two paths from a college degree to the outcome. There is a direct path, which represents the causal effect of college completion on the outcome, and there is, in the language of Judea Pearl, a backdoor path from college completion to precollege characteristics to the outcome.[54] If we adjust for precollege characteristics, we close that backdoor

Figure 3.2 Four-Year College Completion Effects

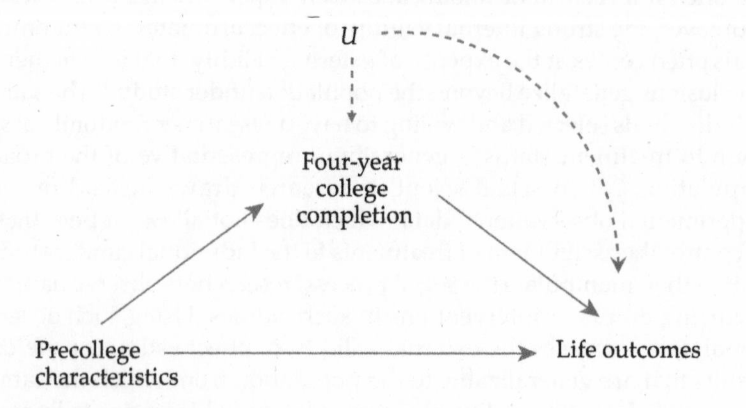

Source: Author's conceptual diagram.
Notes: *U* = unobserved confounders.

path. If unconfoundedness is true, comparisons of outcomes between college and non-college graduates have a causal interpretation. We hold the unconfoundedness condition as an unverifiable assumption. Its plausibility hinges on the richness of the observed precollege characteristics. Measurement of theoretically meaningful precollege characteristics renders the assumption more plausible but not necessarily true. *U* depicts an unobserved confounding factor, and the dashed lines show *U* influencing college completion and the outcome.[55] We can again have a backdoor path from college completion to *Y*, this time through *U*, which is unobserved. To the extent that unobserved factors correlate with observed factors, we may be accounting for many unobserved factors.[56] Let us next consider methods to estimate the effects of college completion on life outcomes.

Matching Methods for Estimating Effects of College Completion

Matching is a transparent and intuitive method for making predictions about counterfactual outcomes.[57] James Heckman and Salvador Navarro-Lozano contend that matching is a popular evaluation approach because it is easy to understand and apply.[58] Matching methods have a long history, dating to experimental work in the first half of the twentieth century.[59] The foundational work in statistics by Donald Rubin and Paul Rosenbaum in the 1970s and 1980s sparked interest and applications in sociology in the 1980s and 1990s.[60] The use of this work became even more widespread throughout the 2000s.[61] Broadly defined, we use matching to balance the distribution of precollege confounders in the college and non–college completion groups.[62] Matched non-college graduates serve to approximate the counterfactual outcomes of each college graduate. Thus, we learn about college completion effects by imputing counterfactual quantities with similar, or matched, comparison units and average outcomes across matched pairs of college and non-college graduates. Matching involves four steps: (1) defining closeness, that is, the distance measure used to determine whether an individual is a good match for another; (2) implementing a matching method given the measure of closeness; (3) assessing the quality of the resulting matched sample (possibly iterating steps 1 and 2 until a well-matched sample is obtained); and (4) estimating the effects.[63]

Suppose we want to match on race, parental education, parental occupation, family structure, high school achievement, psychosocial skills, and high school characteristics. As the number of matching variables increases, the number of bins to subset the population increases exponentially, creating a dimensionality problem.[64] Influential work by Paul

Rosenbaum and Donald Rubin shows that we do not need to compare students of each parental income, racial, and achievement category who did and did not complete college.[65] Instead, matching those with the same estimated probability, or *propensity*, of college as a measure of closeness is sufficient.[66] The propensity, or probability, of college completion provides a single number that summarizes the estimated likelihood that an individual will complete college.[67] The statistician Elizabeth Stuart notes that "grouping individuals with similar propensity scores replicates a mini-randomized experiment, at least for observed covariates."[68] For example, take Nick, who completed college. To estimate the effect of a four-year degree we want to know what would have happened to Nick had he not completed college. Although we cannot observe his life without college, we can observe Rich, who did not complete college but had the same estimated propensity to complete college as Nick. We use Rich to impute the missing counterfactual for Nick and estimate the individual-specific college effect. As we repeat this process across many pairs and average the differences, our attention is focused on counterfactual quantities.[69] Another key advantage of this conceptual apparatus is that it encourages analysts to assess the process of causal exposure—in this case, selection into college completion—and necessitates modeling that process as the first step of data analysis.[70] Analysts must carefully consider which variables are appropriate to condition on and which are irrelevant and may amplify bias.

The sociologists Stephen Morgan and David Harding write that "matching succeeds admirably in laying bare the particular problems of estimating causal effects."[71] Yet matching methods cannot ensure the identification of causal effects any more than standard regression models based on observational data.[72] For example, we know that Nick and Rich had the same estimated propensity for college completion and had similar family backgrounds, high school achievement, and psychosocial skills. Some other characteristics may nonetheless still differentiate Nick and Rich that we do not observe. After all, Nick completed college and Rich did not. Matching, or any other method based on observational data, does not absolve researchers from the problem of selection bias. But neither does it make matters worse than standard regression models. And of course, explicit attention to the assignment mechanism and counterfactual conditions can increase the internal validity of our estimates and better equip analysts to draw causal conclusions.

There are several possible matching algorithms we can use to estimate effects. I use nearest-neighbor matching to construct the counterfactual for each college graduate using four non-college graduates matched on the estimated (linearized) propensity for college.[73] I adopt an iterative stepwise procedure outlined by Guido Imbens and Donald Rubin to estimate propensity scores.[74] This approach allows for a flexible propensity score model specification.[75] I include covariates presumed to affect college completion and life chances and exclude presumed instrumental variables and postcollege mediators.[76] We can introduce more bias if we control for variables that occur after (or during) college.[77] I restrict analyses to high school graduates with comparable propensities for college, or the *region of common support* (also known as "overlap").[78] Figure 3.3 depicts the issue of common support. Suppose there are regions where the range of the college completion propensity does not overlap for college and non-college graduates. In that case, matching is justified only when performed over the region of common support. The counterfactual outcome is unidentified for individuals outside the region of support.

Comparing the incomparable—in other words, violating the common support condition—is an important source of bias in causal effects estimates. Researchers often overlook this source of bias in regression analyses that do not consider potential outcomes. Suppose we have some college graduates with very high propensities for completion, and we

Figure 3.3 Common Support in Matching

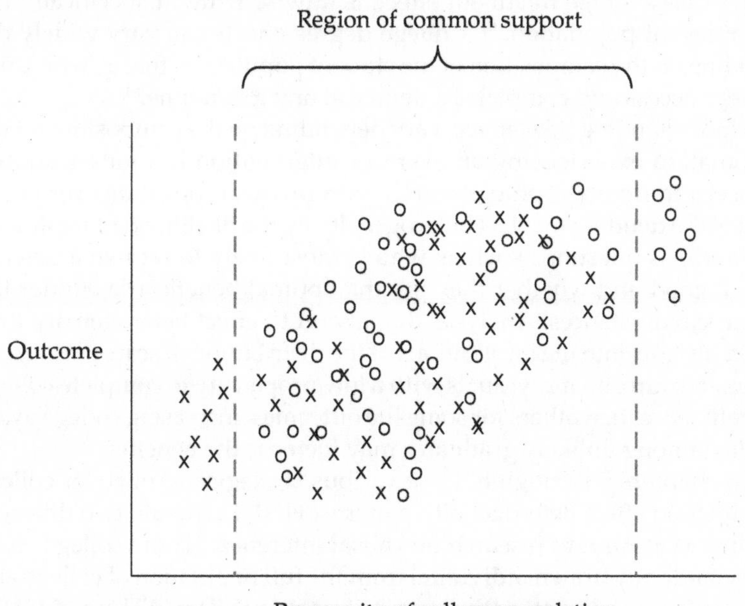

Source: Author's conceptual diagram.
Notes: O data points = college graduates; X data points = non-college graduates.

draw on non-college graduates as control cases who do not have similarly high propensities. In that case, our college completion effect estimates will be biased. I eliminate college graduates with very high propensity scores with no comparable non-college graduates.[79] Likewise, I eliminate non-college graduates with very low propensities with no comparable college graduates. The online methodological appendix provides more matching and propensity score estimation details.[80]

Assessing Variation in the Effects of College Completion

A defining feature of social research is the tension between the reality that people experience circumstances and events differently and the need to aggregate individuals to summarize the effects of those circumstances or events.[81] College degrees affect people in unique ways. Yet statistical analyses of college completion effects generally involve some group-level average, which can mask important effect heterogeneity within groups. When individuals differ in their response to completing college, no single number summarizes the distribution of responses.[82] As the sociologist Herbert Smith writes: "To speak of *the* treatment effect, or *the* average treatment effect, is unwise without specification of the relevant population."[83] College degree effects can vary widely depending on the composition of the student population, that is, who gains college access and completes a degree at any given time.[84]

Understanding how effects vary depending on the composition of the population experiencing an event or intervention is a long-standing concern in demographic research with broad implications for social policy.[85] Attending to effect heterogeneity by the likelihood of treatment, we address questions such as who is most likely to receive a desired social good and whether they are the optimal beneficiaries under the given circumstances. Analyses that attend to effect heterogeneity thus yield insights into the implications of the distribution of scarce resources. If less-resourceful individuals with a low propensity to complete college benefit more than others for some life outcomes, increasing college availability among unlikely graduates may increase the benefits.

In chapters 5 through 8, I use various strategies to uncover college completion effect heterogeneity patterns. First, I estimate two different quantities central to research on causal inference: (1) the college effect for a randomly drawn individual from the full population of college and non-college graduates, or the average treatment effect (ATE); and (2) the college effect among college graduates, or the treatment effect on the treated (TT). For example, if we match Nick to Rich and subtract Rich's wages from Nick's, we get an estimate of the effect of college on Nick's wages. We could also consider a non-college graduate, Josefina, from the population and subtract her wages from those of a matched college graduate, Daniela, to get an estimate of what Josefina's wages would be *had she attended and completed college*. If we average over the whole population of college and non-college graduates, we get the ATE. Averaging over all college graduates, we recover the TT. We have evidence for variation in the college effect by the likelihood of college completion when these estimates do not equal one another. If TT exceeds ATE, college completion effects are greater for those individuals who are more likely to graduate; analogously, if ATE exceeds TT, college effects are greater for those individuals who are less likely to graduate. I estimate the ATE and TT using matching, as described earlier.

Second, I explore patterns of college effect variation by the estimated propensity for college completion. By providing a summary measure of the likelihood of college, propensity-based methods ultimately simplify our task of determining how college effects vary across students who are more or less likely to obtain degrees. I examine effects partitioned according to low-, middle-, and high-propensity scores and the continuous propensity score.[86] Subclassification (or partitioning) on the propensity score dates to Paul Rosenbaum and Donald Rubin's work in the 1980s.[87] I use matching within the three propensity score strata to adjust for the remaining imbalance in propensity scores within strata. I also use two estimation methods in addition to matching as robustness checks, as described later. A decrease in the college effect with an increase in the propensity for college roughly corresponds to the setting where ATE > TT—evidence that the college degree effect decreases as the college degree likelihood increases.[88] Appendix figures C.3 and C.4 for the NLSY79 and NLSY97, respectively, display box plots of the distributions for the propensity-stratified samples. The plots show that matching equalizes imbalances in the distributions.

Third, I use a smoothing-differencing method for estimating heterogeneous college completion effects. The method consists of the following steps: (1) estimating propensity scores of college completion for each individual; (2) for each group (the college and non-college graduates), fitting and plotting separate local polynomial regressions of the outcome variable on the propensity score; and (3) taking the difference in the nonparametric regression line between the college and non-college graduates at different levels of the propensity score to obtain the pattern of college completion effect heterogeneity as a function of the propensity score.[89] I plot step 2 to observe levels of the outcome for college and non-college graduates and determine to what degree college completion equalizes life chances. I plot step 3 to observe college completion effects by completion likelihood. Results from this approach enable us to observe situations in which a nonlinear pattern of college effects emerges across the distribution of the propensity for college completion, with no simple analog to the estimates of ATE and TT.

Fourth, I also compare effects for different groups, including race, parental income, mother's education, and test scores. I group family income, mother's education, and test scores into low, middle, and high strata. At times I combine characteristics, such as low-income racially minoritized students or low-income first-generation students. Family background characteristics like parental income and mother's education are strongly associated with the propensity for college completion. Sometimes analysts question whether running interactions with key covariates would be simpler than using propensity-based methods to uncover effect heterogeneity. For many research questions, heterogeneity by specific covariates is of scientific interest. Of course, as I do here, we can do both. Yet here I am interested in how selection into completing degrees relates to the effects of completing degrees. In this case, the interaction with the propensity score offers the most straightforward approach, one that allows us to make simple summary statements about the unequal distribution of scarce resources. The results have important implications for access to higher education and the effects of higher education. For example, we can make statements like "those unlikely to complete college benefit the most in reducing poverty." Estimating effects by race, parental income, and test scores also indicates selection into college. Yet these analyses do not precisely reveal how unequal access relates to unequal returns.[90] Examining effects by the propensity score also directs attention to heterogeneity in selection processes and causal assumptions.

Fifth, I use a machine learning approach to uncover the subpopulations most responsive to college completion. Uncovering effect heterogeneity represents a promising use of machine learning methods for causal inference.[91] It is difficult to know ex-ante which people benefit most from college degrees. In social scientific practice, researchers routinely consider many possible subgroups to determine if they have meaningful differences in effect estimates and proceed to report the effect estimates of those that do. Yet it may just be chance that the subgroup they focus on is more responsive to college.[92] Moreover, individual characteristics may be most informative when considered jointly, in complex and nonlinear ways—for example, considering Black women who grew up in large families rather than considering just Blacks or Black women. It may be unclear which of many possible joint covariates and covariate thresholds are best to consider before analyses. A new approach based on decision trees, known as causal trees, partitions the population according to effect heterogeneity and estimates effects within each group. Using this approach, I can uncover key subpopulations that may or may not accord with conventional sociodemographic partitions and theoretical priors.[93] I then use matching to estimate effects within the subgroups determined by the causal trees. Appendix A offers estimation details.

Interpreting Variation in the Effects of College Completion

Identifying the effects of completing a college degree is complex. We can match individuals based on the observed characteristics described earlier, but doing so does not eliminate the possibility that our matched comparisons differ in unobserved ways. The situation is further complicated when we aim to uncover the distribution of responses to college completion. Our selection bias problem could be worse for some subpopulations than others. An observed pattern of variation in college completion effects could be due to variation in unobserved selection into college. For example, Black students generally face more barriers to completing college than White students do. Thus, Black students who overcome the odds and complete a degree may have characteristics that render them more selective than White students who face fewer barriers to degree completion. The question is whether we adequately account for all those characteristics in our matched comparisons. We may believe that White college graduates are less selective while overlooking some measures, such as perseverance in the face of discrimination, for Black graduates. If so, our estimates of college completion effects for Blacks could be larger than estimates for Whites, not because Blacks benefit more from college degrees than Whites, but because their tenacity or resilience led them to complete college and have better socioeconomic outcomes.

We can extend this line of reasoning to most of the comparisons we make, whether by family income, parents' education, test scores, the propensity for college completion, or some subgroup identified by the machine learning algorithm. In each case, we may have differential selection bias that complicates our interpretation of effect differences. Researchers often sweep aside differential selection bias that influences stratified effect estimates.[94] Yet we would not eliminate interactions because we suspect differential selection bias and instead restrict attention to the full population. If there is selection bias in subpopulations, this will also generally produce selection bias in the population-average causal effect. Thus, even in the presence of heterogeneous selection, it is helpful to examine subpopulation effect estimates. Such analyses add not only insight into effect heterogeneity but also concreteness to concerns about unobserved selection.

That said, analysts and the public at large too often turn to individual characteristics as the basis for questioning the validity of college degree effects, as if those who do not attain higher levels of education somehow lack motivation or commitment. We may instead assume that individuals who do not complete a degree work hard under difficult circumstances and do not obtain a degree due to social and structural conditions that we observe and for idiosyncratic reasons that do not necessarily bias our results. Although college degree attainment is highly selective, we have rich data to predict that attainment. We know about sociodemographic factors; about family background factors, including parents' education, income, occupation, nativity, and family structure; and about achievement in high school and test scores. We know about college expectations and aspirations, friends' plans, and self-esteem; about delinquent behavior and teenage pregnancy; and about the characteristics of the secondary schools that students attend. As described more fully in chapter 4, I construct a model with many interaction terms between these variables. For example, I include interactions such as whether individuals grew up in large families and lived in the South and whether they were Black and enrolled in college preparatory courses. The unobserved confounding variables we worry about must differ from all the factors I use in this model to bias the estimated effects of college completion.

No one can prove that a causal claim is true or whether it results from selection. Although the assumption that we have accounted for all relevant factors that predict college degree attainment is inherently untestable, we sometimes let critics get away with a lower burden of proof. The costs of this inclination include the risk of dismissing a true result. At worst, we set the bar of evidence so high that we never learn anything about the social world. Peter Blau and Otis Dudley Duncan warned against leaning too heavily on the possible selection bias critique:

> It is all too easy to make a formidable list of unmeasured variables that someone has alleged to be crucial to the process under study. But the mere existence of such variables is already acknowledged by the presence of the residual. It would seem to be part of the critic's task to *show*, if only hypothetically but specifically, how the modification of the causal scheme to include a new variable would disrupt or alter the relationships in the original diagram.[95]

Duncan also warned social scientists of the danger of "statisticism"—the assumption "that statistical formulas exist for evaluating such things as the relative merits of different substantive theories."[96] We cannot adjudicate between the selection and substantive interpretations in the estimation of college degree effects, but we can consider substantive knowledge and the robustness of the pattern of results across many different types of analyses. Angrist and Pischke write, "We're after truth, but truth is not revealed in full, and the messages the data transmit require interpretation."[97] Social scientists should consider the value of statistical methods and empirical findings alongside a substantive understanding of social processes. Selection is part of the process and how we interpret effects. For example, in our earlier work, Yu Xie and I emphasize both selectivity bias and substantive interpretations. We argue that the very pattern of heterogeneous effects of college degrees on earnings by the propensity to complete college suggests that individuals from disadvantaged social backgrounds, for whom college is not a culturally expected outcome, overcome considerable odds to attend college and may be uniquely driven by the economic rationale. We speculate that the observed pattern of negative selection could reflect differential selectivity, with persons of low propensity to complete college more selective than persons of high propensity.[98] Although this is possible, we must also draw on the body of social science evidence. As I discuss in chapter 2, the substantive basis for suggesting significant returns to college degrees for disadvantaged students is compelling. The notion that large college completion benefits among unlikely college graduates must be due to unobserved characteristics is lacking support in the literature in economics and sociology, much less the compelling narrative of the lives of disadvantaged youth completing degrees.[99]

Critics should thus offer a reasonable theoretical and empirical basis for suspecting that unobserved variables differ substantially from observed variables and bias results. Often, instead, critics offer only vague claims that such bias exists. We can demonstrate a pattern of heterogeneous effects under one set of assumptions and show that those effects may reflect differential unobserved selection under another set of assumptions. Both can be consistent with the data. The conclusions we draw depend upon which assumptions are more credible and which findings are more consistent with what we know about the social world. We could assume bias levels for much social scientific work and conclude that effects are erroneous. We could assume differential selection for interactions by race, parental income, or any other common factors to question the validity of observed variation in effects across subgroups.[100] Assumptions of possible bias do not, however, invalidate the approach used in a study and the possibility of real response heterogeneity.[101]

Considering how college completion effects vary by the estimated propensity for college completion encourages analysts to consider selection processes more explicitly and to question the extent to which those processes differ across the population of college graduates. By focusing on possible imbalance or selection bias at the tails of the distribution, the propensity score approach motivates researchers to evaluate the assumptions they make about average college completion effects. In analyses assuming homogeneity, scholars may estimate an "average effect" and possibly state that there may be selection bias, but do not identify where that selection bias is most likely to occur across the population. Considering effects partitioned by propensity scores encourages the assessment of how subpopulations more and less likely to complete college influence the average effect. Herein lies, not a limitation of this approach, but a fundamental strength.

Interpreting the effects of college degrees thus requires consideration of how observable and unobservable characteristics influence selection into college attainment for different subgroups. Disadvantaged youth must overcome the odds to complete a college degree. Although we cannot know the relative strength of observed to unobserved factors, we hypothesize that stronger unobserved factors influence selection into college among those with a low propensity to complete a degree than among those with a high propensity. That is, a high proportion of advantaged youth attend college regardless of their abilities, whereas a more selective group of disadvantaged youth generally does so. The behavior of low-propensity youth may align more closely with (conventional) rational action theory, whereby they positively select into college according to their expected returns to college. We may, in effect, have positive selection among those on the margin of school continuation, even if there is negative selection among the full population. This yields an important policy implication. If we expand college degrees to those on the margin of school continuation across the propensity for college, we have larger expected gains if we target low-propensity youth rather than high-propensity youth.[102]

Robustness Checks and Sensitivity Analyses

Throughout this book, I explore various methods to study college completion effect heterogeneity to learn more about the data. The sociologist Charles Halaby's review of sociological methods notes that "causal inference cannot be reduced to any one formula applied to data."[103] The analytic methods I use throughout have different strengths and weaknesses, but all of them are essentially different ways to identify subpopulations with a varying probability of selection into college. Moreover, in addition to the matching approach I use to assess effects by propensity score strata, I also consider two additional estimation strategies as a robustness check: a doubly robust inverse probability weighted approach, and a machine learning method based on generalized random forests. I describe both methods in appendix A.

We must contend with the reality that our causal effect estimates are uncertain. Albert Einstein observed that, "as far as the laws of mathematics refer to reality, they are not certain; and as far as they are certain, they do not refer to reality."[104] Gary King, Robert Keohane, and Sidney Verba also note that we should not avoid causal language; instead, "we should draw causal inferences where they seem appropriate but also provide the reader with the best and most honest estimate of the uncertainty of that inference."[105] A strategy we can use to address such uncertainty is called a sensitivity analysis. We determine how sensitive the results are by estimating how extensive unobserved confounding would need to be to invalidate the conclusions we draw from the estimated effects.[106] The college completion effect decreases when the unobserved variable strongly affects completing college and the outcome of interest. For example, unobserved resilience might reduce poverty levels and be higher among college graduates. I assess a range of bias values that such an unobserved variable, like resilience, may generate.[107] I also use sensitivity analyses to determine whether patterns of effect heterogeneity are affected by differences in unobserved confounding. I consider unobserved confounding for the stratified effect estimates and use an approach to assess bounds across the continuous propensity score distribution. This latter approach assumes a larger bias for low- and high-propensity college graduates.[108] The procedure is described more fully in Appendix A.

Matched Vignettes

To contextualize the quantitative findings, I construct twelve matched vignettes (or twenty-four individuals) using data from NLSY79. I select one White, one Black, and one Hispanic male college graduate with a low propensity for college, and one White, one Black, and one Hispanic male college graduate with a high propensity for college. I also select one White, one Black, and one Hispanic female college graduate with a low propensity for college, and one White, one Black, and one Hispanic female college graduate with a high propensity for college. For each selected college graduate, I select a matched comparison to serve as the individual-specific counterfactual. I select one match out of four possible matches using nearest-neighbor matching on the estimated propensity score.[109] I also draw on coarsened strata to make these matches, which, in addition to gender and race, include quartiles of parental income and test scores.[110] Although they have the same propensity for college and several key characteristics, this does not mean that all their features are the same.

Among the pairs with a low propensity for college, I select individuals who differ for one or more instrumental variables. An instrumental variable affects college-going, but only the outcome of interest through college. For example, one case who completed college had a four-year public college nearby, while the matched case who did not complete college did not have a college nearby. The idea is that having a college nearby may influence whether some students attend college but does not directly influence their life outcomes (rendering it an "instrument" for establishing the effect of college). Or one individual who completed college lived in an area with a high unemployment rate, while the matched case who did not complete college lived where the local unemployment rate was lower. These cases may indicate the effect of college for an individual on the margin of school continuation induced into college by the instrument.[111] I consider four instrumental variables using private geocode data from the NLSY79 merged with data from various sources. First, I construct the presence of a public four-year college in the county of residence with NLSY79 geocode data merged with data from the Higher Education General Information Survey. Second, I draw on those sources to measure the average public four-year college tuition in the county of residence. Third, I use NLSY79 geocode data merged with the Bureau of Labor Statistics data to create the local-area unemployment rate in the state of residence at age seventeen. Fourth, I construct average wage in the county of residence at age seventeen with NLSY79 geocode data merged with Bureau of Economic Analysis data.

I choose a college graduate between the twenty-fifth and seventy-fifth percentile of the propensity score distribution within each propensity score stratum to avoid extreme cases at the low and high ends.[112] I choose each college graduate based on satisfying these criteria and having the individual college completion effect for three selected outcomes nearest to the average value for that category. The outcomes include time in a low-wage job, time as a single parent, and receipt of social assistance. For example, for low-propensity college graduates, the average effect on the proportion of time in a low-wage job is −0.2. In other words, college is associated with 20 percent less time spent in a low-wage job throughout a career for low-propensity college graduates. I selected low-propensity college graduates with an estimated treatment effect of −0.2.[113] I thus use this selection technique to generate vignettes that represent the average individual for college completion effects on a few key outcomes for that group. Of course, not all cases will perfectly match the average effects for each selected outcome.

Once constructed, I assign gender- and race-specific common names. I also assign names beginning with the letters B, C, and D for low-propensity college graduates, H, I, and J for low-propensity non-college graduates, N, O, and P for high-propensity college graduates, and R, S, and T for high-propensity non-college graduates. That is, the bottom half of the alphabet corresponds to low-propensity vignettes and the top half

Table 3.2 Matched Vignettes

	No Four-Year College Degree	Four-Year College Degree
Low likelihood of college completion		
White		
Male	Henry	Brian
Female	Helen	Brenda
Black		
Male	Isaiah	Caleb
Female	Imani	Chantelle
Hispanic		
Male	Javier	Diego
Female	Josefina	Daniela
High likelihood of college completion		
White		
Male	Rich	Nick
Female	Rebecca	Nancy
Black		
Male	Samuel	Otis
Female	Sydney	Olanna
Hispanic		
Male	Tomas	Pedro
Female	Tia	Paula

Source: Author's calculations using data from the U.S. Bureau of Labor Statistics National Longitudinal Surveys.

corresponds to high-propensity vignettes. Table 3.2 categorizes the individuals according to the criteria for selection.[114] I follow the lives of these twenty-four individuals from adolescence to midlife. I describe their family background circumstances, high school achievement, psychosocial well-being, educational attainment, and broad life outcomes from ages twenty-five to fifty.

The next chapter describes unequal college chances. I consider how social origins influence college attainment. I describe the propensity for college attainment and characteristics of individuals with low and high propensity. I also describe the experiences of the vignettes with varying college chances in narratives that contextualize the quantitative statistics. The subsequent four chapters consider college degree effects across estimated college chances.

Chapter 4

Unequal College Chances

Chantelle had a low likelihood of completing college. A Black woman who grew up in the urban South, she was raised by a single mother and had several siblings. Chantelle's mother did not finish high school, and her family income was in the bottom quartile of the income distribution, under the poverty threshold. Chantelle attended a disadvantaged high school where about 20 percent of the students did not complete a high school degree. She felt that she had little control over her life. Unsatisfied with her high school experience, Chantelle did not expect to continue her schooling. The odds of attaining a college degree were against her. Consider the difference between Chantelle's odds of completing college and Nancy's. Nancy had a high likelihood of obtaining a college degree. A White woman who also grew up in the urban South, Nancy grew up with both of her parents and one sibling. Both of Nancy's parents completed college. Her father had a law degree and worked as a law professor and their income was in the top quartile of the distribution. Nancy attended an advantaged high school where almost all the students received their diplomas. She enrolled in college prep courses, expected to go to college, and felt in control of her life. The odds of attaining a college degree were firmly in Nancy's favor.

Despite their different socioeconomic backgrounds, both Chantelle and Nancy ultimately attended a four-year college immediately after high school and completed a college degree within four years of high school. Their backgrounds reveal some characteristics that differentiate youth with unequal chances of completing a college degree. In this chapter, I introduce estimated college completion propensities. I first offer a conceptual model of social origins, education, and socioeconomic destinations. I then discuss how social origins and structural inequalities impact college attendance and completion. After constructing an estimate of college attendance and completion chances, or propensity, I describe the characteristics of those with a low versus high propensity to complete college.

A Basic Model of Social Origins and College Attainment

Education plays a key role in social mobility. On the one hand, it serves as a vehicle for social reproduction, transmitting social origins to socioeconomic destinations. Disadvantaged social origins decrease educational attainment, and low educational attainment is associated with disadvantaged socioeconomic destinations. On the other hand, education opens opportunities for upward mobility.[1] Individuals who overcome the odds and attain high levels of education can attain high levels of socioeconomic success. Figure 4.1 is a simplified version of Peter Blau and Otis Dudley Duncan's classic path diagram depicting the status attainment model. It models what stratification researchers call the "O-E-D triangle": the relationship between social origins (O), education (E), and socioeconomic destinations (D).[2] In an era characterized by origins-based attainment, when family origins overwhelmingly dictate life chances (that is, path *a* is strong, while path *c* is weak), access to higher education is less consequential for economic outcomes. As we move to a social and economic system characterized by education-based attainment (path *c* is strong), our attention to how origins influence education (the strength of path *b*) is increasingly critical. We ask to what extent the conditions and circumstances of early life influence educational attainment.

In this chapter, I consider path *b*. In subsequent chapters, I consider path *c* and how path *c* varies by levels of social origins, where the pro-

Figure 4.1 The O-E-D Triangle: The Effects of Socioeconomic Origins (O) and Education (E) on Socioeconomic Destinations (D)

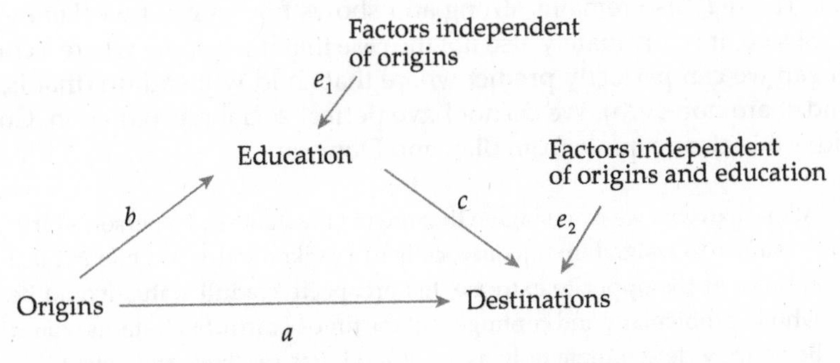

Source: Author's conceptual diagram.

pensity for college completion and other sociodemographic and social background factors constitute social origins.[3]

Education facilitates equal opportunity to the extent that access to higher education results from factors other than social origins (e_1); schools reproduce inequality to the extent that social origins determine access to education (path *b*). The former is variously deemed a "meritocracy," an achievement-based system, or an open system of social mobility.[4] Daniel Bell proclaimed in the 1970s that education is the arbiter of class position in a post-industrial society, as an advantaged social background no longer guarantees access to educational or socioeconomic attainment.[5] Access to higher education constitutes a struggle over the meaning of merit, where the winners always impose their "self-endorsing definition of merit on the losers."[6] Those who succeed are smart, hardworking, and motivated, or so goes the meritocratic narrative.[7]

Notwithstanding that many Americans remain wholly convinced that we operate under such a system and that success in higher education is an unfettered function of effort and achievement, access to schooling still strongly depends on family background and structural inequality (that is, path *b* remains strong).[8] Still, meritocratic conceptions even influence academic debate. The dominant scholarly critique of most studies of the effects of college is that we miss unobservable characteristics of individuals, and most scholars who level this critique assume that the missing variable is some measure of individual motivation or ambition rather than structural conditions, such as unequal access to school resources by class background or racial and ethnic discrimination.

In contrast to the meritocratic narrative, social reproduction refers to the tendency of children to replicate their parents' social status. Since paths *b* and *c* are strong, education preserves privilege across generations and plays a role in social reproduction.[9] Still, the direct association between individuals' origins and their destinations not mediated by education (path *a*) also remains strong and shows few signs of weakening.[10] That said, it is fortunately also not the case that if we know where a child began we can perfectly predict where that child will end up (that is, e_1 and e_2 are non-zero). We do not have perfect social reproduction. Consider this classic quote from Blau and Duncan:

> At one extreme we can imagine that the circumstances of a person's birth . . . suffice to assign him unequivocally to a ranked status in a hierarchical system. At the opposite extreme, his prospective adult status would be wholly problematic and contingent at the time of birth. Such status would be entirely determinate only as adulthood was reached, and solely as a consequence of his own actions taken freely—that is, in the absence of any constraint deriving from the circumstance of his birth or rearing. Such a

> pure meritocratic system is, of course, hypothetical, in much the same way that motion without friction is a purely hypothetical possibility in the physical world. Whenever the stratification system of any moderately large and complex society is described, it is seen to involve both ascriptive and achievement principles.[11]

Blau and Duncan's status attainment model offered early estimates of the degree to which education opens opportunities or reproduces existing inequalities. The main finding from Blau and Duncan's simple status attainment model is that the role of education in fostering equal opportunity and reproducing inequality is not mutually exclusive: education is a primary factor in both opportunity *and* inequality. In other words, Blau and Duncan observed a significant direct effect of socioeconomic origins on education (path *b*) coupled with a significant direct effect of education on socioeconomic destinations (path *c*), such that education transmits origins to destinations. Yet they also observed unexplained factors independent of socioeconomic origins that influence educational attainment (e_1) and are transmitted to socioeconomic destinations via education (path *c*). Thus, variation in education comes from two sources: social origins and all factors independent of origins. The portion of education's variance that comes from origins contributes to reproduction, while the portion that is independent of origins contributes to mobility. Blau and Duncan concluded that education thus serves a key role in social mobility and the intergenerational reproduction of inequality.

Fifty years later, education continues to both promote opportunity and reproduce inequality and serves as a key mechanism linking the social status of one generation to the next. College has rapidly expanded over this period, yet socioeconomic factors still strongly predict the likelihood of educational attainment.[12] Still, even with far more sophisticated models to account for social origins since Blau and Duncan, much unexplained variation in educational attainment remains.[13] In other words, many factors independent of measured social origins influence whether individuals attend and complete college.[14]

Patterns of Social Origins and College Completion

Selection into higher education is one of the key mechanisms by which inequality is reproduced from generation to generation. It influences whether we characterize a society as open or closed, fair or unfair.[15] Socioeconomic inequality in college attainment is high despite the known benefits of college and a college-for-all ethos.[16] America faces an opportunity gap. As listed in table 4.1, a variety of sociodemographic,

Table 4.1 Factors Predicting Four-Year College Attendance and Completion in the NLSY

Predictor	Description of measures
Sociodemographic factors	
Sex	Male (0/1), female reference
Race	Black (0/1), Hispanic (0/1), white/other reference
Residence	Southern age fourteen (0/1), rural age fourteen (0/1), non-south, non-rural reference
Religion	Catholic (0/1), Jewish (0/1), Christian/other reference
Family background factors	
Parental income	$100s (continuous 0–750) / $1,000s (0–250)
Mother's education	Highest education (0–20)
Father's education	Highest education (0–20)
Father's education unknown	Unknown (0/1); if unknown, education was imputed
Father's occupation	Upper-white collar occupation (0/1), reference is all other occupations
Family structure	Two-parent family at age fourteen (binary 0/1), non-two-parent reference
Family size	Number of siblings (continuous 0–19)
Cognitive and psychosocial factors	
Cognitive ability	ASVAB scores (continuous –3–3)
High school academics	College prep program (0/1), no college prep reference
Self-esteem	Rosenberg self-esteem scale (16–30)
Social control	Rotter Locus of Control scale (continuous 4–16)
Educational aspirations	Aspires to attend college (0/1), does not aspire reference
Educational expectations	Expects to attend college (0/1), does not expect reference
Friends' aspirations	Friends aspire to attend college (0/1), do not aspire reference
Juvenile delinquency	Any delinquent activity, 20 measures, (0/1), no delinquency reference
School factors	
School disadvantage	Percentage of students disadvantaged by ESEA guidelines (0–99)
School racial composition	Percentage of black or Hispanic students (0–99)
Family formation factors	
Family attitudes	Standardized of eight measures of family values (0–1)
Marital status	Age eighteen married (binary 0/1), unmarried reference
Had a child	By age eighteen (binary 0/1), childless reference
Instrumental variables	
State unemployment	Average unemployment rate in state at age seventeen
County wage	Average wage in county at age seventeen
Local college tuition	Average college tuition in county at age seventeen
Four-year public college	Four-year public college in county at age seventeen (0/1)

Source: Author's calculations using data from the U.S. Bureau of Labor Statistics National Longitudinal Surveys.
Notes: Instrumental variables are constructed using private geocode data from the NLSY.

family background, cognitive and psychosocial well-being, and school factors influence college attendance and completion.

Throughout the book, I measure college attendance as attending a four-year college by age twenty and college completion as completing a four-year degree by age twenty-five. Let us consider some key factors influencing college attendance and completion, beginning with parental income. While the likelihood of attending and completing college has risen over recent decades, educational inequality by parental income has persisted.[17] As shown in figure 4.2, about half of high-income youth in the NLSY79 cohort (those with parental income above $74,000) attended a four-year college, relative to about one-fifth of low-income youth (those with parental income below $40,000).[18] Nearly two-fifths of high-income youth completed college, relative to only about one-tenth of those with low income.[19] A greater proportion of students with low parental income than those with high parental income began attending a four-year college and did not complete a four-year degree.[20] As shown in figure 4.3, a higher percentage of students attended and completed a four-year college in the more recent NLSY97 cohort, but differentials across income strata persisted.

Research has shown notable parental income differences in not only whether individuals enroll in college and complete degrees but also whether and where they apply, where they attend, and whether they enroll full-time. Low-income youth are more likely to follow nontraditional college pathways characterized by discontinuous college enrollment and frequent transfers between institutions, resulting in a lower likelihood of degree completion.[21] Most of the increase in college attendance among low-income students has occurred at two-year colleges and for-profit colleges—institutions with low four-year completion rates.[22] The selectivity of colleges that students attend differs markedly by parental income. Chetty and his colleagues find that children whose parents are in the top 1 percent of the income distribution are seventy-seven times more likely to attend an Ivy League college than those whose parents are in the bottom 20 percent of the parental income distribution.[23] Caroline Hoxby and her colleagues find that most high-achieving students from low-income families do not apply to even a single selective college or university—the kind of institution that has the highest persistence and completion rates.[24] Despite relatively high qualifications, they are more likely to attend a two-year college or a less-selective institution if they attend college at all.[25] These students exhibit behavior typical of students of their parental income rather than students of comparable achievement. Complex student loan financing discourages many prospective students from applying.[26] Many low-income college students are thus undermatched rather than overmatched, in contrast to what critics who question the value of college for disadvantaged students

Figure 4.2 College Attendance and Completion by Selected Characteristics: NLSY79

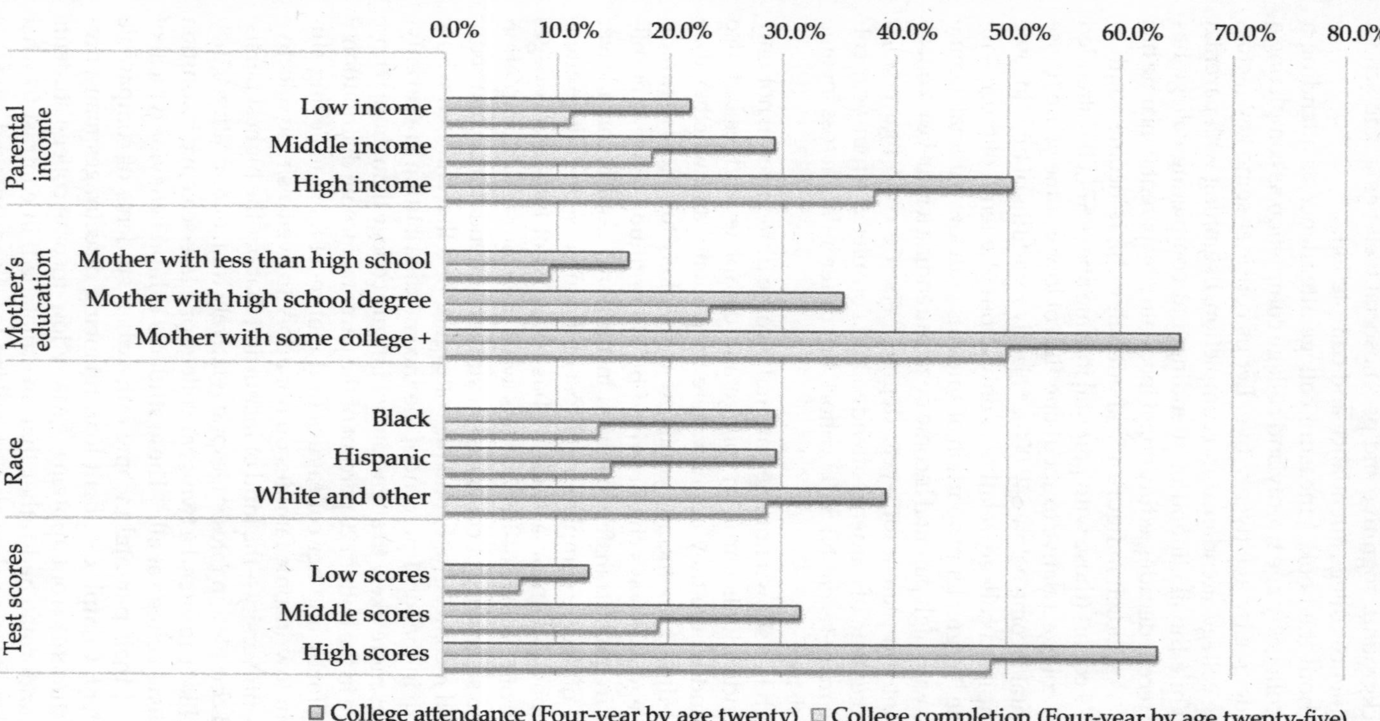

Source: Author's calculations using data from the U.S. Bureau of Labor Statistics National Longitudinal Surveys ($n = 4{,}085$).
Notes: Parental income, divided into terciles, ranges from $0 to $40,500 (in 2020 dollars) for low income, $40,500 to $74,000 for middle income, and $74,000 to $267,000 for high income. Test scores (ASVAB), also divided into terciles, range from −2.48 to −0.24 for low, −0.24 to 0.40 for middle, and 0.40 to 2.39 for high.

Figure 4.3 College Attendance and Completion by Selected Characteristics: NLSY97

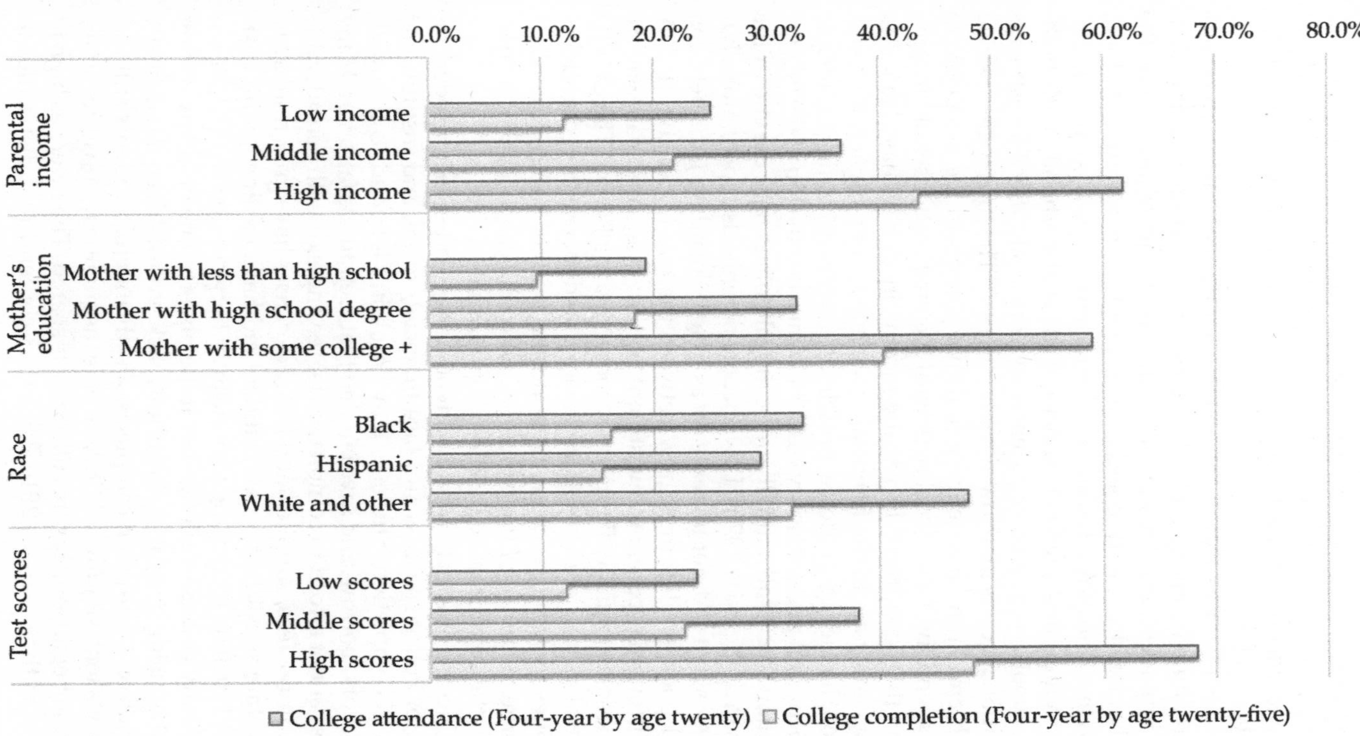

Source: Author's calculations using data from the U.S. Bureau of Labor Statistics National Longitudinal Surveys ($n = 7{,}626$).
Notes: Parental income, divided into terciles, ranges from \$0 to \$49,200 (in 2020 dollars) for low income, \$49,200 to \$88,900 for middle income, and \$88,900 to \$397,400 for high income. Test scores (ASVAB), also divided into terciles, range from –3.10 to –0.37 for low, –0.37 to 0.06 for middle, and 0.06 to 2.46 for high.

would have us believe. Stefanie DeLuca, Susan Clampet-Lundquist, and Kathryn Edin observe that undermatching "could not begin to describe" what they saw in their analysis of low-income students.[27] Such evident educational inequality has implications for our collective sense of opportunity and fairness.[28]

Why does family income have such a substantial impact on educational attainment? First, there is a direct effect of income in that expenditures impact educational attainment. Family income purchases the goods that children need to succeed in school, such as nutritious food, medical care, a healthy environment, educational toys, academic enrichment activities, and homes in advantaged neighborhoods with high-quality schools. High-income parents can more easily afford investments in educational goods than low-income parents.[29] The sociologists Sabino Kornrich and Frank Furstenberg find that parents in the top decile of earners spend five times what parents at the median household income spend on their children.[30] Increasing income inequality has also led to growing class gaps in the financial investments that impact children's education, including childcare, preschool, lessons, schooling, academic enrichment, and postsecondary costs.[31] Parents near the top of the income distribution spent substantially more in real dollars near the end of the 2000s than in the early 1970s. Low-income parents also spent more, but what they spent did not increase by as much. Spending gaps between rich and poor families thus grew between the two NLSY cohorts.[32] A rising differential parental investment pattern offers one pathway by which income inequality limits intergenerational mobility.[33] The COVID pandemic has further exposed and exacerbated increasing educational inequalities by family income. Low-income families and communities have borne the brunt of the pandemic, with consequences that further diminish their children's educational opportunities.[34]

Low-income students who do attend college often lack needed resources for college success and face financial, social, and institutional barriers to completion. Students may enroll in higher education with plans to work, borrow, and save but find that their funds fall short. Many students cannot afford to complete a degree and exit with considerable debt.[35] Tuition, fees, supplies, and living expenses have grown substantially as state subsidization and student aid have declined, with costs and debt burdens increasing significantly between the two NLSY cohorts.[36] Many college students live at the poverty line or below, facing food and housing insecurity.[37] Anthony Jack writes: "Even if they make it to dorms on leafy-green campuses, disadvantaged students still live in poverty's long shadow."[38] Still, income inequalities in postsecondary completion began long before college costs soared. They were as high in the 1980s as they were in 2010.[39] Scholars contend that disparities in family income that influence college access contribute more to unequal completion rates than rising costs.[40]

Parental income also correlates with other demographic and family background factors related to educational attainment, including race, parental education, family structure, and schools and neighborhoods. Racial and ethnic gaps in educational achievement and attainment exist at all levels. In the NLSY79, Black and Hispanic students completed college at about half the rate of White students (see figure 4.2).[41] Over half of Black and Hispanic students who begin college at a four-year school do not complete a degree, compared to 30 percent of White students. While increasing numbers of students of color are transitioning to college, completion rates remain low. Their attendance and completion rates also continue to lag Whites', as shown in figure 4.3 for the NLSY97.[42] Black and Hispanic students are overrepresented in two-year colleges and less-selective institutions with lower completion rates.[43]

Gaps reflect, in part, the broader racial and ethnic hierarchies in the United States.[44] Black and Hispanic students fall into categories with high rates of economic deprivation relative to White and Asian students.[45] Socioeconomic differences by race explain a large percentage of the racial college completion gap.[46] The barriers that low-income youth face are exacerbated for those of color, who face additional obstacles resulting from racism, discrimination, and residence in segregated and impoverished neighborhoods.[47] As DeLuca and her colleagues note: "Family background and a history of racially discriminatory housing policies have continued to yield a strong influence on where children end up in life and being born poor and Black suppresses life chances to a frightening degree."[48] Students of color have high educational aspirations but may be hesitant to enroll in college owing to perceived barriers and risks to completing degrees.[49] Limited support and services on college campuses and a limited sense of belonging can contribute to the lower likelihood of completing a degree among students of color.[50]

In the NLSY79, Black and Hispanic students completed college at lower rates than White students at each parental income level. The percentage of low-income Whites who completed college (14 percent) was most similar to middle-income Blacks (16 percent) and Hispanics (14 percent). However, a larger percentage of high-income Black students (29 percent) and Hispanic students (25 percent) completed college than did low-income (14 percent) or middle-income (19 percent) White students. Despite the low overall college completion rates for students of color, some students overcome the odds. As Prudence Carter writes: "Certainly, not all racially marginalized and economically disadvantaged youth fail to reach the higher rungs of academic success and mobility.

In fact, a critical number will sail the winds of upward mobility by entering the doors of higher education."[51]

Parental education also has a strong intergenerational link to children's education. In fact, parents' education may be the most important family factor in predicting children's educational attainment.[52] Less-educated parents are less able to support and advise their children in college selection, preparation, application, and financial aid processes than college-educated parents.[53] In the NLSY, patterns of college attendance and completion by mother's education were consistent with patterns by parental income terciles, but starker. As shown in figure 4.2 less than 10 percent of NLSY79 respondents whose mothers had less than a high school degree completed college, relative to 50 percent of those whose mother had attended some college. About one-third of respondents who completed college were first-generation college students (neither parent attended college). Mother's education strongly predicts the likelihood of college completion at each parental income level. Only about 13 percent of high-income youth whose mother had less than a high school degree completed college, compared to half of the respondents whose mother had a college degree. Low-income youth with a college-educated mother completed college (19 percent) at higher rates than did high-income youth with a less-educated mother (13 percent).

In the NLSY97 cohort (see figure 4.3), a greater proportion of those with a less-educated mother attended a four-year college and completed a degree than in the earlier cohort. A modestly higher percentage of individuals in the NLSY79 whose mother had attended college completed a degree than their counterparts in the NLSY97. Still, there were far more mothers who attended college in the more recent cohort.

Both parental education and income affect children's education by cultivating cultural and social capital. Cultural capital is the general cultural background, knowledge, disposition, and skills that parents pass on to their children.[54] Social classes differ in their cultural capital, with impacts on social class inequality in academic achievement. Influenced by the social theorists Karl Marx and Max Weber, Bourdieu's cultural capital concept elucidates the process of social reproduction and offers a key mechanism through which educational inequality is preserved.[55] Dispositions and skills are judged differently by school personnel, and by society more broadly, who favor the linguistic and cultural tendencies of middle- and upper-class youth and devalue those of lower-class youth.[56] More-educated parents also increasingly engage in what the sociologist Annette Lareau refers to as "concerted cultivation": spending an increasingly large amount of time on developmental activities that cultivate educational achievement.[57] Middle- and upper-class and more-educated parents also have educated social networks, or social capital, that facilitate academic success.[58] Advantaged youth consequently benefit from a unitary cultural narrative of four-year degree completion, whereas disadvantaged youth lack a cohesive sketch of educational success.[59] Underprivileged youth are exposed to many models of employment and education—low-wage work, trade school, community college, four-year college—and information about four-year colleges is diluted by the various alternatives.

Family structure, such as number of siblings and parental marital status, also correlates with parental income and education and impacts college attendance and completion.[60] In general, the larger the family size (the more siblings there are), the worse a child's educational attainment prospects. This pattern holds partly because low-income and less-educated parents tend to have more children. Increased family size can also dilute parental resources and attention such that each child receives a smaller portion of the ration of family goods. Children and adolescents who experience family disruption and grow up with a single parent also have worse educational outcomes than those who live in stable families with two parents.[61] Yet in the NLSY, family structure differentiates college completion only among high-income families. It does not distinguish children from low-income families, whose completion rates are low across family types.[62]

Parental income and race also impact where families live and the schools children attend. A large literature suggests that neighborhoods matter for social connections, isolation, social organization, neighborhood collective efficacy, and socialization.[63] High rates of poverty, high residential turnover, and low rates of homeownership affect the normative environment and neighborhood resources available to low-income families living in these communities. Raj Chetty and Nathanial Hendren show that every additional year of childhood spent in a neighborhood with more resources improves a child's educational attainment.[64] Different residential environments impact children's cognitive functioning, social development, physical health, and cultural frames by which to interpret social life and make decisions.[65] Concentrated disadvantage limits the mobility prospects of children. As Anthony Jack summarizes:

> Some communities protect us from hurt, harm, and danger. Others provide no respite at all. This process is not random, but the consequence of historical patterns of exclusion and racism. Life in privileged communities means that children traverse safer streets, have access to good schools and interact with neighbors who can supply more than the proverbial cup of sugar. Life in distressed communities can mean learning to distinguish between firecrackers and gunshots.[66]

Schools in more- and less-advantaged neighborhoods also differ markedly in resources allocated to infrastructure, staff salaries, strategic educational investments, and targeted educational programs.[67] As a result, these schools face higher student turnover rates, greater problems recruiting high-quality teachers, and more difficulty creating safe learning environments. Children in school districts with the highest concentrations of poverty score an average of more than four grade levels below children in the wealthiest districts.[68] Despite efforts to equalize financial expenditures per pupil, schools are increasingly unable to deliver anything approximating an equal chance for a quality education.[69] Still, while disentangling family background factors from the neighborhood and school environment is complex, the evidence suggests that variation in children's academic performance is far more strongly associated with family than school characteristics.[70] In the NLSY79, attending a relatively advantaged high school did not overcome the impact of family income: only about 15 percent of low-income youth who attended the most-advantaged schools completed college, relative to 44 percent of high-income youth.[71]

Patterns of Social Origins, Skills and Achievement, and College Completion

Social origins are associated with skills and achievement in schools, and achievement in high school, test scores, and psychosocial skills impact college attainment. For example, in the NLSY79, almost half of students with high Armed Services Vocational Aptitude Battery (ASVAB) test scores (top tercile) completed college compared to about 7 percent of those with low ASVAB scores (low tercile) (see figure 4.2).[72] Among those who completed an elite degree, over 80 percent scored high on the ASVAB. About the same percentage of high-scoring students completed college in the more recent NLSY97 cohort, while a larger percentage (15 percent) of low-scoring students completed college (see figure 4.3).

Scholars have long known that many low-income students have more ability than the educational system allows them to realize.[73] For many low-income children and adolescents, especially low-income students of color, academic promise may not be enough to achieve high educational attainment.[74] Among youth with high test scores in the NLSY79, about 26 percent of low-income youth relative to 60 percent of high-income youth completed a four-year degree. Low-income youth with high test scores completed college at a rate like that of high-income youth with average test scores. Among high-scoring college graduates of highly selective institutions, one in twenty grew up in a low-income family, while three out of four grew up in a high-income family. However, those with low test scores had low rates of college completion across parental income terciles (5 percent among the low-income and 8 percent among the high-income). Fewer than one-third of Black and Hispanic youth with high test scores completed college relative to over half of White youth. Black and Hispanic students with high test scores completed college at much higher rates than those with low scores, but not at the same rate as White students with high scores.

In sum, even within test score categories, we have a social class and race and ethnicity gradient in college completion. Thus, to the extent that such scores represent a measure of academic achievement or ability, such achievement does not fully overcome the influence of class and racial inequality in educational attainment. Moreover, many capable and intelligent low-income and racially minoritized youth are not motivated to score high on such tests or do not receive the educational preparation that facilitates high scores.[75] And so-called ability tests contain biases that lower the scores of disadvantaged and racially minoritized students. Policymakers and academics who argue that we should focus on low-income youth with high test scores overlook this fundamental issue.

Enrolling in college-prep courses in secondary school is also patterned by social class and race and linked to enrolling in college and completing a four-year degree. In the NLSY79, individuals with low-income parents were half as likely to enroll in college-prep courses as those with high-income parents. While the largest difference in course-taking in the NLSY79 is by ASVAB scores—over half of the high-scoring students taking college-prep courses relative to just over 15 percent of low-scoring students—the causal direction of this pattern is unclear.[76] High-scoring students may have access to and choose more challenging courses, more challenging courses may impact students' ASVAB scores, or both factors could be at work. It is difficult to separate student agency in rigorous course-taking and social and structural conditions, including access to resources that facilitate achievement or perceptions of student ability by class and race that constrain student choice. School segregation by class and race also gives students differential access to course-taking opportunities. Among those who take college-prep courses, we continue to see a gradient in college completion by parental income. In the NLSY79, about 56 percent of high-income youth who took college-prep courses completed college, relative to about 24 percent of those who did not take such courses. Low-income youth who took college-prep courses completed college at rates like those of high-income youth who did not take college-prep courses.

Psychosocial or socioemotional skills, such as work habits, independence, and persistence, are also strong determinants of educational success, as argued in several studies by James Heckman and his colleagues.[77] Some recent work has suggested that returns to cognitive skills have declined while returns to psychosocial skills have increased.[78] In the NLSY79, low-income youth with low self-esteem were half as likely to complete college as those with high self-esteem.[79] Social scientists have also long documented the association between educational aspirations and expectations in facilitating higher education.[80] Yet despite increasingly high aspirations to attend college, many low-income youth and people of color have unmet expectations.[81] Socioeconomic constraints, academic preparation, and pressure to expedite a path to economic security, among other factors, dampen college goals.[82]

Estimating the Likelihood of College Completion

Sociodemographic, family background, and achievement factors strongly influence college completion. The next task is to build college attendance and completion models based on these factors. As I discuss in chapter 3, a causal model has two essential components: the use of potential outcomes and the assignment mechanism.[83] The assignment mechanism is a probabilistic model for the college attendance and completion process. To estimate the one-dimensional propensity metric, I consider the precollege measures of sociodemographic, family-background, cognitive, psychosocial, school-level, and family-formation factors described in table 4.1 (except for the instrumental variables).[84] I benefit from a rich set of possible college predictors in the NLSY data.

Descriptive statistics of the NLSY sample of the precollege characteristics are consistent with well-documented socioeconomic differences in educational attainment and the patterns described earlier (see Appendix tables B.1 and B.2 for the NLSY79 and NLSY97 cohorts, respectively). College attendees and graduates are more likely to come from families with high incomes, highly educated parents, both parents present, and fewer siblings. They also have higher average test scores and are more likely to have taken college-prep classes. In addition, they attended more advantaged high schools, have higher educational expectations, and have friends with higher educational expectations.[85]

As discussed in chapter 3, I use an iterative procedure that generates a flexible model specification to estimate college attendance and completion propensities.[86] I estimate propensity scores for four-year college attendance by age twenty and four-year college completion by age twenty-five. In the NLSY79, I restrict the sample to individuals who were fourteen to seventeen years old at the baseline survey in 1979 ($n = 5{,}582$) and who completed at least the twelfth grade ($n = 4{,}548$). I restrict the sample to individuals with overlap in their likelihood of attending and completing a four-year college. I thus eliminate college graduates with values higher than the highest propensity score among the non-college graduates ($p(X) = 0.923$; $n = 13$) and non-college graduates with values lower than the lowest propensity score among the college graduates ($p(X) = 0.003$; $n = 400$). I also eliminate college attendees with values higher than the highest propensity score among the non–college attendees ($p(X) = 0.976$; $n = 7$) and non–college attendees with values lower than the lowest propensity score among the college attendees ($p(X) = 0.004$; $n = 43$). The final analytic sample is 4,085. In the NLSY97, I restrict the sample to individuals who had completed at least the twelfth grade ($n = 7{,}753$). I eliminate college graduates with values higher than the highest propensity score among the non-college graduates ($p(X) = 0.913$; $n = 47$) and non-college graduates with values lower than the lowest propensity score among the college graduates ($p(X) = 0.001$; $n = 63$), as well as college attendees with values higher than the highest propensity score among the non–college attendees ($p(X) = 0.993$; $n = 17$). There are no additional non–college attendees with values lower than the lowest propensity score among the college attendees ($p(X) = 0.005$; $n = 0$). The final analytic sample is 7,626.

Restricting to the region of common support, I essentially omit those individuals with limited infrastructure to attend or complete college and those whose prospects for college were largely secured. For example, those with a low propensity outside the region of support had, on average, parents with an eighth-grade education. Almost none of those with a very low propensity had a father with a professional or managerial job, had enrolled in college-prep courses, or expected to attend college. Their average ASVAB score was below the tenth percentile of the distribution. Nearly half were teenage parents. Those with very high propensity scores outside the region of support had, on average, parents with graduate degrees. Most had a father with a professional or managerial job and had enrolled in college-prep courses. All of these individuals expected to attend college. Their average ASVAB score was above the ninety-fifth percentile of the distribution.

More low-propensity cases lacked support than did high-propensity cases—96 percent of the cases deleted were low-propensity—in the NLSY79. This pattern suggests that while the chances of completing college were secured for a relatively small segment of the sample, there was a far larger share for whom the chances were near zero. Moreover, this restriction is based on a sample who completed high school or a GED. The share would be even larger if we allowed those who did not complete high school to enter the mix. This result questions the opportunities available to all high school students to pursue and successfully persist in postsecondary education. However, in the NLSY97 cohort, the low-

and high-propensity individuals who did not reach common support constituted a smaller share of the total sample. Notably, the percentages of those who were low- or high propensity and who lacked support were evenly split. Thus, in the more recent cohort, we have a larger share whose chances of completing a degree seemed secure, but a smaller share with minimal chances, reflecting historical shifts in the likelihood of college completion. I note, however, that statements about a lack of common support in a sample are limited because a larger sample might enable greater overlap across the propensity score distribution.

Even with the complex model I use to estimate propensity scores, I cannot perfectly predict college attainment.[87] These models explain about 40 percent of the variation in college attendance and completion. In other words, substantial unexplained variation in college attainment remains. Although this suggests uncertainty in our ability to predict the propensity for college attainment, it is expected. We cannot perfectly predict anything in the social world, nor would we want to. This is always true in model estimation. Peter Blau and Otis Dudley Duncan sagely noted:

> Sociologists are often disappointed in the size of the residual, assuming that this is a measure of their success in "explaining" the phenomenon under study. They seldom reflect on what it would mean to live in a society with nearly perfect explanation of the dependent variable. . . . In such a society it would indeed be true that some are destined to poverty almost from birth. . . . By no effort of their own could they materially alter the course of destiny, nor could any stroke of fortune, good or ill, lead to an outcome not already in the cards.[88]

The matching strategy reflects uncertainty in the propensity score estimation.[89] Yet while the propensity score is an imprecise estimate of a person's probability of attending and completing college, this is not to say that it does not give us a pretty good indication of educational trajectories. For example, only 3 percent of cases with a low propensity for college (less than 0.1) complete a four-year degree.

As discussed in chapter 3, I use propensity scores for matching college graduates to non-college graduates. The purpose of matching is to construct a sample in which we roughly balance college chances between college and non-college graduates. For the propensity score and each variable included in the model, matching greatly reduces the percentage bias between college and non-college graduates. In the matched samples in both NLSY cohorts, the standardized bias in the propensity score is reduced about 99.9 percent by matching. I offer box plots of the propensity score distribution before and after matching for the full sample in appendix figures C.1 and C.2 for the NLSY79 and NLSY97, respectively.

The mean estimated propensity score is 0.33 for college attendance and 0.21 for college completion on a scale of 0 to 1 in the NLSY79. In the NLSY97, the mean is 0.40 for attendance and 0.24 for completion.[90]

Trajectories and Characteristics by the Estimated Likelihood of College Completion

I construct three strata to assess the effects of college completion for those with low-, middle-, and high-propensity scores.[91] About two-thirds of the NLSY79 sample was in the low-propensity stratum, but only about 18 percent of the college graduates were. Conversely, about 16 percent of the sample was in the high-propensity stratum, but over half of the college graduates were. In the NLSY97 cohort, about 58 percent of the sample was in the low-propensity stratum, with 21 percent of college graduates. Nineteen percent of the sample was in the high-propensity stratum, with about 35 percent of the college graduates. Thus, the distribution of college graduates across college completion likelihood was spread more evenly in the recent cohort.

Let us consider the educational trajectories of college and non-college graduates across propensity strata. As I report in table 4.2, almost all of the high-propensity college graduates by age twenty-five in both cohorts attended some college by age twenty (98 percent), and most low-propensity college graduates (87 percent in the NLSY79 and 94 percent in the NLSY97) did so as well. Most began at a four-year college. About 18 percent of high-propensity college graduates earned a degree from a highly selective institution, relative to 3 and 4 percent among the low- and mid-propensity college graduates, respectively.[92] About one-fourth of low- and mid-propensity college graduates obtained a graduate degree, while about two-fifths of high-propensity college graduates did so. Still, about 10 percent of elite college graduates and almost 20 percent of graduate degree holders were low-propensity college graduates. Given the large benefits of completing a four-year degree for low-propensity graduates (described in the subsequent chapters), it is notable that they were less likely than high-propensity graduates to obtain a degree from a selective college or to obtain a graduate degree.

Many high-propensity non-college graduates attended either some college (63 percent) or more specifically a four-year college (54 percent) by age twenty. In contrast, far fewer of the low-propensity non-college graduates attended college (15 percent attended any college, and 10 percent attended a four-year college by age twenty). Still, few non-college graduates completed a degree by age thirty (12 percent of the high-propensity non-college graduates, 8 percent of the mid-propensity non-college graduates, and 3 percent of the low-propensity non-college

Table 4.2 Educational Trajectories by Four-Year College Completion Likelihood

	Low Propensity		Mid Propensity		High Propensity	
	No College Completion (Four-Year by Age Twenty-five)	College Completion (Four-Year by Age Twenty-five)	No College Completion (Four-Year by Age Twenty-five)	College Completion (Four-Year by Age Twenty-five)	No College Completion (Four-Year by Age Twenty-five)	College Completion (Four-Year by Age Twenty-five)
NLSY 1979 Cohort						
Attended any college by age twenty	15.1%	87.0%	39.0%	96.6%	63.2%	98.3%
Attended any college by age twenty-five	25.1	100.0	51.0	100.0	76.2	100.0
Attended four-year college by age twenty	9.6	83.2	28.8	94.7	54.0	98.3
Completed four-year college by age thirty	2.7	100.0	7.6	100.0	11.9	100.0
Completed graduate degree by age forty	1.0	26.4	3.5	25.7	7.4	39.2
Sample size	2,538	155	487	252	212	441
NLSY 1997 Cohort						
Attended any college by age twenty	23.5%	93.8%	51.8%	97.2%	77.8%	97.8%
Attended any college by age twenty-five	34.0	100.0	64.4	100.0	85.9	100.0
Attended four-year college by age twenty	12.5	93.6	36.8	96.1	65.4	97.8
Completed four-year college by age thirty	3.2	100.0	11.6	100.0	18.2	100.0
Sample size	4,191	285	1,144	570	446	990

Source: Author's calculations using data from the U.S. Bureau of Labor Statistics National Longitudinal Surveys.

Notes: NLSY79 sample weights used to adjust percentages. NLSY79 sample is restricted to individuals who were fourteen to seventeen years old at the baseline survey in 1979 ($n = 5{,}582$), who had completed at least the twelfth grade ($n = 4{,}548$), and who had common support ($n = 4{,}085$). NLSY97 sample is restricted to individuals who had completed at least the twelfth grade ($n = 7{,}753$) and who had common support ($n = 7{,}626$). College completion likelihood is indicated by three propensity score strata. Low stratum is an estimated propensity score from 0 to less than 0.2, middle stratum score from 0.2 to less than 0.5, and high stratum score from 0.5 to 1.

graduates). None of the twelve non-college graduates in the vignettes completed college by age forty. More youth who did not complete a four-year degree by age twenty-five attended some college in the more recent NLSY cohort across each propensity stratum, and more completed a degree by age thirty, particularly among the high-propensity youth (18 percent).

As expected, those who were likely to complete college had more educated and high-income parents, had high achievement and test scores, attended more-advantaged schools, and held higher expectations for their attainment than those who were unlikely to complete college. Figures 4.4 to 4.11 are stacked bar charts showing the distribution of parental income, mother's education, race, and ASVAB scores by propensity score strata for the NLSY79 and NLSY97 cohorts. As I show in figure 4.4 for the NLSY79, there is a high representation of high-income families among high-propensity youth (72 percent) and a relatively low representation

Figure 4.4 Parental Income Distribution by Four-Year College Completion Likelihood: NLSY79

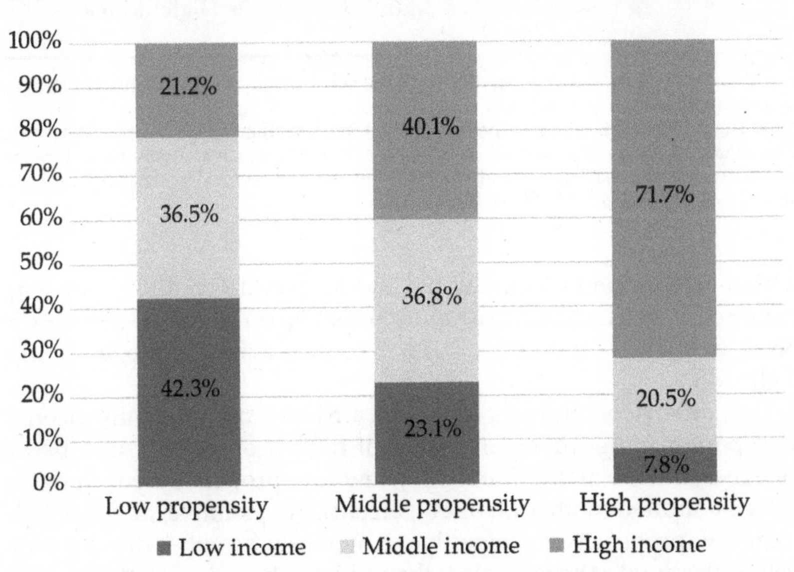

Source: Author's calculations using data from the U.S. Bureau of Labor Statistics National Longitudinal Surveys ($n = 4{,}085$).
Notes: The college completion propensity score is 0 to less than 0.2 for low propensity, 0.2 to less than 0.5 for middle, and 0.5 to 1 for high. Parental income, divided into terciles, ranges from $0 to $40,500 (in 2020 dollars) for low income, $40,500 to $74,000 for middle income, and $74,000 to $267,000 for high income.

Figure 4.5 Parental Income Distribution by Four-Year College Completion Likelihood: NLSY97

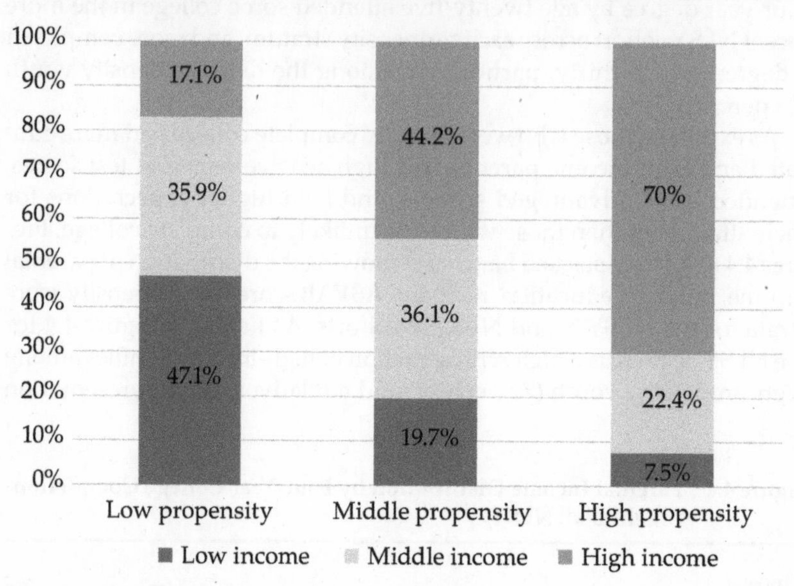

Source: Author's calculations using data from the U.S. Bureau of Labor Statistics National Longitudinal Surveys ($n = 7{,}626$).

Notes: The college completion propensity score is 0 to less than 0.2 for low propensity, 0.2 to less than 0.5 for middle, and 0.5 to 1 for high. Parental income, divided into terciles, ranges from $0 to $49,200 (in 2020 dollars) for low income, $49,200 to $88,900 for middle income, and $88,900 to $397,400 for high income.

of high-income families among the low-propensity youth (21 percent). The income distribution in the more recent NLSY97 cohort (figure 4.5) looks similar to the older NLSY cohort across college degree likelihood.

The patterns for mother's education are like those for family income. As reported in figure 4.6, over half of high-propensity youth had a college-educated mother, and very few low-propensity youth had a college-educated mother (about 8 percent). For example, all six people in the low-propensity vignettes had a mother who either did not complete high school or held no more than a high school degree. By contrast, all people in the high-propensity college graduate vignettes had a mother who completed high school or attended college. As I report in figure 4.7 for the more recent cohort, mothers had significantly higher levels of education across propensity score strata, with almost 30 percent of mothers having attended college. The patterns reflect the increasing educa-

Figure 4.6 Mother's Education Distribution by Four-Year College Completion Likelihood: NLSY79

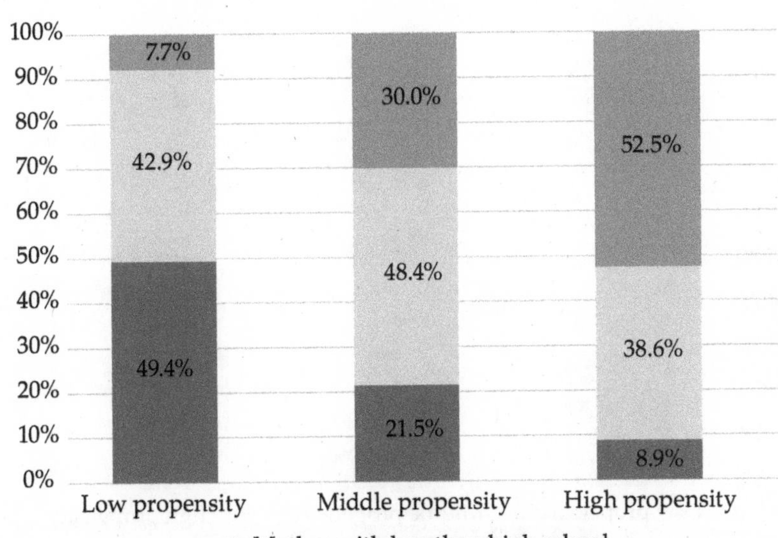

Source: Author's calculations using data from the U.S. Bureau of Labor Statistics National Longitudinal Surveys ($n = 4{,}085$).
Notes: The college completion propensity score is 0 to less than 0.2 for low propensity, 0.2 to less than 0.5 for middle, and 0.5 to 1 for high.

tional attainment across cohorts of women. Differentials across strata, however, are similar.

A little over half of those with a low propensity for college completion were White (or other), about one-third were Black, and 17 percent were Hispanic (figure 4.8). About 84 percent were White among those with a high propensity for college completion, under 10 percent were Black, and about 7 percent were Hispanic. Racial and ethnic patterns remain similar in the NLSY97 (figure 4.9); the greater proportion of Hispanics in the low-propensity stratum reflects population demographic change.

Test scores are unequally distributed across college chances. As reported in figure 4.10, very few high-likelihood college graduates had low ASVAB scores (fewer than 1 percent), while about 85 percent had high ASVAB scores. All the high-propensity college graduate vignettes

Figure 4.7 Mother's Education Distribution by Four-Year College Completion Likelihood: NLSY97

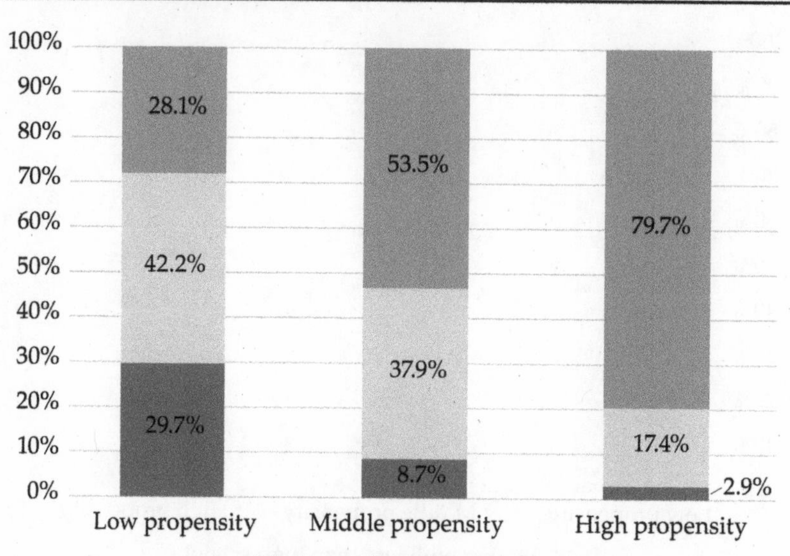

Source: Author's calculations using data from the U.S. Bureau of Labor Statistics National Longitudinal Surveys ($n = 7{,}626$).
Notes: The college completion propensity score is 0 to less than 0.2 for low propensity, 0.2 to less than 0.5 for middle, and 0.5 to 1 for high.

had high test scores, except for Nick, a White male whose ASVAB score was average. Test scores were more evenly distributed among those with a low likelihood for college completion, suggesting that a range of factors underlie a low likelihood of obtaining a degree. The people in the low-propensity college graduate vignettes had a mix of low and average scores, except for Caleb, a Black male who had high scores. Generally, low-propensity youth tended to be a combination of low-income and middle-scoring or mid-income and low-scoring. Fewer than 4 percent of low-propensity youth were high-income and high-scoring, compared to about three-fifths of the high-propensity youth. The remaining high-propensity individuals were mid-income and high-scoring or high-income and mid-scoring. Most low-income and high-scoring youth had a low propensity for college, although some had a mid or high propensity

Figure 4.8 Racial and Ethnic Distribution by Four-Year College Completion Likelihood: NLSY79

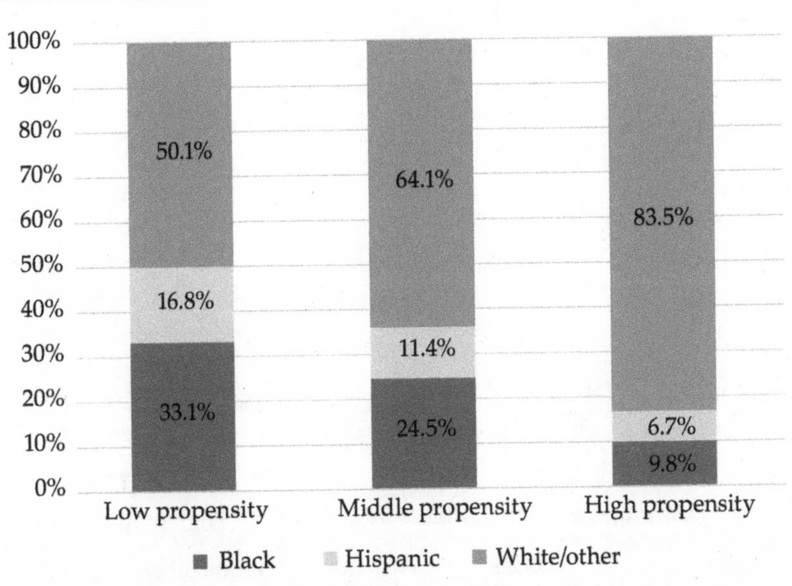

Source: Author's calculations using data from the U.S. Bureau of Labor Statistics National Longitudinal Surveys ($n = 4{,}085$).
Notes: The college completion propensity score is 0 to less than 0.2 for low propensity, 0.2 to less than 0.5 for middle, and 0.5 to 1 for high.

for completion.[93] As I report in figure 4.11 for the more recent NLSY cohort, I observe a larger proportion of individuals with low test scores and a high propensity for degree completion. The distribution of ASVAB scores among low-propensity individuals is roughly the same across NLSY cohorts.

Propensity and Policy

Some analysts argue that, for policy purposes, we may want to focus on increasing college access among the low-income population with high measured aptitude, whose propensity for college is low for financial rather than for achievement reasons. That is, they question why we would want to study the impact of college by the propensity for completion rather than by subgroups partitioned by income and achievement. Some analysts also contend that it is hard to make sense of what "low

Figure 4.9 Racial and Ethnic Distribution by Four-Year College Completion Likelihood: NLSY97

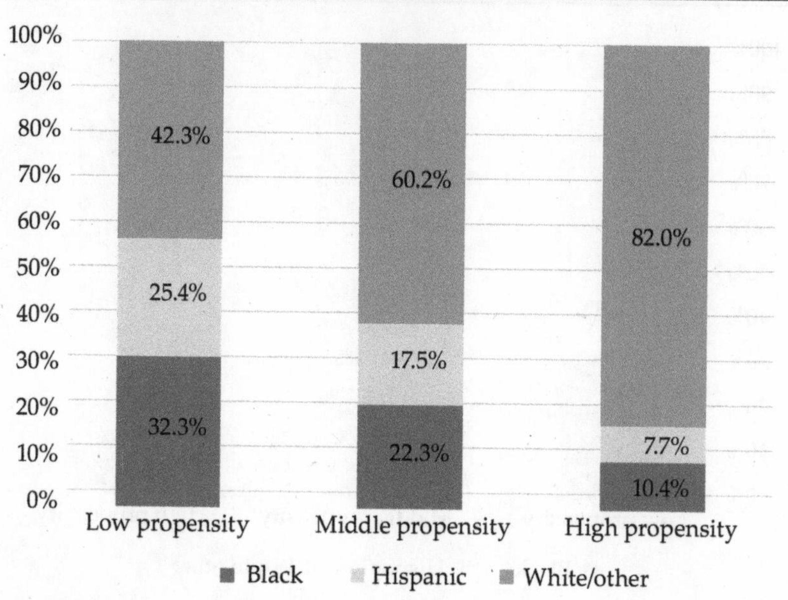

Source: Author's calculations using data from the U.S. Bureau of Labor Statistics National Longitudinal Surveys ($n = 7{,}626$).
Notes: The college completion propensity score is 0 to less than 0.2 for low propensity, 0.2 to less than 0.5 for middle, and 0.5 to 1 for high.

propensity" means, characterizing it is a heterogeneous group of individuals relative to low-income youth or low-income and high-ability youth. I have several responses to these arguments.

First, we can do both. There is no reason we cannot look at the interaction between college and the propensity for completing college and the interaction between other measures of socioeconomic background and achievement. I do so repeatedly throughout the analyses of college completion effects.

Second, while individuals are heterogeneous across propensity strata, they are also heterogeneous across income and test score strata. Whichever way we subdivide the population, we face the ontological reality of the heterogeneity underlying the population. Yet to isolate low-income, high-scoring youth is to focus on a relatively small proportion of the population—for example, about 7 percent of the NLSY79 sample. Among low-income, high-scoring youth, almost half were low-propensity, more than one-third were mid-propensity, and about 15 percent were high-

Figure 4.10 Test Score Distribution by Four-Year College Completion Likelihood: NLSY79

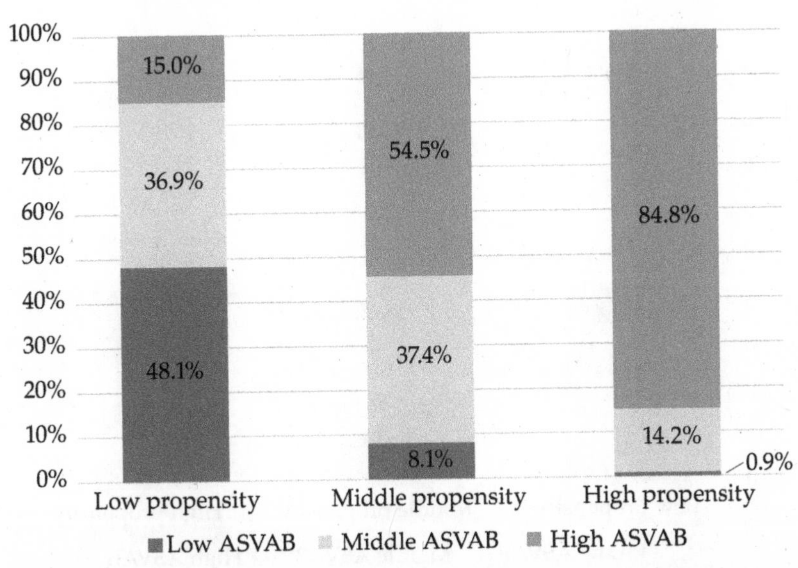

Source: Author's calculations using data from the U.S. Bureau of Labor Statistics National Longitudinal Surveys ($n = 4{,}085$).
Notes: The college completion propensity score is 0 to less than 0.2 for low propensity, 0.2 to less than 0.5 for middle, and 0.5 to 1 for high. ASVAB scores, divided into terciles, range from −2.48 to −0.24 for low, −0.24 to 0.40 for middle, and 0.40 to 2.39 for high.

propensity. As I noted earlier, the largest proportion of low-propensity youth were low-income and low-scoring. Most of the remaining cases had low to average parental income coupled with low to average test scores. Fewer than 10 percent were high-income and low-scoring. In contrast, nearly 60 percent of high-propensity youth were high-income and high-scoring; the remaining were high-income and mid-scoring or mid-income and high-scoring. High-propensity, low-income youth tended to have notably high test scores—higher than those of the typical high-scoring youth.

Third, why should we exclude students who score below average on standardized tests—who make up a large share of low-propensity individuals—from a policy focus? It would be a considerable disservice to these students to assume that their standardized test scores represent an underlying deficiency in their capability or potential. The same argument applies if we focus on grades in high school. Socioeconomic and structural impediments, discriminatory forces, and leveled future attainment

Figure 4.11 Test Score Distribution by Four-Year College Completion Likelihood: NLSY97

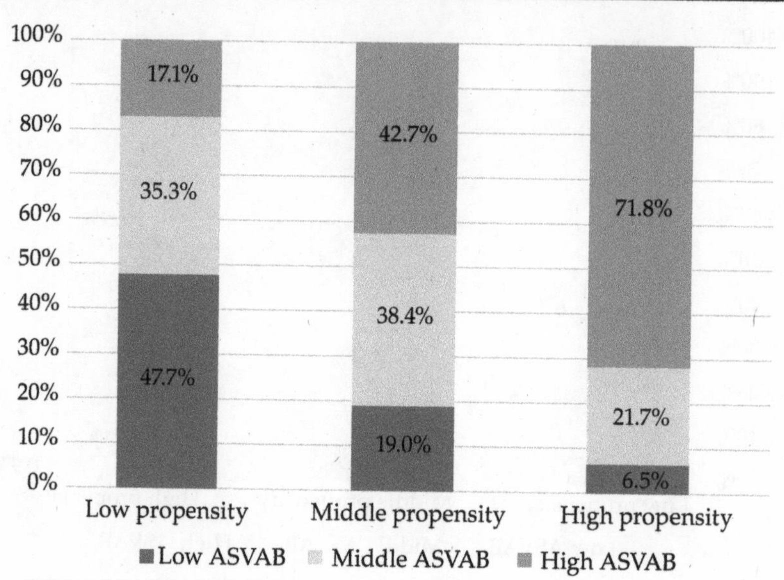

Source: Author's calculations using data from the U.S. Bureau of Labor Statistics National Longitudinal Surveys ($n = 7{,}626$).
Notes: The college completion propensity score is 0 to less than 0.2 for low propensity, 0.2 to less than 0.5 for middle, and 0.5 to 1 for high. ASVAB scores, divided into terciles, range from −3.10 to −0.37 for low, −0.37 to 0.06 for middle, and 0.06 to 2.46 for high.

expectations strongly influence achievement. If we say that we should focus on low-income and high-scoring or high-achieving youth, we imply that students who do not score high on such metrics are less deserving. Mid- or low-scoring students who have average parental income—perhaps because a parent works long hours, such as Caleb's or Diego's parents—would be overlooked. If we exclude these students from our policy focus, we contribute to the reproduction of inequality inherent in the system of academic testing and achievement in schools. There are many dimensions of achievement that we do not capture by these measures. Indeed, disadvantaged students have the skills to navigate considerable issues in their daily lives.[94]

Fourth, analyses by propensity score strata speak more explicitly about the impact of particular educational expansion policies. Some policies, like increasing educational access by building more colleges or making colleges more accessible, affect students on the margin of school continuation. These policies are not explicitly targeted at particular sociodemographic groups, like students of color or low-income students, but instead impact students who struggle to attend college for various reasons. Of course, these policies may have a substantial impact on low-income youth. Yet they also affect students facing varied obstacles to attending college, such as students with average income who attend disadvantaged schools or who have experienced household disruption.

Finally, there is a message about social inequality and the distribution of scarce resources that we miss if we focus only on measures of sociodemographic characteristics and not the propensity for college completion. It is one thing to say that low-income, high-achieving youth benefit the most from completing college. It is quite another thing to say that those unlikely to complete college benefit the most. The latter is a powerful message about how we distribute societal goods in an unequal society.[95]

In chapters 5 through 8, I consider the impact of college on life outcomes. In addition to quantitative estimates describing the long-term impact of college for about 4,100 individuals in the NLSY79 sample and 7,600 individuals in the NLSY97, I closely follow the life histories of twenty-four selected individuals. Although no single case can encapsulate the life histories of the diverse students I study, I draw on these individuals to provide a narrative arc to the quantitative estimates of variation in the effects of a four-year college degree.

Chapter 5

Cultivating Privilege and Circumventing Precarity

Diego and Javier are Latinos with a low propensity for college. Neither Diego's nor Javier's parents completed high school. Both their families had incomes in the bottom quartile of the distribution. Diego and Javier each attended a high school in an urban area in the West. They had ASVAB scores in the second quartile of the distribution. Neither enrolled in college-prep courses, although both expected to attend college. When Diego was twenty-four years old, against the odds, he completed a four-year degree. Javier completed two years of a four-year college but did not complete a four-year degree. Javier serves as Diego's matched counterpart.[1]

After college, Diego worked as a stocks and bonds salesman and then as a financial manager, a job he held for fifteen years. Diego saw steady wage growth from his mid-twenties through his late forties. After college, he earned about $44,000 annually (in 2020 dollars); by his late forties, he was making almost $160,000 annually. He lost his job in his early forties and subsequently became a personal financial adviser. He saw a drop in his earnings around the 2008 recession, but his earnings climbed in his mid-forties. Diego was almost continuously employed throughout his career. He spent less than 10 percent of his career in a low-wage or low-skilled job.

Javier, by contrast, frequently changed jobs. He worked as a farm laborer, gas station attendant, and garbage collector. In his mid-thirties, he began working as a machine operator. Around the 2008 recession, he was unemployed and remained without a job through 2014. He earned roughly $26,000 annually (in 2020 dollars) in his late twenties and saw little wage growth over his career. He spent over three-quarters of his career in a low-wage and low-skill job. Diego's average wage over his career was almost four times higher than Javier's average wage, and he experienced far less low-wage work and job precarity than Javier did.

If Javier represents Diego's alternative trajectory, completing college is associated with considerable socioeconomic benefits for Diego. Can we assume that Javier represents Diego's counterfactual socioeconomic trajectory without completing college? Perhaps Diego has characteristics that Javier did not possess that facilitated his college degree and subsequent socioeconomic success. Alternatively, we may feel reasonably confident that Javier's trajectory is an approximate counterfactual for Diego. Perhaps some local circumstances facilitated Diego's educational attainment, like having a local college nearby, rather than something fundamentally different about their socioeconomic potential. Even if Javier is not the perfect match for Diego, we may wonder whether Diego would have had a trajectory fundamentally different from Javier's had he not completed college. Would he have been as successful in his career had he not completed college, or would his labor market prospects have been limited by the obstacles faced by less-educated, disadvantaged youth?

In this chapter, I first review the literature on the effects of college on socioeconomic outcomes. This section is abbreviated as I already considered the existing literature on earnings in depth in chapter 2. There is also far less literature on the effects of college on other measures of socioeconomic destinations. Using data from the NLSY cohorts, I assess how four-year college completion impacts socioeconomic outcomes across the career. I consider average and heterogeneous effects on earnings, unemployment, not being in the labor force, low-wage work, low-skill work, and employment instability. I describe levels of each outcome for college and non-college graduates and ask whether college equalizes the range of outcomes I consider. Finally, I discuss how college circumvents socioeconomic disadvantage for different population segments.

Background on College Completion Effects on Socioeconomic Outcomes

As I discuss in chapter 2, college-educated workers have substantial wage returns over the life course. Many studies point to an approximately 90 percent advantage associated with a college degree.[2] Of course, much of the premium results from the characteristics that individuals bring to college. After adjusting for selection into college, researchers find that anywhere from a 20 to 40 percent advantage is associated with a college degree relative to a high school degree. College-educated workers benefit from a steeper age-earnings profile, supporting predictions from human capital theory.[3] College graduates are also more likely to be employed, to hold high-status jobs and jobs that require more advanced skills, and to report higher levels of job satisfaction.[4] The unemployment rate among college graduates is about half to one-third that of high school graduates.[5] This gap in unemployment has increased over the last two decades.[6] David Card writes that hundreds of studies have confirmed that "better-educated individuals earn higher wages, experience less unemployment, and work in more prestigious occupations than their less-educated counterparts."[7]

A college degree can also circumvent low-wage work and job precarity. As Paul Attewell and his colleagues note, the "appropriate measures of success for mass higher education should not just be the earnings and occupational attainment . . . but also whether, by going to college students from underprivileged backgrounds break the cycle of disadvantage."[8] As described by Arne Kalleberg, recent decades have been marked by a more precarious and polarized economy, particularly in the post-1979 period that I consider with the NLSY data.[9] Indeed, job polarization has been one of the labor market's defining features since 1970, and a feature that correlates strongly with education.[10] I emphasized in chapter 1 that the trend we have seen in the growth in demand for skilled, educated workers has paralleled the growth of low-wage jobs for less-skilled workers.[11] Institutions that support stable wages, like unions and public-sector employment, have weakened over the last four decades, significantly affecting less-educated workers.[12] The incidence of low-wage jobs with little room for advancement, labor market instability, and wage volatility grew dramatically for workers with less than a college degree.[13] We have thus seen a substantial decline in overall job quality and employer-offered benefits and an increase in precarious and nonstandard work for less-educated workers.[14]

The sociologist Matthew Desmond writes: "What kinds of jobs are available to people without much education? By and large, the answer is jobs that do not pay enough to live on."[15] A 2019 U.S. Census Bureau report showed that 4 percent of college graduates lived in poverty relative to 13 percent of high school graduates.[16] David Deming and Sue Dynarski maintain that getting low-income youth to attend college will reduce their risk of poverty.[17] They state that for college to "function as an anti-poverty strategy, policies must be implemented to ensure that more students from low-income backgrounds stay enrolled and complete their degrees."[18] Yet this work largely focuses on increasing poor students' access to college rather than on directly assessing the effects of college on low-wage work or job instability. Given the high poverty rates among the less-educated, this work simply assumes that college will decrease labor market disadvantage for low-income youth.

As I discuss in chapter 2, there is considerable evidence not only for large average socioeconomic benefits to completing college but for large benefits to disadvantaged youth who complete college. An article in the *Chronicle of Higher Education* asks us to "imagine a young person who looks, on paper, highly unlikely to go to college. If this person does manage to enroll in college despite all those obstacles, is he wasting his time and money?" Far from it, the "college graduates from the against-the-odds stratum seem to have the best results, relative to their peers."[19] Likewise, Douglas Webber notes that "it may be tempting to believe that college doesn't pay off for the students who barely make the college admission cutoffs, so-called 'marginal' students. This does not appear to be the case, as the consensus of the recent literature is that these students have financial returns that are quite large."[20] Paul Attewell and his colleagues conclude: "Our analyses of earnings data fly in the face of criticism that expanding access would produce at best puny economic benefits. Going to college paid off for all, and the earnings boost was sometimes greater for minority students. . . . Opening the gates to academe to minorities and the less affluent has not undermined the earnings-boosting power of academic degrees."[21]

Research is more limited as to variation in the effects of college on measures of socioeconomic well-being beyond wages. Yet if more-disadvantaged college graduates are at a greater risk of low-wage work and job precarity than their more privileged peers, we should expect them to benefit more on these outcomes from completing a degree. The results I present here strongly support this expectation.

College Completion Cultivates Socioeconomic Advantage and Circumvents Socioeconomic Disadvantage

Otis and Samuel were Black males with a high propensity for college completion. Both grew up in the South. Both their mothers and fathers attended college but did not complete a degree, and both had two siblings. Otis and Samuel had high test scores. They both expected to attend college and had friends who aspired to attend college. Otis attended a four-year college after high school, completed his degree after six years, and obtained a master's degree. Samuel attended one year of community college and did not complete a four-year degree. Samuel serves as Otis's matched counterpart.

After completing his degrees, Otis worked as a supervisor. He was continuously employed throughout his career. He saw career wage growth, from an annual salary of $70,000 to over $100,000, with some decline following the 2008 recession. Samuel worked as a freight and stock mover. He was also steadily employed but saw little wage growth, earning about $35,000 for most of his career. Otis's wage trajectory significantly differed from Samuel's, suggesting labor market advantages for Otis associated with completing a four-year degree.

Researchers' traditional focus is on how college increases wages, often at only one or a few points in time. As I have argued, this is a restrictively narrow assessment of the impact of higher education on socioeconomic destinations. Here I expand the socioeconomic outcomes to include a consideration of how college also circumvents socioeconomic disadvantage. For the NLSY79, I consider six measures indicating outcomes from 1990 to 2014, when respondents were ages twenty-five through fifty. For the NLSY97, I consider outcomes measured from 2010 to 2019, when respondents were twenty-five to thirty-five. I use an inflation-adjusted measure of hourly wages averaged over the career. I also consider the proportion of time spent unemployed; out of the labor force; in low-wage work, defined as two-thirds of the median hourly wage in any given year; and in low-skilled work, defined as clerical, service and sales, craft, trade, or plant and machine operator and assembler occupations.[22] I also assess employment instability with a variable indicating a count of jobs lost due to layoffs or plant closings from ages twenty-five through fifty for the NLSY79 and one for job loss during the COVID-19 pandemic for the NLSY97. I thus expand the typical socioeconomic outcomes and consider returns over the life course.

I use a matched analysis to compare pairs like Otis and Samuel and then average the differences in their outcomes across the sample. For example, Brian, a low-propensity male who completed college, received an average wage of $28.50 per hour (or 3.35 if we take the natural log of that value). Henry, Brian's matched counterpart, did not complete college and received an average wage of $9.50 per hour over his career (or 2.25 if we take the natural log). The difference between the two logged values of their average wages over their careers is 1.1. The exponentiated value of 3 suggests a 200 percent wage increase associated with a college degree. As another example, Chantelle, who completed college, did not report being unemployed. Imani, Chantelle's matched counterpart who did not complete college, reported that she was unemployed 20 percent of the time over twenty-five years. If we take the difference between these two values, the college effect is a 20 percent reduction in time spent unemployed.

As reported in appendix table B.5 for the NLSY79, four-year college attendance and completion significantly increase wages over the life course. The average wage for college graduates is $28 per hour (in 2020 dollars) and $19 per hour for non-college graduates. The average wage over the career is thus more than 50 percent greater for college graduates than for non-college graduates ($e^{0.412}$). The return to four-year college attendance is smaller than the return to completing a degree but still considerable (a 36 percent advantage). There is a modest, though insignificant, difference between estimates of the average college completion effect (*ATE*) and the average college completion effect for college graduates (*TT*). When the average effect for a randomly selected person from the population (*ATE*) exceeds that for college graduates (*TT*), we have evidence suggesting that those people with a lower propensity for completing college have larger benefits than those with a higher propensity; in other words, we have evidence of negative selection. For measures of average earnings, the direction points toward negative selection, but the evidence is not strong.

It is also important to consider how college circumvents socioeconomic disadvantage across the working career. College completion is associated with significantly lower levels of unemployment and time out of the labor force (6 to 9 percent less time out of the labor force), low-wage and low-skilled work (20 percent less), and job instability (fewer jobs lost). College attendance also has a sizable effect, but effects associated with completion tend to be larger. For all socioeconomic disadvantage measures, the average college completion effects for the full population (*ATE*s) exceed those for college graduates (*TT*s), suggesting a pattern of negative selection. The *ATE* and *TT* differences for college attendance suggest greater homogeneity, with no significant differences indicated.

In appendix table B.6, I report the more recent NLSY97 cohort results. I find a similar college completion career average wage return (49 percent higher) and college attendance return (30 percent higher). Given the younger age of the cohort, who were mostly in their thirties at the last data collection, the return does not yet capture expected wage growth for more-educated workers. I find a similar reduction (by seven to nine percentage points) associated with college attendance and completion for the time in unemployment and out of the labor force and a reduction (by twenty percentage points) in low-wage work. Since most low-wage work among more-educated workers is concentrated in the early career, the similarity in effects across cohorts indicates a possible larger effect over the careers of the younger cohort. I also note larger college attendance and completion effects on reducing low-skilled work in the recent cohort than in the older cohort. The effects of college on reducing socioeconomic disadvantage are, again, greater for the *ATE* than for the *TT*, particularly for college completion effects, suggestive of negative selection. Let us now consider patterns of heterogeneity in more detail.

College Completion Increases Wages for Low- and High-Likelihood Graduates

Caleb was a Black male with a low propensity for college completion. Caleb's father had a high school degree, and his mother did not complete high school. His father was a mechanic, his mother was a cleaning person, and their income was below average. Caleb attended a disadvantaged, primarily Black and Hispanic high school in an urban area in the Northeast. He scored in the top quartile of the test score distribution, yet he did not enroll in college-prep courses in high school, did not expect to attend college, and did not have friends who aspired to attend college. Against the odds, He enrolled in a four-year college after high school and completed his degree in six years.

Isaiah was a Black male with the same college completion propensity as Caleb, yet Isaiah did not complete college. Like Caleb, Isaiah's mother did not have a high school degree and worked as a cleaning person. Their family income was low. Isaiah attended a disadvantaged, racially mixed high school in an urban area in the Northeast. Like Caleb, Isaiah scored in the top quartile of the test score distribution, did not enroll in college-prep courses in high school, did not expect to go to college, and had no friends who aspired to attend college.[23] Isaiah serves as Caleb's matched counterpart.

After college, Caleb worked in his late twenties through his forties as an air traffic controller, a job requiring higher education. He earned about $60,000 in his twenties and thirties, and his earnings climbed to over $100,000 annually in his late forties (in 2020 dollars). Caleb was continuously employed throughout his career, from his mid-twenties through age fifty. By contrast, Isaiah worked a series of different jobs. In his twenties, he worked as a carpenter, then as a salesclerk, and then as an upholsterer. In his thirties, Isaiah worked as a wood finisher and then as a warehouseman. In his forties, he worked as a carpenter again. His earnings, about $30,000 annually, climbed to about $60,000 in his early forties.

While Isaiah also saw wage growth, he earned considerably less than Caleb throughout his career. The difference in their average wages suggests that Caleb made one and a half times what Isaiah earned over his career. Isaiah was also not continuously employed over his career. Thus, while their social origins were very similar, their socioeconomic destinations were quite different. If we consider Isaiah a plausible counterfactual career trajectory for Caleb, comparing Caleb's and Isaiah's careers suggests that a large socioeconomic advantage is associated with a college degree.

Now consider the career trajectories of Nick and Rich, White males with a high propensity for college completion. Both grew up with both parents. Both had one college-educated parent and one who held a high school degree. Nick's father worked as a manager, and his mother worked as a registered nurse. Rich's father was an engineer, and his mother was a childcare worker. Both had family incomes in the top quartile of the income distribution. Nick and Rich attended relatively advantaged high schools in the Northeast and scored in the second quartile of the distribution of test scores. Nick completed a four-year college degree, while Rich attended one year of a four-year college but did not complete a degree. Rich serves as Nick's matched counterpart.

After college, Nick worked as an accountant throughout his career and was continuously employed, having earned about twelve years of tenure at his current job by age forty. He saw steady wage growth, from about $50,000 annually in his early career to about $170,000 in his late forties. Rich worked a few jobs as a mechanic and as a bartender in his twenties. In his late twenties, he began working as an engineering technician. He reported working as a civil engineer through his late forties, a job that did not require a college degree at the time. Although not as steep as Nick's, Rich saw wage growth over his career, from about $40,000 annually in his early career to $110,000 in his late forties. He was continuously employed. Comparing Nick to Rich, we observe considerable wage returns to college. Yet Nick's and Rich's average wages over their careers are more comparable than Caleb's and Isaiah's.

The trajectories of several matched women with a low and high propensity for college completion also illustrate the variation in returns. Chantelle was a Black female with a low likelihood of completing college, but she completed a degree in four years. Imani was also a Black female with a low likelihood of completing college, and she did not attend college. Chantelle grew up with her uncle, Imani grew up with her single mother, and they both had several siblings. Both also had a parent or guardian who did not complete high school and family incomes in the bottom quintile of the income distribution. Chantelle's uncle worked as a garbage collector, and Imani's mother worked as a cleaning person. Chantelle and Imani both had below-average test scores. Neither enrolled in college-prep courses, nor did either expect to attend college. They both attended a racially mixed, disadvantaged high school in the South. Imani serves as Chantelle's matched counterpart.

Chantelle worked as a manager and administrator in her mid to late twenties and then held a job as a financial adviser in her thirties and forties. She made about $32,000 annually (in 2020 dollars) in her twenties, about $40,000 annually in her forties, and was continuously employed. Imani worked as a waitress from her twenties to early forties. Her wages were very low, roughly $12,000 annually. Her wage trajectory was irregular—up some years and down others. Chantelle's career relative to Imani's suggests considerable college degree returns. The difference in their average wages over their careers suggests an advantage of over 150 percent, similar to Caleb's return.

Compare Nancy, a White female who had a high propensity for college completion and who completed her degree, to Rebecca, a White female with the same high propensity who attended one year of community college but did not complete a degree. They both had college-educated parents and high incomes. They both attended a primarily White high school in an urban area in the South and scored in the second quartile of the test score distribution. Rebecca is Nancy's matched counterpart.

After college, Nancy, like her father, got a law degree. She worked as a lawyer from her mid-twenties to early fifties and saw wage growth to about $64,000 in her late forties. Her wage profile was below what we might expect a lawyer to earn, partly because she worked part-time for about one-third of her career. Her total household income was far higher—over $160,000 annually in her forties. In her mid-twenties to late forties, Rebecca worked as a restaurant manager. She was also continuously employed and saw a steady increase in her wages, from about $46,000 to $90,000. Rebecca's wages were higher than Nancy's, presumably because Rebecca worked full-time throughout her career. Rebecca's household income, however, was substantially lower than Nancy's, at about $75,000. (I discuss the difference in household income and the family formation patterns that underlie this pattern in chapter 6.) The individual wage return appears to be greater for Chantelle, a low-propensity woman, than for Nancy, a high propensity woman.

I report propensity-score-stratified matching estimates in figure 5.1 and appendix table B.7(a). I observe the largest wage effect for low-propensity college graduates. I also note a larger effect for high-propensity than mid-propensity college graduates, suggesting a roughly *u*-shaped pattern across the propensity distribution. Low-propensity college graduates have a 56 percent return, relative to 44 percent for high-propensity college graduates and 40 percent for mid-propensity college graduates. In appendix table B.7(a), I also report the differences between the low- and high-propensity estimates. The difference between the wage coefficients is insignificant, as expected, given the U-shaped pattern in returns. I combine men and women, as the patterns do not tell a markedly different story by gender, except that there is a stronger pattern of negative selection among women. Earnings returns are also larger for men than for women.

The economic returns to college degrees by propensity score strata are largely consistent with recent work that takes a long-term perspective

Figure 5.1 Effects of Four-Year College Completion on (Log) Wages by College Completion Likelihood: NLSY79

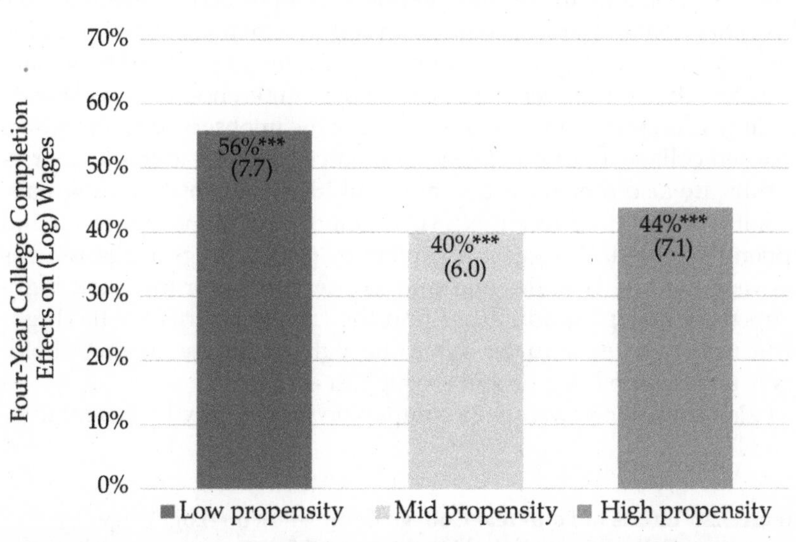

Source: Author's calculations using data from the U.S. Bureau of Labor Statistics National Longitudinal Surveys ($n = 4{,}085$).
Notes: The college completion propensity score is 0 to less than 0.2 for low propensity, 0.2 to less than 0.5 for middle, and 0.5 to 1 for high. Analyses are based on matching on the linearized propensity score. Numbers in parentheses are standard errors.
*** $p \leq 0.001$; two-tailed tests

and focuses on how wage returns accrue over the life course, suggesting large returns at both tails of the distribution of college chances. The larger wage return for high-likelihood college graduates results from them also holding graduate degrees and some being very high earners. As I noted in chapter 4, almost 40 percent of high-propensity college graduates have an advanced degree. If I eliminate holders of an advanced degree, college effects on wages remain the same for low-propensity graduates, while the effects for high-propensity graduates are reduced to the level for mid-propensity graduates. I then observe a pattern of negative selection. Likewise, if I eliminate the top 5 percent of earners, I also observe a pattern of negative selection.

To check the robustness of the results to the matching approach, I report estimates using doubly robust inverse probability weighting and generalized random forests in appendix table B.7(b). The results suggest even greater similarity in returns for low- and high-propensity college graduates. I also conduct sensitivity analyses in which I suppose that some factor unobserved in the data—for example, resilience—increases wages over the career and is higher among individuals who completed college than among those who did not.[24] As reported in appendix table B.10, I find that the effect of college on wages remains significant for the low-propensity college completers at each value of potential bias that I consider. This is true even when unobserved differences have a substantial impact on wages and the prevalence of the unobserved factor differs between college and non-college graduates by a considerable degree. Results are also robust for the mid- and high-propensity individuals. Results for the more recent NLSY97 cohort reported in figure 5.2 and appendix table B.8 suggest a similar pattern of large wage returns between the mid-twenties and mid to late thirties for low- and high-propensity college graduates. I find the largest returns for the high-propensity college graduates; again, the high returns are driven by holders of an advanced degree and the highest earners.[25]

I also consider how college completion effects vary by parental in-

Figure 5.2 Effects of Four-Year College Completion on (Log) Wages by College Completion Likelihood: NLSY97

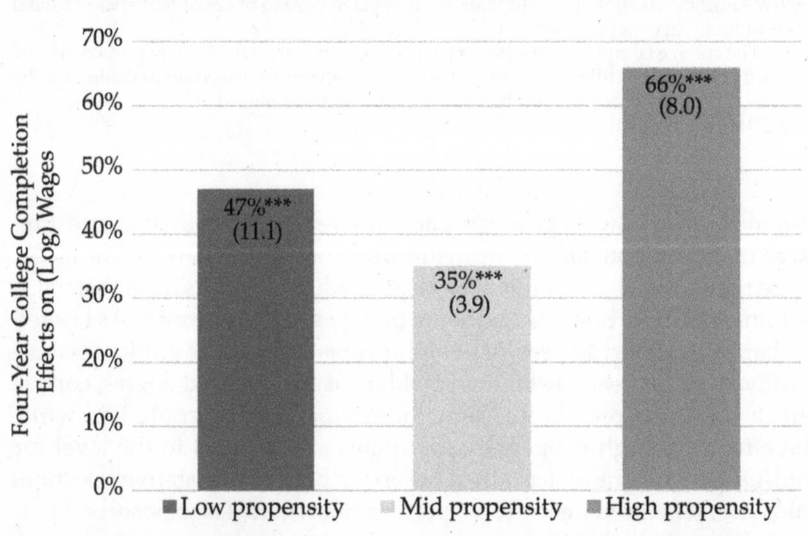

Source: Author's calculations using data from the U.S. Bureau of Labor Statistics National Longitudinal Surveys ($n = 7{,}626$).

Notes: The college completion propensity score is 0 to less than 0.2 for low propensity, 0.2 to less than 0.5 for middle, and 0.5 to 1 for high. Analyses are based on matching on the linearized propensity score. Numbers in parentheses are standard errors.

*** $p \leq 0.001$, two-tailed tests

come, mother's education, ASVAB test scores, and race (reported in appendix table B.9[a]). I find a pattern of negative selection for the effects of college completion on average wages by parental income and mother's education. Wage returns are also particularly large for Hispanics. College graduates with low test scores have the largest wage gains, but high-scoring graduates also have large gains. These patterns are likely to affect the *u*-shaped patterns by propensity score strata reported earlier. Intersecting these characteristics, I find that low-income, first-generation college graduates have a 60 percent average wage return over their career relative to a 47 percent return for high-income graduates with college-educated parents.

Finally, I apply machine learning models based on causal trees that search for subgroups with the largest effects of college completion. In appendix table B.9(b), I provide the estimated treatment effect for the most responsive subgroup as determined by the causal trees and describe the splits that identified that subgroup. I then offer some descriptive statistics of the group identified as most responsive by the causal tree. For average wages, Hispanics have notably high returns (60 percent average wage return). Among non-Hispanics, there was a large effect among men who reported delinquent activity, grew up in a large family, and had high social control (68 percent average wage return).[26]

College Completion Circumvents Socioeconomic Disadvantage for Unlikely Graduates

Caleb and Isaiah had very similar social origins and the same low propensity for college completion, yet Caleb completed a college degree and Isaiah did not. After completing his four-year degree, Caleb spent no time unemployed or out of the labor force. He spent less than 10 percent of his career in low-wage work and about one-third in a low-skilled job. By contrast, Isaiah spent over one-third of his career unemployed or out of the labor force. He spent 40 percent of his career in low-wage work and 80 percent in low-skilled work. If we compare Caleb's career to Isaiah's, it appears that college enabled Caleb to circumvent considerable socioeconomic disadvantage. The comparison between Diego and Javier also suggests that college enables Diego to avoid economic precarity.

Similarly, Chantelle spent no time unemployed or out of the labor force and worked 20 percent of her career in a low-skilled job and less than 15 percent in a low-wage job. By contrast, Imani, Chantelle's matched counterpart, spent most of her career in low-wage work. She also spent 20 percent of her career out of work, mostly in her late forties. Again, the comparison between Chantelle, who completed college, and

Imani, who did not, suggests that a college degree can substantially lessen socioeconomic disadvantage.

The trajectories of Daniela and Josefina, Latinas with a low propensity for college, are similar. Both of their mothers immigrated from Mexico, and both of them were born in the United States. Daniela's mother, who did not complete high school, worked as a machine operative. Neither of Josefina's parents finished high school. Her mother did not work, and her father worked as a meat cutter. Daniela's and Josefina's family incomes were in the second quartile of the income distribution. Daniela and Josefina scored in the bottom quartile of the distribution of test scores, and neither enrolled in college-prep courses in high school or expected to attend college. Yet Daniela attended community college, transferred to a four-year school, and completed a four-year degree in six years. Josefina did not attend college.[27] Daniela spent no time unemployed and about 10 percent of her career in low-wage work. Josefina spent about 85 percent of her time out of work, and her time employed was spent in low-wage work.

Now consider the trajectories of Nick and Rich, both high-propensity White men. Nick completed a college degree, and Rich did not. Nick spent no time in a low-wage or low-skilled job throughout his career, and he never lost a job. Although he worked in a low-skilled job in his mid-twenties, Rich, like Nick, spent no time in low-wage work and never lost a job. Our comparison of Rich's and Nick's lives suggests that college did not protect Nick from socioeconomic disadvantage as much as it did Caleb. Indeed, the socioeconomic disadvantage was essentially equalized between Caleb and Nick but was quite dissimilar for Isaiah and Rich, a point I return to later. Likewise, Nancy and Rebecca did not spend time in low-skilled work, both spent little time in low-wage jobs, and neither lost a job. On these measures of socioeconomic disadvantage, we do not see a difference in these two high-propensity women's trajectories, despite their difference in college degree status. This story differs considerably from the one that emerges when we compare Chantelle's and Imani's trajectories.

Figures 5.3(a), 5.3(b), and 5.3(c) display the effects of college completion on five measures of socioeconomic disadvantage: the proportion of time in unemployment, the proportion of time not in the labor force, the proportion of time in low-wage work, the proportion of time in low-skilled work, and a count of lost jobs. I reverse the y-axis so that higher bars indicate larger college-reducing effects on socioeconomic disadvantage. Appendix table B.7(a) provides the complete matching estimates, and table B.7(b) reports robustness checks. I again describe estimates by three propensity score strata (low, mid, and high). When I reported earnings by strata, I noted that effects were largest for low- and high-

Figure 5.3(a) Effects of Four-Year College Completion on Unemployment and Not in the Labor Force (NILF) by College Completion Likelihood (y-Axis Reversed): NLSY79

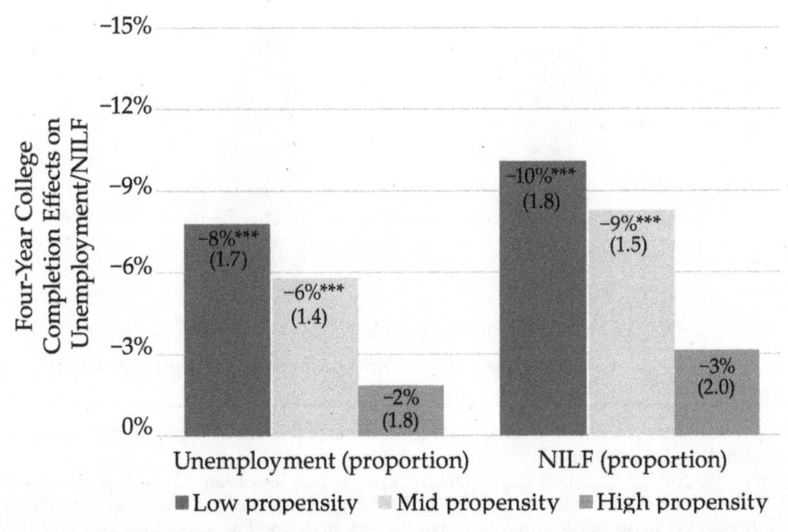

Source: Author's calculations using data from the U.S. Bureau of Labor Statistics National Longitudinal Surveys (n = 4,085).
Notes: The college completion propensity score is 0 to less than 0.2 for low propensity, 0.2 to less than 0.5 for middle, and 0.5 to 1 for high. Analyses are based on matching on the linearized propensity score. Numbers in parentheses are standard errors.
*** $p \leq 0.001$; two-tailed tests

propensity college graduates. Here I find a clear pattern of negative selection across measures of socioeconomic disadvantage: a college degree reduces socioeconomic disadvantage most strongly for low-propensity graduates. For example, I find an eight- and ten-percentage-point lower level of unemployment and not in the labor force (NILF), respectively, for low-propensity college graduates relative to a two- and three-percentage-point (insignificant) lower level among high-propensity college graduates (see figure 5.3[a]).

College graduates with low completion chances have a twenty-three-percentage-point-lower level of low-wage work compared to a nine-percentage-point-lower level for those with high completion chances (figure 5.3[b]).[28] Employment stability also suggests that the largest effect is for low-propensity graduates (figure 5.3[c]), but in this case the effect for high-propensity graduates exceeds the effect for mid-propensity graduates. I find significant differences between college effect

Figure 5.3(b) **Effects of Four-Year College Completion on Low-Wage and Low-Skilled Work by College Completion Likelihood (y-Axis Reversed): NLSY79**

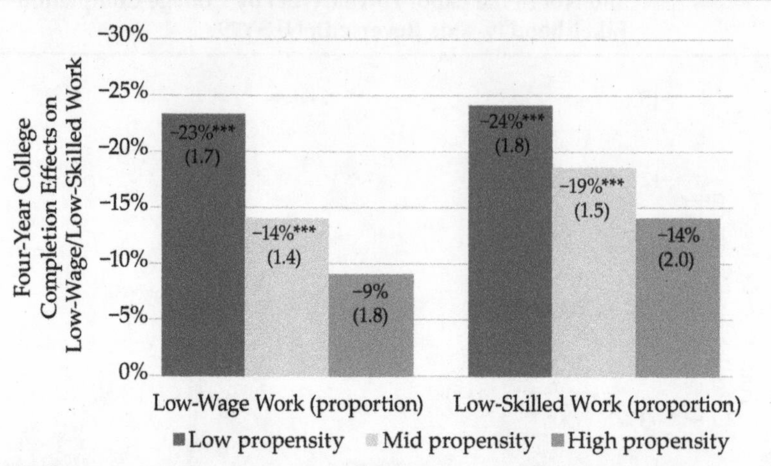

Source: Author's calculations using data from the U.S. Bureau of Labor Statistics National Longitudinal Surveys ($n = 4{,}085$).
Notes: The college completion propensity score is 0 to less than 0.2 for low propensity, 0.2 to less than 0.5 for middle, and 0.5 to 1 for high. Analyses are based on matching on the linearized propensity score. Low-wage work is defined as two-thirds of the median hourly wage in any given year, and low-skilled work is defined as clerical, service and sales, craft, trade, and plant and machine operator and assembler occupations. Numbers in parentheses are standard errors.
*** $p \leq 0.001$; two-tailed tests

Figure 5.3(c) **Effects of Four-Year College Completion on Job Instability by College Completion Likelihood: NLSY79**

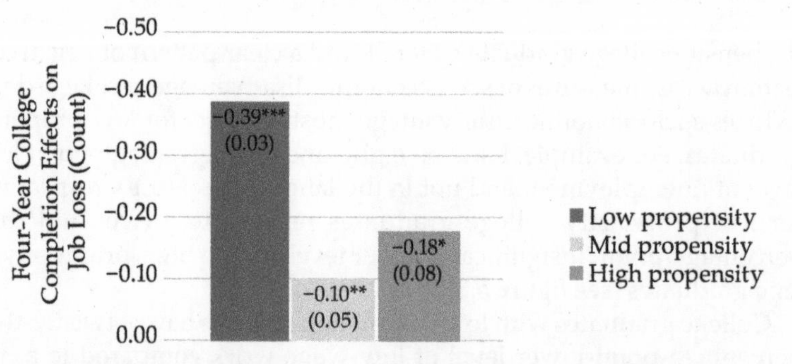

Source: Author's calculations using data from the U.S. Bureau of Labor Statistics National Longitudinal Surveys ($n = 4{,}085$).
Notes: The college completion propensity score is 0 to less than 0.2 for low propensity, 0.2 to less than 0.5 for middle, and 0.5 to 1 for high. Analyses are based on matching on the linearized propensity score. Job instability is measured as a count of jobs lost due to layoffs or plant closings. Numbers in parentheses are standard errors.
* $p \leq 0.05$; ** $p \leq 0.01$; *** $p \leq 0.001$; two-tailed tests

estimates for low-propensity and high-propensity graduates for each outcome (see appendix table B.7[a]). The results are robust to alternative estimation strategies (see appendix table B.7[b]), and effect estimates for the low-propensity remain significant at various levels of assumed unobserved confounding (see appendix table B.10). These results represent a key finding that has been largely overlooked in the prior literature: college allows unlikely graduates to reduce intergenerational persistence of socioeconomic disadvantage. Assessing a broader set of socioeconomic outcomes provides this fuller understanding of the returns for disadvantaged college graduates.

Results for the more recent NLSY97 cohort reported in figures 5.4(a), 5.4(b), and 5.4(c) (and appendix table B.8) suggest a similar pattern between the mid-twenties and mid-thirties. College completion has the largest impact on reducing socioeconomic disadvantage among low-propensity graduates.[29] College effects on reducing low-skilled work are larger for the more recent cohort for all subgroups (figure 5.4[b]) and significantly larger for low-propensity graduates relative to high-propensity graduates. At least for early career outcomes, advantaged

Figure 5.4(a) Effects of Four-Year College Completion on Unemployment and Not in the Labor Force (NILF) by College Completion Likelihood (y-Axis Reversed): NLSY97

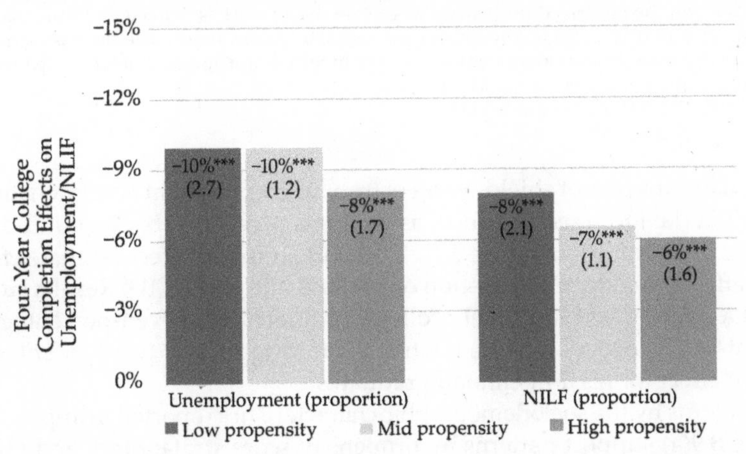

Source: Author's calculations using data from the U.S. Bureau of Labor Statistics National Longitudinal Surveys ($n = 7{,}626$).
Notes: The college completion propensity score is 0 to less than 0.2 for low propensity, 0.2 to less than 0.5 for middle, and 0.5 to 1 for high. Analyses are based on matching on the linearized propensity score. Unemployment analyses are based on doubly robust estimation. Numbers in parentheses are standard errors.
*** $p \leq 0.001$; two-tailed tests

Figure 5.4(b) Effects of Four-Year College Completion on Low-Wage and Low-Skilled Work by College Completion Likelihood (y-Axis Reversed): NLSY97

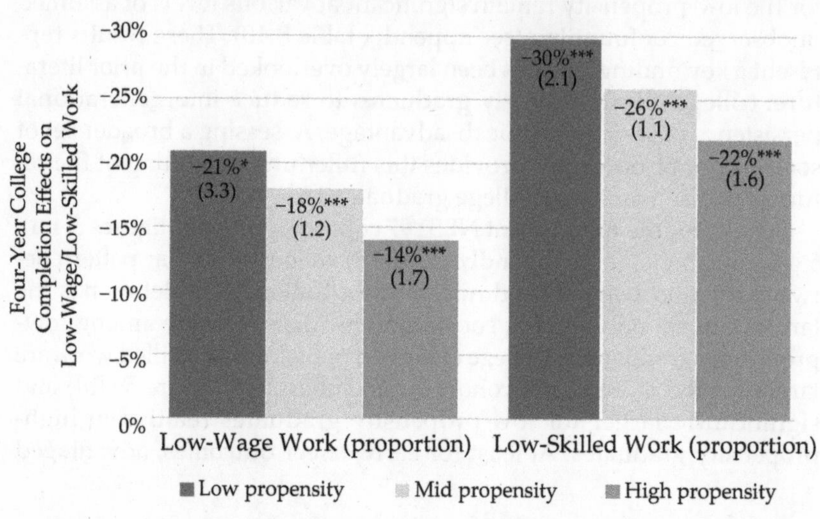

Source: Author's calculations using data from the U.S. Bureau of Labor Statistics National Longitudinal Surveys (n = 7,626).
Notes: The college completion propensity score is 0 to less than 0.2 for low propensity, 0.2 to less than 0.5 for middle, and 0.5 to 1 for high. Analyses are based on nearest-neighbor matching on the linearized propensity score. Low-wage work is defined as two-thirds of the median hourly wage in any given year, and low-skilled work is defined as clerical, service and sales, craft, trade, and plant and machine operator and assembler occupations. Numbers in parentheses are standard errors.
* $p \leq 0.05$; *** $p \leq 0.001$; two-tailed tests

social origins do not shield workers from unemployment and low-wage work in the more recent cohort as well as a privileged background did in the prior cohort. In figure 5.4[c], I report stratified effect estimates for the effects of college completion on job loss due to COVID. Results suggest a large effect for unlikely college graduates, an eleven-percentage-point-lower level of job loss relative to an insignificant two-percentage point effect for high-likelihood graduates.

Patterns by the sociodemographic characteristics reported in appendix table B.9(a) support patterns by propensity score strata: Black and Hispanic college graduates with low parental income, low test scores, or low mother's education experienced higher disadvantage-reducing effects of college than did White college graduates and those with high parental income, high test scores, and college-educated parents. For example, college graduates with low parental income had a twenty-nine-percentage-

Figure 5.4(c) Effects of Four-Year College Completion on Job Loss during the COVID-19 Pandemic by College Completion Likelihood: NLSY97

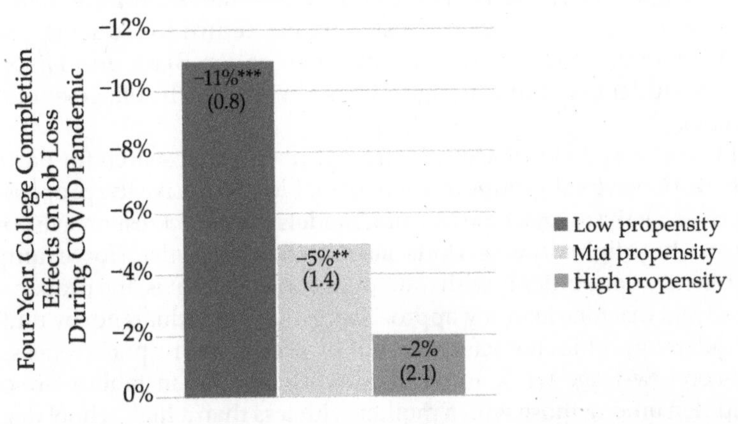

Source: Author's calculations using data from the U.S. Bureau of Labor Statistics National Longitudinal Surveys ($n = 7{,}626$).
Notes: The college completion propensity score is 0 to less than 0.2 for low propensity, 0.2 to less than 0.5 for middle, and 0.5 to 1 for high. Analyses are based on matching on the linearized propensity score. Job loss during the COVID-19 pandemic indicates a job lost in 2020 because of the pandemic. Numbers in parentheses are standard errors.
** $p \leq 0.01$; *** $p \leq 0.001$; two-tailed tests

point-lower level in low-wage work, those with middle parental income had a twenty-one-percentage-point-lower level, and those with high parental income had a nine-percentage-point-lower level. Patterns are similar for the mother's education and test score categories. Likewise, college graduates with low parental income had a ten-percentage-point-lower level of unemployment, while there was no effect among those with high parental income. The patterns are similar across the other sociodemographic groups, suggesting larger reductions in socioeconomic disadvantage for more-disadvantaged college graduates.

Examining selected subgroups leads to the same substantive conclusion. For example, Black and Hispanic college graduates with low parental income had an eleven-percentage-point-lower level of time in unemployment and a twenty-seven-percentage-point-lower level of time in low-wage work than matched non-college graduates. Their time spent in low-skilled jobs was twenty-eight percentage points lower, and they experienced fewer job losses. By contrast, White college graduates with high parental income had a six-percentage-point-lower level of time in unemployment and an eighteen-percentage-point-lower level in low-wage work than comparable non-college graduates. They had a twenty-one-percentage-point-lower level of time in low-skilled jobs and experienced fewer job displacements, although this reduction was not as large as it was for Black and Hispanic college graduates with low parental income. These differences suggest a greater return to reducing disadvantage among low-income and first-generation Black and Hispanic college students relative to high-income Whites with college-educated parents.

I report results for machine learning models that search for particularly responsive subgroups in appendix table 8.9(b). Like the propensity-stratified analyses, machine learning models that select responsive populations highlight intersections across characteristics (for example, first-generation students with low social control). That is, the propensity-based and machine learning approaches group individuals not by unitary sociodemographic characteristics but by access and responsiveness. Effects on low-wage work, low-skilled work, and job instability are concentrated among those with a mother with less than a high school degree and with low parental income. I find that college completion reduces unemployment most among those with low to mid propensity scores, a mother who did not complete high school, and low test scores. College reduces low-wage work for those whose mother did not complete high school and who grew up in a large family and reduces time in a low-skilled job for men who grew up without both parents and for men with low parental income who report low social control. Recent work by Stefanie DeLuca and her colleagues suggests that anticipation of disruptive events, or low social control, is a key factor limiting the educational attainment of disadvantaged youth.[30] Here I find that youth who complete a degree despite low social control reap significant socioeconomic returns. The machine learning algorithm also identifies those with low propensity scores as experiencing the largest effect of college completion on reducing job instability. Notably, the most responsive subgroups have low propensity scores for all five outcomes.

College as the Great Equalizer: Exploring Levels of Socioeconomic Outcomes across College Completion Likelihood

Nick was a White male from a high-income, college-educated family. He had high test scores and secondary school achievement. Diego was a first-generation Latino with low-income parents. He had below-average test scores and low secondary school achievement. Nick had a high likelihood of completing college, and Diego had a low likelihood, yet both completed a four-year degree. Nick was continuously employed from his mid-twenties through age fifty, as was Diego. In his early thirties, Nick earned nearly $100,000 annually, a wage that steadily increased to about $160,000. Diego's wages also grew, but his earnings were not as consistently high as Nick's. Like Nick, he was earning about $160,000 at his peak, but he saw his wages decline later to about $130,000. Nick's average wage over his career was about 12 percent higher than Diego's. If we consider only earnings, we might conclude that college does not perfectly equalize the destinations of men like Nick and Diego.

Let us compare the wage levels of Nick and Diego to those of Rich and Javier. Rich is Nick's matched counterpart, a high-propensity White male who did not complete college. Diego's counterpart, Javier, is a low-propensity Latino who did not complete college. Rich's wages rose from about $80,000 annually in his mid-thirties to $100,000 in his late forties. Javier's earnings remained at about $26,000 annually throughout his career. Rich's average wage over his career was four times higher than Javier's. Notably, Rich's wages were more like Nick's than Javier's; in other words, Rich's earnings looked more like those of a college graduate of high social origins than those of a non-college graduate of low social origins. While a comparison between Nick's and Rich's wages suggests considerable economic returns to college, especially in terms of wage growth, the economic returns suggested by the comparison between Diego's and Javier's wage profiles are even more substantial. Thus, although wages were unequal between Nick and Diego, the wage returns to college were larger for Diego than for Nick. We reach a similar conclusion if we compare Nick and Rich to Brian and Henry—that is, to low-propensity White men.

An influential set of studies has considered whether education acts as a great equalizer. As discussed in chapter 2, most of this scholarship focuses on whether college equalizes wages or occupational status. In other words, scholars ask whether the wages and status of college graduates are similar regardless of social origins. Generally, we observe a strong positive correlation between social origins (or family income) and socioeconomic destinations (or earnings). If we observe a weaker relationship between social origins and socioeconomic destinations among college graduates, we have evidence that college serves as an equalizer. I have emphasized that this is a question of considering heterogeneity in socioeconomic outcomes among college graduates rather than heterogeneity in the effects of college on those outcomes. Considerable misrepresentation of the value of college is due to expectations of equalization of *levels* of (mostly) wages across college graduates by social origin rather than attending to the *effects* of completing college on wages by social origin. Moreover, we get an incomplete understanding of college benefits if we consider only wages.

In this section, I turn to the variation across outcome levels for the matched sample of college and non-college graduates. Depiction of outcome levels not only speaks to the debate on equalization; it is informative about the mechanisms underlying the differential benefits of college completion and differences in those mechanisms across different socioeconomic outcomes. Yet I remind the reader that we can have unequal socioeconomic destinations for college graduates by social origin and still have larger college completion effects on socioeconomic destinations by social origin.

Figures 5.5(a) to 5.5(f) show two panels: on the left, I show earnings levels for college graduates (solid line) and non-college graduates (dashed line) by the propensity for college; on the right, I show the difference in levels between college graduates and non-college graduates. In figure 5.5(a), the x-axis is the propensity for college, and the y-axis indicates (log) earnings. The x-axis also identifies the three propensity score strata corresponding to the earlier analyses: the low stratum, ranging from 0 to 0.2; the middle stratum, ranging from 0.2 to 0.5; and the high stratum, ranging from 0.5 to 1.0. As I noted previously, the average propensity score value is 0.2. Values above 0.75 represent only 5 percent of cases, and values below 0.005 represent the bottom 5 percent. I eliminate the bottom and top 5 percent of the distribution to avoid the tails unduly influencing the pattern.

As I show in figure 5.5(a), non-college graduates with disadvantaged social origins or a low propensity for college completion had low wages. That level increased with the likelihood of completing a degree until it leveled off for the high-propensity non-college graduates. Among college graduates, earnings also increased as propensity increased, but not as steeply as that for non-college graduates, particularly at the low end of the propensity distribution. We do not see full equalization in earnings for college graduates across their career. Advantaged college graduates had high wage growth that exceeded that of disadvantaged college graduates.[31] This is not to say that college does not equalize other important socioeconomic outcomes. And again, this does not mean that the return to high-propensity graduates is greater, as we see larger returns for unlikely graduates. The right panel shows the large wage returns for those with a low propensity for college, which decline after about the average propensity score. If I had included the top 5 percent of the propensity score distribution, we would have seen a greater return to the high-propensity graduates and more of a *u*-shaped curve.

If we instead consider indicators of socioeconomic disadvantage, we draw a firmer conclusion regarding the equalization of socioeconomic outcomes. Both Nick and Diego spent no time unemployed. Nick spent

Figure 5.5(a) Levels of Wages and Effects of Four-Year College Completion on Wages by College Completion Likelihood: NLSY79

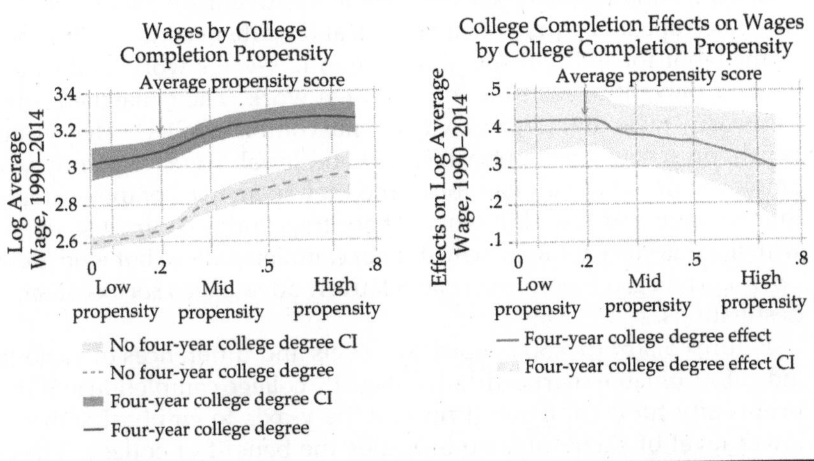

Source: Author's calculations using data from the U.S. Bureau of Labor Statistics National Longitudinal Surveys ($n = 4{,}085$).
Notes: CI indicates confidence interval. Analyses are based on local polynomial smoothing.

about 15 percent of his career in low-wage work and Diego spent 7 percent; both spent under 7 percent of their time in low-skilled work. The comparison suggests an almost complete equalization of indicators of socioeconomic disadvantage for men who grew up under different socioeconomic circumstances but completed a college degree. Consider the comparable indicators of disadvantage for Rich and Javier, who did not complete college. Rich spent no time unemployed, while Javier spent 40 percent of his time unemployed. Rich spent about a year out of the labor force, while Javier spent over half of his time out of the labor force. Rich spent no time in low-wage work, while Javier spent 80 percent of his career in low-wage work. Rich spent 20 percent of his career in low-skilled work, a considerably larger share than Nick's share, but Javier spent about three-quarters of his time in low-skilled work. The socioeconomic trajectories of men with different social origins who did not complete college diverged sharply.

In summary, while we see almost complete equalization of indicators of socioeconomic disadvantage for Nick and Diego, the difference in these outcomes between Rich and Javier is considerable. Diego, who grew up in a disadvantaged family and completed college, experienced considerable upward intergenerational mobility. In contrast, Javier, who had similarly disadvantaged social origins and did not complete college continued to experience socioeconomic disadvantage. The trajectories of Brian and Caleb, both low-propensity college graduates, aligned with Diego's for indicators of socioeconomic disadvantage. Neither Brian nor Caleb spent any time unemployed, and neither spent any time out of the labor force. Brian spent no time in low-wage work, and Caleb spent 7 percent of his time in low-wage work. Their matched low-propensity male counterparts who did not complete college, Henry and Isaiah, present a stark contrast. Henry and Isaiah were frequently unemployed or out of the labor force, and they spent most of their careers in low-wage and low-skill work. These trajectories contrast strongly with the trajectory for Rich, who did not complete college but who grew up in a privileged family. Rich had relatively advantaged socioeconomic destinations.

Figures 5.5(b) to 5.5(f) depict the levels and differences of various indicators of labor market disadvantage by college completion and the propensity for completion. I reverse the y-axis to emphasize that a lower level of each outcome indicates the benefit of college. These figures mirror the pattern I depict in the stylized figure 2.1: the pattern for college graduates across the levels of unemployment (figure 5.5[b]), time out of the labor force (figure 5.5[c]), low-wage work (figure 5.5[d]), low-skilled work (figure 5.5[e]), and job instability (figure 5.5[f]) is generally flat, suggesting equalization. For non-college graduates, the levels decrease as the propensity increases. Low-likelihood non-college graduates experience the highest levels of socioeconomic disadvantage. As I discussed earlier (and report in appendix table B.7[a]), the effect of college on reducing unemployment, time out of the labor force, low-wage work, low-skilled jobs, and job instability is greatest for those with a low propensity and decreases as the propensity increases. In figures 5.5(b) to 5.5(f), we see the levels that generate those stratified results. The pattern of negative selection results from the equalization of socioeconomic disadvantage for college graduates across the propensity for college completion relative to the strong relationship between social origins and socioeconomic destinations for non-college graduates.

Consider the proportion of time spent in unemployment and out of the labor force reported in figures 5.5(b) and 5.5(c), respectively. We see largely equal levels for college graduates across degree likelihood, except insofar as low-propensity graduates had even lower unemployment and time out of the labor force than high-propensity graduates. By contrast, there is a steep slope among non-college graduates by the propensity for college completion. Suppose we focus on the low stratum, with a propensity for 0 to 0.2. These non-college graduates spent about 13 percent of their time unemployed, relative to about 5 percent for college gradu-

Figure 5.5(b) Levels of Unemployment and Effects of Four-Year College Completion on Unemployment by College Completion Likelihood (y-Axis Reversed): NLSY79

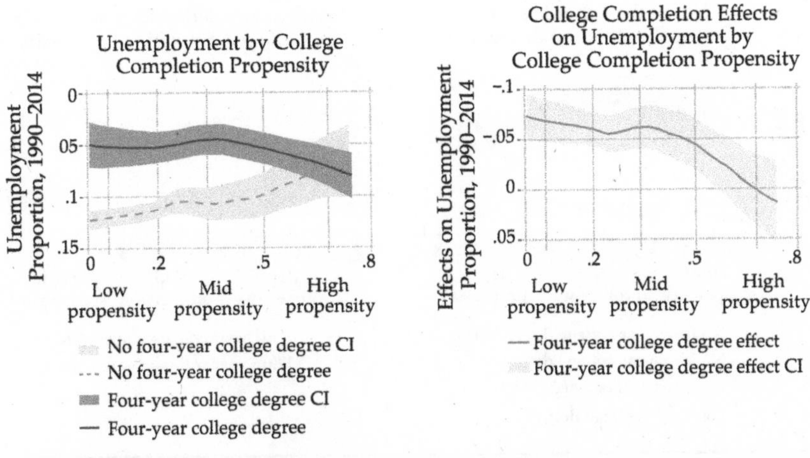

Source: Author's calculations using data from the U.S. Bureau of Labor Statistics National Longitudinal Surveys ($n = 4{,}085$).
Notes: CI indicates confidence interval. Analyses are based on local polynomial smoothing.

ates, yielding an estimated effect of college of seven to eight percentage points. At the high-propensity score stratum, above 0.5, we see levels of 5 to 7 percent overlapping, yielding no significant difference between college graduates and non-college graduates. The right-side panel of figure 5.5(b) shows that the effect estimate for high-propensity individuals is about 0. The pattern for time out of the labor force, reported in figure 5.5(c), mirrors that for unemployment.

Now consider low-wage work as reported in figure 5.5(d). College graduates spent about 24 percent of their time in low-wage work, often in their early career. This was true regardless of their social background and achievement before college. By contrast, non-college graduates spent more time in low-wage work if they had disadvantaged social origins than did non-college graduates with more-advantaged origins. Disadvantaged non-college graduates spent about 44 percent of their time in low-wage work relative to about 31 percent for advantaged non-college graduates. Taking the difference, we have a roughly 20 percent reduction for disadvantaged low-propensity college graduates compared with an approximately 7 percent reduction in low-wage work for advantaged high-propensity college graduates (see right-side panel of figure 5.5[d]).

Figure 5.5(c) Levels of Not in the Labor Force (NILF) and Effects of Four-Year College Completion on NILF by College Completion Likelihood (y-Axis Reversed): NLSY79

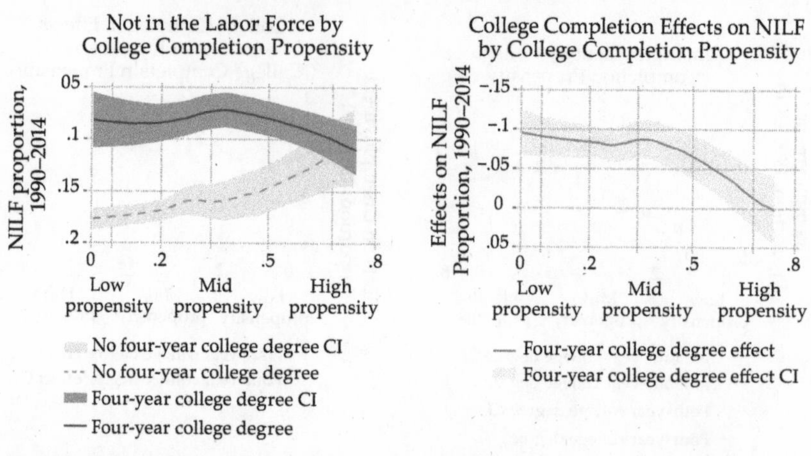

Source: Author's calculations using data from the U.S. Bureau of Labor Statistics National Longitudinal Surveys ($n = 4{,}085$).
Notes: CI indicates confidence interval. Analyses are based on local polynomial smoothing.

Figure 5.5(d) Levels of Low-Wage Work and Effects of Four-Year College Completion on Low-Wage Work by College Completion Likelihood (y-Axis Reversed): NLSY79

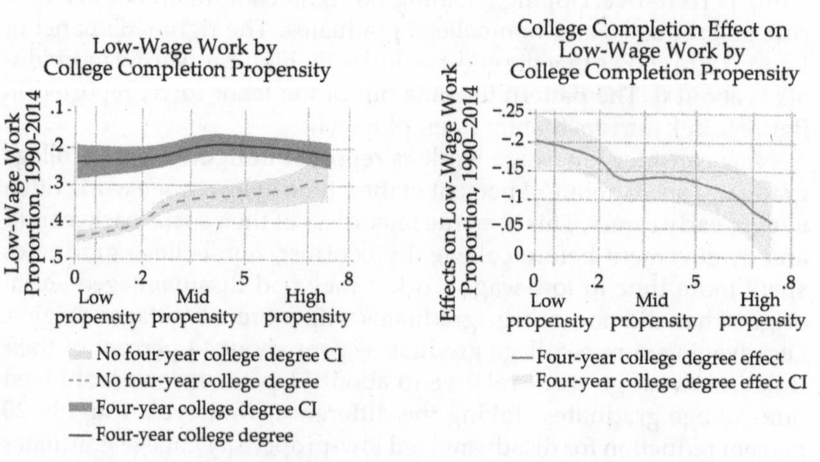

Source: Author's calculations using data from the U.S. Bureau of Labor Statistics National Longitudinal Surveys ($n = 4{,}085$).
Notes: CI indicates confidence interval. Analyses are based on local polynomial smoothing. Low-wage work is defined as two-thirds of the median hourly wage in any given year.

Figure 5.5(e) Levels of Low-Skilled Work and Effects of Four-Year College Completion on Low-Skilled Work by College Completion Likelihood (y-Axis Reversed): NLSY79

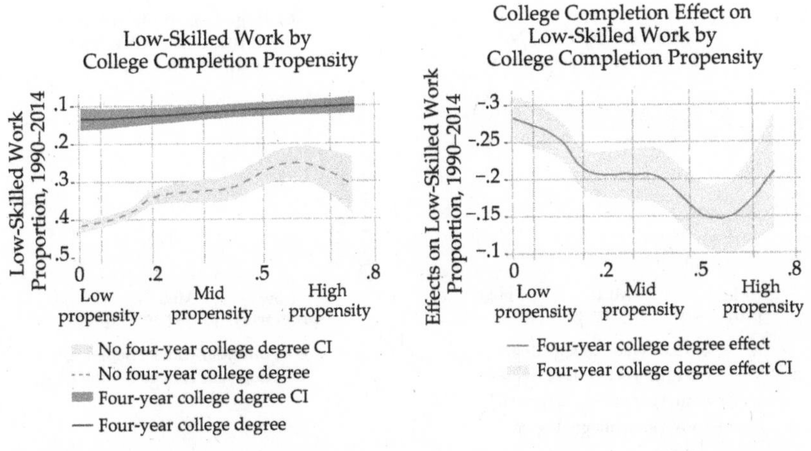

Source: Author's calculations using data from the U.S. Bureau of Labor Statistics National Longitudinal Surveys (n = 4,085).
Notes: CI indicates confidence interval. Analyses are based on local polynomial smoothing. Low-skilled work is defined as clerical, service and sales, craft, trade, and plant and machine operator and assembler occupations.

The pattern for the proportion of time spent in a low-skilled job, reported in figure 5.5(e), is similar. College graduates spent about 10 percent of their career in low-skilled work, regardless of degree likelihood or social origins. There is a gradient for non-college graduates by social origins: low-propensity non-college graduates spent 35 to 40 percent of their time in low-skilled work relative to 25 to 30 percent among high-propensity non-college graduates. Thus, a roughly 27 percent difference is associated with college among the low-propensity relative to a 15 to 20 percent difference among the high-propensity (right-side panel of figure 5.5[e]). The number of involuntary job losses reported in figure 5.5(f) shows the same pattern: equalization among college graduates relative to a steep slope for non-college graduates, yielding a notably large return for low-propensity graduates (right-side panel of figure 5.5[f]). The sum of the findings reported in figures 5.5(b) through 5.5(f) speaks to the consequential equalizing role of college in socioeconomic disadvantage. I assess the sensitivity of the pattern of college effect heterogeneity to unobserved confounding by the continuous propensity for college and find that the patterns I observe are reasonably robust (see appendix figure C.6).[32]

Figure 5.5(f) Levels of Job Instability and Effects of Four-Year College Completion on Job Instability by College Completion Likelihood (y-Axis Reversed): NLSY79

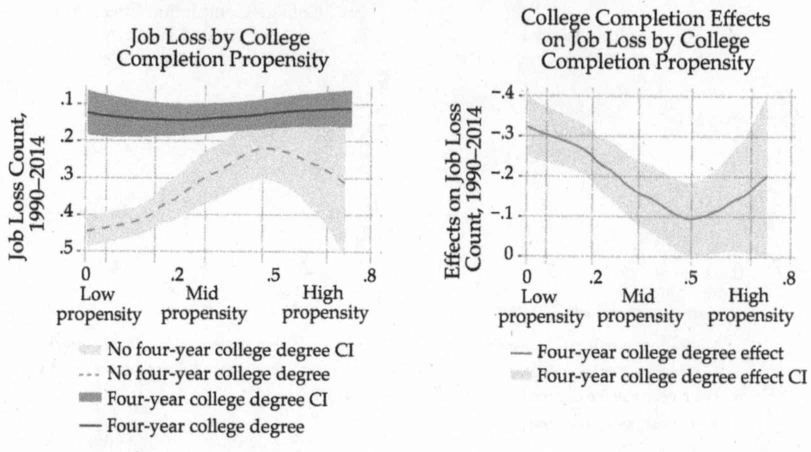

Source: Author's calculations using data from the U.S. Bureau of Labor Statistics National Longitudinal Surveys ($n = 4{,}085$).
Notes: CI indicates confidence interval. Analyses are based on local polynomial smoothing. Job instability is measured as a count of jobs lost due to layoffs or plant closings.

Results from the NLSY97 cohort indicate similar patterns, with a few important differences, reported in figures 5.6(a) to 5.6(f). In figure 5.6(a), we do not see as steep a rise in wage levels among non-college graduates as the propensity for college increases, suggesting that high-propensity high school graduates are facing increasing difficulties in the labor market. Results for wages suggest a modest *u*-shaped pattern, with larger effects for high-propensity graduates. We continue to see equalization among college graduates for unemployment (figure 5.6[b]), time out of the labor force (figure 5.6[c]), low-wage work (figure 5.6[d]), low-skilled work (figure 5.6[e]), and job instability (figure 5.6[f]). Equalization does not hold for non-college graduates, yielding larger college degree returns for those with a low propensity for college completion (see right-side panels of figure 5.6[b] to 5.6[f]). Gaps are greater, however, between high-propensity college graduates and high-propensity non-college graduates for the younger than the older cohort. Advantaged social origins no longer appear sufficient to avoid labor market precarity without a college degree, at least not in the early career.

Figure 5.6(a) Levels of (Log) Wages and Effects of Four-Year College Completion on (Log) Wages by College Completion Likelihood: NLSY97

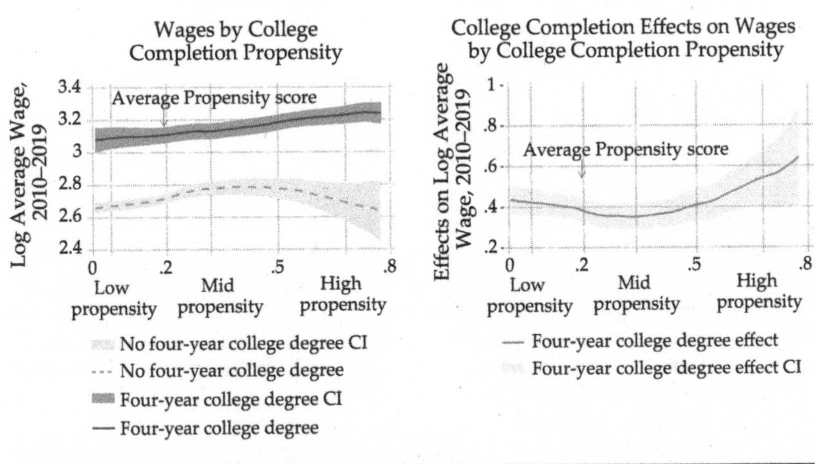

Source: Author's calculations using data from the U.S. Bureau of Labor Statistics National Longitudinal Surveys ($n = 7{,}626$).
Notes: CI indicates confidence interval. Analyses are based on local polynomial smoothing.

Figure 5.6(b) Levels of Unemployment and Effects of Four-Year College Completion on Unemployment by College Completion Likelihood (y-Axis Reversed): NLSY97

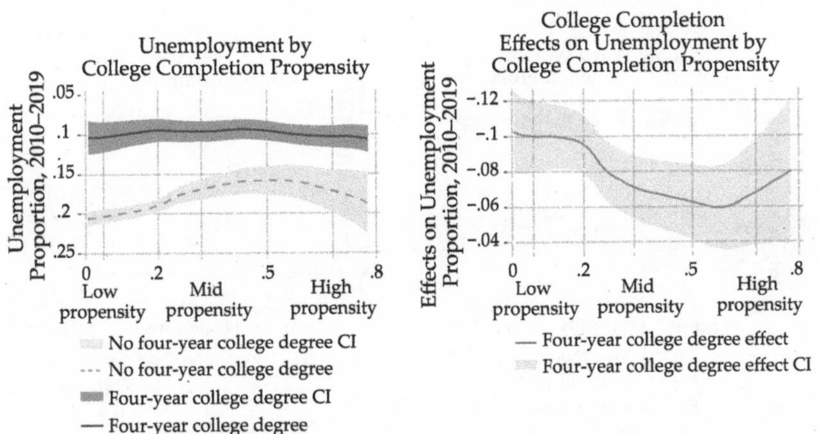

Source: Author's calculations using data from the U.S. Bureau of Labor Statistics National Longitudinal Surveys ($n = 7{,}626$).
Notes: CI indicates confidence interval. Analyses are based on local polynomial smoothing.

Figure 5.6(c) Levels of Not in the Labor Force (NILF) and Effects of Four-Year College Completion on NILF by College Completion Likelihood (y-Axis Reversed): NLSY97

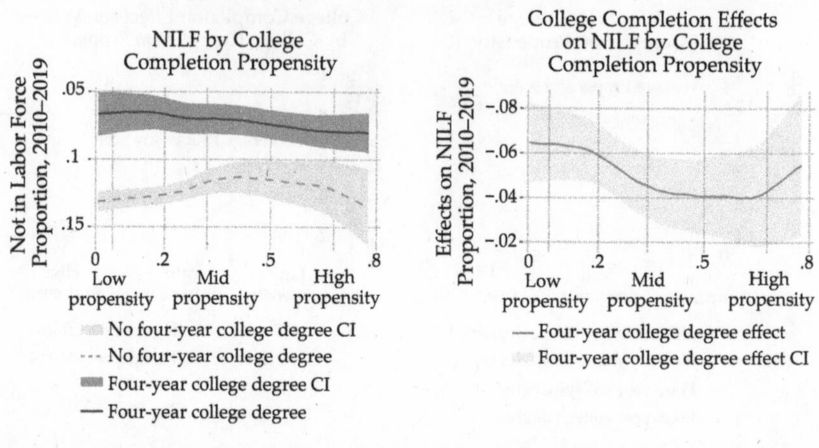

Source: Author's calculations using data from the U.S. Bureau of Labor Statistics National Longitudinal Surveys ($n = 7{,}626$).
Notes: CI indicates confidence interval. Analyses are based on local polynomial smoothing.

Figure 5.6(d) Levels of Low-Wage Work and Effects of Four-Year College Completion on Low-Wage Work by College Completion Likelihood (y-Axis Reversed): NLSY97

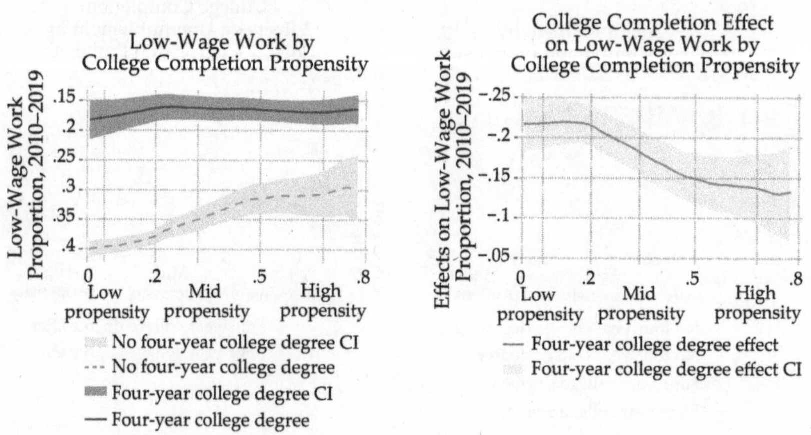

Source: Author's calculations using data from the U.S. Bureau of Labor Statistics National Longitudinal Surveys ($n = 7{,}626$).
Notes: CI indicates confidence interval. Analyses are based on local polynomial smoothing. Low-wage work is defined as two-thirds of the median hourly wage in any given year.

Figure 5.6(e) Levels of Low-Skilled Work and Effects of Four-Year College Completion on Low-Skilled Work by College Completion Likelihood (y-Axis Reversed): NLSY97

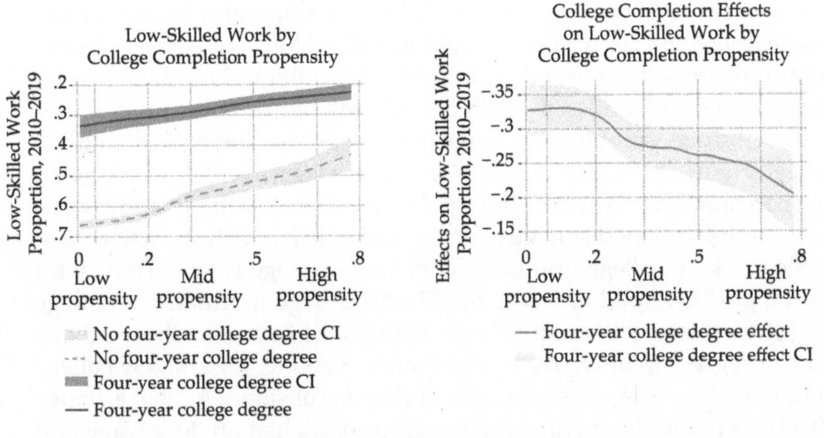

Source: Author's calculations using data from the U.S. Bureau of Labor Statistics National Longitudinal Surveys ($n = 7{,}626$).
Notes: CI indicates confidence interval. Analyses are based on local polynomial smoothing. Low-skilled work is defined as clerical, service and sales, craft, trade, and plant and machine operator and assembler occupations.

Figure 5.6(f) Levels of Job Loss during the COVID-19 Pandemic and Effects of Four-Year College Completion on Job Loss during the Pandemic by College Completion Likelihood (y-Axis Reversed): NLSY97

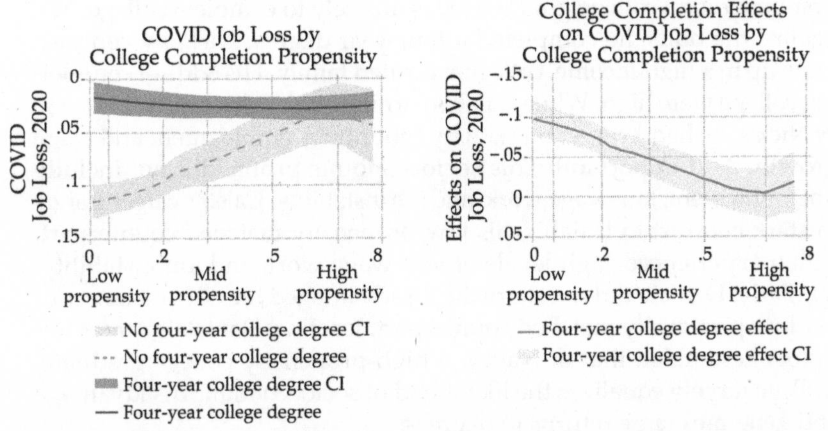

Source: Author's calculations using data from the U.S. Bureau of Labor Statistics National Longitudinal Surveys.
Notes: CI indicates confidence interval. Analyses are based on local polynomial smoothing.

Cultivating Privilege and Circumventing Precarity

In this chapter, I have emphasized that our assessment of college benefits should attend to not only earnings but also the effect of college on a person's overall socioeconomic standing that operates by stabilizing employment and circumventing low-wage and low-skilled work. These latter outcomes have broad and pressing sociological implications for the lives of disadvantaged youth considering higher education.

The findings point to large wage returns for low-and high-likelihood college graduates over the life course. I have suggested that two different mechanisms lead to similarly high wage returns at the low and high ends: high-likelihood college graduates establish a high-growth career, while unlikely college graduates avoid a low-wage career. That is, for both high-likelihood and low-likelihood college graduates, a college degree cultivates a life of privilege. However, I have also shown that a college degree circumvents socioeconomic precarity for unlikely college graduates. I have demonstrated this finding in considering college degree effects on unemployment and labor force participation, low-wage and low-skilled work, and job instability. The large impact on reducing socioeconomic disadvantages among unlikely graduates for each of these measures results from the relative equalization of disadvantage among college graduates across social origins. I have noted that whether college is a great equalizer depends on which indicators of socioeconomic status we consider. A college degree may not perfectly equalize wages while it does equalize low-wage and low-skilled work and labor market precarity.

As an illustration, I presented several vignettes. Caleb, a low-income, first-generation college graduate, was unlikely to complete college. Yet, against the odds, he completed a four-year degree. Nick, by contrast, grew up in a high-income, college-educated family. His odds of completing college were high. While Caleb's earnings trajectory was not as steep as Nick's, he had a career marked by continuous employment and wage growth. And importantly, his socioeconomic profile did not include unemployment, low-wage work, and job instability. Caleb's career stands in stark contrast to Isaiah's, his low-propensity matched counterpart. Isaiah experienced high levels of low-wage work and job instability. Similarly, Daniela did not share the disadvantaged life circumstances of her low-propensity matched counterpart, Josefina. Daniela's career trajectory resembled that of Nancy, a high-propensity college graduate. College largely equalizes the likelihood of socioeconomic disadvantage and generates large returns to degrees.

These findings suggest meaningful and differential ways in which a college degree impacts socioeconomic trajectories. As college access reaches broader segments of the population, it impacts broader outcomes. Expanding college access to youth from underprivileged backgrounds increases its influence along diverse indicators of socioeconomic well-being. If low-income youth experience greater returns to college than high-income youth, increasing their representation among college graduates should reduce intergenerational income persistence.[33] Although inequality in some socioeconomic outcomes, like wages, may persist among college graduates, college degrees equalize socioeconomic disadvantage. In sum, these findings suggest that completing college is acutely consequential for unlikely college graduates. In chapter 6, I consider the impact of college degrees on family-level outcomes.

Chapter 6

Forming Families and Preventing Poverty

Olanna and Sydney were Black women with a high likelihood of college completion. Olanna's mother attended college, and Sydney's mother had an advanced degree. Their mothers raised them on their own, and their family income was below average, but both Olanna and Sydney had high test scores, expected to attend college, and had friends who aspired to attend college. They both expected to marry in their twenties and expressed a commitment to combining marriage with work. Olanna attended college after high school and completed a degree in four years. Sydney, Olanna's matched comparison, attended college for two years after high school but did not complete a four-year degree.

Olanna worked as a teacher. She was married in her twenties, and her husband worked as a precision production worker. She divorced her first husband and was later remarried. She had two children and had spent most of her life married. Olanna's average household income was about $110,000. Her family did not spend any time in poverty. Sydney worked as a secretary most of her career and then as an account collector. She was single throughout her life and had no children. Sydney's average household income was about $45,000, and she spent about 15 percent of her time in poverty. Neither Olanna nor Sydney spent time as a single mother, Olanna because she was married with children and Sydney because she was single without children. If we believe that Sydney represents Olanna's counterfactual destinations, college appears to be associated with forming a family and having a higher household income, but completing college makes little difference in time spent in poverty for these women and their families.

Now let us consider Chantelle and Imani, both low-propensity Black women whose similarity in social origins I described in chapter 5. Chantelle completed college in four years, and Imani attended some community college but did not complete a degree. Like Olanna and Sydney, Chantelle and Imani expressed similar family formation preferences and values in adolescence, and both expected to get married in their twenties. Chantelle was single until her late twenties and then got married. She would remain married and have no children. Her husband worked in construction in his early career and later as a service technician. Imani was single through her late forties. She had her first child in her mid-twenties—unintentionally, she reported—and then she had a second child. She spent most of her life as a single mother.

Although we see no difference in single parenthood between Olanna and Sydney, we observe a large difference in the time spent as a single parent between Chantelle and Imani. Chantelle had a significantly higher household income than Imani, but the differential was not as large as it was with Olanna and Sydney. Chantelle did not spend any of her time under the family poverty threshold, while Imani and her family spent about 85 percent of their time in poverty. Assuming Imani's trajectory represents Chantelle's possible counterfactual, a college degree markedly reduced family-level disadvantages for Chantelle.

These trajectories illustrate the variations in college completion effects that I explore in this chapter. Completing a four-year degree significantly affects marriage and household income for high-likelihood college graduates. Conversely, completing college is associated with significant reductions in single parenthood and family-level poverty for unlikely graduates. I first review the literature on the effects of college on family-level outcomes and assess the impact of completing a four-year college degree on family outcomes. I consider average and heterogeneous effects on household income, family poverty, marriage, spousal status, and single parenthood. I describe levels of each outcome for both college graduates and non-college graduates and ask whether college equalizes family outcomes. I conclude with a discussion of the differential impacts of college on family formation and family socioeconomic well-being.

Background on College Completion Effects on Family-Level Outcomes

Family formation patterns are an important dimension of stratification and inequality.[1] College degrees are associated with higher household income and a lower likelihood of family-level poverty.[2] Household income and family poverty depend on both the individual socioeconomic outcomes I consider in chapter 5 and family formation factors. College graduates are more likely, on average, to get married and to stay married than non-college graduates, and they are more likely to have children and to raise them within marriage.[3] The less-educated are more likely to raise their children outside of marriage, in less stable contexts, and with limited resources.[4] Men's economic prospects and financial stability have long been positively associated with marriage and family formation, and women's economic opportunities have become similarly associated with marriage.[5] Those who do not meet the economic bar to marriage are less likely to form marital unions.[6] Scholars have noted a growing educational family divide, such that marriage is increasingly reserved for those with higher education. Education is also associated with a delay in the onset of childbearing and with having fewer children overall.[7] The less-educated also delay or forgo marriage but not fertility, leading to high fertility and single parenthood.[8] Women with less than a college degree are more likely to have children outside marriage and with multiple partners.[9] The number of nonmarital births is almost four times higher for women with a high school degree than for those with a college degree.[10]

As I discuss in chapter 2, the human capital model assumes that youth take a lifetime perspective when making choices. They foresee a future trajectory of schooling and family formation and choose the sequence and timing of events.[11] That is, young people with high educational expectations may strategically aim to postpone family formation to finish higher education, gain work experience, and build economic resources.[12] Although being in school can delay family formation, college-educated men and women also wait to form families because they face higher opportunity costs.[13] By contrast, less-educated women with limited career prospects may have minimal economic incentive to delay childbearing. Instead, motherhood offers a valid social role for women who perceive, as the sociologists Kathryn Edin and Maria Kefalas write, that they have "little access to the academic degrees, high-status marriages, and rewarding professions that provide many middle- and upper-class women with gratifying social identities."[14] The sociologists Heather Rackin and Christina Gibson-Davis similarly note that financial prerequisites act as a barrier to marriage but not to fertility because "low-income parents believed that financial well-being had little bearing on their ability to raise children."[15] And less-educated women have little incentive to marry men with limited employment stability and economic prospects.[16] As a result, many disadvantaged less-educated women view childbearing and marriage as separate decisions.[17] Births to less-educated mothers are also more likely to be reported as unintended.[18]

The sociologist Sara McLanahan argues that the second demographic transition widened social class disparities by leading to two different trajectories for women: "One trajectory—the one associated with delays in childbearing and increases in maternal employment—reflects gains in resources, while the other—the one associated with divorce and nonmarital childbearing—reflects losses. Moreover, the women with the most opportunities and resources follow the first trajectory, whereas the women with the fewest opportunities and resources follow the second."[19] The sociologists Pamela Smock and Christine Schwartz describe a continuation of the trends described by McLanahan in their recent review of family demography research.[20]

Some prior research has considered heterogeneity in the effects of college on family-level outcomes. For example, college effects on household income appear greater for White women than for women of color.[21] Nevertheless, given what we know from the results in chapter 5 about patterns across a range of indicators of socioeconomic precarity, college may still have a greater effect on reducing family poverty among unlikely college graduates. Moreover, studies show that a college degree has a larger impact on the likelihood of ever marrying for Black women than for White women.[22] The sociologist Megan Sweeney notes that Blacks place greater emphasis on economic stability in marital decision-making than Whites do, and college may thus be more critical for Blacks to form marital unions.[23] Likewise, Paul Attewell and his colleagues follow students admitted under the City University of New York's open admissions policy and find that underprivileged college-educated women tend to raise their children in stable two-parent households and to earn high incomes.[24] However, these researchers do not compare college completion effects for the underprivileged to effects for more-privileged graduates.

Notwithstanding these findings, evidence from several studies suggests that a college education does not fully equalize differences by social origins in the process of family formation.[25] For example, Chetty and his colleagues find that more than half of Princeton students born in upper-income families were married by their mid-thirties, in contrast to only one-third of Princeton students from low-income families. The same pattern holds at other elite institutions.[26] Other research suggests that college completion is not a great equalizer for marriage and assortative mating.[27] What do these findings mean for the effects of college attendance and completion? In a study that considers college attendance and completion effects, Kelly Musick, Dwight Davis, and I find that advantaged high-propensity men and women have a larger positive effect on marrying than more-disadvantaged low-propensity men and women.[28]

Marital homogamy—the tendency to marry others with similar characteristics—implies social similarity between groups as a prerequisite for union formation.[29] More schooling makes individuals more attractive not only to employers in the labor market but also to high-status mates in the marriage market.[30] As a result, college graduates are more likely to have college-educated and high-status spouses.[31] Yet, while similarities in education and earnings potential play key roles in marriage market matches, so too do similarities in social origins and racial and ethnic background.[32] Elizabeth Armstrong and Laura Hamilton's work discuss the limits on social interaction and dating on college campuses encountered by more-disadvantaged women. At the same time, these women distance themselves from lower-achieving peers and potential romantic partners from the communities of their youth.[33] As a result, more-disadvantaged college graduates may have difficulty forming or maintaining social relationships and partnerships with both higher-status peers and those who share their social origins.[34] That is, their socioeconomic destinations may not match those of potential mates who share their social origins, while their origins do not match the origins of potential mates who share their destinations. Marriage market mismatch can limit the equalizing role of college on marriage patterns by social origins.

In contrast to effects on marital formation, Dwight Davis and I, in another study, find that college reduces births more among women who are unlikely to attend and complete college.[35] College does not reduce fertility for those whose social origins make college very likely. Research also shows that the effect of education on decreased fertility is higher for Black women than for White women.[36] The strong economic motives of disadvantaged women who complete a degree may dictate reduced fertility. By contrast, underprivileged less-educated women have poor labor market prospects, and the attendant low economic opportunity costs, coupled with cultural norms of success via motherhood, motivate their relatively high fertility. The difference between disadvantaged women's fertility in the presence and absence of college results in a sizable fertility-decreasing effect. Davis and I note that we would not describe low-propensity women's lower fertility as necessarily a benefit of college. On the one hand, college may alter the path that these women might have taken, one marked by single motherhood in young adulthood and socioeconomic adversity. On the other hand, upward mobility for women from disadvantaged social backgrounds comes with a potential cost: fewer or no children. Taken together, these findings suggest that more-disadvantaged college graduates may be less likely to get married and have children.[37] Thus, while high-propensity graduates see education and family formation as an interconnected privileged pathway, low-propensity graduates may understand education and family formation as mutually exclusive pathways. These processes could also lead to a larger college effect on reducing single parenthood for unlikely college graduates.

College Completion Increases Marriage and Household Income and Decreases Single Parenthood and Family Poverty

Paula and Tia were Latinas with a high propensity for college. Both had parents who completed high school but did not attend college. They grew up with their parents, and each had two siblings. Paula and Tia were second-generation immigrants. Their mothers did not work, their fathers were in the armed forces, and their families had above-average income. Paula and Tia both had high test scores, enrolled in college-prep courses, and expected to attend college. They reported having high levels of control over their lives and believed that their motivation and determination would pay off. Paula attended college after high school and completed a degree in four years. Tia attended a year of college in her late twenties and did not complete a degree. Tia serves as Paula's matched comparison.

Paula got married around age thirty and had two children. Her husband worked as a computer systems administrator. She divorced after twelve years of marriage and was a single mother for a few years. Tia was married and had two children in her early twenties. Her husband worked as a mechanic. She was then unmarried around age twenty-five and cohabitated for a period with a partner. Tia married again around age forty and then divorced in her late forties. She spent several years as a single mother. Paula spent half as much time as a single mother as Tia and had fewer family transitions. Neither woman spent any time in poverty. If we believe that Tia represents Paula's counterfactual, college increased the time married to a high-status spouse and decreased the time spent as a single parent. But for a high-likelihood college graduate like Paula, college did not appear to reduce family poverty.

I assess college degree effects on average household income—the total net family income for all household members—from ages twenty-five to fifty. I also consider the proportion of time spent in family poverty, which is based on total net family income. These measures correspond to when respondents were twenty-five to fifty years old. I consider the time spent married and married with a spouse in high-skilled work, measured from ages thirty to fifty. Finally, I consider how college reduces the proportion of time spent as a single parent.[38] Respondents are coded as single parents if unmarried with a child under eighteen.[39] I estimate the effect of college attendance and college completion and both the average college effect (the average treatment effect [*ATE*] and the average college effect for college graduates [the treatment effect on the treated (*TT*)]). Results are reported in appendix table B.11 for the NLSY79 and B.12 for the NLSY97.

Average household income is about 60 percent greater for college graduates than for non-college graduates. College completion generates larger effects than attendance. *TT* effects exceed *ATE* effects for household income, suggesting a greater impact of college for more-advantaged college graduates.[40] College attendance and completion reduce family poverty by seven to nine percentage points. These effects for the *ATE* are about twice those of the *TT*, suggesting the reverse pattern from what we observe for household income. A college degree appears to have a larger impact on reducing family poverty for more-disadvantaged college graduates.

Effects of college on household income and family poverty reflect, in part, effects on family formation processes. I find a significant effect of college attendance and completion on the proportion of time spent married, with a larger effect for completing than attending college. Effect estimates suggest a larger effect of college on forming marital unions among individuals with a relatively high likelihood of college (*TT* > *ATE*). Thus, comparing Brenda and Helen (see next section) suggests a minimal college effect on marriage, while comparing Nancy and Rebecca, as described earlier, indicates a larger effect. I also find evidence of assortative mating: college attendance and completion increase the time spent with a spouse with a high-skilled occupation, which also influences household income. The proportion of time spent married to a spouse in a high-status occupation is ten to fifteen percentage points higher for college graduates than for non-college graduates. College attendance and completion also reduce time spent as a single parent. I find an eight-percentage-point-lower level of time spent as a single parent associated with college attendance and completion. This effect is greater for the *ATE* than the *TT*, again suggesting a larger college-reducing impact among those with a lower likelihood of college attendance and completion, paralleling the pattern for family poverty.

Findings from the more recent NLSY cohort also suggest college attendance and completion are associated with higher household income, less time spent in poverty, increased time spent married, and less time spent as a single parent. Effect sizes appear similar to those for the older cohort, except that neither the increase in household income nor the decrease in time in poverty is as large at this stage in the life course. This is expected, as socioeconomic advantages associated with a college degree accumulate over time. We see a larger increase in time spent married among more-disadvantaged college graduates and an effect that appears the same across the population. Taken together, these results suggest that college increases the likelihood of forming families and increases overall family socioeconomic status, with a stronger college completion effect than an attendance effect.[41] These effects appear to be larger for high-likelihood college graduates than for unlikely graduates. However, college also reduces family poverty and single parenthood, and here I observe larger effects for unlikely college graduates. Let us now more systematically consider variation in the impact of college on family-level outcomes.

College Completion Increases Household Income for High-Likelihood Graduates and Decreases Poverty for Low-Likelihood Graduates

Brian and Henry were White males with a low propensity for college. Neither Brian nor Henry had college-educated parents. Brian's mother worked as a salesclerk, and his family was in the bottom quartile of the income distribution. Henry's father was a repairman, and his mother was a healthcare worker. His family had about average income. Neither Brian nor Henry enrolled in college-prep courses in high school or expected to attend college. They both attended an urban high school where dropout rates were relatively high and about one-third of the students were disadvantaged. Although they had the same estimated propensity for college, Brian began college immediately after high school and completed a degree in four years, and Henry did not attend college. Henry serves as Brian's matched counterpart.[42] Brian's average annual household income was over twice as much as Henry's. Brian spent almost no time in poverty, and Henry spent about one-third of his time in poverty.

Brenda and Helen, two low-propensity White women, offer a similar comparison. Neither Brenda nor Helen had parents who attended college. Brenda's mother worked as a bookkeeper. Helen's father worked as a laborer, and her mother did not work. Both of their families had below-average family income. Both Brenda and Helen had above-average test scores. Neither Brenda nor Helen enrolled in college-prep courses in high school, nor did either of them expect to attend college. Neither had friends who aspired to go to college. Yet Brenda attended a four-year college after high school and completed her degree, while Helen did not attend any college. Helen serves as Brenda's matched counterpart.[43] Brenda's household income was about 25 percent higher than Helen's, and Brenda spent no time in poverty, while Helen spent about 15 percent of her time in poverty.

Daniela and Josefina were Latinas with a low college completion propensity. Daniela, who completed college, spent no time in poverty, while Josefina, who did not complete college, spent two-thirds of her time in poverty. The difference in poverty levels between Chantelle and Imani, two Black low-propensity women, was also sizable: no time spent in poverty for Chantelle and about 85 percent of her time spent in poverty for Imani. Diego, a Latino low-propensity college graduate, spent almost no time in poverty, while Javier, his matched counterpart, spent about 40 percent of his time in poverty. Caleb and Isaiah were Black men with the same low likelihood of college completion. Caleb completed college, and Isaiah did not. Caleb spent no time in poverty, while Isaiah spent almost 30 percent of his time in poverty. The comparisons of low-propensity college graduates and non-college graduates suggest considerable reductions in family poverty.

Although I observe notable differences in household income for high-likelihood college graduates, the differences in poverty are minimal. Pedro and Tomas are Latinos with a high college completion propensity. They both had college-educated professional fathers and working high school–educated mothers. Their family income was above average. They grew up with both parents and several siblings in the South. They had high test scores, expected to attend college, and had friends who expected to attend as well. Pedro completed a four-year degree, while Tomas attended a two-year college but did not complete a four-year degree. Tomas serves as Pedro's matched counterpart. After college, Pedro's income neared $225,000, while Tomas's was $110,000, suggesting a large return to household income. Pedro spent no time in poverty, and Tomas spent only about 7 percent of the time in poverty. Similarly, Nancy's average household income was about $135,000, while Rebecca's was about $65,000. Olanna's average household income was $110,000, while Sydney's was $45,000. Yet Nancy and Rebecca, and Nick and Rich, were never in poverty. Differences in poverty are also small for high-propensity Black matched pairs. However, some high-propensity Black non-college graduates, including Sydney and Samuel, spent 10 to 15 percent of their time in poverty. In contrast, their matched comparisons who graduated from college, Olanna and Otis, spent no time in poverty.

The vignettes illustrate variation in college completion effects on household income and poverty status by the likelihood of completing a degree. College completion effects are considerable for household income for both high- and low-likelihood graduates. However, effects of college completion on reducing poverty are the largest for unlikely college graduates. Figure 6.1 displays matching estimates for household income, having ever been in poverty, and the proportion of time spent in poverty between about ages twenty-five and fifty (1990–2014) in the NLSY79 cohort (see also appendix table B.13[a]). Matching estimates align with the vignettes: for both low- and high-likelihood college graduates, the effects of college completion on household income were large. I observe a 73 percent household income advantage for high-likelihood college graduates and a 59 percent advantage for the unlikely graduates, but

Figure 6.1 Effects of Four-Year College Completion on (Log) Household Income and Family Poverty by College Completion Likelihood: NLSY79

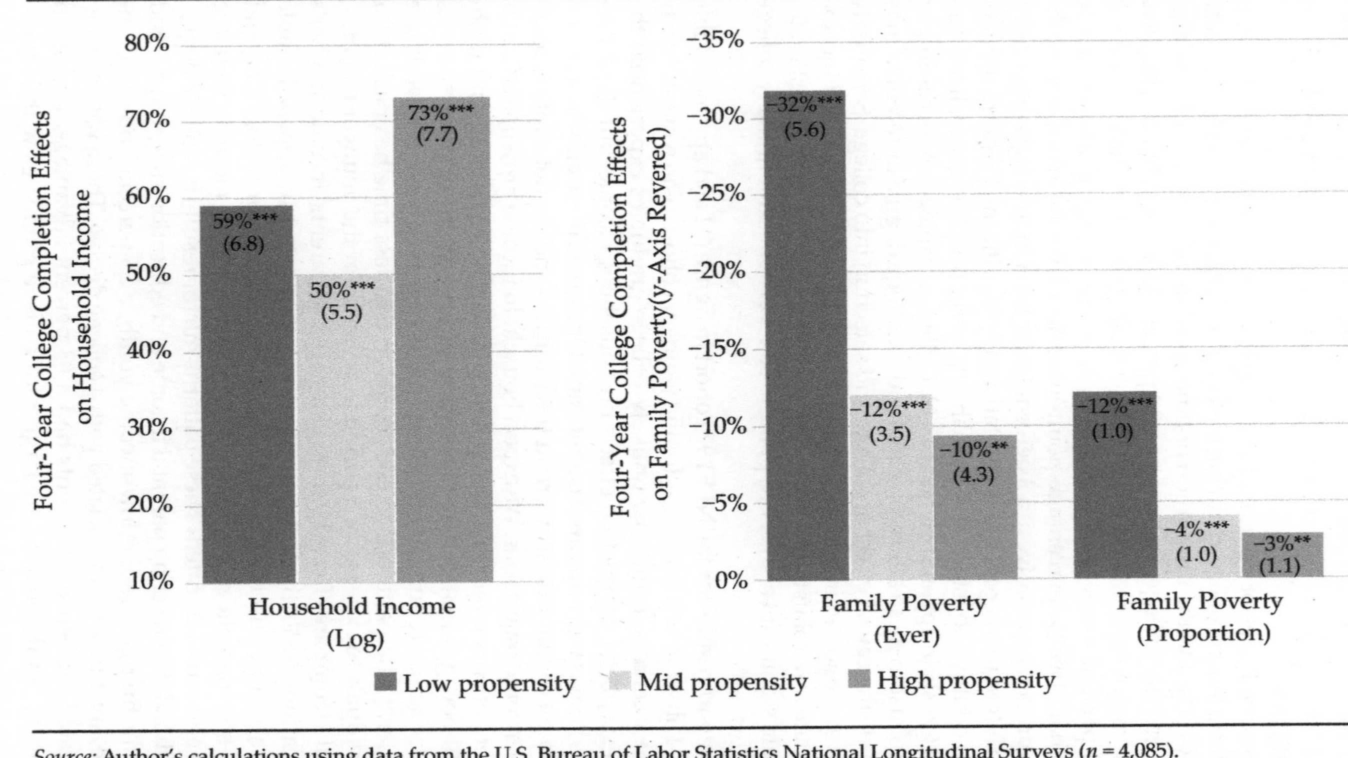

Source: Author's calculations using data from the U.S. Bureau of Labor Statistics National Longitudinal Surveys ($n = 4{,}085$).
Notes: The college completion propensity score is 0 to less than 0.2 for low propensity, 0.2 to less than 0.5 for middle, and 0.5 to 1 for high. Analyses are based on nearest-neighbor matching on the linearized propensity score. Numbers in parentheses are standard errors.
** $p \leq 0.01$; *** $p \leq 0.001$; two-tailed tests

that gap is insignificant. This pattern reflects a combination of large wage returns for low- and high-likelihood college graduates and a greater likelihood of marriage and a high-status spouse for high-likelihood graduates.

For measures of poverty, I reverse the y-axis so that the higher bars indicate larger college-reducing effects. The patterns for having ever been in poverty and the proportion of time spent in poverty are notably large for unlikely college graduates: a 32 percent lower level of having ever been in poverty for low-propensity college graduates relative to about a 10 percent lower level for high-propensity college graduates. I also observe a twelve-percentage-point-lower level of time in poverty for the low-propensity relative to a 3 percent lower level for the high-propensity. The differences across strata are statistically significant. I report estimates from doubly robust inverse probability weighting and generalized random forests in appendix table B.13(b). College completion effect estimates are robust to these alternative methods. College degree differences may include the causal effect of college and selection into college. Sensitivity analyses reported in appendix table B.16 suggest that household income estimates are robust to confounding for all groups. For poverty, estimates remain significant at every hypothesized level of bias for unlikely college graduates.[44]

I report results for the NLSY97 cohort in figure 6.2 and appendix table B.14. I observe smaller effects for the younger cohort, who were still early in their careers. I find that unlikely college graduates experienced the largest college completion effects on household income, but the differences between groups are insignificant. Of course, these effects occurred when these individuals were in their thirties and do not capture long-term income trajectories. We expect household income growth that yields larger returns over time and potentially larger growth among high-likelihood graduates. The proportion of time spent in poverty looks similar across cohorts, while effects on having ever been in poverty are smaller.[45] The pattern is expected, given that less time has passed for individuals to experience a period in poverty for the younger cohort.

I also compare effects by three categories of parents' income, mother's education, ASVAB test scores, and race (reported in appendix table B.15[a]). For household income, I find large effects for low-scoring and high-scoring college graduates and for those whose mothers were the least and most educated. These patterns mirror results by college degree likelihood. Intersecting parental income and education subgroups, I find that for first-generation low-income youth, a 55 percent household income advantage was associated with a college degree. Those with college-educated high-income parents had a 63 percent advantage. Effects on reducing family poverty are largest for college graduates with low pa-

Figure 6.2 Effects of Four-Year College Completion on (Log) Household Income and Family Poverty by College Completion Likelihood: NLSY97

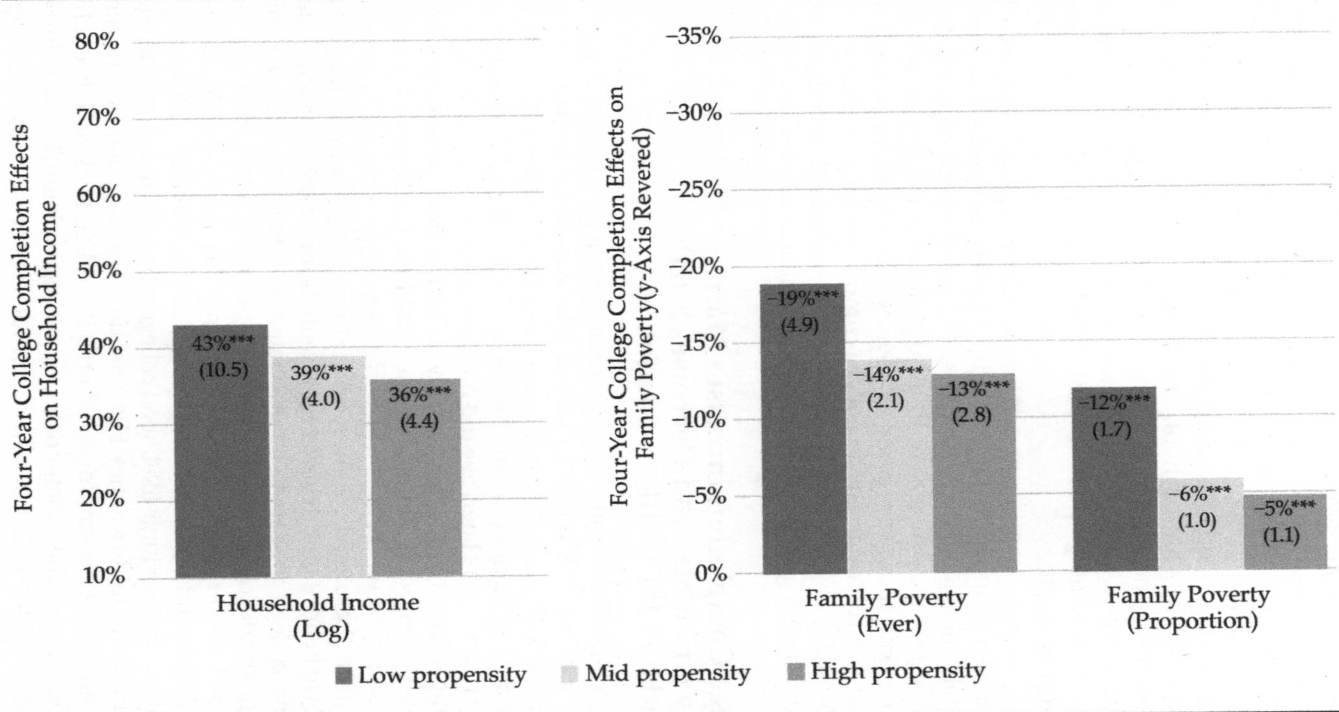

Source: Author's calculations using data from the U.S. Bureau of Labor Statistics National Longitudinal Surveys ($n = 7{,}626$).
Notes: The college completion propensity score is 0 to less than 0.2 for low propensity, 0.2 to less than 0.5 for middle, and 0.5 to 1 for high. Analyses are based on nearest-neighbor matching on the linearized propensity score. Single parenthood measures the time spent unmarried with at least one child. Numbers in parentheses are standard errors.
*** $p \leq 0.001$; two-tailed tests

rental income—a fifteen-percentage-point reduction in time spent in poverty and a twenty-five-percentage-point reduction of time ever spent in poverty. College reduces time in poverty by nine percentage points among those who grew up mid-income and by four percentage points among those who grew up high-income. College also significantly reduces poverty among those with low test scores, those whose mothers did not complete high school, and Blacks and Hispanics. For first-generation low-income youth, a fifteen-percentage-point-lower level of time spent in poverty is associated with college degree status compared to a seven-percentage-point-lower level among continuing-generation high-income youth.

Using machine learning models that search for particularly responsive subgroups (see appendix table B.15[b]), I find large effects of college on household income among Hispanics. The machine learning algorithm identified low-propensity youth as experiencing the largest effect on reducing time spent ever being in poverty. Time spent in poverty was also particularly responsive to college completion for low-income individuals who grew up in large families. Both subgroups identified were more-disadvantaged, unlikely college graduates.

College Completion Increases Marriage for Likely Graduates and Decreases Single Parenthood for Unlikely Graduates

Nancy, a high-likelihood college graduate, got married in her late twenties and had two children in her thirties. She was stably married throughout her life. Rebecca's family life was more unstable than Nancy's. Rebecca was single until her late thirties, when she married, and then got divorced a few years later. She did not have any children. Nancy worked part-time intermittently, presumably using her time to manage family responsibilities, while Rebecca worked full-time throughout her career. Nancy's spouse worked as a geoscientist, while Rebecca was a sole earner (thus the large difference in their household incomes I noted earlier). If we believe that Rebecca represents Nancy's counterfactual destinations, college appears to be associated with forming a stable family and higher household socioeconomic well-being. Neither Nancy nor Rebecca was ever a single mother—Nancy because she was married with children and Rebecca because she was single without children.

Similarly, Nick, a high-likelihood college graduate, was stably married beginning in his mid-twenties. His wife did not work in her twenties and thirties and was later employed as a retail worker. Nick had three children. Rich, his matched comparison, was unmarried until his early forties and had no children. Neither Nick nor Rich spent any time as a single parent. Nick, like Nancy, spent more time married than their matched comparisons, Rebecca and Rich. Olanna, a high-likelihood college graduate, was stably married beginning in her mid-thirties. Her husband worked in retail trade. She had two children. Sydney, her matched comparison, never married and had no children. Neither woman spent time as a single parent. In summary, these high-likelihood college graduates spent more time married with children and married to high-status spouses than did their non-college graduate counterparts, but no less time as single parents.

Now consider several matched pairs of unlikely college graduates and non-college graduates. I observe little difference between Brenda and Helen, two low-propensity women, in the time they spent married, nor between Brian and Henry, two low-propensity men who were married for most of their lives. Brenda's husband worked as a computer support specialist, and Helen's husband worked as a property manager. Brian's and Henry's wives did not work. Chantelle was stably married beginning in her early thirties but had no children. Her husband worked as an industrial truck operator. Imani was never married and had two kids. Chantelle spent no time as a single parent, while Imani spent almost all her time from ages thirty to fifty as a single parent. Caleb, a low-likelihood college graduate, married in his mid-thirties and had one child. His wife worked as a travel ticket agent. Isaiah, Caleb's matched counterpart, was married in his mid-twenties and divorced in his early thirties. He had five children. Caleb spent a year as a single father, while Isaiah spent over half his time as a single parent. These low-likelihood college graduates spent less time as single parents than did their non-college graduate counterparts.

These comparisons illustrate the variation in college completion effects on family formation patterns by the likelihood of completing a degree. While college completion increases marriage and marriage to a high-status spouse among those with a high probability of completing a degree, it generally does not decrease single parenthood. By contrast, while college completion does not generally increase marriage and marriage to a high-status spouse among unlikely college graduates, it decreases single parenthood. These family formation patterns help elucidate some of the mechanisms influencing household income and poverty status described earlier. Figure 6.3 and appendix table B.13(a) display the effects of college completion on the proportion of time married, time with a spouse with high-skilled work, and single parenthood by college likelihood in the NLSY79 cohort. I again show estimates for three propensity score strata (low, mid, and high). For single parenthood, I reverse the y-axis so that the higher bars indicate larger college-reducing effects. I find that high-propensity college graduates experienced significantly larger effects of college on forming marriages and marriages with a high-status spouse than did mid- or low-propensity graduates. Effects on having a high-status spouse are significant for all the propensity score strata but substantially larger among the high-propensity graduates. We see the reverse pattern for reducing single parenthood. The proportion of time spent as a single parent is about eight percentage points lower among the low- and mid-propensity college graduates than the non-college graduates and four percentage points lower among the high-propensity college graduates.

Once again, I report estimates from doubly robust inverse probability weighting and generalized random forests in appendix table B.13(b). Estimates for the high-propensity graduates are robust to these alternative specifications, and estimates for low-propensity graduates are somewhat larger. The patterns remain the same. Sensitivity analyses suggest that the effects of college completion on marriage and spouse's occupation remain significant for high-likelihood college graduates at each value of confounding I consider (see appendix table B.16). This result holds even when unobserved differences substantially impact these outcomes, and the prevalence of the unobserved factor differs between college and non-college graduates by a considerable amount. Spousal occupational status is sensitive to confounding among the low-propensity college graduates. For single parenthood, estimates remain significant at every level of bias for unlikely college graduates.

I also show results for the more recent NLSY cohort in figure 6.4 (and in appendix table B.14). For the younger cohort, I do not observe a difference between high- and low-propensity graduates regarding time spent married. For all three groups, a nine- to ten-percentage-point increase is associated with college completion. Differences may emerge as the cohort ages. Reduction in the proportion of time as a single parent is greater in the younger cohort and notably greater for unlikely college graduates. Yet this may also reflect a greater likelihood of being unmarried in the twenties and thirties relative to the forties, as captured with the older cohort.

Finally, I estimate college effects on family outcomes by parents' income, mother's education, ASVAB test scores, and race (see appendix table B.15[a]). I observe a pattern supporting the propensity strata results for marriage and high-status spouse outcomes: the more-advantaged experienced larger college completion effects on these measures of family formation. However, college completion effects on time spent married were greatest for Blacks. High-income continuing-generation youth experienced sizable effects of college completion on forming marital unions and having a high-status spouse, while first-generation low-income youth experienced no significant effects. I observe the largest college

Figure 6.3 Effects of Four-Year College Completion on Family Formation by College Completion Likelihood: NLSY79

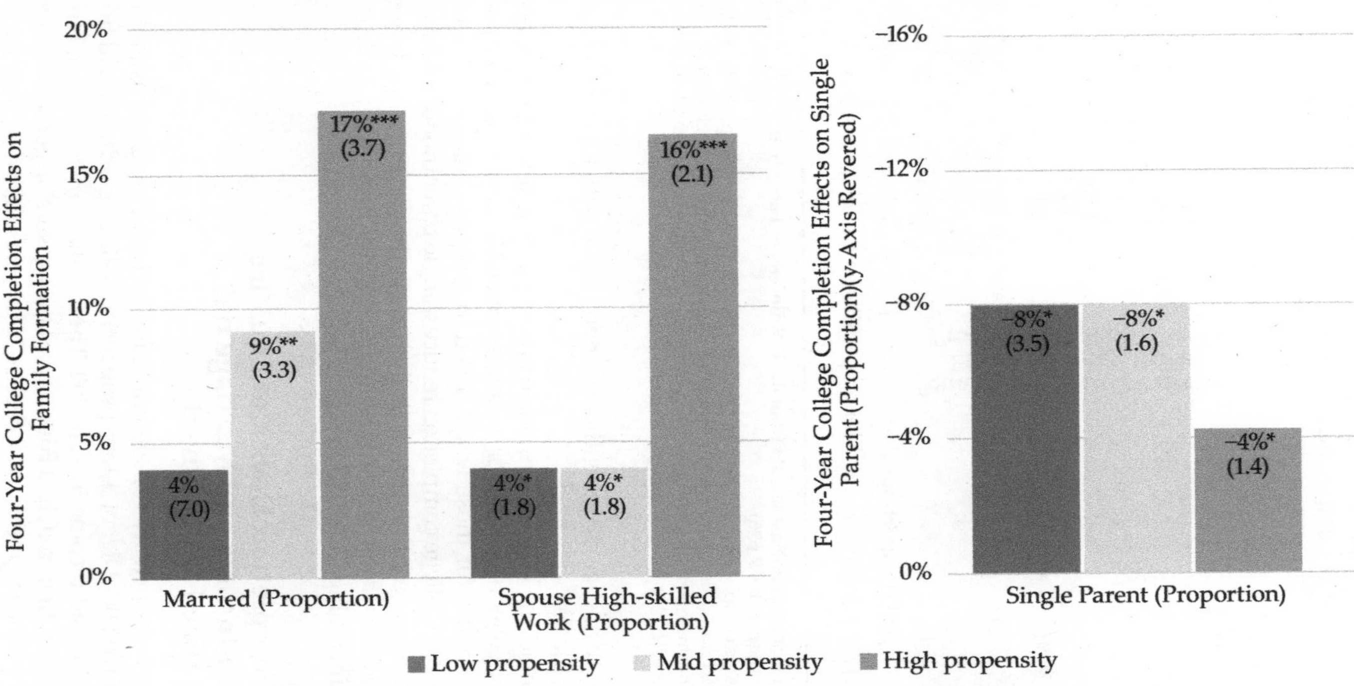

Source: Author's calculations using data from the U.S. Bureau of Labor Statistics National Longitudinal Surveys ($n = 4{,}085$).
Notes: The college completion propensity score is 0 to less than 0.2 for low propensity, 0.2 to less than 0.5 for middle, and 0.5 to 1 for high. Analyses are based on nearest-neighbor matching on the linearized propensity score. Single parenthood measures the time spent unmarried with at least one child. Numbers in parentheses are standard errors.
* $p \leq 0.05$; ** $p \leq 0.01$; *** $p \leq 0.001$; two-tailed tests

Figure 6.4 Effects of Four-Year College Completion on Family Formation by College Completion Likelihood: NLSY97

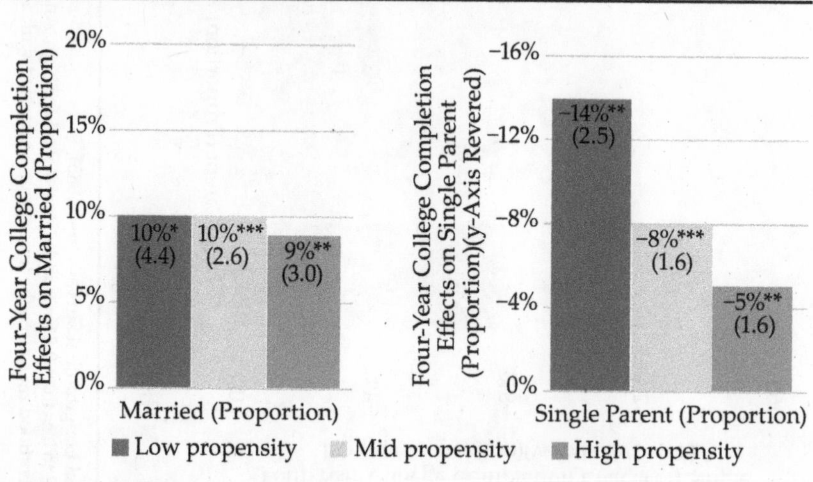

Source: Author's calculations using data from the U.S. Bureau of Labor Statistics National Longitudinal Surveys ($n = 7{,}626$).
Notes: The college completion propensity score is 0 to less than 0.2 for low propensity, 0.2 to less than 0.5 for middle, and 0.5 to 1 for high. Analyses are based on nearest-neighbor matching on the linearized propensity score. Numbers in parentheses are standard errors.
* $p \leq 0.05$; ** $p \leq 0.01$; *** $p \leq 0.001$; two-tailed tests

effects on reducing single parenthood among those with low test scores and among Blacks.

I report machine learning results in appendix table B.15(b). Findings suggest that college completion increases marriage and marriage to a high-status spouse for those who aspired to complete college and had high test scores. College completion reduces single parenthood for those who reported low control over their lives and who grew up in a large family. These characteristics represent many low-propensity college graduates, including Caleb, Chantelle, Diego, and Brenda.

College Completion Does Not Equalize Household Income and Marriage but Does Equalize Family Poverty

Nancy, a high-propensity college graduate, had an average household income of $135,000. Diego, a low-propensity college graduate, had an average household income of $110,000. These values are not equal, but a comparison of their matched counterparts suggests a larger difference between non-college graduates. Rebecca, Nancy's matched counterpart, had an average household income of $65,000, and Javier, Diego's matched counterpart, had an average household income of $35,000. In contrast to household income, we see equalization in poverty rates across social origins among college graduates and large differences across origins among non-college graduates. For example, Nancy, Paula, and Nick, high-propensity graduates, did not spend time in poverty. Likewise, Caleb, Chantelle, and Daniela, low-propensity graduates, did not spend time in poverty. Yet the differences in non-college graduates' time spent in poverty are significant. While Rebecca, Tia, and Rich, high-propensity non-college graduates, did not spend time in poverty, Isaiah spent 25 percent of his time in poverty, Imani spent 85 percent, and Josefina spent 65 percent.

Figures 6.5(a), 6.5(b), and 6.5(c) display household income, ever spent time in poverty, and proportion of time in poverty, respectively. The left panels show college graduates' and non-college graduates' outcome levels by college likelihood. The solid lines (and shaded confidence intervals) indicate college graduates, and the dashed lines (and shaded confidence intervals) indicate non-college graduates. The x-axis is the college completion propensity, and the y-axis is the outcome level. The difference between the two lines gives us the college effect, shown in the right panels. Propensity values between 0 and 0.2 correspond to low-propensity college graduates, 0.2 and 0.5 to the mid-propensity graduates, and 0.5 and 1.0 to the high-propensity graduates.[46] I find a gradient in household income, with high-likelihood college graduates having higher household income (an average of $110,000) than those with a low likelihood (an average of $90,000). I observe large completion effects for low- and high-propensity college graduates because household income for unlikely non-college graduates is low (an average of $50,000), as is household income for high-likelihood non-college graduates (an average of $65,000). This produces the roughly *u*-shaped curve in the right panel, demonstrating the high returns for both low- and high-propensity individuals.

Results for poverty (figure 6.5[b]) and proportion of time in poverty (figure 6.5[c]) suggest an equalization among college graduates. About 18 percent of college graduates experience a spell of poverty, which did not differ by social origin. Yet almost half of the low-propensity non-college graduates experienced poverty, while about 28 percent did so among high-propensity non-college graduates. This yields the difference shown in the panel on the right, which suggests that about a thirty-percentage-point advantage is associated with college completion for low-propensity college graduates relative to less than a ten-percentage-point advantage among high-propensity graduates. College graduates also spent very little time in poverty—about 3 percent of the time be-

Figure 6.5(a) Levels of (Log) Household Income and Effects of Four-Year College Completion on (Log) Household Income by College Completion Likelihood: NLSY79

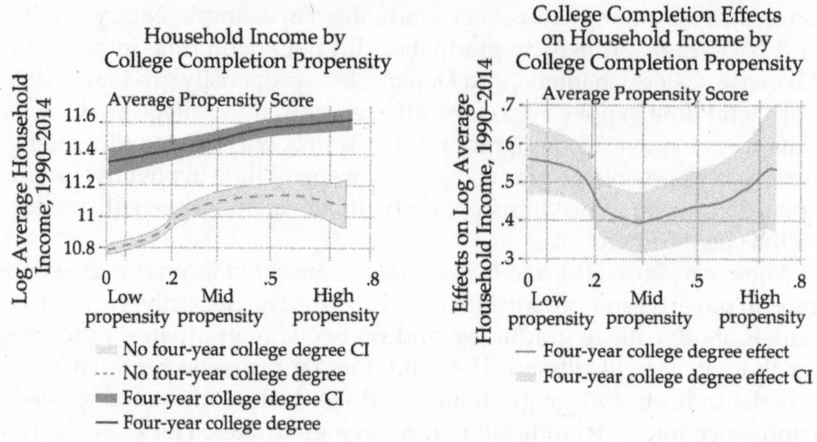

Source: Author's calculations using data from the U.S. Bureau of Labor Statistics National Longitudinal Surveys ($n = 4{,}085$).
Notes: CI indicates confidence interval. Analyses are based on local polynomial smoothing.

Figure 6.5(b) Levels of Family Poverty and Effects of Four-Year College Completion on Family Poverty by College Completion Likelihood (y-Axis Reversed): NLSY79

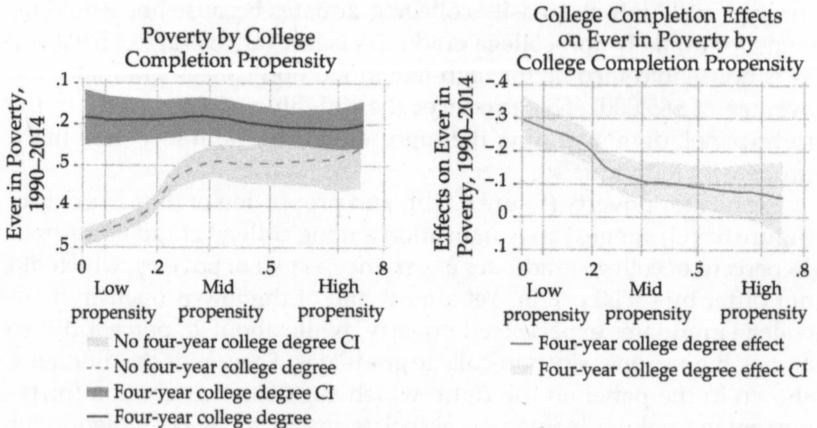

Source: Author's calculations using data from the U.S. Bureau of Labor Statistics National Longitudinal Surveys ($n = 4{,}085$).
Notes: CI indicates confidence interval. Analyses are based on local polynomial smoothing. Measure indicates whether ever in poverty.

Figure 6.5(c) Levels of Family Poverty and Effects of Four-Year College Completion on Family Poverty by College Completion Likelihood (y-Axis Reversed): NLSY79

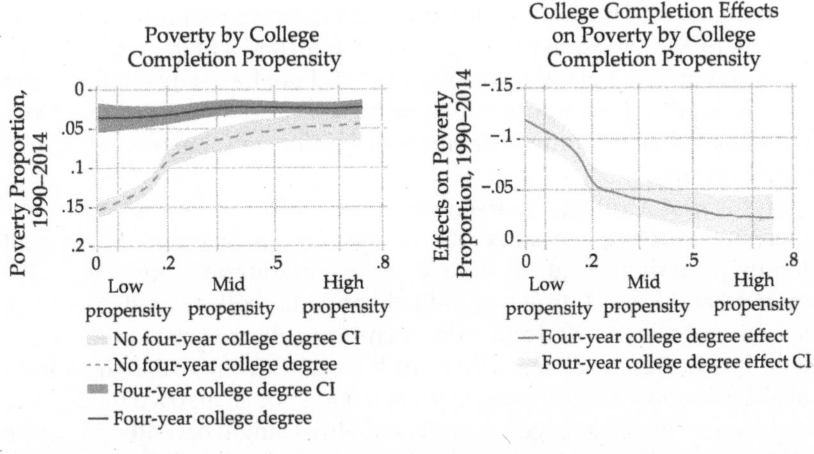

Source: Author's calculations using data from the U.S. Bureau of Labor Statistics National Longitudinal Surveys ($n = 4{,}085$).
Notes: CI indicates confidence interval. Analyses are based on local polynomial smoothing. Measure indicates proportion of time in poverty.

tween ages twenty-five and fifty—and this did not differ by social origins. We can juxtapose this pattern with the gradient among non-college graduates. Low-propensity non-college graduates spent about 15 percent of their time in poverty relative to 6 percent among high-propensity non-college graduates. This results in a 12 percent difference in poverty among low-propensity college and non-college graduates and a 3 percent difference among high-propensity college and non-college graduates, shown in the right panel. I thus observe sizable effects of circumventing poverty for unlikely college graduates. Moreover, the results are reasonably robust to unobserved selection (see appendix figure C.7).

Now let us consider family formation outcomes. Nancy, a high-propensity college graduate, married in her late twenties, and Chantelle, a low-propensity college graduate, married around age thirty. Both women remained stably married. Nancy had two children, while Chantelle did not have any children. Nancy's husband worked in a professional occupation, and Chantelle's did not. Nick, a high-propensity college graduate, was stably married, beginning in his mid-twenties, and had three children. Caleb, a low-propensity college graduate, experienced more marital instability and had one child. College does not perfectly equalize family formation across social origins.

Let us compare family formation levels of Nancy, Chantelle, Nick, and Caleb to those of Rebecca, Imani, Rich, and Isaiah, their non-college-graduate matched counterparts. Rebecca spent a few years married, and Imani was never married. Rebecca had no children, and Imani had two children. As Rebecca was married for only a few years and Imani was never married, neither woman had a high-status spouse. Rich was married in his early forties but did not have any children, and Isaiah experienced marital instability and had five children. Non-college graduates' family formation also differs in some respects across social origins.

Yet just as a college degree does not equalize some socioeconomic measures but does equalize others, the same is true for measures of family formation. High-likelihood college graduates were likely to be married and have children; high-likelihood non-college graduates were less likely to be married and to have children. By contrast, unlikely college graduates were less likely to have children, while their low-likelihood non-college graduate peers tended not be married but to have children. In effect, college generally equalizes single parenthood, while we see a gradient in single parenthood among non-college graduates by social origins. For example, Nancy was never a single mother, but neither was Chantelle. Among non-college-educated women, family patterns diverge by social origins. Rebecca's trajectory did not differ from Nancy's, while Imani's differed substantially from Chantelle's. The same is true when we compare high- and low-propensity men. Nick spent no time as a single father, and Caleb spent a year as a single father. By contrast, Rich spent no time as a single father, while Isaiah spent most of his time as a single father.

Figures 6.5(d), 6.5(e), and 6.5(f) display proportion of time married (from ages thirty to fifty), proportion of time married to a high-skilled spouse (from ages thirty to fifty), and proportion of time as a single parent (from ages twenty-five to fifty), respectively. We see a gradient in the likelihood of time in a marital union for college graduates and non-college graduates (figure 6.5[d]). The trend for non-college graduates flattens at the upper end of the propensity distribution, yielding a large difference in marriage for high-propensity college graduates, as shown in the right panel. A similar pattern holds for having a spouse with a high-status occupation (figure 6.5[e]). For the proportion of time as a single parent (figure 6.5[f]), there is a modest slope for college graduates such that college does not completely equalize single parenthood. Yet we have a much steeper slope for non-college graduates. The relative equalization of single parenthood across social origins among the college-educated yields a larger college-reducing effect for unlikely graduates.

Figure 6.5(d) Levels of Marriage and Effects of Four-Year College Completion on Marriage by College Completion Likelihood: NLSY79

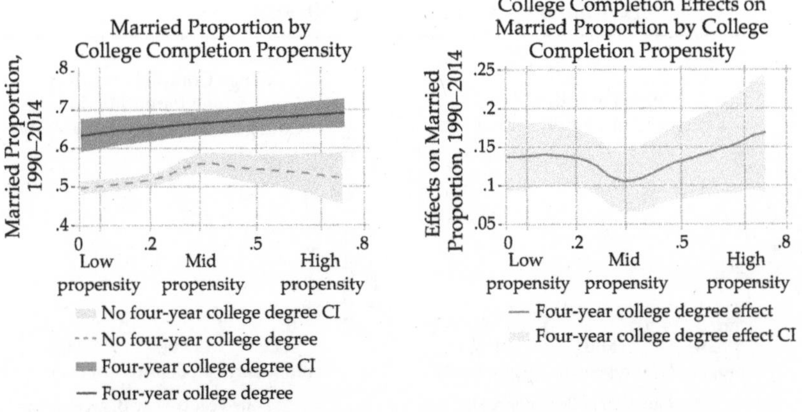

Source: Author's calculations using data from the U.S. Bureau of Labor Statistics National Longitudinal Surveys.
Notes: CI indicates confidence interval. Analyses are based on local polynomial smoothing. Measure indicates proportion time married.

Figure 6.5(e) Levels of Spouse with High-Skilled Work and Effects of Four-Year College Completion on Spouse with High-Skilled Work by College Completion Likelihood: NLSY79

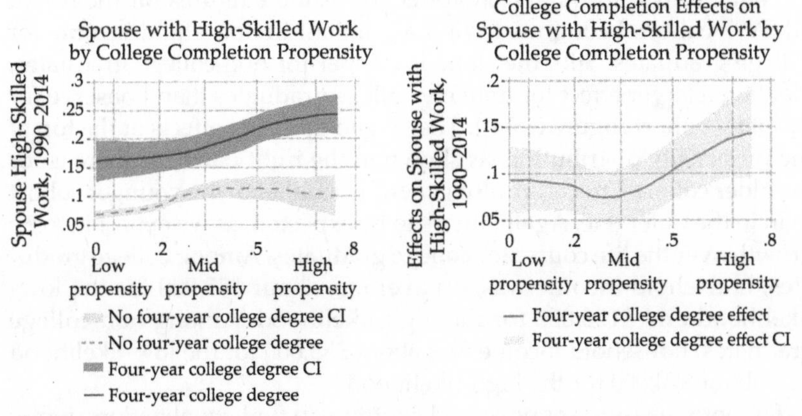

Source: Author's calculations using data from the U.S. Bureau of Labor Statistics National Longitudinal Surveys.
Notes: CI indicates confidence interval. Analyses are based on local polynomial smoothing. Measure indicates proportion of time married. Spouse with high-skilled work measures the time a respondent had a spouse who held a job in a managerial, professional, technical, or associated professional occupation.

Figure 6.5(f) Levels of Single Parenthood and Effects of Four-Year College Completion on Single Parenthood by College Completion Likelihood (y-Axis Reversed): NLSY79

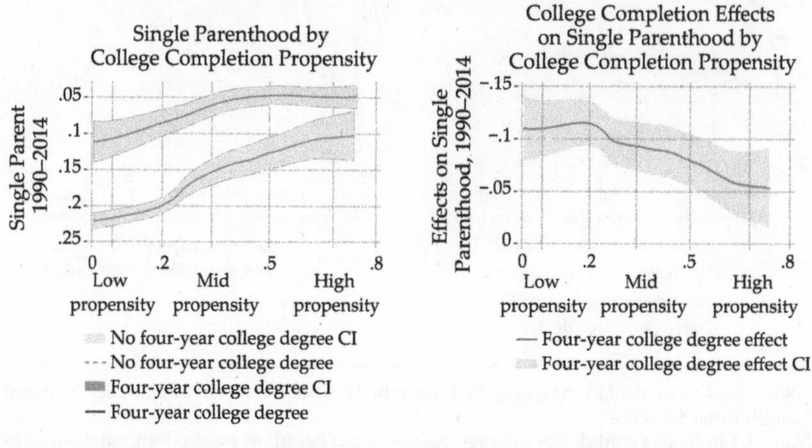

Source: Author's calculations using data from the U.S. Bureau of Labor Statistics National Longitudinal Surveys.
Notes: CI indicates confidence interval. Analyses are based on local polynomial smoothing. Measure indicates time spent unmarried with at least one child.

Figures 6.6(a) through 6.6(e) offer comparable figures for the recent NLSY97 cohort. I continue to find a gradient in household income for college graduates. Still, the slope is steeper for non-college graduates, yielding a larger effect for unlikely college graduates than I observe for the older cohort (figure 6.6[a]). There is no uptick in effects at the top of the propensity distribution, as shown in the right panel, as there is for the older cohort. Effects are also generally smaller in the younger cohort than in the older one. Again, this is to be expected, as we expect income growth over the life course for college graduates. Among college graduates, household income was, on average, about $85,000 for the low-likelihood and $100,000 for the high-likelihood. Among non-college graduates, household income was about $55,000 for the low-likelihood and about $70,000 for the high-likelihood.

For both measures of poverty, I continue to find equalization among college graduates and a steep slope among non-college graduates by college completion likelihood (figures 6.6[b] and 6.6[c]). College graduates spent 3 to 4 percent of the period between ages twenty-five and thirty-five in poverty, a rate that did not differ much by their social origins. Low-propensity non-college graduates spent about 15 to 17 percent of their time in poverty relative to about 8 percent among high-propensity

Figure 6.6(a) Levels of (Log) Household Income and Effects of Four-Year College Completion on (Log) Household Income by College Completion Likelihood: NLSY97

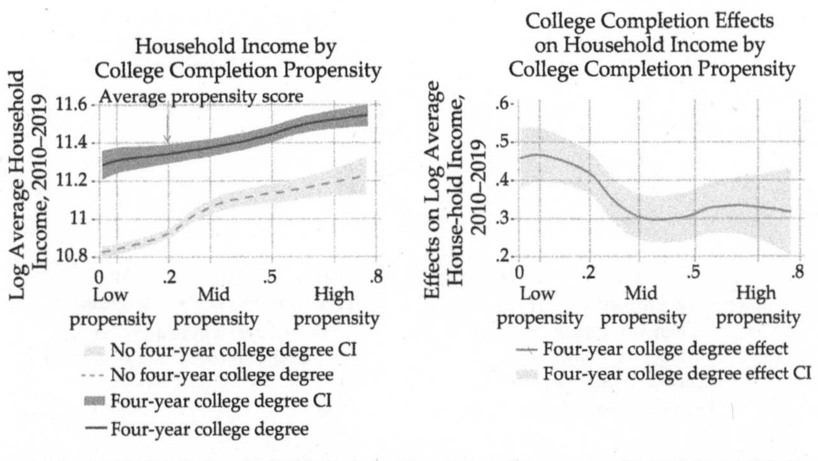

Source: Author's calculations using data from the U.S. Bureau of Labor Statistics National Longitudinal Surveys (n = 7,626).
Notes: CI indicates confidence interval. Analyses are based on local polynomial smoothing.

Figure 6.6(b) Levels of Poverty and Effects of Four-Year College Completion on Poverty by College Completion Likelihood (y-Axis Reversed): NLSY97

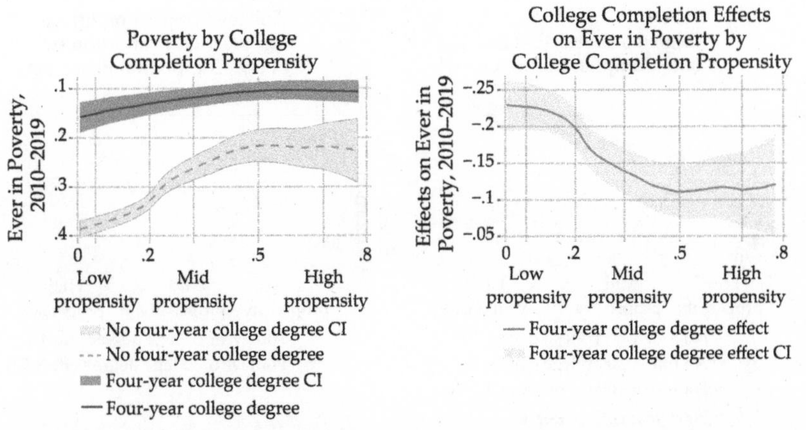

Source: Author's calculations using data from the U.S. Bureau of Labor Statistics National Longitudinal Surveys (n = 7,626).
Notes: CI indicates confidence interval. Analyses are based on local polynomial smoothing. Measure indicates whether ever in poverty.

Figure 6.6(c) Levels of Poverty and Effects of Four-Year College Completion on Poverty by College Completion Likelihood (y-Axis Reversed): NLSY97

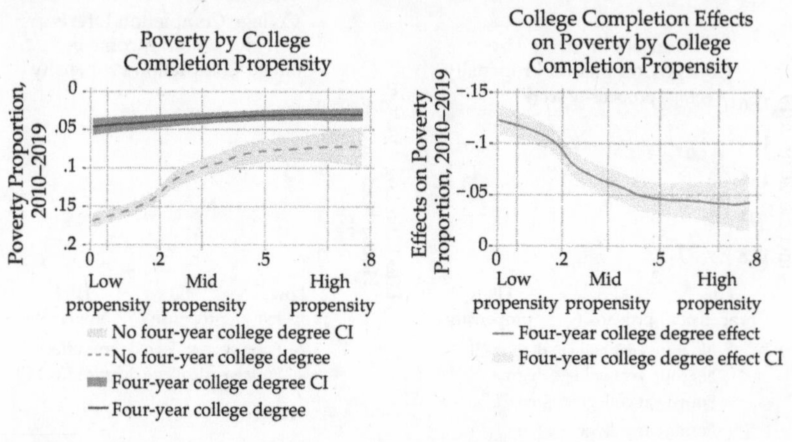

Source: Author's calculations using data from the U.S. Bureau of Labor Statistics National Longitudinal Surveys ($n = 7{,}626$).
Notes: CI indicates confidence interval. Analyses are based on local polynomial smoothing. Measure indicates proportion of time in poverty.

Figure 6.6(d) Levels of Marriage and Effects of Four-Year College Completion on Marriage by College Completion Likelihood: NLSY97

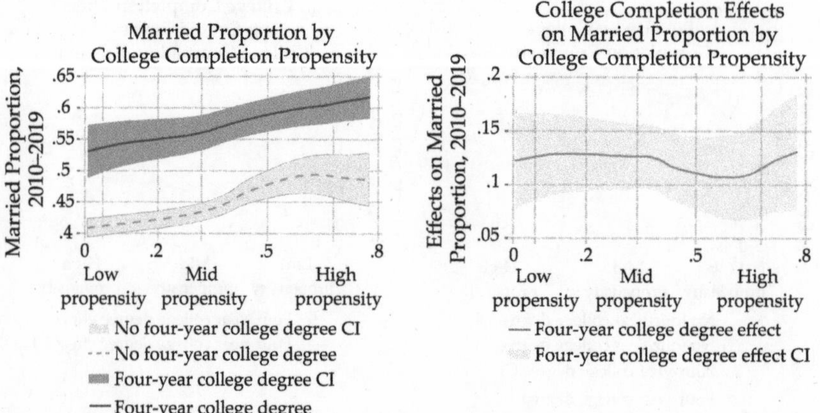

Source: Author's calculations using data from the U.S. Bureau of Labor Statistics National Longitudinal Surveys ($n = 7{,}626$).
Notes: CI indicates confidence interval. Analyses are based on local polynomial smoothing. Measure indicates proportion of time married.

Figure 6.6(e) Levels of Single Parenthood and Effects of Four-Year College Completion on Single Parenthood by College Completion Likelihood (y-Axis Reversed): NLSY97

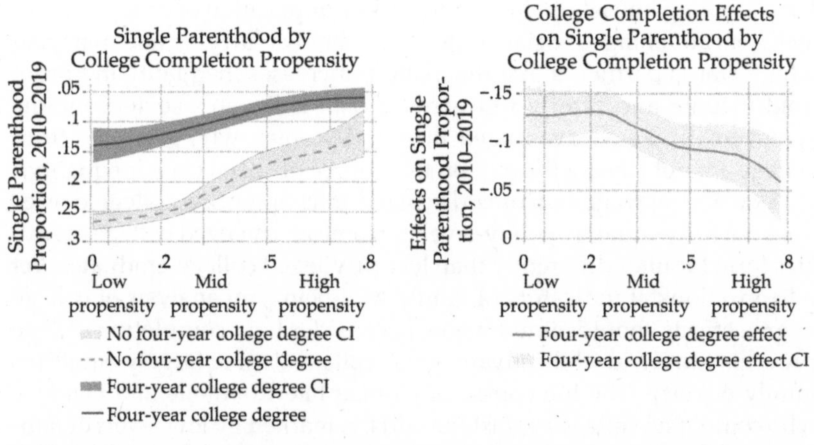

Source: Author's calculations using data from the U.S. Bureau of Labor Statistics National Longitudinal Surveys ($n = 7{,}626$).
Notes: CI indicates confidence interval. Analyses are based on local polynomial smoothing. Measure indicates time spent unmarried with at least one child.

non-college graduates. This produces the patterns of negative selection observed in the right panels of the poverty figures—for example, a twelve-percentage-point difference in poverty proportion among the low-propensity compared to a five-percentage-point difference among the high-propensity.

For poverty, patterns look nearly identical across the two cohorts. As I noted earlier, patterns for time spent married are more homogenous across college likelihood for the NLSY97 cohort (figure 6.6[d]), probably reflecting the increasing age of marriage and the shorter period observed. Patterns for single parenthood (figure 6.6.[e]) look very similar across cohorts.

Forming Families and Preventing Poverty

In this chapter, I have considered how college impacts family formation and family socioeconomic well-being. The socioeconomic characteristics of families and family formation patterns are central to analyses of inequality and mobility. A large literature indicates that family patterns are associated with various conditions that affect children's future life chances and ability to move up the income ladder.[47] I have found that while more-advantaged college graduates simultaneously achieve socioeconomic success and form families, less-advantaged college graduates often achieve socioeconomic success at the expense of forming a family. With growing educational homogamy between spouses, we also have growing household inequality. A key implication of college graduates from advantaged social origins increasingly marrying and marrying a high-status partner is that this pattern increases inequality in household income and family resources and in children's socioeconomic achievement. Less-advantaged men and women who graduate from college are not closing the gap on this source of social class inequality.

As with the wage outcome discussed in chapter 5, a college degree does not fully equalize family-level outcomes. Privileged college graduates form families differently than less-privileged college graduates. Yet when we look at indicators of family well-being, an analysis of college degree effects should simultaneously consider how completing college prevents family-level disadvantage. A college degree largely equalizes family poverty. The life course of women like Chantelle and Daniela, who completed college against the odds, is marked by low levels of family instability and no time spent in poverty. By these markers, Chantelle's and Daniela's life courses resemble those of Nancy and Olanna, high-likelihood college graduates, far more than those of Imani and Josefina, their matched non-college graduate counterparts. Similarly, Caleb's likelihood of family poverty and instability resembles Nick's and Otis's more than Isaiah's.

I conjecture that the mechanisms leading to the patterns observed in this chapter parallel those for individual socioeconomic outcomes described in chapter 5. While advantaged college graduates cultivate privilege and form traditional families, disadvantaged college graduates avoid precarious conditions and circumvent poverty. The equalizing role of college in reducing family instability and poverty across social origins has important implications for intergenerational inequality. It also has implications for social policy. Much policy discussion centers on the cycle of poverty. Higher education can serve to break the cycle of disadvantage.[48] In chapter 7, I consider how the impact of completing a four-year degree and the variation in its effects extend to indicators of social assistance.

Chapter 7

Reducing Social Assistance

Brian and Henry had the same low likelihood of completing college, yet Brian obtained a degree and Henry did not. After college, Henry received unemployment assistance, while Brian did not receive any aid. Daniela and Josefina were Latinas with low college degree likelihood, but Daniela completed college and Josefina did not. As we know from chapter 5, Daniela had a considerably more successful career than Josefina did. Daniela received no social assistance, while Josefina received Temporary Assistance to Needy Families (TANF) benefits and Supplemental Nutrition Assistance Program (SNAP) benefits (food stamps), mostly in her forties. If we believe that Henry's and Josefina's receipt of aid indicates what Brian and Daniela's outcomes might have looked like in the absence of a college degree, we see notable reductions in aid associated with college completion among unlikely college graduates.

In this chapter, I first briefly review the limited research on the effects of college on reducing social assistance. I report estimated effects of four-year college attendance and degree completion on whether respondents ever received aid, the type of aid received, and the amount of aid received. I then consider heterogeneous effects, paralleling the analyses in chapters 5 and 6. I describe levels of each outcome for college graduates and non-college graduates and ask whether college equalizes receipt of aid. I conclude with a discussion on the implications of findings suggesting that college completion is associated with a reduction in social assistance among unlikely graduates.

Background on College Completion Effects on Social Assistance

As discussed in chapters 5 and 6, a college degree is critical for mitigating unemployment, low-wage work, economic instability, and poverty. Policymakers often advance higher education as a means to reduce poverty among low-income youth.[1] For example, President Barack Obama declared in his 2010 State of the Union Address that "the best anti-poverty program around is a world-class education."[2] Statements such as these imply that low-income youth benefit, potentially more than high-income youth, from a college education in reducing poverty. A reduction in poverty generally leads to a reduction in social assistance. Lessening the population's dependence on the nation's safety net is an important factor in considering the costs of not educating youth and how we spend public dollars.

The U.S. safety net is a patchwork system composed of several programs designed to respond to worsening economic conditions. Most programs provide cash (or a near-equivalent) to working-age adults and families. The Temporary Assistance to Needy Families program (TANF), previously Aid to Families with Dependent Children (AFDC) (commonly called "welfare"), provides cash assistance to low-income families with children.[3] The Supplemental Nutritional Assistance Program (SNAP, previously known as "food stamps") enables low-income families to acquire unprepared foods. SNAP reaches higher into the income distribution than AFDC/TANF and serves the working and nonworking poor. The Special Supplemental Nutrition Program for Women, Infants, and Children (WIC) provides nutrition education, breastfeeding support and referrals, and nutritious foods based on an applicant's situation (pregnant, breastfeeding, postpartum woman, infant, or child). Supplemental Security Income (SSI) provides income support to low-income disabled, blind, or elderly individuals. Individuals may be eligible for SSI if they meet the program's criteria for disability and financial need. When determining SSI eligibility, the Social Security Administration (SSA) considers factors such as the individual's medical condition, work history, and ability to earn a living. Finally, unemployment insurance (UI) provides benefits to formerly employed workers who are experiencing unemployment. UI eligibility and benefit levels are a function of an individual's earnings history. For this reason, the support provided by UI tends to reach people with higher incomes.[4]

Since the mid-1990s, during the labor market period experienced by both NLSY cohorts, U.S. social assistance policies expanded support for the working poor while minimizing the cash safety net for the nonworking poor. TANF replaced AFDC over concerns that the program disincentivized work, encouraged single parenthood, and created a long-term dependency on aid. The share of low-income families receiving cash welfare fell from 68 percent in 1996 to 23 percent in 2014.[5] Participation in food stamps declined during the 1990s but then, as SNAP, grew steadily in the early 2000s. Overall, we have seen a dramatic shift from need-based to work-based aid. Assistance has thus moved cash away from the neediest families to the working poor. The sociologists Laura Tach and Kathryn Edin note that work is the "litmus test by which deservedness is judged."[6] After welfare reform, single-mother employment rates rose from about 64 percent to 73 percent. Some of those changes reflected increased reporting of work rather than actual increases in work activity. Yet the number of nonworking single mothers grew throughout the 2000s and is now higher than before welfare reform.[7] The changes in the safety net appear to have had little impact on family formation and stability. Many families are increasingly experiencing deep poverty. And despite the increased emphasis on work, Americans continue to harbor negative views about welfare.

A college degree is associated with lower levels of social assistance. Research suggests that the government spends between $800 and $2,000 per year less on social programs (including TANF, SNAP, UI, and other social assistance programs) for thirty-year-old college graduates than for high school graduates.[8] For example, about 8 percent of high school graduates age twenty-five and older reside in households that rely on SNAP, compared to about 1 percent for those with a college degree.[9] Yet these are descriptive results of social assistance by higher education level. Few studies assess the effects of college attendance and completion on reducing aid, and few studies consider variation in the impact.[10] One study of single-mother college students in New York found that 100 percent of former welfare recipients who obtained a four-year degree stopped relying on social assistance compared to 81 percent of those who obtained a two-year degree. Yet there is no comparison to effects among more-advantaged college graduates.[11]

Perhaps the most relevant research on college completion effects on social assistance is a study by Heckman and his colleagues.[12] Using data from the NLSY79, they find that college attendance and completion were associated with lower welfare use between 1996 and 2006, among many other "nonmarket" benefits. In addition, they show that college attendance and completion decrease welfare more for low-achieving than high-achieving youth. The authors state that this finding contrasts with market returns to higher education. Discounting these benefits could lead policymakers to "greatly underestimate the benefits of supporting education."[13]

Social assistance is intertwined, of course, with socioeconomic and family outcomes. If there are larger effects of college completion on reducing low-wage work, unemployment, job instability, and poverty among disadvantaged college graduates, we should reasonably expect to observe larger effects on reducing social assistance.

College Completion Reduces Social Assistance

I consider a range of social assistance measures, including any social assistance, AFDC/TANF, SNAP, SSI, UI, and the cumulative amount of assistance received. In the NLSY79, I consider measures when respondents were in their mid-twenties to early fifties and in the NLSY97 when respondents were in their mid-twenties to mid-thirties.[14] As in chapters 5 and 6, I estimate the effect of college attendance and college completion and both the average college effect (the average treatment effect, *ATE*) and the average college effect for college graduates (the treatment effect on the treated, *TT*). As reported in appendix table B.17 for the NLSY79, I find that college attendance and completion reduce the likelihood and amount of assistance. College effects are larger (that is, their assistance-reducing effects are larger) for the *ATE* than for the *TT*. College completion effects are larger than college attendance effects: college completion is associated with a twenty-two-percentage-point-lower level of receipt of assistance, and attendance is associated with a sixteen-percentage-point-lower level. I observe notable reductions in aid received from AFDC/TANF, SNAP, SSI, and UI. For college completion effects, differences between the *ATE* and *TT* are significant for every measure. These patterns suggest larger aid-reducing effects for unlikely college graduates than for high-likelihood graduates.

Results for the more recent NLSY97 cohort are very similar, with larger effects for the *ATE* than the *TT* and larger effects of college completion than attendance (see appendix table B.18). College completion is associated with a twenty-seven-percentage-point reduction in any assistance, that is, it is larger than the estimate reported for the older cohort. The reduction in TANF in the recent cohort is not as large as it was for the older cohort, but the reduction in SNAP is larger.

College Completion Reduces Social Assistance Most for Unlikely Graduates

Chantelle and Imani had the same low propensity to complete a four-year degree. Chantelle completed college, and Imani did not. As discussed in chapters 5 and 6, Chantelle was continuously employed throughout her career, spent little time in low-wage work, and never experienced poverty. By contrast, Imani's wages were very low, her work was unstable, and she spent most of her time in poverty. Chantelle received no social assistance, while Imani received AFDC/TANF and SNAP benefits throughout her twenties and into her late forties, and she received UI benefits in her late forties. Caleb and Isaiah also had the same low propensity for college. Caleb completed college, and Isaiah did not. Caleb was continuously employed and spent less than 10 percent of his time in low-wage work, while Isaiah spent one-third of his career unemployed and 40 percent of his time in low-wage work. Caleb spent no time in poverty, and Isaiah spent over one-quarter of his time in poverty. Caleb did not receive any AFDC/TANF, SNAP, or SSI benefits. Isaiah received UI benefits in his mid-twenties and SSI benefits in his forties. Brenda and Helen had the same low propensity for college. Brenda completed college, and Helen did not. Brenda received no aid, and Helen received SSI benefits throughout her thirties. These comparisons suggest that a college degree may reduce the assistance received by unlikely graduates.

Comparisons between high-propensity college graduates and noncollege graduates tell a different story. Nick, Nancy, and Olanna were high-propensity graduates. Rebecca, Rich, and Sydney were high-propensity non–graduates. They all spent little time unemployed or in low-wage work. None of these high-propensity men and women received AFDC/TANF, SNAP, or SSI benefits from their mid-twenties to their early fifties. Sydney received UI benefits in her forties, and Nick received one year of UI benefits in his mid-twenties. Comparing these cases to those described earlier, college appears to differentiate the receipt of social assistance by those unlikely to complete college while having little to no impact on those with a high likelihood of completing college.

Figures 7.1(a) and 7.1(b) offer estimates of college completion effects stratified by propensity scores for measures of social assistance (see also appendix table B.19[a]). Figure 7.1(a) shows the effects of college completion on any assistance received and the cumulative amount received. Figure 7.1(b) shows the effects on AFDC/TANF, SNAP, SSI, and UI receipt. AFDC/TANF measures assistance received through the Temporary Assistance to Needy Families program, previously Aid to Families with Dependent Children; SNAP measures assistance received through the Supplemental Nutritional Assistance Program; SSI measures assistance received through the Supplemental Security Income; and UI measures assistance received through the unemployment insurance benefits program. Effects of completing college on reducing social assistance decrease as the propensity for college completion increases. Unlikely college graduates have a 25-percentage-point-lower level of receiving social assistance relative to a roughly 11-percentage-point-lower level for mid and high likelihood graduates. The reduction in the cumulative amount received associated with a college degree is five times greater for low likelihood relative to high likelihood graduates.

Turning to college completion effects for specific programs, I find significant differences between low- and high-likelihood college gradu-

Figure 7.1(a) Effects of Four-Year College Completion on Social Assistance by College Completion Likelihood (y-Axis Reversed): NLSY79

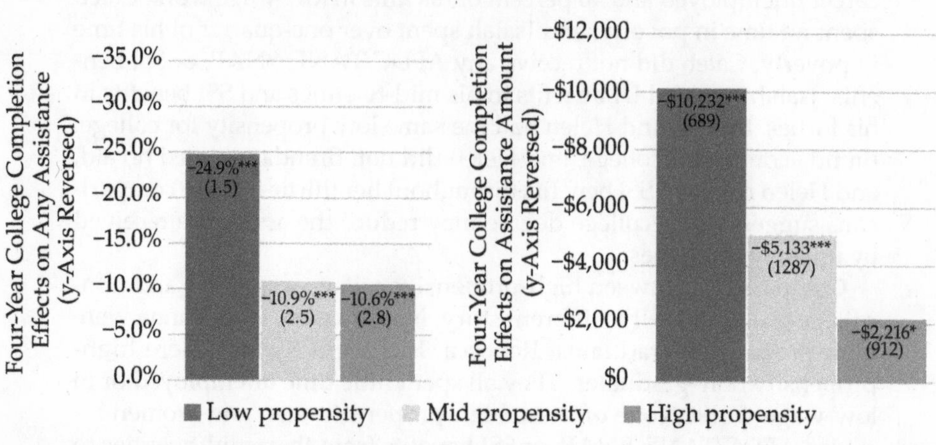

Source: Author's calculations using data from the U.S. Bureau of Labor Statistics National Longitudinal Surveys ($n = 4{,}085$).
Notes: The college completion propensity score is 0 to less than 0.2 for low propensity, 0.2 to less than 0.5 for middle, and 0.5 to 1 for high. Analyses are based on nearest-neighbor matching on the linearized propensity score. Social assistance includes AFDC/TANF, SNAP, SSI, and UI. Numbers in parentheses are standard errors.
* $p \leq 0.05$; *** $p \leq 0.001$; two-tailed tests

ates for the effects of college on reducing all forms of social assistance. For several measures, the college-reducing impact for low-likelihood graduates is more than twice what it is for mid-likelihood graduates, which is often more than twice the impact for high-likelihood graduates. The largest effects of completing college are for reducing SNAP and UI. Appendix table B.19(b) provides estimates, based on alternative model specifications, that suggest that results are robust to the estimation method. Sensitivity analyses indicate that estimates of college completion effects for low-propensity graduates are robust to unobserved confounding for all outcomes (see appendix table B.22). Mid- and high-propensity college effect estimates are generally robust to unobserved confounding except when I assume high bias levels.

As I show in figure 7.2, results for the more recent NLSY97 cohort reflect the same pattern of a significant reduction in social assistance received, with the largest effects for unlikely college graduates (see also appendix table B.20). For the NLSY97, the measure of SNAP includes receipt of WIC, which measures assistance received through the Special Supplemental Nutrition Program for Women, Infants, and Children. Although the pattern is the same across cohorts, the effects are even

Figure 7.1(b) **Effects of Four-Year College Completion on Social Assistance by College Completion Likelihood (y-Axis Reversed): NLSY79**

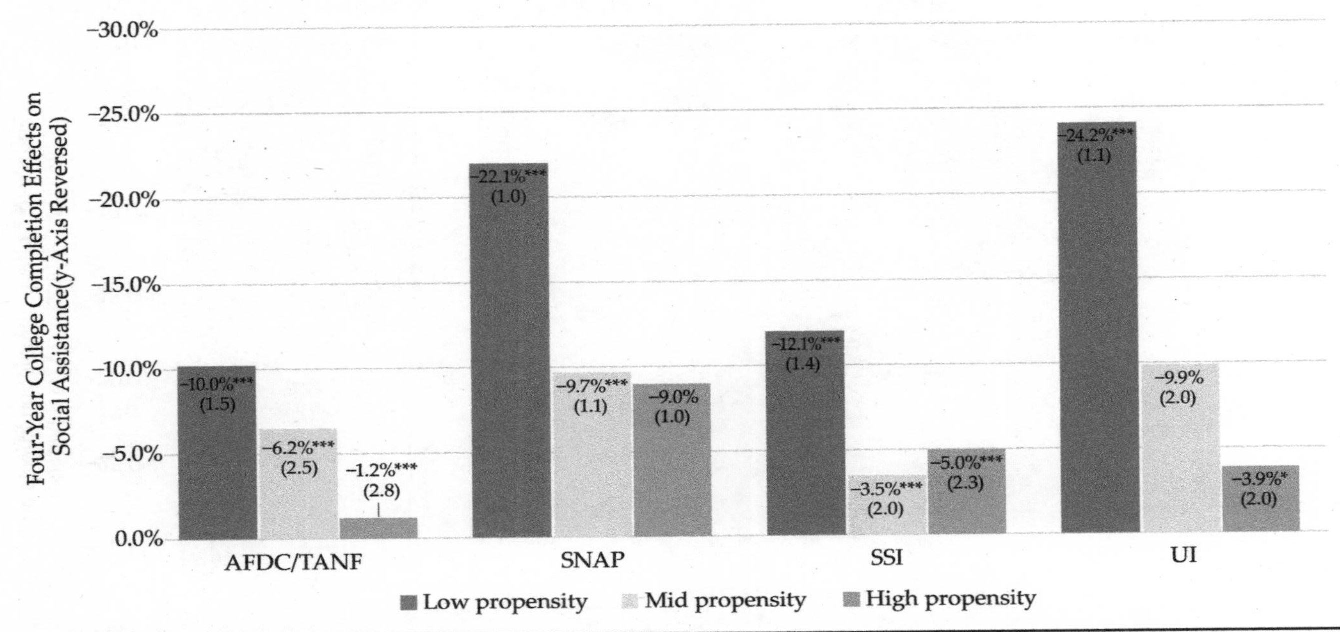

Source: Author's calculations using data from the U.S. Bureau of Labor Statistics National Longitudinal Surveys ($n = 4{,}085$).
Notes: The college completion propensity score is 0 to less than 0.2 for low propensity, 0.2 to less than 0.5 for middle, and 0.5 to 1 for high. Analyses are based on nearest-neighbor matching on the linearized propensity score. Numbers in parentheses are standard errors.
* $p \leq 0.05$; *** $p \leq 0.001$; two-tailed tests

Figure 7.2 Effects of Four-Year College Completion on Social Assistance by College Completion Likelihood (y-Axis Reversed): NLSY97

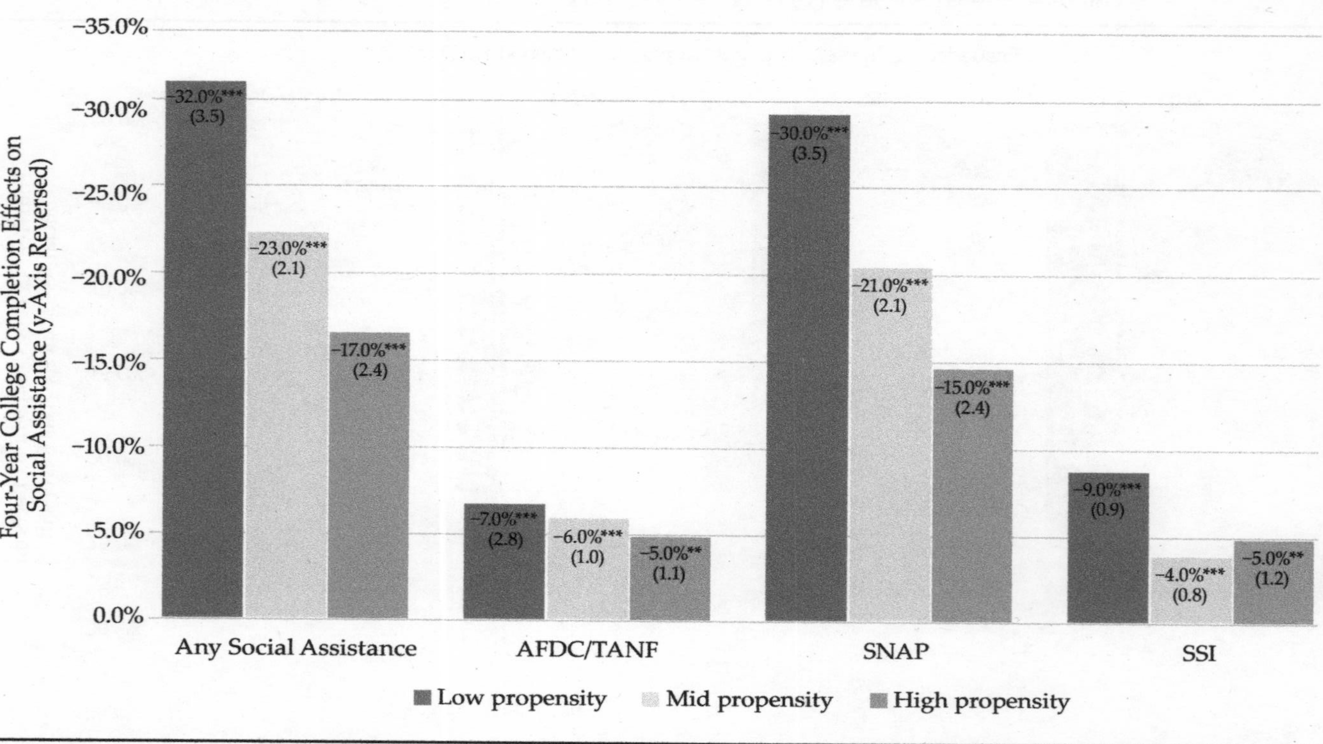

Source: Author's calculations using data from the U.S. Bureau of Labor Statistics National Longitudinal Surveys ($n = 7{,}626$).
Notes: The college completion propensity score is 0 to less than 0.2 for low propensity, 0.2 to less than 0.5 for middle, and 0.5 to 1 for high. Analyses are based on nearest-neighbor matching on the linearized propensity score. Numbers in parentheses are standard errors.
** $p \leq 0.01$; *** $p \leq 0.001$; two-tailed tests

greater for the younger cohort. I find a thirty-two-percentage-point reduction in any assistance among unlikely college graduates and a fifteen-percentage-point reduction for high-likelihood graduates. This pattern may reflect a greater likelihood to receive some aid earlier in the life course or a larger effect associated with college for the more recent cohort.

I compare college effects on social assistance by parents' income, mother's education, ASVAB test scores, and race (see appendix table B.21[a]). The effect estimates mirror propensity-stratified estimates for parental income, mother's education, and test scores for each outcome. I observe the largest assistance-reducing college effects among those with low parental income, a mother without a high school degree, and low test scores. For example, I observe a twenty-four-percentage-point-lower level in aid received for low-parental-income college graduates and a fifteen-percentage-point-lower level for high-parental income graduates. In addition, I observe a twenty-nine-percentage-point-lower level among those with low test scores compared to a thirteen-percentage-point-lower level among those with high test scores. I also find larger college effects for Black and Hispanic graduates than for White graduates. For Black college graduates, I observe about a twenty-nine-percentage-point-lower level of assistance received, which is twice the effect for Whites. I also consider subsets of college graduates. Low-income racially minoritized college graduates and low-income first-generation graduates experienced notably large effects. Chantelle and Caleb fell into both categories. Low-parental-income graduates with high test scores did not experience large effects, as we would expect, given the smaller effects for high-scoring graduates. We would overlook more responsive subgroups if we focused policy efforts singly on this subgroup rather than on those with lower test scores.

I report results using machine learning models that search for the most responsive subgroups in appendix table B.21(b). I find substantial college completion effects on receiving social assistance for those with low college chances. On average, the most responsive groups had the lowest propensity scores, parental income, mother's education, and test scores. For any social assistance, as well as SNAP, SSI, and UI, the average propensity score is under 0.05. Leaves with the most responsive groups often split along gender, college aspirations, and test scores. For example, low-income females whose friends did not aspire to attend college were the most responsive group with respect to reductions in the amount of assistance received. Black females were the most responsive to the effects of a college degree in reducing ADFC/TANF assistance—Black female college graduates received a twenty-percentage-point-lower level of ADFC/TANF benefits than their matched counterparts (Black female non-college graduates). The findings parallel those in figure 7.1, suggesting the large effects at the low end of the college likelihood distribution.

College Completion Equalizes Social Assistance

As discussed earlier, completing college equalized social assistance levels for Chantelle, Caleb, and Brenda but not for Rebecca, Nick, and Olanna. That is, college graduates spent little or no time receiving aid, while the experiences of non-college graduates differed markedly by their social backgrounds. Figures 7.3(a) to 7.3(f) show levels and differences in levels of any assistance, levels of ADFC/TANF, SNAP, SSI, and UI assistance, and amount of assistance. The left panels show levels for college graduates and non-college graduates by college likelihood, and the right panels show differences in levels. All the figures display the same clear result of low levels of assistance received and equalization among college graduates by college completion chances. By contrast, we see a steep gradient among non-college graduates by college chances, such that non-college graduates with disadvantaged social origins are far more likely to receive assistance than those with advantaged social origins. Thus, social assistance levels are about the same among advantaged college graduates and non-college graduates and starkly dissimilar among disadvantaged college graduates and non-college graduates.

In figure 7.3(a), for any assistance received over twenty-five years, we see that the level for college graduates is about 8 percent, which is the same across the college completion likelihood. For low-likelihood non-college graduates, we see a level of about 25 to 30 percent receiving assistance, which levels off to about 18 percent among mid- to high-likelihood non-college graduates. This pattern results in the difference we see in the right panel, a roughly twenty-two-percentage-point-lower level of aid associated with completing a college degree among low-propensity respondents and an eleven-percentage-point-lower level among mid- to high-propensity respondents. For receipt of AFDC/TANF (figure 7.3[b]), college graduates' level hovers around 1 percent. About 10 percent of low-likelihood non-college graduates received aid, as did 5 percent of mid-likelihood non-college graduates and 1 to 4 percent of high-likelihood non-college graduates. This results in a linear pattern in the difference plot, with low-propensity respondents seeing a roughly ten-percentage-point-lower level and high-propensity respondents a two- to three-percentage-point-lower level of aid received associated with completing a college degree. There is a modest gradient in SNAP

Figure 7.3(a) Levels of Social Assistance and Effects of Four-Year College Completion on Social Assistance by College Completion Likelihood (y-Axis Reversed): NLSY79

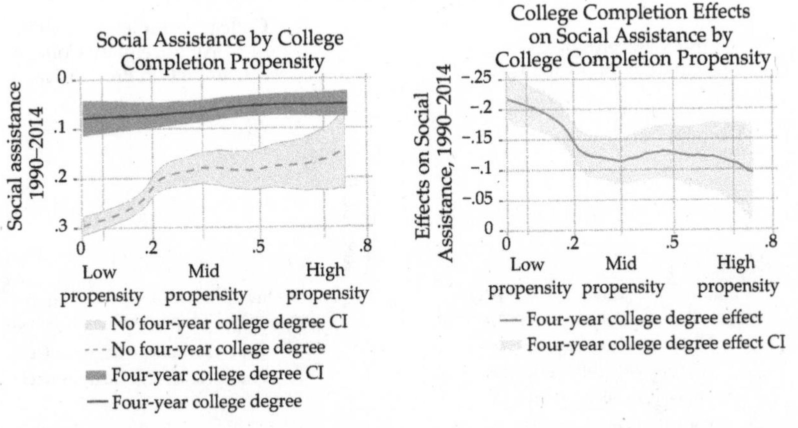

Source: Author's calculations using data from the U.S. Bureau of Labor Statistics National Longitudinal Surveys ($n = 4{,}085$).
Notes: CI indicates confidence interval. Analyses are based on local polynomial smoothing. Social assistance includes AFDC/TANF, SNAP, SSI, and UI.

Figure 7.3(b) Levels of AFDC/TANF Receipt and Effects of Four-Year College Completion on AFDC/TANF Receipt by College Completion Likelihood (y-Axis Reversed): NLSY79

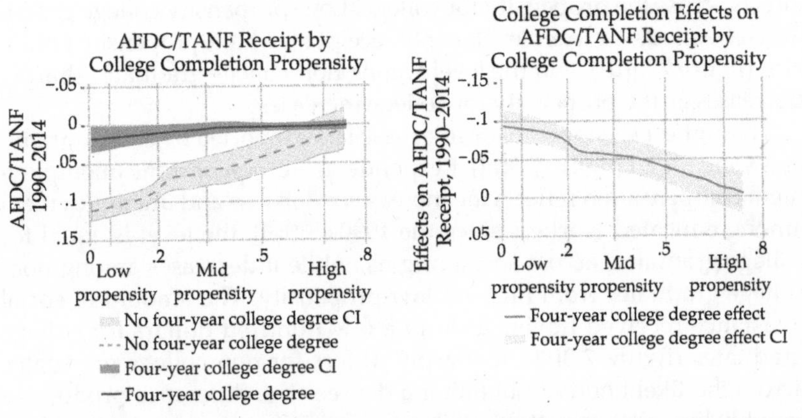

Source: Author's calculations using data from the U.S. Bureau of Labor Statistics National Longitudinal Surveys ($n = 4{,}085$).
Notes: CI indicates confidence interval. Analyses are based on local polynomial smoothing.

Figure 7.3(c) Levels of SNAP Receipt and Effects of Four-Year College Completion on SNAP Receipt by College Completion Likelihood (y-Axis Reversed): NLSY79

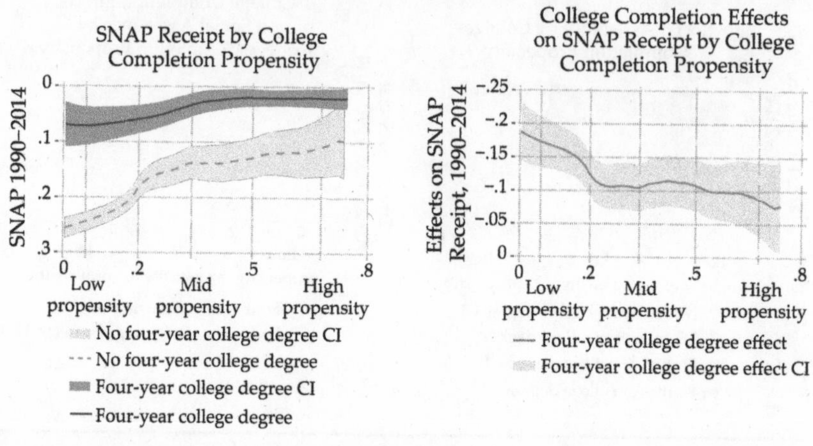

Source: Author's calculations using data from the U.S. Bureau of Labor Statistics National Longitudinal Surveys ($n = 4{,}085$).
Notes: CI indicates confidence interval. Analyses are based on local polynomial smoothing.

benefits received among college graduates (figure 7.3[c]). The gradient is far less steep, however, than the slope observed among non-college graduates. The difference produces a pattern of declining college degree effects across the propensity for college. Low-propensity college graduates have modestly *lower* levels of SSI receipt than high-propensity graduates (figure 7.3][d]), and the level among non-college graduates sharply decreases as the propensity for college increases.

The highest levels of the forms of assistance reported by college graduates were for UI (figure 7.3[e]). Respondents' receipt of some unemployment compensation reflects the increases in job loss and unemployment among educated workers since the 1990s.[15] Still, the level is equal for college graduates across social origins, while it decreases among non-college graduates from high- to low-propensity. The amount of social assistance received hovers around a few hundred dollars for college graduates (figure 7.3[f]). It sharply differs for non-college graduates across the likelihood of obtaining a degree. The difference produces a roughly linear effect pattern, with a more significant aid-reducing effect among the low-likelihood that nears zero as the likelihood increases. The results are robust to unobserved selection at most assumed bias levels (see appendix figure C.8).

Figure 7.3(d) Levels of SSI Receipt and Effects of Four-Year College Completion on SSI Receipt by College Completion Likelihood (y-Axis Reversed): NLSY79

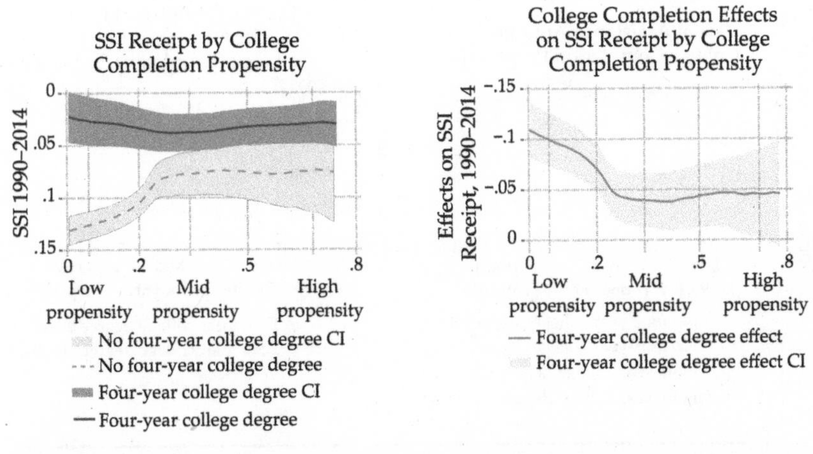

Source: Author's calculations using data from the U.S. Bureau of Labor Statistics National Longitudinal Surveys (n = 4,085).
Notes: CI indicates confidence interval. Analyses are based on local polynomial smoothing.

Figure 7.3(e) Levels of UI Receipt and Effects of Four-Year College Completion on UI Receipt by College Completion Likelihood (y-Axis Reversed): NLSY79

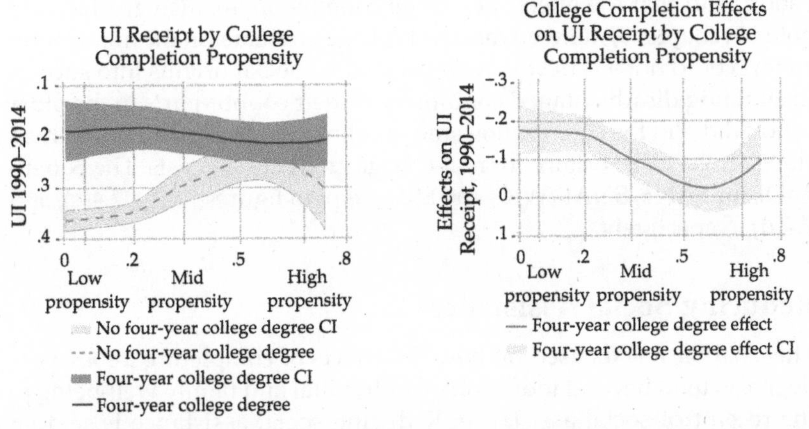

Source: Author's calculations using data from the U.S. Bureau of Labor Statistics National Longitudinal Surveys (n = 4,085).
Notes: CI indicates confidence interval. Analyses are based on local polynomial smoothing.

Figure 7.3(f) Levels of Social Assistance and Effects of Four-Year College Completion on Social Assistance by College Completion Likelihood (y-Axis Reversed): NLSY79

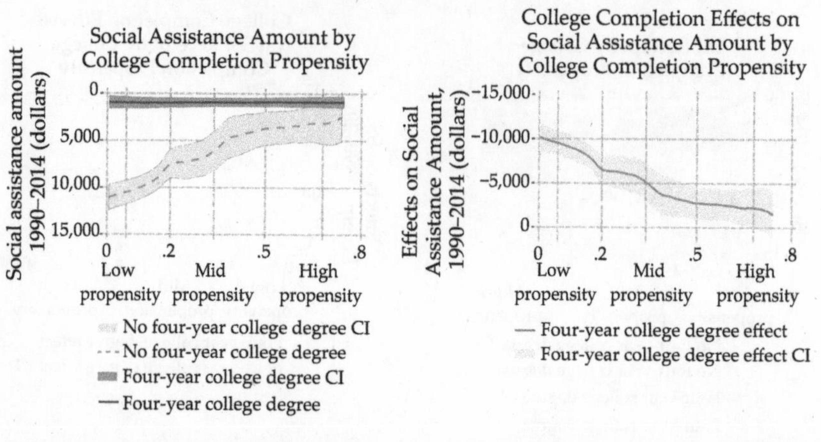

Source: Author's calculations using data from the U.S. Bureau of Labor Statistics National Longitudinal Surveys ($n = 4{,}085$).
Notes: CI indicates confidence interval. Analyses are based on local polynomial smoothing. Social assistance includes AFDC/TANF, SNAP, SSI, and UI.

As depicted in figures 7.4(a) to 7.4(d), I find the same pattern for the more recent NLSY97 cohort. Figure 7.4(a) suggests that social assistance levels are higher for college graduates and non-college graduates in this cohort, and that the effects of college completion are also greater. As I noted in chapter 5, more-advantaged college graduates in the more recent cohort could not as effectively translate their social origins into success in avoiding disadvantaged conditions as their counterparts in the older cohort did. But the equalization among college graduates and the marked slope across social origins for non-college graduates persists. The pattern holds for TANF, SNAP/WIC, and SSI receipt in figures 7.4(b), 7.4(c), and 7.4(d), respectively.

Reducing Social Assistance

This chapter has focused on how the effects of completing a four-year degree extend beyond indicators of individual and family well-being to the receipt of social assistance. Reducing social assistance is seldom studied in assessing college degree effects. Yet it can be a key benefit for more-disadvantaged college graduates whose backgrounds put them at a greater risk of poverty and welfare. I have found large college effects

Figure 7.4(a) Levels of Social Assistance and Effects of Four-Year College Completion on Social Assistance by College Completion Likelihood (y-Axis Reversed): NLSY97

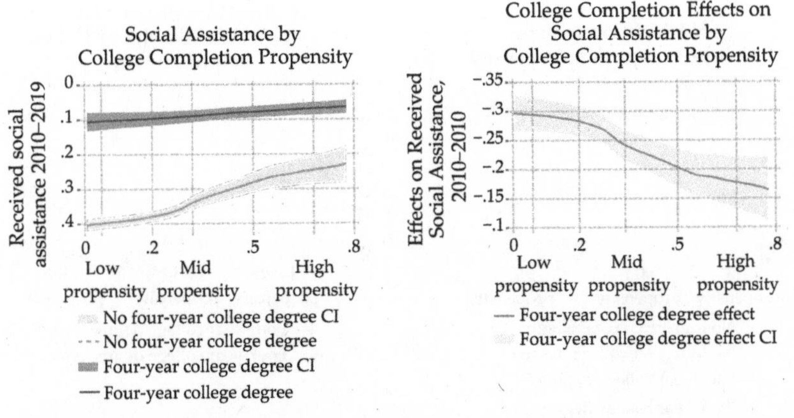

Source: Author's calculations using data from the U.S. Bureau of Labor Statistics National Longitudinal Surveys ($n = 7{,}626$).
Notes: CI indicates confidence interval. Analyses are based on local polynomial smoothing. Social assistance includes TANF, SNAP, and SSI benefits.

Figure 7.4(b) Levels of TANF Receipt and Effects of Four-Year College Completion on TANF Receipt by College Completion Likelihood (y-Axis Reversed): NLSY97

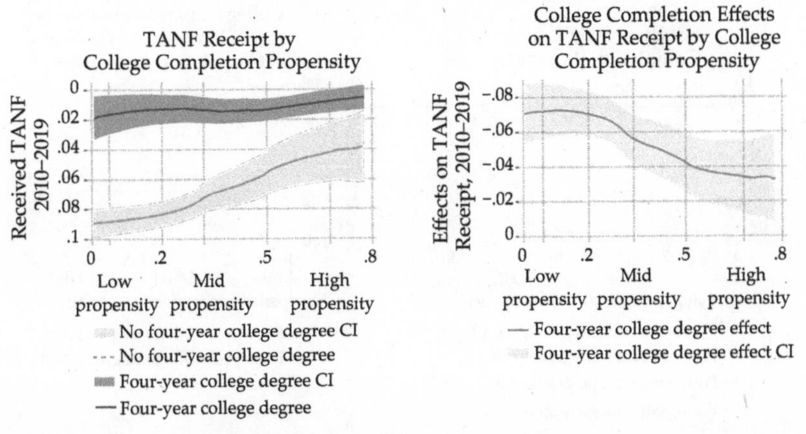

Source: Author's calculations using data from the U.S. Bureau of Labor Statistics National Longitudinal Surveys ($n = 7{,}626$).
Notes: CI indicates confidence interval. Analyses are based on local polynomial smoothing.

Figure 7.4(c) Levels of SNAP/WIC Receipt and Effects of Four-Year College Completion on SNAP/WIC Receipt by College Completion Likelihood (y-Axis Reversed): NLSY97

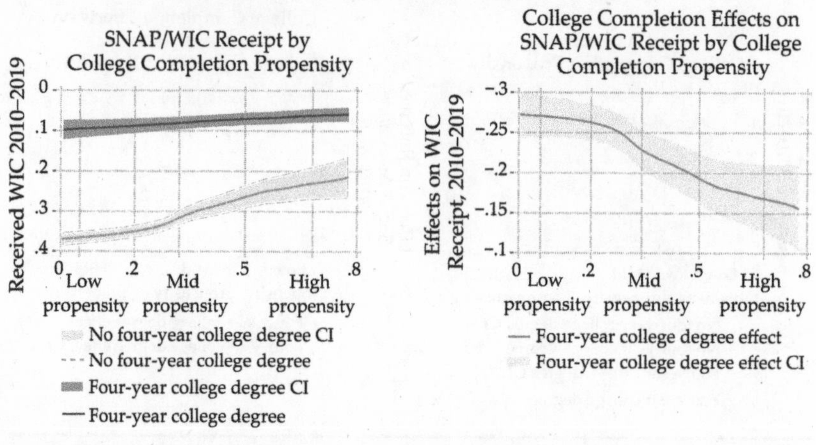

Source: Author's calculations using data from the U.S. Bureau of Labor Statistics National Longitudinal Surveys ($n = 7{,}626$).
Notes: CI indicates confidence interval. Analyses are based on local polynomial smoothing.

Figure 7.4(d) Levels of SSI Receipt and Effects of Four-Year College Completion on SSI Receipt by College Completion Likelihood (y-Axis Reversed): NLSY97

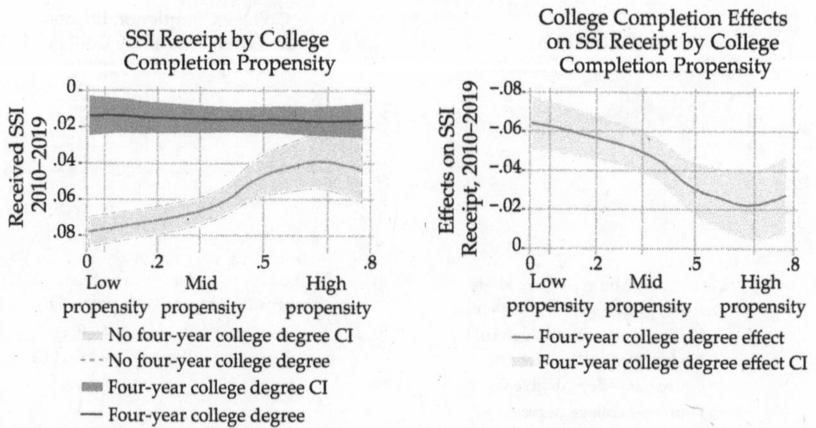

Source: Author's calculations using data from the U.S. Bureau of Labor Statistics National Longitudinal Surveys ($n = 7{,}626$).
Notes: CI indicates confidence interval. Analyses are based on local polynomial smoothing.

on reducing social assistance, with the strongest effects concentrated among unlikely college graduates. We would expect lower aid levels among college graduates who, as I demonstrated in chapters 5 and 6, largely circumvent unemployment, low-wage work, employment instability, and family poverty. I have found that college graduates' receipt of social assistance does not differ by social origins, indicating another way in which college equalizes life chances. The equalizing effect of college on measures of socioeconomic disadvantage is a central finding revealed throughout the analyses of chapters 5, 6, and 7.

Although reductions in social assistance are seldom studied in assessments of college effects, such reductions can be a key benefit for more-disadvantaged college graduates whose backgrounds put them at a greater risk of poverty and welfare. Chantelle, Daniela, Caleb, and Diego grew up in circumstances that decreased their likelihood of completing four-year college. Yet, after completing a four-year degree, their lives bore little resemblance to those of Imani, Josefina, Isaiah, and Javier, their matched non-college-graduate counterparts. They did not hold low-wage, unstable jobs. They did not experience poverty. And they did not receive welfare. Although college enriched Nancy's and Nick's lives, it did not prevent them from experiencing poverty, precarity, or aid. By these metrics, their lives resembled Rebecca's and Rich's.

These findings suggest meaningful and differential ways in which college degrees impact both individual and societal well-being. Reducing dependence on social assistance can alleviate strains on public resources and allow us to allocate resources to other aims. Public dollars invested in college education for students on the margin of school continuation can reduce the amounts that go toward social assistance. In chapter 8, I consider how college completion affects societal well-being via civic participation.

Chapter 8

Engaging in Civic Society

Brian and Henry had the same low likelihood of completing college, yet Brian obtained a degree, and Henry did not. After college, Brian not only worked in a high-skilled occupation but also spent substantial time engaged in volunteer work. In his thirties and forties, he volunteered ten hours a week in schools, youth groups, and civic and community groups. By contrast, Henry, who held lower-status jobs and was sometimes unemployed, spent no time volunteering. Brian reported that he followed politics, trusted the government, and voted in the 2006 midterm election. Henry reported that he neither followed politics nor trusted the government. He also reported that he did not vote in the midterm election.

Daniela and Josefina were Latinas with a low college likelihood; Daniela completed college, and Josefina did not. As we know from chapter 5, Daniela had a considerably more successful career than Josefina did. Daniela also spent time volunteering in educational groups in her thirties and forties. Josefina did not spend any time volunteering. Daniela reported voting in the 2006 midterm election, and Josefina did not. Suppose that Henry's and Josefina's civic engagement indicates what Brian's and Daniela's civic outcomes might have looked like if they had not earned a college degree. In that case, we see considerable civic benefits associated with college completion among unlikely college graduates.

In this chapter, I first review the research on the effects of college on civic and political engagement, expanding on my discussion on the civic role of education in chapter 2. I report the estimated effects of four-year college attendance and degree completion on voting in a midterm election, government trust, volunteering in any form, as well as civic, educational, and charitable volunteering specifically. I consider heterogeneous effects and describe levels of each outcome for college graduates and non-college graduates, paralleling the analyses in chapters 5 through 7. I conclude with a discussion of the importance of the civic benefits of higher education.

Background on the Effects of College Completion on Civic and Political Engagement

Education for democracy has a history that extends from Aristotle and Plato to John Dewey, Jane Addams, W.E.B. Du Bois, and many other contemporary social theorists.[1] Education supports an informed and engaged citizenry. Early conceptions of the role of education in U.S. society reflected socialization into civic life and societal integration.[2] Some troubling aspects of this socializing role followed mass migration in the early twentieth century that aimed to "Americanize" immigrant children.[3] Still, the civic effects of education have offered a central justification for public policy promoting equal access to schooling. Many American colleges and universities were established with a civic mission to prepare students for active participation in a diverse democracy and develop skills to facilitate community enhancement.[4] Education solidified the solidarity of social purpose. W.E.B. Du Bois said that higher education gave one access to freedom while also bestowing great responsibility to give back to civic society. Jane Addams, like Du Bois, minimized the emphasis on individual rewards and self-reliance and stressed instead social responsibility and civic engagement. For Addams, education should "result not in the snare of preparation, but in a turning of the individual toward public engagement."[5] The social theorist Émile Durkheim stated that education teaches students "how one should act on behalf of the collective interest."[6]

A civic culture moves us from individual competition to collective cooperation. Surely this should be a key goal of higher education. An important justification for expenditures on education is its civic impact, not just its economic impact.[7] The theorist Henry Giroux poignantly calls for us to "rethink what kind of education matters to a democracy and to restate our commitment to public and higher education in terms of its value for political culture and democratic public life in addition to its contributions to economic prosperity."[8] Andrew Delbanco sees a renewed commitment to cultivating civic engagement on college campuses: "Perhaps the brightest spot in the contemporary landscape of American higher education is the resurgence of interest in engaging students in civic life beyond campus. . . . Such actions bespeak a recognition that in any genuine community—an aspiration fundamental to the original conception of college—self-interest and public interest are not at odds but are two names for the same thing."[9]

Scholars have long argued that education is a key determinant of civic and political engagement.[10] The political scientists Gabriel Almond and Sidney Verba remarked as early as the 1960s that the less-educated person is "a different political actor from the man who has achieved a higher level of education."[11] The political scientist Philip Ernest Converse notably summarized the association between education and engagement in the 1970s when he wrote that education facilities cognitive matters, including factual information about politics; motivational matters, such as involvement and investment in civic society; and behavioral matters, including engagement and voting. "The educated citizen," he noted, "is attentive, knowledgeable, and participatory and the uneducated citizen is not."[12] More recently, the sociologist John Wilson has argued that education is the most consistent predictor of self-reported volunteering.[13] Robert Putnam likewise states: "Education is one of the most important predictors—usually, in fact, the most important predictor—of many forms of social participation—from voting to associational membership, to chairing a local committee to hosting a dinner party to giving blood. The same basic pattern applies to both men and women and to all races and generations."[14] He further contends that "education is by far the strongest correlate that I have discovered of civic engagement in all its forms."[15]

Observed associations between college degrees and civic and political engagement support these assertions. College graduates report volunteering at more than twice the rate of high school graduates. In 2009, 43 percent of people with a bachelor's degree or higher reported having volunteered, compared to 19 percent of high school graduates.[16] Similarly, 77 percent of bachelor's degree recipients ages twenty-five to forty-four reported voting in the 2008 presidential election, compared to 45 percent of those with a high school diploma. In the 2014 midterm election, the voting rate of college graduates ages twenty-five to forty-four was twice the rate of high school graduates.[17] College graduates also report greater trust in government than the less-educated; trust in government is linked to engagement in civic society.[18]

College facilitates civic and political engagement in various ways. First, individuals learn civic norms and responsibilities governing democratic society via socialization in higher education. Colleges and universities generally encourage students' civic and political engagement during their time in college. Research suggests that engagement in service and community-based projects during college positively affects students' long-term commitment to their communities as well as their leadership ability, social self-confidence, and conflict resolution skills.[19] Second, college also increases the knowledge, skills, and resources that facilitate civic involvement, such as cognitive, communicative, and bureaucratic proficiency and social and civic trust.[20] Acquired skills and social trust improve social interaction and foster community involvement. Social science and humanities coursework is also associated with civic engagement.[21] Third, more-educated members of society are more likely to be asked to participate, given their valued skills and resources, including their higher income and status.[22] Finally, beyond the direct effects, there are also potential indirect effects of a college degree on civic involvement. Completing college increases an individual's socioeconomic status and family stability, both of which are associated with higher rates of civic involvement.[23]

Another possibility is that educated people would have participated at high rates in civic and political activities even if they had not completed college. In other words, selection into college may bias the observed association between higher education and self-reported civic engagement. It may be that civically active parents tend to have children who are more engaged at school and in their communities, leading to the intergenerational transmission of civic engagement. Or it is possible that certain characteristics, like strong work commitment, contribute to educational success and civic involvement. Civic-minded communities may do more to ensure that they have well-funded and high-quality schools, and students from such schools may be more likely to attend college and complete a degree. The evidence suggests, however, that even with extensive controls for precollege characteristics and natural experiment study designs, the link between higher education and civic engagement persists.[24] The political scientists Norman Nie and Sunshine Hillygus state that the causal link between education and reported civic engagement is "largely uncontested."[25]

In some research on education and engagement, scholars use instrumental variables (IV) models to address selection into college and continue to find significant effects on political involvement.[26] In fact, effects on voting behavior based on IV models exceed ordinary least squares regression estimates. Similar to effects on wages, these findings suggest possible heterogeneity in college effects on civic and political participation, whereby students on the margin of school continuation experience larger effects than average students. The economist Thomas Dee states that his IV results could "indicate that the civic returns associated with college entrance are substantial for the nonrandom subset of individuals whose postsecondary attainments were influenced by the instruments (e.g., those from disadvantaged backgrounds)."[27]

Heckman, Humphries, and Veramendi, using data from the NLSY79 cohort, observe that the returns to education for many "non-market outcomes," including self-reported voting, "appear to be larger for low-ability individuals" than for those with higher test scores.[28] The education scholars William Doyle and Benjamin Skinner, using data from the NLSY97 cohort, find that IV estimates of postsecondary effects exceed standard OLS estimates for self-reported voting in the 2004, 2006, 2008, and 2010 elections and volunteering and charitable donations from 2005 to 2013. They use seven different instrumental variables, all of which suggest larger effects than OLS estimates. They conclude that there are civic benefits to higher education, and that they appear to accrue largely for individuals on the margins of attendance: "We take this finding as evidence that even in the nonmarket realm, the focus of policy and funding should be on those low-income and underrepresented young people who would not otherwise attend postsecondary education."[29]

My prior work using propensity-based methods yields the same conclusion. I find that a college degree raised the civic participation of unlikely college graduates more than it raised participation among traditional college graduates.[30] The effect of completing college on volunteering in civic and community activities decreases as the likelihood of completing college increases. Skinner and Doyle similarly find larger effects of college enrollment on volunteering and voting among those with a lower propensity to enroll.[31] In recent work Caitlin Ahearn, Xiang Zhou, and I also show the same pattern for self-reported voting.[32] Using causal mediation analysis, we find that most of the effect of college attendance on voting is not explained by increased socioeconomic status or family formation patterns but by the direct effect of college. These results suggest that the civic returns to attending college are not contingent upon socioeconomic returns. Expanding higher education, regardless of how college shapes economic outcomes, can narrow the socioeconomic gap in political participation and influence.

As unlikely college graduates generally have less-educated parents who are probably also less civically engaged, college may be especially consequential to them for learning civic norms and responsibilities and developing expanded, educated, civically active social networks. Additionally, civic responsibility accompanies educational opportunities. Disadvantaged individuals may maintain contact with the communities of their youth and be motivated to give back to those communities with the skills and resources they acquired through their schooling.[33]

College Completion Increases Civic and Political Engagement

I consider the effects of college attendance and completion on several self-reported civic and political engagement measures. First, I evaluate the effects of college on any volunteer activity (not-for-profit organizations) between 2010 and 2014, when NLSY79 respondents were in their forties.[34] Then I assess college effects for three specific participation measures: (1) volunteering in civic, community, or youth groups; (2) volunteering in educational groups; and (3) volunteering in charitable organizations or social welfare groups. I also assess self-reported voting in the 2006 midterm election and government trust.

Self-reported voting was based on a question asked of respondents about which statement best described them: (1) "I am sure I voted"; (2) "I usually vote, but didn't in 2006"; (3) "I thought about voting in 2006, but didn't"; and (4) "I did not vote in the November 2006 election."[35] Some respondents refused to answer or reported that they didn't know. I coded those who stated they were sure they voted as voting and all other categories as not voting. This coding coincides with the Current Population Survey coding procedure for voting measures.[36] Among NLSY79 respondents with at least a high school degree, 69 percent reported voting.[37] Although this is higher than the 57 percent who reported voting in this age and education category in the CPS, the gap between college graduates and non-college graduates is roughly the same (about a 20 percent gap).[38] Finally, I consider a 2008 measure of government trust that indicates that the respondent reported that the "government does what people want."

As in chapters 5 through 7, I estimate the effect of college attendance and college completion and both the average effect (average treatment effect, *ATE*]) and the average effect for college graduates (treatment effect on the treated, *TT*). As reported in appendix table B.23, I find a significant impact of college attendance and completion on civic and political participation. For the *ATE*, I find an eleven- to fourteen-percentage-point-higher level of self-reported volunteering and a seventeen- to eighteen-percentage-point-higher level of self-reported voting in the midterm election associated with college completion. College also significantly affects government trust. College effects on volunteering and self-reported voting are larger for the *ATE* than the *TT*, suggesting larger effects among individuals with a low college likelihood. College completion increases engagement more than attendance does, but not by much. Effects are larger for civic and educational volunteering than for charitable volunteering. Differences between the *ATE* and *TT* are not significant for volunteering but are for voting.

For the NLSY97 cohort (see appendix table B.24), I consider a measure of any volunteering and a measure of voting in the 2010 midterm election. Volunteering indicates any unpaid volunteer work between 2011 and 2013, when respondents were in their late twenties, including activities aimed at changing social conditions, such as work with educational groups, environmental groups, landlord-tenant groups or other consumer groups, women's groups, or minority groups. College attendance and completion significantly increase the likelihood of volunteering and voting. Effect sizes for volunteering are similar across cohorts, despite the younger age of the NLSY97 respondents. But effect sizes are smaller for voting. NLSY97 respondents were voting in their late twenties, while the NLSY79 respondents were voting in their early forties, when voting rates are generally substantially higher.

College Completion Increases Civic Engagement for Low- and Mid-Likelihood Graduates

Diego and Javier were both unlikely to complete college, yet Diego completed college and Javier did not. Diego reported voting in the 2006 midterm election, while Javier did not. Likewise, both Daniela and Josefina had a low likelihood of getting a college degree. Daniela completed college, and Josefina did not. As with Diego and Javier, Daniela reported voting, and Josefina did not. Daniela also reported volunteering in educational groups, while Josefina did not. Brian volunteered for civic, community, and educational groups, while his matched noncollege graduate counterpart Henry did not. Brian also voted in the midterm election and trusted the government, while Henry did not vote and did not express such trust. By contrast, we do not see any difference in reported voting by college completion when we compare Nick and Rich and Nancy and Rebecca, all of whom had a high college propensity. All four reported voting in 2006. Neither Rebecca nor Nancy reported any volunteering time. Paula and Tia were high-propensity women but on the low end of that distribution. Both reported voting, but they differed in their volunteering. Paula volunteered for community and education groups, and Tia did not. The same pattern holds for Pedro and Tomas. These descriptions help elucidate the patterns in college degree effects I observe across the likelihood of completion.

Figure 8.1(a) offers propensity-score-stratified matching estimates of civic engagement measures (see also appendix table B.25[a]). The effects are largest for mid-propensity college graduates for any volunteering.[39] Effects for unlikely and high-likelihood college graduates are marginally significant; the estimate for unlikely graduates is larger than that for high-likelihood college graduates. Effects for mid-likelihood college graduates suggest an eighteen-percentage-point-higher level of ever volunteering. This pattern departs from measures of socioeconomic, family, and social assistance outcomes. If I consider more specific forms of participation, I find large effects for low- and mid-likelihood college graduates on civic, youth, and community group volunteering. I observe a seventeen-percentage-point-higher level for unlikely graduates and a sixteen-percentage-point-higher level for mid-likelihood graduates. The effect for high-likelihood graduates is insignificant. For educational volunteering, effects are largest for the unlikely graduates and similar

Figure 8.1(a) Effects of Four-Year College Completion on Volunteering by College Completion Likelihood: NLSY79

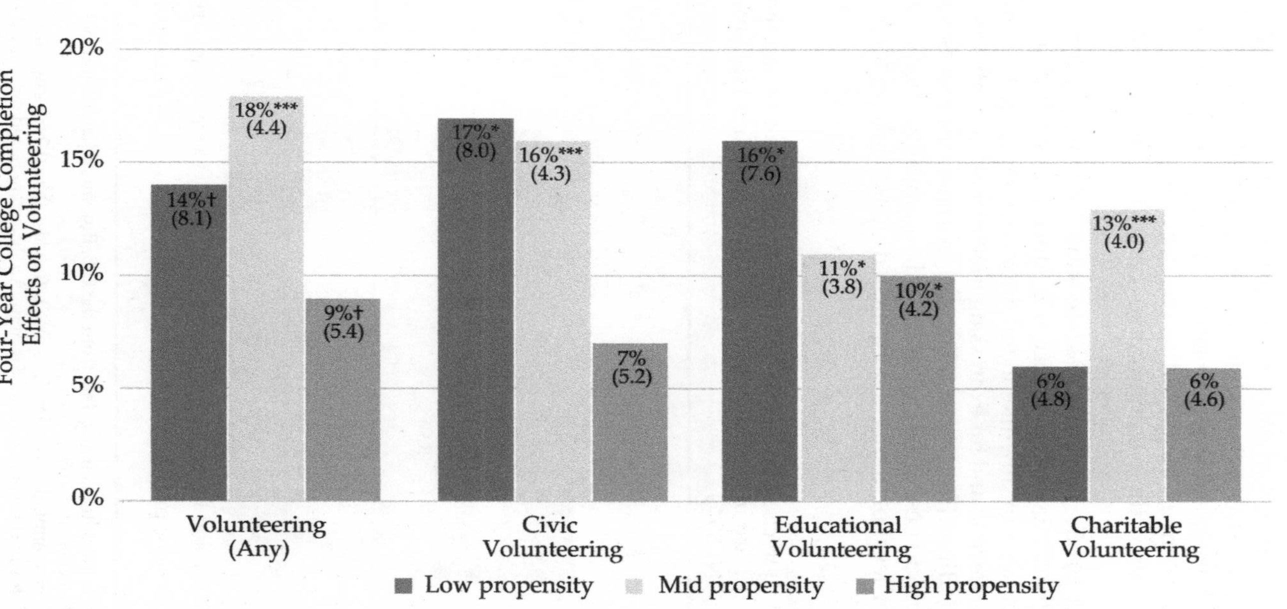

Source: Author's calculations using data from the U.S. Bureau of Labor Statistics National Longitudinal Surveys ($n = 4{,}085$).
Notes: The college completion propensity score is 0 to less than 0.2 for low propensity, 0.2 to less than 0.5 for middle, and 0.5 to 1 for high. Analyses are based on nearest-neighbor matching on the linearized propensity score. Civic volunteering includes civic, community, and youth groups; educational volunteering includes organizations promoting education; charitable volunteering includes charities or social welfare groups. Numbers in parentheses are standard errors.
† $p \leq 0.10$; * $p \leq 0.05$; *** $p \leq 0.001$; two-tailed tests

among mid- and high-likelihood graduates. Finally, effects for volunteering in charitable and social welfare groups are largest among mid-likelihood graduates and insignificant for the other groups. While advantaged college graduates reap large individual economic benefits of college, they are no more likely than their advantaged noncollege peers to report serving their communities or participating in charitable activities.

Figure 8.1(b) offers propensity-score-stratified matching estimates on voting and trust in government (see also appendix table B.25[a]). College completion effects for low-likelihood graduates are largest for voting in the midterm election and for expressing trust in government; these effects significantly differ from the smaller and insignificant effects for high-likelihood graduates. College graduates had a twenty-one-percentage-point-higher level of voting than matched non-college graduates who

Figure 8.1(b) Effects of Four-Year College Completion on Voting and Trust in Government by College Completion Likelihood: NLSY79

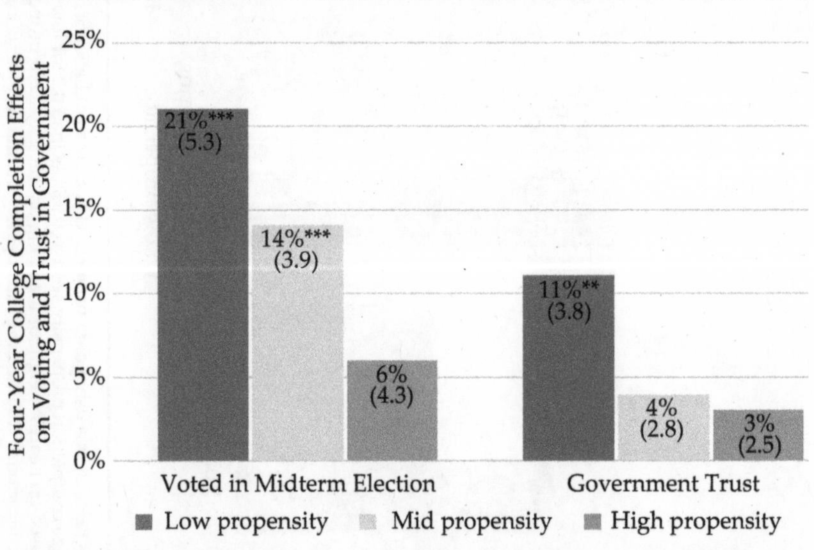

Source: Author's calculations using data from the U.S. Bureau of Labor Statistics National Longitudinal Surveys ($n = 4{,}085$).

Notes: The college completion propensity score is 0 to less than 0.2 for low propensity, 0.2 to less than 0.5 for middle, and 0.5 to 1 for high. Analyses are based on nearest-neighbor matching on the linearized propensity score. Voted indicates the respondent is sure that they voted in the 2006 election. Trust in government indicates stated belief that the government does what people want it to do. Numbers in parentheses are standard errors.

** $p \leq 0.01$; *** $p \leq 0.001$; two-tailed tests

were unlikely to complete a degree.[40] They also had an eleven-percentage-point-higher level of trust in government.

To check the robustness of the results to the matching approach, I report estimates using doubly robust inverse probability weighting and generalized random forests in appendix table B.25(b). The findings are generally the same using these alternative estimation strategies. I conduct sensitivity analyses where I suppose that some unobserved factor affects engagement and college completion. College effects on engagement are relatively robust to unobserved confounding.[41] In figure 8.2, I report results for the NLSY97 cohort for civic volunteering and voting in a midterm election. Findings indicate that the effect of completing college on volunteering is largest for low- and high-likelihood college graduates and that the effect on voting is largest for unlikely graduates.[42] The pattern for volunteering differs from that of the older cohort, but the out-

Figure 8.2 Effects of Four-Year College Completion on Volunteering and Voting by College Completion Likelihood (y-Axis Reversed): NLSY97

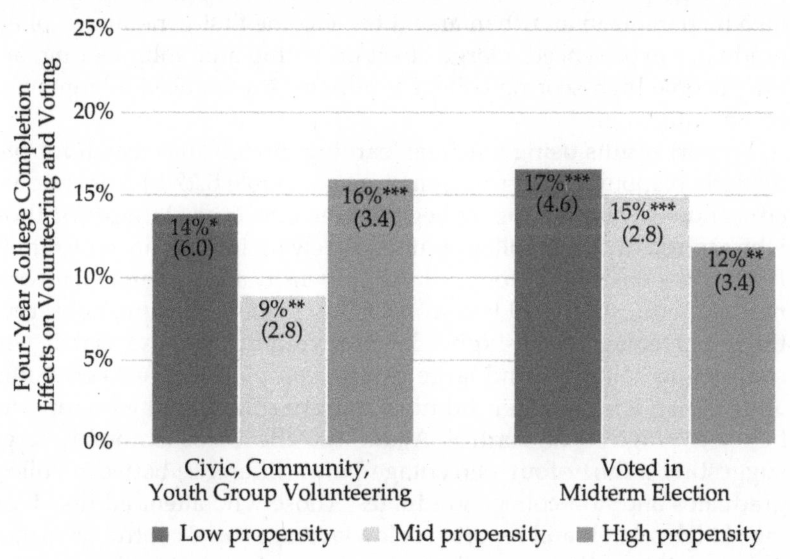

Source: Author's calculations using data from the U.S. Bureau of Labor Statistics National Longitudinal Surveys ($n = 7{,}626$).

Notes: The college completion propensity score is 0 to less than 0.2 for low propensity, 0.2 to less than 0.5 for middle, and 0.5 to 1 for high. Analyses are based on nearest-neighbor matching on the linearized propensity score. Voted indicates the respondent is sure that they voted in the 2010 election. Volunteering includes civic, community, and youth groups. Voting analyses are based on doubly robust estimation. Numbers in parentheses are standard errors.

* $p \leq 0.05$; ** $p \leq 0.01$; *** $p \leq 0.001$; two-tailed tests

come measures correspond to civic participation in the late twenties to early thirties, when engagement differs notably from that in the forties.

In appendix table B.27(a), I compare effects by parents' income, mother's education, ASVAB test scores, and race. The college completion effect on volunteering in civic and community groups and educational groups is largest for those from low-income families and for Blacks. Effects are also large for those whose mother completed at least a high school degree and who had average test scores. I observe a notably large college degree effect on voting among those with low test scores. This pattern is reflected in the comparisons between Brian and Henry relative to Nick and Rich. Brian, Nick, and Rich all voted in the midterm election, while Henry, a low-scoring non-college graduate, did not vote, yielding a large benefit for Brian and no benefit for Nick. Among college graduates who had low-income parents and who grew up in an urban area, college had a sizable effect on reported voting. I observe a twenty-eight-percentage-point-higher level of voting for low-income urban college graduates versus non-college graduates relative to an eleven-percentage-point-higher level for those who did not grow up with low-income parents in an urban area. Low-income first-generation college graduates experienced a large effect on voting and volunteering, and low-income high-scoring college graduates experienced a large effect on volunteering.

I report results using machine learning models that search for particularly responsive subgroups in appendix table B.27(b). For civic and educational volunteering, college degree effects are largest for those who aspired to attend college but who grew up in a low-income family. For this responsive subgroup, whose propensity scores, parental income, mother's education, and test scores fell in the low stratum, I observe a thirty-percentage-point-higher level of volunteering associated with completing college. I find large college completion effects on voting among men whose father did not complete college and who reported below-average social control. Again, the effect size is notably large, suggesting a thirty-four-percentage-point difference between college graduates and non-college graduates. Those who attended disadvantaged high schools and reported below-average social control were most responsive to college completion's effect of facilitating their trust in government. These patterns essentially mirror results suggesting significant effects on civic and political participation among low-propensity college graduates and, to a lesser extent, among mid-propensity college graduates. The effect for the most-advantaged college graduates is negligible.

College Completion Equalizes Some Forms of Civic and Political Engagement

College degrees serve to equalize some forms of civic and political engagement. For example, Brian and Danielle, low-propensity college graduates, had participation levels like those of Paula and Pedro, both high-propensity graduates. In figures 8.3(a) to 8.3(f), the left panels provide levels of civic and political engagement separately for college and non-college graduates across the likelihood of college completion. The right panels provide differences in those levels. Levels are more similar among high-likelihood college graduates and non-college graduates than among unlikely college graduates and non-college graduates. Accordingly, college graduates' engagement levels across social origins are more similar than non-college graduates' levels across social origins, suggesting some degree of equalization for college graduates (for example, see figure 8.3[a]).

For example, about 35 to 40 percent of college graduates reported volunteering in civic activities (figure 8.3[b]), with only a few percentage points' difference between low- and high-propensity graduates. By contrast, only 10 to 12 percent of low-propensity non-college graduates re-

Figure 8.3(a) Levels of Volunteering and Effects of Four-Year College Completion on Volunteering by College Completion Likelihood: NLSY79

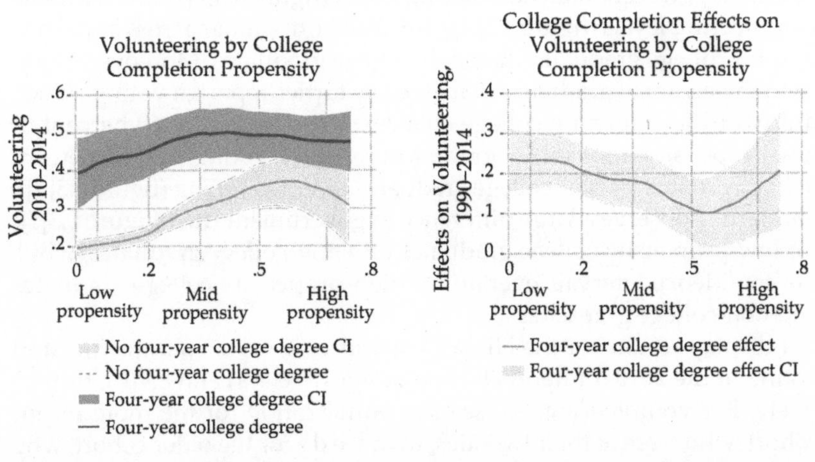

Source: Author's calculations using data from the U.S. Bureau of Labor Statistics National Longitudinal Surveys ($n = 4{,}085$).
Notes: CI indicates confidence interval. Analyses are based on local polynomial smoothing.

Figure 8.3(b) Levels of Civic Volunteering and Effects of Four-Year College Completion on Civic Volunteering by College Completion Likelihood: NLSY79

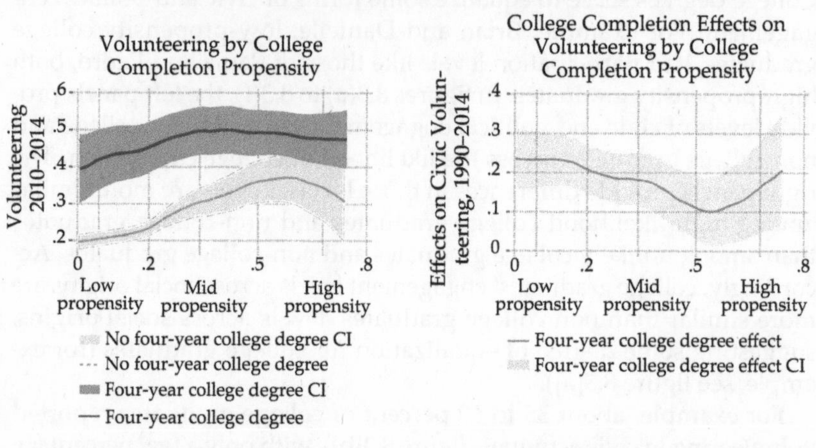

Source: Author's calculations using data from the U.S. Bureau of Labor Statistics National Longitudinal Surveys ($n = 4{,}085$).
Notes: CI indicates confidence interval. Analyses are based on local polynomial smoothing. Civic volunteering includes civic, community, and youth groups.

ported volunteering, relative to about 25 percent of high-propensity graduates. Educational volunteering levels (figure 8.3[c]) and charitable volunteering levels (figure 8.3[d]) are also more similar across social origins for college graduates than non-college graduates. Moreover, about 80 to 85 percent of graduates in their early forties reported voting, which did not differ much by college chances. In comparison, 60 percent of low-propensity non-college graduates reported voting, and 75 percent of high-propensity non-college graduates reported voting (figure 8.3[e]). Similarly, I observe a large difference in government trust (figure 8.3[f]) for low-propensity college graduates and non-college graduates, while the confidence intervals overlap for high-propensity college graduates and non-college graduates.

I display results for the NLSY97 measures of civic volunteering and voting in the 2010 midterm election in figures 8.4(a) and 8.4(b), respectively. For volunteering, we see less equalization for the more recent cohort, who were in their twenties, than we do for the older cohort, who were in their forties. As another possible explanation for this divergence, the measure of volunteering also differs across cohorts.[43] However, we see relative equalization of voting, even in the twenties, for college gradu-

Figure 8.3(c) Levels of Educational Volunteering and Effects of Four-Year College Completion on Educational Volunteering by College Completion Likelihood: NLSY79

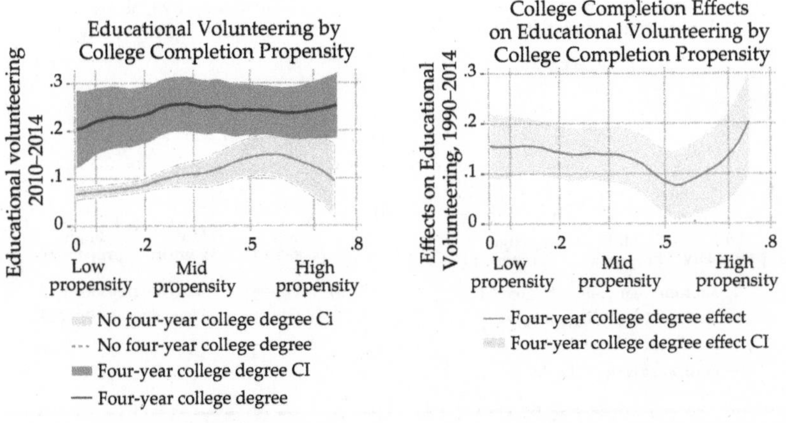

Source: Author's calculations using data from the U.S. Bureau of Labor Statistics National Longitudinal Surveys ($n = 4{,}085$).
Notes: CI indicates confidence interval. Analyses are based on local polynomial smoothing. Educational volunteering includes organizations promoting education.

Figure 8.3(d) Levels of Charitable Volunteering and Effects of Four-Year College Completion on Charitable Volunteering by College Completion Likelihood: NLSY79

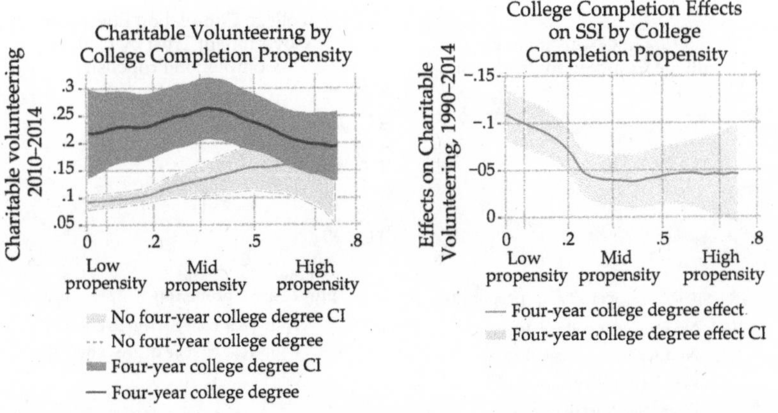

Source: Author's calculations using data from the U.S. Bureau of Labor Statistics National Longitudinal Surveys ($n = 4{,}085$).
Notes: CI indicates confidence interval. Analyses are based on local polynomial smoothing. Charitable volunteering includes charities or social welfare groups.

Figure 8.3(e) Levels of Voting and Effects of Four-Year College Completion on Voting by College Completion Likelihood: NLSY79

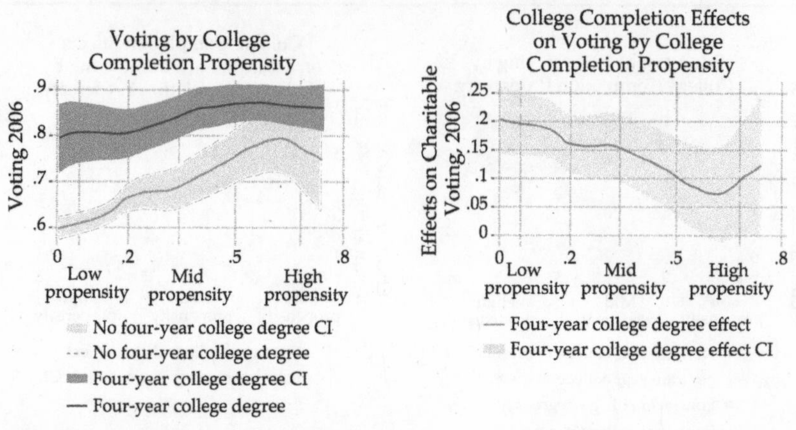

Source: Author's calculations using data from the U.S. Bureau of Labor Statistics National Longitudinal Surveys ($n = 4{,}085$).
Notes: CI indicates confidence interval. Analyses are based on local polynomial smoothing. Voted indicates the respondent is sure that they voted in the 2006 election.

Figure 8.3(f) Levels of Trust in Government and Effects of Four-Year College Completion on Trust in Government by College Completion Likelihood: NLSY79

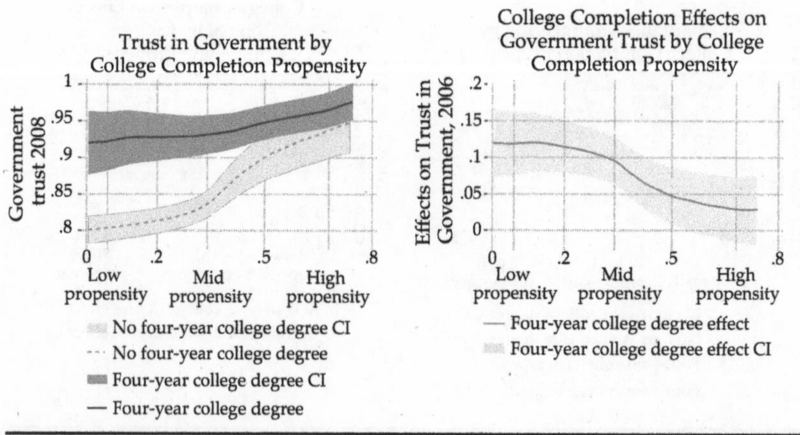

Source: Author's calculations using data from the U.S. Bureau of Labor Statistics National Longitudinal Surveys ($n = 4{,}085$).
Notes: CI indicates confidence interval. Analyses are based on local polynomial smoothing. Trust in government indicates stated belief that the government does what people want it to do.

Figure 8.4(a) Levels of Volunteering and Effects of Four-Year College Completion on Volunteering by College Completion Likelihood: NLSY97

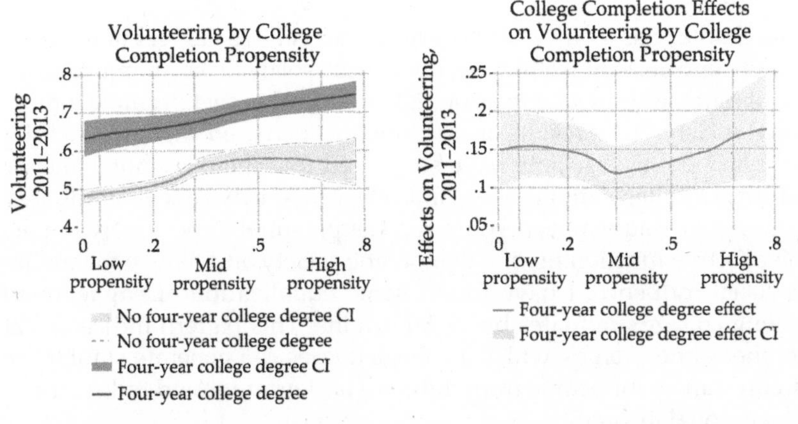

Source: Author's calculations using data from the U.S. Bureau of Labor Statistics National Longitudinal Surveys ($n = 7{,}626$).
Notes: CI indicates confidence interval. Analyses are based on local polynomial smoothing. Volunteering includes any form of participation in civic, youth, or community groups.

Figure 8.4(b) Levels of Voting and Effects of Four-Year College Completion on Voting by College Completion Likelihood: NLSY97

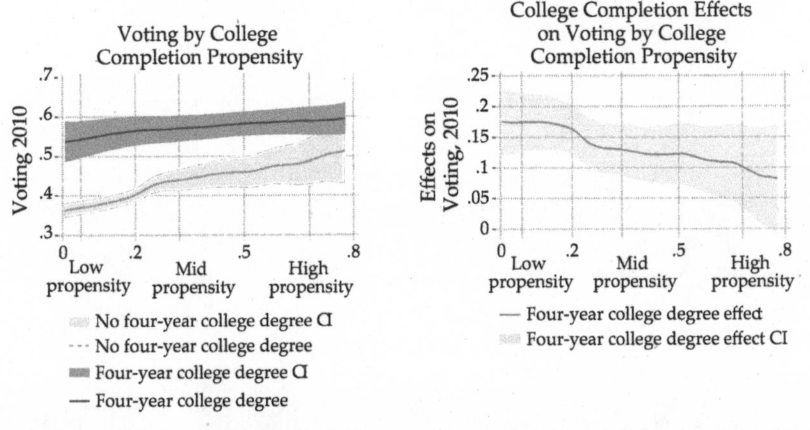

Source: Author's calculations using data from the U.S. Bureau of Labor Statistics National Longitudinal Surveys ($n = 7{,}626$).
Notes: CI indicates confidence interval. Analyses are based on local polynomial smoothing. Voted indicates the respondent is sure that they voted in the 2010 election.

ates relative to non-college graduates, resulting in a pattern of the largest effects being seen for unlikely graduates.[44]

Engaging in Civic Society

This chapter has focused on how four-year college degrees affect community and societal well-being. If we focus solely on economic returns, we obscure additional effects of higher education that promote a more equal society.[45] The results of assessing the increased engagement with civic and political society have suggested that there are notable civic returns to college among low- and mid-propensity college graduates. Educating disadvantaged youth has the potential to positively impact the effective functioning of a democratic society and reduce inequality in social influence. I have found some equalization of engagement among college graduates by social origins. This pattern indicates yet another dimension by which a college degree can generate similar life circumstances for people from different backgrounds and reduce intergenerational inequality.

Understanding patterns of heterogeneity in civic returns to completing college is critical to assessing the societal benefits of increasing access to higher education. If the effect of college on civic and political involvement is strong among relatively disadvantaged college graduates, educational expansion can enhance societal engagement and decrease inequality in social influence. In the final chapter, I consider the implications of the findings reported throughout the book.

Chapter 9

Inequality and Investment

Caleb was unlikely to complete college. Neither of his parents went to college, and he attended a disadvantaged high school. Despite high test scores, he did not take college-prep courses in high school and did not expect to attend college. Isaiah's background was very similar to Caleb's. Yet Caleb ultimately completed a four-year college degree, and Isaiah did not. Their subsequent life trajectories look markedly different. Considering possible college counterfactuals, like the differences between Caleb and Isaiah, motivates a conceptual frame to understand returns to schooling. Of course, the fundamental problem of causal inference is that we never observe an individual's counterfactual state. I underscore the need to conceptually attend to counterfactuals while acknowledging that they are unobserved quantities.

Too often, rhetoric on the value of attending and completing college is based on comparisons rather than counterfactuals. These comparisons often lead to misleading conclusions about the value of college degrees for subsets of students. Misleading comparisons are frequently applied to suggest that college does not pay off for students who are underachieving in high school or for low-income or racially minoritized youth. We cannot know the counterfactual trajectory for a Black college graduate with low-income parents like Caleb. But we can at least conceptually know that we should be considering his life chances in the absence of completing college rather than the life chances of a White college graduate with high-income parents. The latter comparison allows us to assess racial or social class inequality controlling for educational attainment, but it does not tell us about the value of a college degree for low-income youth. Comparing the earnings levels, for example, for college graduates with advantaged backgrounds to those of graduates from less-advantaged backgrounds does not give us the *effect* of going to college. Misleading comparisons beget misleading conclusions.

Throughout this book, I have acknowledged that individuals with different backgrounds differ in how they benefit from completing college.

Yet, in contrast to those who would limit access for underprivileged youth, I argue that those unlikely to complete college benefit the most for a range of life outcomes. Without a college degree, those with disadvantaged social backgrounds have limited family resources and networks and limited labor market prospects. By contrast, in the absence of a college degree, individuals from more-advantaged social backgrounds can still rely on their privileged resources, networks, and job opportunities; as a result, there is a smaller difference by educational attainment in their socioeconomic and family well-being.

The original goals of mass education were centered on its philosophical, moral, and civic benefits and on the collective utility in educating the nation's citizens, but contemporary discussions about the role of schooling overwhelmingly focus on the impact of higher education on job prospects. Most policy discussions of higher education rest on the assumption that the central purpose of going to college is to get a good-paying job. Yet economic conditions do not capture all the utility-enhancing effects of education. I argue that the benefits of attending and completing college extend far beyond the typically studied wage gains. College impacts many socioeconomic, family-level, social assistance, and civic engagement outcomes, among other life conditions.

The benefits of college are also not all immediate. Long-term gains often compensate for short-term costs. Debates about access and returns to college degrees need to recognize both the far-reaching and long-term benefits. I ask not only how a four-year college degree increases wages over the career but also how it reduces the risk of unemployment, a low-wage career, and job instability. I ask not only how completing college increases family income but also how it prevents family poverty. I explore how college reduces social assistance and how it increases civic and political engagement. Evaluating the differential response to four-year degree completion and, in particular, the benefits for unlikely college graduates hinges upon taking a holistic view of life outcomes. As college reaches a more diverse population, its benefits become more diverse.

I have shown that if we view college with a counterfactual lens and expand our accounting to the diversity of long-term benefits for diverse students, we better understand how college transforms lives. For advantaged youth, I find that large and increasing wage growth, high household income, and the formation of stable families are associated with college completion. For disadvantaged youth unlikely to complete college, I find that increases in wages and household income, as well as civic and political participation, are associated with college completion, but also that completing college circumvents unemployment, low-wage work, job instability, family poverty, and social assistance. Patterns were essentially the same across the two cohorts of college graduates. College appears to be even more consequential for circumventing some measures of precarity and poverty for more recent graduates.[1] In sum, the findings I present throughout this book suggest that completing college has larger benefits for a range of indicators among disadvantaged college graduates, findings that are consistent with a large literature.

Large benefits of completing college for unlikely college graduates result from the equalizing role of college on life outcomes. Although a college degree does not fully equalize some outcomes across social origins, it equalizes others. Notably, college equalizes most of the disadvantaged life outcomes I consider. Thus, although college may not equalize the cultivation of privilege, it equalizes the circumvention of poverty. Education is not a panacea. School improvements cannot solve all economic and social problems and may not fully eliminate the impact of social origins for outcomes like wages and household income. Yet even when outcomes are unequal in a way that benefits privileged youth, college degrees may bring large returns to disadvantaged youth.

Large returns to disadvantaged youth suggest that educating broad segments of the U.S. population can reduce social inequality and increase societal well-being. Disinvestment in college serves to stratify and maintain social inequality. Those who perceive that they benefit from a system of inequality and from an unequal distribution of scarce resources may resist sharing resources. Yet educating youth is not just about individual economic returns. Investment in higher education benefits our collective well-being and our democratic society. Greater long-term earnings (and thus more tax revenue), less reliance on public assistance, and high levels of volunteering indicate that public investment in higher education for students from disadvantaged backgrounds yields far-reaching societal benefits. If we frame education in terms of individual rewards, it is more challenging to garner widespread public support to expand to a more diverse population. We should demand a society based on collective good rather than individualism and scarcity. It is better for our society when more people complete a four-year degree.

Overcoming the Odds: Selection into College and Benefits for Unlikely Graduates

Daniela had a low likelihood of completing college. She grew up with a single mother who had immigrated to the United States from Mexico and who had little education. Her family income was below average. Daniela had low test scores and did not take college-prep courses in high school. She attended a disadvantaged high school, one in which she felt unsafe. Yet Daniela aspired to attend college. After high school, she enrolled in and completed college within four years. Daniela overcame the odds to complete a college degree.

This book has invited readers to consider how the life of a college graduate like Daniela would have unfolded in the absence of college. It has also asked readers to consider the variations in counterfactual life chances across the college-educated population. We cannot observe counterfactuals. Yet even if we believe that Daniela's life would not have looked like Josefina's, her matched counterpart, in the absence of a college degree, do we believe that it would instead have looked like Nancy's? Or would Caleb's life without a college degree have looked more like Isaiah's, his matched counterpart, or like Nick's, a high-propensity graduate? That is, while factors that we do not observe may facilitate educational and socioeconomic success among unlikely college graduates, this does not necessarily mean that college effects among disadvantaged youth are driven by those characteristics rather than by the causal effects of completing college.

Low-propensity youth who attend and complete college do so against the odds.[2] But to what extent does this mean that they are atypical individuals or that some atypical circumstance facilitated their college pathway? Considerations of what enables unlikely college graduates to overcome the odds often focus on personal attributes, like motivation or tenacity. Yet particular social and structural factors often play a role, such as an uncommonly supportive nonparental family or community member, a charismatic teacher or counselor, or an effective high school program designed to facilitate underprivileged students' achievement.[3] Students on the margin may continue their schooling because of other factors, like having access to a nearby college, low local college tuition, or high local unemployment that induces them to attend. It need not be an unobserved individual factor.

This book has considered various ways to define students who are unlikely to complete college, including propensity to complete college, parental income, parental education, test scores, race, and the intersection of precollege characteristics. The propensity score approach invites questioning of differential selection into college. Low-propensity college graduates may be more self-selective than high-propensity graduates, for whom college-going is a social norm. Yet strong self-selection into college may also be true for subgroups defined by parental income, parental education, race, or test scores.[4] To invalidate the observed pattern of results, we must believe that unobserved characteristics influence college completion and each outcome beyond the observed factors I include. As I have detailed, I draw on rich precollege characteristics that indicate social background, test scores, achievement, psychosocial factors, expectations, and secondary school characteristics. I estimate a flexible model that combines the interactions of many of these factors. What we do not observe must sufficiently differ from the factors we observe and the interactions between those factors to invalidate the results. Sensitivity analyses throughout the book also generally suggest that unobserved factors would need to have large effects on completing college and life outcomes to invalidate the observed effects of college completion for unlikely graduates.

We must also overlook substantial theoretical and empirical support in the college effects literature to question the story told here. Negating the selection bias argument among unlikely college-goers, Florencia Torche contends that while selection decreased as education expanded over the last quarter-century, college returns did not correspondingly decrease.[5] She concludes that the evidence is inconsistent with selection playing a strong role in mobility patterns.[6] Paul Attewell and his colleagues similarly write: "Mass education has not made a college degree worth less. . . . On a national scale, greater access to higher education has been accompanied by growth in the earnings premium for a college degree."[7]

Still, the pattern of the largest returns for low-propensity college graduates does not invariably hold. As shown in the summary of results in table 9.1, we do not always find the largest effects among "against the odds" cases. Indeed, some patterns suggest larger effects among high-propensity college graduates, and some indicate no significant observable heterogeneity across the population. Some patterns even suggest that the largest effects are in the middle of the distribution, such as college effects for some forms of civic participation. Many of the most interesting analyses with implications for social inequality, however, indicate large effects among unlikely college graduates, particularly those suggesting that unlikely graduates circumvent a wide range of disadvantaged life conditions.

The critique about unobserved factors influencing large college returns for disadvantaged students adopts, at least implicitly, much of the public rhetoric on limiting college access—including the assertion that students on the margin of college could not have larger benefits than privileged youth, and thus the analyses must be wrong. Yet interestingly, the assumption that there is strong selection for unlikely graduates is precisely the argument one could use to counter claims that underprivileged students are "taking" traditional students' spots on college campuses. If unlikely college graduates are not less qualified but instead more selective, they have enhanced qualifications to compensate for disadvantaged socioeconomic factors. They may select into college based on motivation,

Table 9.1 Summary of Results from Chapters 5 to 8

	Order of Four-Year College Completion Effect Size by College Completion Likelihood	
Outcomes	NLSY79	NLSY97
Chapter 5		
Earnings (log average)	low-high-mid	high-low-mid
Unemployment (proportion)	low-mid-high	low- mid-high
Not in the labor force (proportion)	low-mid-high	low-mid-high
Low-wage work (proportion)	low-mid-high	low-mid-high
Low-skilled work (proportion)	low-mid-high	low-mid-high
Job instability	low-high-mid	low-high-mid
Chapter 6		
Household income (log average)	high-low-mid	low-mid-high
Family poverty (ever)	low-mid-high	low-mid-high
Family poverty (proportion)	low-mid-high	low-mid-high
Married (proportion)	high-mid-low	low-mid-high
Spouse in high-skilled work (proportion)	high-mid-low	
Single parenthood (proportion)	low-mid-high	low-mid-high
Chapter 7		
Social assistance (any)	low-mid-high	low-mid-high
AFDC/TANF (any)	low-mid-high	low-mid-high
SNAP (any)	low-mid-high	low-mid-high
SSI (any)	low-mid-high	low-mid-high
UI (any)	low-mid-high	
Social assistance (amount)	low-mid-high	
Chapter 8		
Volunteering (any)	mid-low-high	high-low-mid
Civic volunteering (any)	low-mid-high	
Educational volunteering (any)	low-mid-high	
Charitable/social welfare volunteering (any)	mid-low-high	
Voted in midterm election	low-mid-high	low-mid-high
Trust in government	low-mid-high	

Source: Author's calculations using data from the U.S. Bureau of Labor Statistics National Longitudinal Surveys.

Notes: College completion likelihood is indicated by estimated propensity score strata. Low propensity is a four-year college completion propensity score from 0 to less than 0.2, middle from 0.2 to less than 0.5, and high from 0.5 to 1. Results are shown in figures 5.1, 5.3, 6.1, 6.3, 7.1, 7.3, 8.1, and 8.3 and the corresponding tables in appendix B (online).

tenacity, and other distinctive qualities that set them apart and allow them to succeed. This is a population well worthy of occupying seats in our nation's colleges.

Consider Chantelle, a Black woman who grew up with her uncle in a low-income household. She attended a high school in the South with few resources. Even though her social origins made her unlikely to complete college, Chantelle attended college immediately after high school and completed a four-year degree. She became a financial adviser, was continuously employed throughout her career, and spent no time in poverty. She did not receive any social assistance from her twenties to her fifties, and she reported voting in the midterm election. Would Chantelle's life conditions have been the same had she not completed college? A lower likelihood of completing college correlates with more unobserved selection, or characteristics necessary to overcome the odds to complete a degree.[8] Perhaps Chantelle had high ambition, tenacity, and goal-oriented behavior that enabled her to complete college despite her disadvantaged origins. The selectivity argument maintains that these qualities would have led to largely the same life path irrespective of whether she earned a degree. But would they have? Or would her social background and lack of a degree have limited her opportunities? Did college serve as a mechanism that linked her ambition and tenacity to socioeconomic success?

Many low-propensity college graduates, who may be more selective on unobservable characteristics, are precisely those who utilize a college degree most effectively. Even if their counterfactual is one in which they are exceptionally motivated, this is not to say that they would be able to transcend their disadvantaged backgrounds and translate their unique drive into beneficial life conditions without the values and rights conferred by a college degree. Being a more selective population does not bias our estimated impact of college completion if it is difficult to translate those qualities to life outcomes in the absence of a college degree—that is, if they do not strongly impact outcomes for these individuals in the absence of completing college. Many jobs require a college degree, and tenacity is unlikely to overcome that barrier. Employers and other networks value educational credentials. And individuals themselves may perceive their abilities and opportunities differently without a college degree.

College can be transformative for students whose early life trajectory gave them low odds of completing a degree.[9] The unfamiliar setting encountered by students who are unlikely to complete college, like Chantelle, can disrupt their life trajectory. As Andrew Delbanco writes, "It is often students of lesser means for whom college means the most—not just in the measurable sense of improving their economic competitiveness, but in the intellectual enlargement it makes possible." He continues:

> If I were pressed to say what my main conclusion has been from the many campus gatherings I've attended over the past few years . . . it's that college matters most to those who do not take it for granted. . . . Those of us who were privileged to know from childhood that college was a scheduled stop along the way to adulthood have a great deal to learn from those who struggle to get to college, stay in college, and take from college something commensurate to the effort they put in. In the matter of making college accessible to students below the sector of privilege, no serious person can doubt that we should be doing much better.[10]

College becomes a site to access resources these students lacked in childhood and adolescence. Increased capability and confidence can be particularly salient among those who acquired limited social and cultural capital during their youth. For those whose childhood was resource-rich, a college degree has less additive value. The incremental gain of a scarce resource is greater for those with fewer resources. Analyses by the propensity to complete college demonstrate this pattern of social inequality and encourage a critical sociopolitical perspective. The distribution of scarce educational resources is such that resources are often unlikely to be received by those who gain the most.

Is Negative Selection a General Pattern?

Negative selection is an important process of social stratification. In chapter 2, I described various studies suggesting that negative selection underlies the benefits of college attendance and completion and in selective college attendance. But there is also evidence suggesting that negative selection is at work in the distribution of other scarce educational resources; in other words, those unlikely to receive resources are often the most significantly impacted. In the context of primary and secondary schooling, research suggests that the resources of affluent schools substantially benefit poor children (who are the least likely to receive these resources) and offer few benefits to wealthy children (who are the most likely to receive these resources). Jonathan Kozol contends in his classic work that cities should allocate more resources to poor schools than wealthy schools because students who attend poor schools will benefit more from them.[11] Likewise, the education scholar Norton Grubb shows that the effects of smaller classes, which reflect resource allocation, are larger for the students who are the least likely to be assigned to them, such as poor and minority children.[12]

In other recent work, the sociologists Emily Rauscher and Yifen Shen argue that school spending has the largest return in counties with low prior investment, which tend to be counties with a high percentage of Black students.[13] In other words, schools and student populations that benefit most from additional spending tend to be the more-disadvantaged schools unlikely to receive higher spending allotments. Moreover, Stephen Morgan finds that private Catholic school effects are strongest among low-SES and disproportionately Black or Hispanic students, who are unlikely to attend private schools.[14] Morgan offers several possible explanations for the pattern: for example, disadvantaged students may utilize the opportunity more than more-advantaged students do, or these students may have poor public schooling alternatives. Scholars have also shown that the benefits of Head Start are greatest for the most-disadvantaged children, who would otherwise have stayed at home, relative to children who otherwise would have attended a state-funded day-care center.[15] These findings suggest that those who have few academic enrichment options benefit most. Additionally, research suggests that cultural resources are more consequential for the educational attainment of low-SES children (who lack access to such resources) than for high-SES children.[16] For example, the sociologists Mads Meier Jaeger and Kristian Karlson show that the "return to cultural capital is asymmetric in the sense of being higher for low-SES children (who tend to occupy schooling environments with little cultural capital) than for high-SES children (who tend to occupy schooling environments with high levels of cultural capital)."[17]

Studies also suggest that secondary school resources have stronger effects on more-disadvantaged than advantaged students, indicating a pattern of negative selection.[18] Summarizing this research, Michael Hout contends that research on secondary school effects shows a pattern that closely resembles negative selection.[19] For example, Rauscher finds that school revenue increases achievement among low-SES students but not high-SES students.[20] She hypothesizes that while higher-SES students may receive more academic input at home, lower-SES students depend more critically on school facilities. Her findings are also consistent with work suggesting that there are large benefits of school resources for disadvantaged students and students who attend school in poor or low-income districts—those least likely to receive those resources.[21] Policy researchers find that rigorous course-taking increases high school graduation more among students who attend a high-poverty school, where they have less access to rigorous courses, than among those who attend a more affluent school.[22]

Research also suggests patterns of negative selection across educational settings. The economist Joshua Angrist and his colleagues show that disadvantaged and underserved students benefit most from a charter school program that provides educational resources.[23] Likewise, the economist Christopher Walters, in his study of charter schools with randomized admission lotteries, observes a pattern of negative selection: "Charter schools generate larger gains for disadvantaged students, but demand for charters is stronger among more advantaged students. Similarly, gains are inversely related to unobserved preferences for charters. As a result, counterfactual simulations indicate that charter expansion is likely to be most effective when accompanied by efforts to target students who are unlikely to apply."[24] Walters continues: "Charter school choices are therefore inconsistent with sorting based on comparative advantage in academic achievement."[25] Outreach efforts to low-income youth would be beneficial, as his results suggest that "efforts to target students who are otherwise unlikely to participate in school choice programs may yield high returns."[26] Charter expansion draws in students who receive larger gains.

Similarly, the economist Ying Shi finds larger effects of elite boarding school attendance on selective college admissions for the least-privileged students, including racially minoritized students, students with lower achievement, students from rural neighborhoods, and students from low-achieving sending schools.[27] Research by the economist Kirabo Jackson and his colleagues assesses the long-run effects of attending "effective high schools," or schools that improve students' test scores and socio-emotional development.[28] They find that while more-advantaged students are the most likely to attend these schools, disadvantaged students see the largest improvements in their likelihood of high school graduation, college-going, and school-based arrests. They show that underprivileged students reap these large benefits because the high-quality school environment improves their psychosocial skills. Other work in economics suggests that high school completion effects on reducing welfare receipt are larger for individuals from troubled family backgrounds and low-income neighborhoods (who are less likely to complete a degree).[29] Likewise, Heckman, Humphries, and Veramendi find that effects for "low-skill" individuals of completing high school on reducing the likelihood of incarceration are larger than for "high-skill" individuals.[30] Finally, Susan Dynarski and her colleagues use a large-scale experiment to test an early commitment of free tuition at a flagship university.[31] Studying heterogeneity along the propensity for highly selective college attendance, they find that the intervention increased applications most among students who were the least likely to attend a highly selective school. The effects were also large in the middle of the propensity distribution, but near zero at the top.[32]

Michael Hout comments on the implications of research, suggesting negative selection in education: "This is a crucial policy point. It means that throughout the history of American higher education, we have seen appreciable gains by pushing the frontier of opportunity further up the achievement ladder and further down the selection ladder."[33]

Determining Who Deserves Access to College

Implicit in much of the discussion of the distribution of educational resources is who *deserves* access. The capitalist economy and worldview are based on quid pro quo. The exchange of goods dominates our cultural frame, including our social and political views, social relationships, and self-image. Self-reliance and individualism are the foundation of meritocracy. Americans use this frame to decide who is deserving and who is undeserving. If we believe that we live in a meritocracy, those with fewer societal goods are deemed undeserving. Seymour Lipset has commented that the greater the income and wealth inequality—the greater the divide between the top and the bottom of the class distribution—"the greater the pressure on the upper strata to treat the lower as . . . innately inferior," to disparage the sharing of resources, and to treat those with less as undeserving.[34]

Despite Americans' general belief that broad access to higher education is an essential component of the nation's ideal as a land of opportunity,[35] we have seen reduced public support for higher education. A political movement in the 1970s and 1980s emphasized that higher education should be financed by the private sector and not by the government. Americans in recent years are overwhelmingly split along political party lines, with conservatives increasingly questioning not only public financing of higher education but the value of a college degree.[36] Responsibility is placed on individuals to finance their education—an expectation that, of course, disproportionately limits the access of students for whom college costs are a barrier to entry, or students who are unlikely to complete a degree. The sociologist Sara Goldrick-Rab argues that student debt punishes the purported "undeserving poor" for trying to get ahead and overcome the odds.[37]

Costs and Benefits of Expanding Access to College

College attendance rates, costs, and student debt have changed over the last several decades. A larger share of high school graduates attended college between the two NLSY cohorts, and an even larger share do so today. However, degree completion rates have remained problematically low.[38] Many students who begin college do not complete a four-year degree and do not obtain the benefits associated with degree completion. Nevertheless, as Douglas Webber estimates, a college education has an expected rate of return considerably greater than that of a high school degree, even considering the uncertainty of completing a degree.[39] This holds for the entire domain of college costs that students may face.[40] Webber argues that, assuming low to average college costs, most degrees pay for themselves by the early to mid-thirties. It takes longer to realize returns from a degree earned at a higher-cost private institution. Simulations nevertheless suggest that economic returns are large across colleges and majors for students at the twenty-fifth percentile of the measured ability distribution. According to Marcus Winters, "the best economic research suggests that the wage return for a year of college course work is more than enough to justify pursuing at least some higher education." He continues: "Those who argue that the bachelor's degree has lost its luster in the labor market are ignoring empirical evidence to the contrary."[41] Winters contends that it is not the case that too many students are going to college.

Michael Hout summarizes the literature on economic returns to college degrees:

> Even the most cautious reading of the evidence confirms that earning a college degree will pay back the cost of obtaining it several times over. In a 40-year work life, men with college degrees can expect to earn $1.1 million more than high school graduates. . . . At a public university, five years at full cost works out to $70,500. That investment will pay off 18 times over for men and ten times over for women. . . . The returns to higher education are large enough to offset even the full costs students now face. The difference between the earnings of college graduates and high school graduates has risen almost as much as tuition in the past 25 years, so the yield now is almost as large as it was when tuition was lower.[42]

The economists Philip Oreopoulos and Uros Petronijevic likewise contend that a college degree pays off for both average and marginal students.[43] While costs have increased over the last several decades, so too have long-term returns. We should expect that more recent cohorts of college graduates who overcome the odds to complete a degree will continue to see notably large returns on investment.

While the benefits outweigh the costs, college costs are far too high for individuals. Every one of the fifty states offers free public education and requires school attendance at least through age sixteen. Americans collectively determined that all young people deserve free education through the secondary years. Despite primary and secondary school shortcomings, that policy has helped equalize opportunity and prepare American youth to participate productively in society. By itself, free enterprise would not do this. But the public decided to spread some of its wealth to all citizens through education. We do not operate out of a vision of scarcity with respect to primary and secondary schooling that compels us to limit access to the deserving. We neither question who benefits from primary and secondary schooling nor see it as an individual reward-based system; we agree that benefits accrue to the whole population when we educate our citizens.[44] Yet Americans do not maintain the same vision of equal educational opportunities beyond high school. A high school education was the route to the middle class many decades ago, but a college education is the route today. And despite some factions of conservative anti-intellectualism, the public knows it. Affluent, middle-class, and low-income parents alike, in overwhelming numbers, aspire to see their children attend college. Indeed, there is remarkable agreement about the value of college when people speak of their own children. Claims that too many students are going to college always seem to apply to other people's children.[45]

College cannot be the great equalizer if low-income youth do not get in the door and are not supported once they are there. As the U.S. Department of Education recently commented, college remains the greatest driver of socioeconomic mobility in America, but we need to have more students completing a degree.[46] Differential access to college degrees is a key factor in the reproduction of inequality. It is not that underprivileged youth have limited benefits from completing college, but that they complete college in limited numbers.[47] That is, education maintains socioeconomic inequalities not primarily because advantaged students benefit more from college but because advantaged students are more likely to attend and complete college. Americans are willing to tolerate a certain level of inequality as inevitable and even fair in a competitive system. But they also hold to the notion of equal opportunity for success, and education has long been held as essential to that opportunity. For higher education to transform lives, communities, and societies, we need to find ways to increase college access and create more similar college experiences that enable higher levels of four-year degree completion.[48]

Beyond Monetizing Higher Education

Debates about college access are based mainly on the extent to which it will equip students to get good-paying jobs and play an important role in the economy. Education is something that an individual purchases, and it needs to pay off. With the increase in college costs and student debt over the last several decades, even more attention is placed on whether students are getting a return on investment.[49] As I have discussed, the evidence that attending college and completing a four-year degree generate high individual economic rewards is extensive. Yet the benefits to educating a broad population go beyond individuals to families, communities, and civic society. A narrow focus on economic rewards to college marketizes and monetizes higher education, which can lead to calls for limiting access. Critics of educational expansion argue that broad segments of the population do not need higher education because they will occupy jobs that do not require a college degree and so they should not incur the costs. Thus, some of these critics contend that college is not for everybody. If a college degree is not applied directly to vocational pursuits, in this view, it is not worth obtaining.

Of course, the assumption that more-disadvantaged college graduates will occupy less-skilled positions throughout their careers is riddled with questionable ideas about their long-term career prospects and often does not consider counterfactual life paths. But even if this assumption held true, why should less-skilled vocations not be accompanied by a four-year degree? As Michael Roth writes: "The bartender with a chemistry degree is the contemporary version of the farmer who reads the classics with pleasure and insight, or of the industrial worker who can quote Shakespeare. Where once these 'incongruities' might have been hailed as signs of a healthy republic, today they are more likely to be cited as examples of a 'wasted'—nonmonetized—education."[50] What is wrong with a more-educated plumber? What prevents us from having a society with a different distribution of occupational rewards characterized by less differentiation in income across occupational categories like plumbers and lawyers? Roth further notes that many critics of expanding higher education seem too comfortable with the inequality that characterizes society.[51]

How we portray the purpose of college influences the type of education we foster and how we progress as a society. Enabling students to acquire job-related knowledge and skills is an important mission of higher education, but it is not the only or most admirable mission. Higher education is not solely a means to an occupational end. The forceful focus on measurable economic benefits and costs risks sidestepping the less-tangible benefits of postsecondary education: a society whose citizens have skills in higher-order problem-solving, reasoning, critical thinking, and creativity is ultimately a better-functioning society.[52] Henry Giroux contends:

> While providing students with technical mastery and marketable skills is important, such an approach is too narrow in terms of the competencies

> such an effort provides and the vision it offers young people. At the end of the day, we need much more than that. . . . Reducing the purpose of schooling to the teaching of work-related skills not only opens the door to defining education as a private rather than a public good; such a view also limits the horizon of what a critical education might be by confusing training with education while offering reforms that are both narrowly instrumental and ideologically suspect.[53]

If we treat education as narrowly instrumental, we severely limit the vision we offer to the next generation.

Decades-long marketization of higher education has convinced many politicians that a university education is valuable only insofar as it is immediately profitable. One of the consequences of the monetization and marketization of higher education has been disinvestment in public education and a broad curriculum toward more narrowly instrumental vocational programs that deliver immediate economic returns. In protest, a group of scholars at colleges and universities worldwide recently declared support for funding humanities and social sciences programs: "The purpose of higher education is not to produce 'immediate returns' on investments. The purpose of higher education must always be to produce an educated, enriched society that benefits from the collective endeavor to create human knowledge. Higher education is a purpose in and of itself. Education in the full range of the arts and sciences is the cornerstone of a liberal arts education."[54] Likewise, Andrew Delbanco writes: "The best reason to care about college—who goes and what happens to them when they get there—is not what it does for society in economic terms but what it can do for individuals, in both calculable and incalculable ways. . . . We owe it to posterity to educate our citizens."[55]

The emphasis on individual costs and returns detracts from the considerable benefits that extend beyond the individual to the collectivity. We should not send the message, particularly to disadvantaged youth, that they need to bear high educational costs as individuals. We should minimize college costs because it is an investment in our society. Both liberal and conservative constituencies benefit from educating the nation's youth. College graduates receive higher wages and can pay more in taxes, contributing to the funding of important government programs and services. Because they are less likely to be unemployed or reliant on government assistance, the burden on social safety net programs is reduced.[56] And for more-disadvantaged college graduates, effects on these outcomes are notably large. By investing in the education of our youth, we foster the development of new ideas and technologies and meet the demand for skilled workers that can drive national economic growth and enable the United States to remain competitive in the global economy. Alisa Cunningham, director of the Higher Education Policy Institute, states that "it isn't just the individuals who have gone to college who benefit; the larger society also gains. . . . Each benefit leads to others, producing a cascade of benefits from postsecondary education."[57] "All gain when more are educated," writes Michael Hout.[58] We underestimate the value of higher education when we do not include the societal benefits and the spillover effects of a more-educated community.[59]

Early discourse on college benefits also long centered on values other than jobs and wages and the narrowly utilitarian purpose of developing a skilled workforce. In this vein, Roth writes: "Liberal education matters because by challenging the forces of conformity, it promises to be relevant to our professional, personal, and political lives. That relevance isn't just about landing one's first job."[60] Students engage with questions of truth, responsibility, and justice. The educated learn to question ideas and to critically consider the arguments advanced on all sides of debates, including those that some may seek to immunize from critical scrutiny.[61] By bringing to campus students with different backgrounds and viewpoints, colleges promote the consideration of diverse perspectives.[62]

Higher education increases our capacity to understand the world and contribute to it. Open-mindedness, critical thinking, and debate are essential to our democratic society. Patricia McGuire, president of Trinity Washington University, notes: "Higher education should be the great counterweight to government, the reliable steward of truth and knowledge against the corrupting tendency of politics to manipulate facts and tell outright lies as a means to gain and secure public support."[63] "If you want democracy to work," Michael Crow points out, and "if you want more participation in the democratic process, then educational attainment is really important."[64] Will Bunch comments that politicians and others who say that America cannot afford a radical change in higher education are missing the much bigger picture: "The nation can't afford the implosion of democracy that's taking place without a dramatic change in thinking. This generation and the ones that follow not only need learning to become better citizens, but they need to respect the basic notion that knowledge is the only way to stave off today's threats."[65] We cannot afford *not* to invest in higher education.

Propensity-Conscious Policies

Propensity-based analyses of college effects offer clear statements about the distribution of scarce resources and social inequality and the implications for educational policies. First, we need to clearly convey the message that unlikely college graduates receive far-reaching benefits. Students who overcome the odds and continue their schooling should consider their counterfactual pathways and what college could mean for them across multiple domains and over the life course. Messages conveying the benefits of higher education should not be limited to high-achieving students or even to low-income high-achieving students. Students with low test scores who grow up in middle-class households or students with average test scores and unstable family circumstances also need to hear the message.

Students are unlikely to attend college and complete a degree for a variety of reasons. One reason, noted by the economist Seth Zimmerman, is that students unlikely to attend college have large returns but tend to invest less in educational production while in high school, perhaps because they are "unaware of the returns to higher education."[66] Adolescents and their families considering college should understand the large and far-reaching benefits they forgo if they do not attend college and persist in completing a degree. Several scholars have noted the harm done by suggestions to unlikely college graduates that returns to college for them are low. Rishawn Biddle contends that limiting college access "wrongfully perpetuates a century-old philosophy—that poor and minority kids aren't capable of high quality, college-level education." This message "condemn[s] far too many young men and women to poverty."[67] David Autor notes that "it's genuinely destructive to give people the message that we're overinvesting in college. . . . That's not a message you would want to give to anyone you know who has kids."[68]

Educational policymakers and commentators must also embrace the message that unlikely college graduates receive far-reaching benefits. Those who question the value of college often (at least implicitly) assume that college is the right path for high-likelihood youth and the wrong path for low-likelihood youth, who are variously claimed to be either "unprepared" for college or otherwise unlikely, for a variety of reasons, to complete a four-year degree.[69] In such debates, it tends to be a foregone conclusion that "prepared" students will attend and complete college and that these are the "college-worthy" youth who benefit from obtaining a degree. The language used often suggests that unlikely graduates are undeserving of a seat on campus and that they crowd the job market with degrees and reduce the returns to college. Or the language may be shrouded in concern for unlikely college graduates' uncertain path to completing a degree, their economic plight, and possible limited returns. Regardless, the arguments reflect thinly veiled attempts to retain spots for the elite and more effectively reproduce social inequality.

Second, propensity-conscious policies should include educational outreach, recruitment, and retention efforts that target students with a low likelihood of completing a degree. Many low-propensity students do not have access to good information about college costs and financial aid.[70] Students may be aware of the potential benefits of higher education but overestimate the costs or are uninformed about financial aid.[71] As Susan Dynarski and her colleagues have argued, complex program eligibility and delivery moderates the impact of financial aid.[72] Because low-income students respond to sticker prices, they are more likely to attend college when they know up front that they will not have to pay (or will have to pay very little). Waiting for complicated forms to be filled out and processed depresses college completion among disadvantaged young people. Moreover, state-subsidized tuition combined with grants to cover living expenses for prospective and returning students with family incomes below a low threshold may reduce financial barriers for the students who stand to benefit most from college completion.[73]Alan Krueger urged selective colleges to "recognize that the most disadvantaged students benefit most from your instruction" and to set financial aid and admission policies accordingly.[74]

We also need to support the physical and psychological well-being of low-likelihood students on college campuses, confront racial and class biases, and meet students' basic needs.[75] Policies that focus exclusively on reducing disparities in college attendance but not on completion are insufficient to increase social mobility.[76] Getting more students into selective colleges with high completion rates is one strategy. Derek Thompson admonishes admissions officers of elite colleges: "Do better. America's most selective colleges can, it seems, change the lives of minorities and low-income youth. But they're still bastions of privilege. . . . In this way, elite institutions are like factories of social mobility being used as storage facilities for privilege; they have the potential to use their space to manufacture opportunity at scale, but mostly they clear out real estate for the already rich, who are going to be fine, anyway."[77]

Third, we need to reinvest in increasing educational capacity to meet demand and decrease costs.[78] Significant public support transformed American higher education in the first three-quarters of the twentieth century. However, public support for higher education has diminished both as a share of state expenditures and as a percentage of institutional revenue.[79] Although the revenue sources of American institutions are diverse, two sources are of particular importance to most public institutions: state appropriations and tuition and fees.[80] Traditionally, state appropriations have made up the bulk of institutional revenue at public institutions.[81] Over the last several economic downturns, states cut spending on higher education as state tax revenue fell. As institutions are expected to make up the difference through tuition increases, students and families have increasingly subsidized college costs.[82] They have been expected to do so precisely when they face reduced income themselves from economic downturns and more low-propensity students are seeking higher education given limited labor market prospects.

Access and success in higher education continue to be stratified.[83] Demand for college has increased alongside college costs.[84] As Sara Goldrick-Rab remarks, "We've made it less possible for people to go to college at a time they really want to go."[85] We have a divide between the elites who can afford college and those who cannot.[86] Goldrick-Rab writes: "As college became a place that was more acceptable to regular people, the government pulled back on the funding for it. It really speaks volumes. . . . That's the trend. It has to reverse. . . . Today's students are receiving less support than almost any prior generation of college students."[87] Likewise, Richard Greenwald writes: "When we shift risk onto students' shoulders, it is the more vulnerable students who struggle the most with that weight. . . . Investing in public colleges and universities is an investment in our collective future and that of the American Dream."[88] David Leonhardt writes, "It's as if our society were deliberately trying to restrict opportunities and worsen income inequality."[89]

Faced with declining state support, public colleges and universities are improving efficiencies and diversifying and expanding revenue streams. Yet these efforts do not and should not compensate for less public support. The United States has fallen short in educating enough workers to fill employer demand for educated workers.[90] Policy institutes are projecting that demand for educated workers will substantially outpace supply.[91] The 2023 Economic Report of the President, in the chapter on "Building Stronger Postsecondary Institutions," states: "The United States no longer leads the world in postsecondary attainment, and large gaps by income and race have widened over the past several decades. This has consequences both for individuals, who miss out on the personal benefits of postsecondary education, and for society, which forgoes the increased civic participation, lower reliance on public benefits, increased tax revenues, higher economic growth, and other benefits that such education brings."[92]

Disinvestment in educational capacity disproportionately impacts low-propensity students who might otherwise, for example, be induced to attend college if a college is nearby or if costs are minimized.[93] In the middle of the twentieth century, the United States invested heavily in building colleges to create opportunities for social mobility.[94] Michael Hout and Alexander Janus write: "Most of the increasing mobility from 1930 to 1975 reflected the growth and expansion of educational institutions, not an increase in openness. The subsequent slowdown in mobility from 1975 to the present reflects the stasis in educational institutions. . . . To restart the engine of upward mobility, the United States will have to build more colleges and universities, substantially expand the capacity of today's colleges and universities, or improve the productivity of those colleges and universities."[95] Likewise, Seth Zimmerman writes: "If many students are capable of making high return human capital investments but cannot because they are constrained in some way, then policies aimed at relaxing these constraints will be enough to increase the supply of college graduates. . . . Supply constraints on spots in state universities bind in the sense that they prevent students from making investments that would have high private and social returns."[96] We must encourage states to reverse a quarter-century-long trend of disinvestment and increase capacity. Making college a lot more accessible is a challenge that the government can meet.[97] People look to formal schooling to realize the America Dream,[98] and there are some indications that an increasing percentage of Americans believe that higher education should be more accessible and affordable.[99]

The economist David Deming describes the unequal distribution of educational resources: "Right now, we have made a choice, implicit or explicit, to ration access to college or college quality based on family income. . . . We can decide not to ration access to college at all. . . . We were ambitious once upon a time in this country when it came to the high school graduation rate. There is no law of nature that says that everybody in this country should get free high school education, it's accessible to everyone it's free, but for some reason, we're going to stop at college." He continues to describe the need to dramatically expand access to high-quality education. "I don't think about it as a cost, I think about it as an investment in the economic success of this country, and I think we can do it."[100] Deming also argues that reducing college tuition may cost far less than most people think. If we think more broadly of college as an antipoverty policy, we could factor in the expenditures on social assistance programs. He contends that reduced costs that attract more low-income youth to college is "unequivocally a good thing" and the "long-term payoff of these policies could be enormous."[101] David Leonhardt writes: "Creating a path to economic prosperity means opening the doors of higher education to more Americans. Millions of people with the ability to earn a bachelor's degree are not doing so, and many would benefit greatly from it."[102]

Concluding Comments

As I have shown throughout this book, many benefits, including some benefits not often considered, are larger for more-disadvantaged students than for more-advantaged students. Limiting the education of unlikely college graduates constrains their social mobility and maintains the reproduction of inequality. Greater access to college for disadvantaged groups is part of the solution to reducing intergenerational persistence and broadening prosperity.[103] Across the two cohorts I study throughout this book, more people could have escaped low-income backgrounds if more low-income youth had completed college.[104] Large gains for unlikely students should not be surprising, yet they challenge rhetoric that "college isn't for everyone." Although some people increasingly contend that higher education is overrated (at least when it comes to other people's children), the research I have described is a reminder that the country also underinvests in enrolling students in four-year colleges and making sure they graduate.

Expanding education not only broadens prosperity but also enhances our communities and strengthens our democratic society. Education should not be reserved for the wellborn and the well-off.[105] Universities have long held the ideal that higher education should extend beyond traditionally served students—that the task of modern democracy is to preserve the principle of liberal education and to extend it as far as possible to all the members of the population.[106] Educating disadvantaged students not only expands opportunities but furthers the development of a healthy democratic society, from which all benefit.[107] Yet higher education is at a crossroads, flagging both relatively and absolutely.[108] Education has historically served America well. In a commitment to educating the masses, the nation grew economically and reduced inequality. America should strive to lead the world once again in educational attainment and to reduce economic and racial inequalities. We must reimagine and enact education's equitable possibilities and invest in the educational attainment of diverse youth.[109]

Resistance to progress is common. If fewer people attend and complete college, those who complete college will have less competition. If fewer people obtain a college degree, the political voices of those who have a degree will be more powerful. College completion rates in the United States are problematically low. Those who contend that college attendance and completion have limited benefits reinforce existing inequalities and harm the lives of disadvantaged youth. These arguments are flawed because a college degree is especially beneficial for individuals who are unlikely to complete a degree. We should acknowledge the widespread benefits and collectively invest in policies that enable more students to obtain a four-year college degree.

Notes

Chapter 1: Expanding Access to Higher Education

1. Autor, Katz, and Kearney 2008; Hout 2012.
2. In 2018, the unemployment rate for twenty-five- to thirty-four-year-olds was 2.2 percent for the college-educated compared to 5.7 percent for those with only a high school diploma (Ma, Pender, and Welch 2019).
3. Oreopoulos and Salvanes 2011.
4. Ma, Pender, and Welch 2019.
5. Baum 2014; Hout 2012; Oreopoulos and Petronijevic 2013.
6. Autor 2014; Autor, Katz, and Kearney 2008; Baum, Ma, and Payea 2013; Goldin and Katz 2008; Rosenbaum, Ahearn, and Lansing 2018; see also Day and Newburger 2002. However, some recent research suggests a flattening in the college premium (for example, Ashworth and Ransom 2019).
7. Delbanco 2012; Eckel and King 2004; Hanson and Zogby 2010.
8. See, for example, Baum et al. 2009; Steinbery 2009; Wilson 2010.
9. See the discussion in Barrow and Malamud 2015; see also Leef 2014. As the 2019 College Board report states: "Media headlines highlight stories of college students saddled with debt without gainful employment" (Ma, Pender, and Welch 2019).
10. Pew Research Center 2016.
11. More than half of Americans say that colleges fail to provide students with good value for the cost. See Quadlin and Powell 2022; Pew Research Center 2011; Public Agenda 2016. Nevertheless, 86 percent of college graduates say that college was a good investment for them personally. Most state that it helped them grow intellectually, mature as a person, and prepare them for a career.
12. Critique noted in Attewell et al. 2009, 1.

13. These critiques echo the questioning in a past era of the value of secondary schooling for masses of students.
14. Blau and Duncan 1967.
15. This research was conducted with restricted access to Bureau of Labor Statistics (BLS) data. The views expressed here are those of the author and do not reflect the views of the BLS. Scholars have used NLS data in over 3,700 journal articles and over 1,200 dissertations and master's theses, predominantly in economics, sociology, education, child development, psychology, and health (Bureau of Labor Statistics 2015).
16. Bloome, Dyer, and Zhou 2018.
17. Goldin and Katz 2008.
18. Fischer and Hout 2006.
19. Goldin and Katz 2008.
20. The National Center for Education Statistics (NCES) currently reports about 4,300 degree-granting institutions, divided into about 1,600 public colleges, 1,700 private nonprofit schools, and 1,000 for-profit schools.
21. Community colleges number over 1,200 and serve nearly one-third of undergraduate students (Delbanco 2012). As an archetypal example, Clark Kerr's three-tier system of community colleges, state colleges, and research universities, beginning in the 1960s, enabled widespread access to college for a large population in the state of California. Access for underrepresented groups also increased via the founding of women's colleges and Black colleges, affirmative action, and the GI bill.
22. Bailey and Dynarski 2011.
23. Ibid.
24. McFarland 2017.
25. Baum, Kurose, and McPherson 2013.
26. Brewer and Ehrenberg 1996; Persell, Catsambis, and Cookson 1992. Some institutions are engines of social mobility. For example, schools in the University of California (UC) and City University of New York systems are doing significantly better than other public four-year colleges in enrolling and graduating students from low-income backgrounds. According to data released by the Equal Opportunity Project, almost 40 percent of undergraduate students at UCLA are Pell grant recipients, and their completion rate is close to 90 percent. For-profit institutions have the lowest completion rates. Pell Grant recipients make up almost two-thirds of attendees at these institutions, and only 20 percent of full-time Pell students graduate within six years. Tressie McMillam Cottom (2017) argues that for-profit colleges are distinct from not-for-profit colleges in that they depend on sustained socioeconomic inequalities. See also Whistle and Hiler 2018; Harris 2018.

27. Hamilton and Nielsen 2021.
28. Ibid.
29. Carlson 2016.
30. Goldin and Katz 2008.
31. We are also seeing less educational mobility in the United States in recent decades. Until about 1970, fewer than 10 percent of individuals had completed less schooling than their parents; by the 1990s, that figure had increased to more than 20 percent (Hout and Janus 2011).
32. Goldin and Katz 2008.
33. Goldrick-Rab 2016; Hout 2009; Hout and Janus 2011; Kane 2004; Rosenbaum, Ahearn, and Lansing 2018; Voss, Hout, and George 2022.
34. Voss, Hout, and George 2022.
35. Bailey and Dynarski 2011.
36. Blinkley 2023; Jimenez 2023.
37. Goldin and Katz 2008; U.S. Department of Education 2018.
38. Hout 2009.
39. Hout and Janus 2011, 165.
40. Barrow, Brock, and Rouse 2013.
41. For example, the state covered 70 percent of instructional costs at the University of Michigan in the 1960s and less than 10 percent of instructional costs in the 1990s. Since the early 2000s, state support for higher education in Michigan has continued to decline (Wermund 2017).
42. U.S. Department of Education 2018. Tuition at private universities also increased, by about 130 percent. Moreover, for-profit institutions have entered the higher education marketplace. Deregulation of accreditation standards in the mid-2000s made students attending for-profit schools eligible for federally guaranteed student loans. Completion rates are low at these institutions, and their students carry high levels of debt.
43. However, in recent years the share of Americans who believe that the government should be responsible for higher education funding increased to about one-third, and it increased to one-half for those who believe that the government should be partly responsible (Russell Sage Foundation 2018).
44. Baum, Kurose, and McPherson 2013. Nevertheless, laments over the increasing costs of higher education were voiced as far back as the nineteenth century (Ripley 2018).
45. Eckel and King 2004.
46. Student debt in the United States is over $1 trillion. Millions of young adults are in default. Recent evidence suggests that parents are also increasing their debt to help pay for education for their children (Bernard and Russell 2018).

47. Baum, Kurose, and McPherson 2013.

48. Steinbaum 2017.

49. See Ripley 2018.

50. See the Harvard Kennedy School's "5 Big Ideas in Inequality Series: Videos," https://inequality.hks.harvard.edu/5-big-ideas-inequality-series-2020-2021.

51. See National Center for Education Statistics, Institute of Education Sciences, "Undergraduate Enrollment," https://nces.ed.gov/programs/coe/indicator/cha/undergrad-enrollment (last updated May 2022); see also Hamilton and Nielsen 2021. Disinvestment has also happened alongside bans on affirmative action to increase racial diversity on college campuses.

52. Hamilton and Nielsen 2021.

53. Baum, Kurose, and McPherson 2013, 20.

54. Greenwald 2018.

55. Delbanco 2012; Eckel and King 2004.

56. Karabel 2006. Jewish representation in Ivy league schools is an example.

57. Autor 2014; Autor, Katz, and Kearney 2008; Baum, Ma, and Payea 2013; Rosenbaum, Ahearn, and Lansing 2018; see also Day and Newburger 2002.

58. Autor, Goldin, and Katz 2020; see also James 2012.

59. Oreopoulos and Petronijevic 2013.

60. Bloome, Dyer, and Zhou 2018; Oreopoulos and Petronijevic 2013; Schneider 2018.

61. Median annual earnings in 2022 among millennials ages twenty-five to thirty-two were $45,500 for those with a college degree and $28,000 for those with a high school degree.

62. Autor, Katz, and Kearney 2008.

63. Dickson and Harmon 2011.

64. See Tamborini, Kim, and Sakamoto (2015) for a detailed analysis of lifetime earnings returns. See also U.S. Department of Education 2018.

65. In 2018, the unemployment rate for twenty-five- to thirty-four-year-olds was 2.2 percent for the college-educated compared to 5.7 percent with a high school degree (Ma, Pender, and Welch 2019; Caumont 2014).

66. Hout 2012.

67. Ma, Pender, and Welsh 2019; Caumont 2014.

68. Pew Research Center 2014; see also Baum 2014.

69. See Ma, Pender, and Welch 2019. Moreover, the overwhelming majority of college graduates state that their investment in college paid off (Pew Research Center 2014).

70. See Harvard Kennedy School, "5 Big Ideas in Inequality Series: Videos."

71. Baum et al. 2009.

72. Becker 1964; Blau and Duncan 1967; Mincer 1974.

73. Hout 2012, 379.

74. For example, Collins 1979/2019.

75. Collins also contends in a new preface to *The Credential Society* (2019) that education expands based on the ideology that it will produce more equality of opportunity, but that social class mobility has been stagnant. As Deidre Bloome, Shauna Dyer, and Xiang Zhou (2018) discuss, however, educational expansion needs to reach people who are unlikely to attend college to increase social mobility. If unlikely college graduates have high returns, then expanding access to this group should increase social mobility.

76. Hout 2012, 391.

77. Some scholars contend that in addition to skill requirements, structural and institutional mechanisms lead to college graduates' economic advantage. Some recent work contends that college graduates increasingly hold jobs that require a lower level of cognitive skills, peripheral to the knowledge economy, than positions held by prior cohorts of college graduates (see, for example, Horowitz 2018). Some also suggest that a college degree marks a status distinction in the workplace, one that places college graduates in advantageous positions in the labor market that are associated with better career prospects (Granovetter and Tilly 1988; Tilly 1999). Others argue that a college degree overcomes institutional barriers surrounding high-status occupations and promotions within firms (Tomaskovic-Devey et al. 2009; Weeden 2002; Weeden and Grusky 2012). Yet whether skills or social closure serve as the primary mechanism, college is associated with significant economic rewards.

78. Hout 2012, 391.

79. A recent study of Google employees found that more than STEM expertise and coding skills, Google's top employees had communication, empathy, and critical thinking skills (Davidson 2017).

80. Autor 2010, 2014.

81. Deming 2017.

82. Edsall 2021.

83. Baum, Kurose, and McPherson 2013.

84. Blair and Deming 2020, 363, 365.

85. Carnevale and Rose 2011.

86. U.S. Department of Education 2018. Most declining occupations are those filled by workers with less than a college degree (Song et al. 2023).

87. Baum 2014; Carnevale, Rose, and Cheah 2013; Oreopoulos and Petronijevic 2013.

88. Hufford 2019.
89. Investments in automation also reduce the number of employees needed. Laid-off manufacturing workers with no more than a high school degree see few comparable reemployment opportunities.
90. Baum 2014.
91. U.S. Department of Education 2018.
92. Torche and Johnson 2019; see also Pew Research Center 2014.
93. Duncan and Murnane 2011a.
94. Andrew Delbanco (2012) states that a "college degree long ago supplanted the high school diploma as the minimum qualification for entry into the skilled labor market" (25).
95. Kalleberg and Howell 2019.
96. Howell and Kalleberg 2019.
97. DeLuca, Clampet-Lundquist, and Edin 2016.
98. Torche and Johnson 2019, 21.
99. Horrigan 2015.
100. I construct a measure of elite college attendance using private geocode data from the NLSY. I match institutions to the 1980 *Barron's Profiles of American Colleges* and define the top two Barron's selectivity categories as "elite."
101. While I do not consider the effects of two-year college completion, some students who complete a two-year degree go on to complete a four-year degree.
102. A large literature also attends to the relationship between education and health (Zajacova and Lawrence 2018). I do not assess health outcomes in this book, but it is another important dimension that should be considered in evaluating the far-reaching benefits of completing college.

Chapter 2: Diverse Benefits for Diverse Graduates

1. "Human capital" refers to the stock of competencies, knowledge, and attributes, often gained through education, training, and experience, embodied in the performance of labor to produce economic value.
2. Barrow and Malamud 2015.
3. Kurlander and Hibel 2018.
4. Boudon 2003.
5. Bourdieu 1977; Bowles and Gintis 1976; Brand and Xie 2010; Coleman 1988; MacLeod 1989; Sewell, Haller, and Ohlendorf 1970.

6. Becker 1964.
7. The actual return on human capital nevertheless varies around the expected return because of uncertainty about several factors, including mortality and morbidity, ability, and unanticipated events. Pedro Carneiro, Karsen Hansen, and James Heckman (2003) contend that while, ex-ante, there is considerable uncertainty surrounding the return to schooling, ex post, very few college graduates regret their college experience.
8. Roy 1951. For example, plumbers (who are primarily high school–educated) may have a limited capacity to perform well as highly schooled lawyers. Similarly, lawyers may not do as good a job being a plumber as actual plumbers.
9. Willis and Rosen 1979.
10. Carneiro, Heckman, and Vytlacil 2010, 2–3. They also contend that Charles Murray's claim that too many students go to college appears correct (Carneiro, Heckman, and Vytlacil 2011, 2755).
11. Bourdieu 1977.
12. We can nevertheless consider their decisions to be rational. That privileged youth attend college in such high numbers reflects upper-class families' strong motivation to prevent their children from becoming downwardly mobile and recognition that education is a crucial component to their continued success.
13. Oreopoulos and Salvanes 2011.
14. Breen and Goldthorpe 1997; DiPrete and Engelhardt 2004. Heckman and his colleagues have also noted the importance of psychic costs in explaining why many students do not continue their schooling "even though it is financially rewarding to do so" (Heckman, Stixrud, and Urzua 2006, 28). Elizabeth Bruch, Fred Feinberg, and Kee Yeun Lee (2016) argue that decision-makers have limited time for learning about choice alternatives and that a great deal of behavior is habitual, automatic, or governed by simple rules or heuristics. Moreover, psychologists argue that individuals are unskilled at drawing accurate causal judgments of expected returns (Roese 1997). Rather than at the decision-making stage, individuals may activate counterfactuals and consider potential outcomes only ex post facto, long after their college-going years.
15. Brand and Xie 2010.
16. DiPrete and Engelhardt 2004; Kahneman and Tversky 1979, 1984; Tversky and Kahneman 1986, 1992.
17. Oreopoulos and Petronijevic 2013. The financial aid system is exceedingly complex and may itself deter low-income youth from pursuing higher education.
18. Breen and Goldthorpe 1997.
19. Goldthorpe and Jackson 2008, 109; see also Breen and Goldthorpe 1997.

20. Ovink 2017.

21. Brand and Xie 2010.

22. Heckman 1998, 107.

23. See also Arcidiacono, Bayer, and Hizmo 2010; Bjerk 2007; Johnson and Neal 1998; Lang and Manove 2011. Findings across European nations are also consistent with a negative selection pattern (see, for example, Bernardi and Ballarino 2016; Breen and Jonsson 2007; Breen and Luijkx 2007; Tolsma and Wolbers 2014; Vallet 2004). A recent study finds a pattern of negative selection in medieval China (Wen, Wang, and Hout 2023). Andrea Forster, Herman van de Werfhorst, and Thomas Leopold (2021), however, argue that returns to college are homogenous rather than heterogeneous in the United States and the Netherlands, with some leaning toward positive selection for men and negative selection for women in the United States on one selectivity dimension. However, they fit a linear model for returns to schooling. A nonlinear heterogeneity pattern could be interpreted as homogeneity with a linearity assumption.

24. Henderson, Polachek, and Wang 2011, 1212.

25. Backes, Holzer, and Velez 2014, 1.

26. Eide and Showalter 1999, 266.

27. Attewell and Lavin 2007; Attewell et al. 2009; Cheng et al. 2019; Sakamoto, Tamborini, and Kim 2018.

28. Giani, Attewell, and Walling 2020.

29. Moreover, some recent work in Germany finds no earnings returns for academic track schools relative to non-academic track schools for disadvantaged students and large earnings returns for advantaged students. Academic track placement, however, improved students' measured cognitive abilities across backgrounds (Zühlke, Kugler, and Ruberg 2022).

30. Barrow and Malamud 2015; Card 2001; for a review, see Hout 2012.

31. Card 1995, 2001. The economist Zvi Griliches (1977) noted in the 1970s that estimates of the return to schooling for students on the margin of school continuation exceeded estimates for average college-goers. In the 1990s and 2000s, Card found that estimates of economic returns to college attendance for more-disadvantaged students affected by college accessibility exceeded those for average college-goers by about 30 percent (see also Ashenfelter and Rouse 1998; Deaton 2010).

32. Card 1999, abstract.

33. Hout 2012, 383, abstract. The claim is based on findings that instrumental variable estimates in many leading studies are uniformly larger than ordinary least squares regression estimates.

34. Hout 2012, 384.

35. Goldin and Katz 2008.

36. Oreopoulos and Petronijevic 2013; Ost, Pan, and Webber 2018.
37. The approach compares individuals just above and individuals just below the admission threshold and assumes that they have very similar observed and unobserved characteristics. They then use this discontinuity as the instrumental variable.
38. Zimmerman 2014, 742.
39. Kejriwal, Li, and Totty 2020.
40. Barrow and Malamud 2015, 538. Still, some studies find larger returns for more advantaged college-goers. Notably, however, all of these studies focus on wages.
41. Leonhardt 2015.
42. Bialik 2011.
43. Cheng et al. 2021.
44. Bartik and Hershbein 2018a.
45. Cheng et al. 2021.
46. Research finds that large returns are associated with graduate degrees (Altonji and Zhong 2021).
47. Brand and Halaby 2006; see also Attewell and Lavin 2007.
48. Dale and Krueger 2011, 5.
49. Conwell and Quadlin 2021.
50. Black, Denning, and Rothstein 2020; Bowen and Bok 1998.
51. See the discussion in Carey 2019.
52. Thompson 2018; see also Black, Denning, and Rothstein 2020; Small and Winship 2007.
53. Hout 1988, 1391.
54. Ibid.
55. Precollege schooling also serves an equalizing role. For example, Douglas Downey, Paul von Hippel, and Beckett Broh (2004), in showing that socioeconomic gaps in reading and math skills grow primarily in the summer months rather than during the school year, contend that schools serve as equalizers.
56. Eckel and King 2004.
57. Chetty et al. 2017; Hauser and Logan 1992; Hout 1984, 1988, 2018; Pfeffer and Hertel 2015; Torche 2011. In countries besides the United States, the finding has been replicated in France, Sweden, Germany, and Britain by Richard Breen and his colleagues (Breen 2010; Breen and Jonsson 2007; Breen and Luijkx 2007), by John Goldthorpe and Michelle Jackson (Goldthorpe 2007b; Goldthorpe and Jackson 2008), and by Julie Falcon and Pierre Bataille (2018). For example, Goldthorpe and Jackson (2008)

find little difference in the chance of entering the salariat regardless of social origins among those with higher education, while gaining access differed markedly for those with less education in Britain in the 1970s and 1990s.

58. Pfeffer and Hertel 2015.

59. Torche (2011) finds some reemergence among the subset of the population who obtain degrees beyond a bachelor's degree, but finds little association between parents' education and adult children's earnings among PhD holders (Torche 2018).

60. Torche 2011, 764.

61. Hout 2018. See also Webber (2018), who emphasizes the large difference in returns between individuals who attend college and do not complete a degree and those who complete their degree.

62. Chetty et al. 2017.

63. Bowen, Chingos, and McPherson 2009.

64. Quoted in Flaherty 2018.

65. See Harvard Kennedy School, "5 Big Ideas in Inequality Series" Videos,"https://inequality.hks.harvard.edu/5-big-ideas-inequality-series-2020-2021.

66. Bloome, Dyer, and Zhou 2018.

67. See also Eide and Showalter 1999.

68. Bartik and Hershbein 2018a; Bloome, Dyer, and Zhou 2018; Dale and Krueger 2011; Goldthorpe and Jackson 2008; Karlson 2019; Torche 2011.

69. Goldthorpe and Jackson 2008, 105; see also Goldthorpe 2007b, vol. 2, chap. 7.

70. Jack 2019a, 29.

71. Ibid., 44–45, 47.

72. Webber 2019.

73. Wright 1945. Torche (2011) and Breen and Jonsson (2007) hypothesize that another possible explanation for equalization is that college graduates sort to segments of the labor market in which meritocratic selection is more prevalent and origin characteristics matter less than in the labor market for less-educated workers. Higher educational qualifications act as a signal for employers that overshadows social network effects.

74. Dale and Krueger 2011, 24. A Gallup study showed that employee engagement was equalized by race and ethnicity and by parents' education among college graduates. See Gallup 2014.

75. Lang and Manove 2011; Spence 1973; Weiss 1995; Zhou and Pan 2021. Of course, college does not eliminate labor market racial discrimination (see, for example, Gaddis 2015).

76. See discussion in Baum et al. 2009.

77. The Population Reference Bureau, reporting on the Brand and Xie (2010) findings, concludes that the "college bonus" for disadvantaged students "stemmed in part from the deteriorating income and opportunities for less-educated workers." See Kent 2010.

78. Bloome, Dyer, and Zhou 2018.

79. Mitnik, Cumberworth, and Grusky 2016; Rivera 2015; Stuber 2011.

80. Witteveen and Attewell 2017, 2020; Zhou 2019.

81. Karlson 2019.

82. Chetty et al. 2017; Posselt and Grodsky 2017. Corporate recruiters for finance, consulting, and high-tech jobs on elite college campuses select elite college students into high-status occupations (Binder, Davis, and Bloom 2016).

83. Ma, Pender, and Welch 2019.

84. Witteveen and Attewell 2020; Lubrano 2019; see also Armstrong and Hamilton 2013.

85. Rivera 2015.

86. Pager 2003; see also *New York Times* 2017. Research likewise suggests considerable and growing differences in the wage gap between Black and White college graduates (see Carnevale, Rose, and Cheah 2013). Michael Gaddis (2015) also shows that Black job candidates with an elite college degree only do as well as White candidates with a less selective degree. Moreover, employers offer Black job candidates with lower wages and status than what they offer White candidates.

87. Mare 1980; see also a discussion of Mare's work in Hout, forthcoming.

88. Brand and Xie 2010, 294. Indeed, one of the main motivations to study results by the propensity for college is to uncover sources of probable unobserved selection into college. The *New York Times* blog "Freakonomics: The Hidden Side of Everything" (Levitt 2010) reported on Brand and Xie (2010): "A new study finds that the students who are least likely to go to college (based on family background, abilities, and friend group) are the ones with the most to gain from a degree. . . . The authors believe that the tough labor market faced by non-college educated, disadvantaged students partly explains the results, but they point to an additional factor: economic motivation."

89. DeLuca, Clampet-Lundquist, and Edin 2016. More-advantaged students who pursue advanced degrees are more likely to say that college is a time for personal and intellectual growth and less likely to see it as a time for skill development (Pew Research Center 2016).

90. Roksa 2011; Settersten and Ray 2010.

91. Fisher 1930.

92. Cheng et al. 2021; Grossman 2006; Johnson, Blum, and Cheng 2014; Koenig, Swanson, and Harter 1980; Lawrance 1991; Nurmi 1991; O'Rand and Ellis 1974; Guthrie, Butler, and Ward 2009. Having faced significant disruption in their lives and limited control over the events that befall them, they anticipate future shocks that may derail their educational attainment. Some disadvantaged youth thus opt for shorter and more flexible educational programs (DeLuca et al. 2021).
93. Brand and Xie 2010; Goyette and Mullen 2006; Ma 2009; Quadlin 2017.
94. Altonji and Zhong 2021.
95. Grasgreen 2014; see also Cheng 2017.
96. Grubb and Lazerson 2004.
97. Delbanco 2012, 7.
98. Jefferson 2017.
99. Roth 2013.
100. Du Bois 1903/2014, 14–15.
101. Ibid., 47.
102. See Roth 2014.
103. Dewey 1916.
104. Mill 1867.
105. Roth 2014, 111. Many educators, however, also saw schooling as a means to "Americanize" immigrant youth in the twentieth century.
106. Rawlings 2015. See also Rose (2023) for a discussion of the transformative quality of education and learning.
107. Roth 2014, 101. The emphasis on training nontraditional students with allegedly limited economic prospects to occupy "appropriate" economic roles has long roots. In the early 1900s, many organizations developed two-track vocational and liberal learning systems. Those individuals deemed ill suited for broader forms of learning would be sorted into training to perform the tasks in demand by industry.
108. Roth 2014, 2.
109. Attewell et al. 2009.
110. Dickson and Harmon 2011, 1119; Wolfe and Haveman 1984.
111. Heckman, Humphries, and Veramendi 2018, 303.
112. Goldin and Katz 2008.
113. Brand 2010. Research on the health benefits of education support a resource substitution theory that people whose parents had low levels of education are more dependent on their own educational attainment for good health than are people from more-advantaged backgrounds (Ross and Mirowsky 2011).

114. Giroux 2002.
115. Carter 2018, 24.
116. Roth 2014, 230.
117. Jefferson and Adams quoted in Cappon 1971, 480.
118. Du Bois 1903/2014, 14–15.
119. Alexander 2019.
120. Strauss 2011.
121. Rose 2010.
122. Ibid.
123. Du Bois 1903/2014, 14–15.
124. Roth 2014, 78.

Chapter 3: College Counterfactuals and Estimating Effects

1. Holland 1986.
2. Lewis 1973/2001, 161.
3. John Stuart Mill's (1843) definition of causation led cigarette lobbyists to argue that unless cigarette smoking causes lung cancer in every case, cigarettes are not a cause of lung cancer (Rubin 2017).
4. Musk 2018.
5. This model is also called the Rubin Causal Model, a term coined by Holland (1986). The framework builds on earlier work by the statisticians Jerzy Neyman (1923) and Ronald A. Fisher (1925). Although formal notation for potential outcomes first appears in Neyman's 1920s work on agricultural experiments, the notation was not used for causal inference more generally until Rubin's work in the 1970s. There is some early discussion of potential outcomes in economic theory, such as in the work of Trygve Haavelmo (1943) and Andrew Roy (1951).
6. Imbens 2008, 5.
7. Abadie and Cattaneo 2018.
8. Imbens 2008. Citations of Rubin's work exceed hundreds of thousands, but even this is an understatement of its impact. The potential outcome approach became so widely accepted that citation was no longer necessary.
9. Pearl, Glymour, and Jewell 2016. Andrew Gelman and Aki Vehtari (2020) remarked recently that the counterfactual model of causal inference is one of the most important statistical ideas of the past fifty years.
10. Bind and Rubin 2019.
11. Baum et al. 2009; Steinbery 2009.

12. See *Chicago Ideas Week* 2011.
13. Murray 2008.
14. Fischer et al. 1996; Hauser and Huang 1997.
15. Sander and Taylor 2012.
16. Vedder 2018.
17. Ibid.
18. Raj Chetty and his colleagues (2017) report that low-income, first-generation students' college GPA, higher order learning, and civic engagement exceed those of their more-advantaged peers (Flaherty 2018).
19. Will 2014.
20. Habibi 2015.
21. Caplan 2018a, 226, 278.
22. Caplan 2018b. See also the response by Sean Illing (2008). Richard Arum and Josipa Roksa (2011) also lament that undergraduate learning quality is startlingly low, but they suggest solutions that increase academic rigor on college campuses. Nevertheless, in a 2014 Pew Research report, "The Rising Cost of Not Going to College," the authors report that new college graduates are significantly more likely than high school graduates to say that their education has been "very useful" in preparing them for work and that they have acquired the necessary education and training to advance in their careers.
23. A *Bloomberg* article (Smith 2017) describes Caplan's arguments against college as "deeply flawed," citing evidence suggesting large gains to students' cognitive, quantitative, and verbal skills, as well as their personal development.
24. Picchi 2016.
25. See also *PBS News Hour* 2016.
26. Shell 2018.
27. Bartik and Hershbein 2018a.
28. Bartik and Hershbein 2018b.
29. Wilson and Rodgers 2016; see also *New York Times* 2017.
30. See chapter 2 for evidence on college degree returns by race.
31. Armstrong and Hamilton 2015, 251–52.
32. Jack 2019a.
33. See Arum et al. 2018.
34. For example, Bourdieu 1984.
35. Quintana 2019.
36. Small and Winship 2007, abstract.

37. Darity et al. 2018; Hamilton et al. 2015.

38. The difference in log net worth is 3.2 for Blacks and 0.8 for Whites—a substantial gain for both Blacks and Whites, but a significantly larger gain for Blacks (Killewald, Pfeffer, and Schachner 2017).

39. Zeglen 2019.

40. Vedder 2018.

41. Former Secretary of Education Betsy DeVos made related statements in her 2018 U.S. Department of Education report.

42. Chetty et al. 2017; Hout 1988; Karlson 2019; Pfeffer and Hertel 2015; Torche 2011.

43. Carnevale, Rose, and Cheah 2013; Gregg et al. 2017; Laurison and Freidman 2016; Witteveen and Attewell 2017.

44. Ultimately, we will need to do more to approximate potential outcomes and identify college effects, as detailed in the next sections.

45. Holland 1986.

46. These calculations are based on 2014 wages for NSLY79 respondents.

47. As another example from the NLSY79 data, I observe high school graduates earning $17 per hour and college graduates $36 per hour, suggesting a more than 100 percent economic advantage. After adjusting for selection into college, studies, including this one, suggest that college is associated with about 40 percent higher wages on average; this is a substantial payoff, but considerably less than 100 percent (see also Angrist and Pischke 2009).

48. Brand, Zhou, and Xie 2023.

49. William Cochran (1965, 234) defined an observational study as an empirical investigation in which the "objective is to elucidate cause-and-effect relationships . . . [in settings in which] it is not feasible to use controlled experimentation."

50. Statisticians regularly recite the mantras that "correlation does not imply causation" and that there is "no causation without manipulation." Nevertheless, as the economists Joshua Angrist and Jörn-Steffen Pischke (2009, 113) write, "correlation can sometimes provide pretty good evidence of a causal relation, even when the variable of interest has not been manipulated by a researcher or experimenter."

51. Imbens 2008; Imbens and Woolridge 2009.

52. College and non-college graduates can differ by unobserved characteristics if those characteristics affect only whether they complete college and if they do not directly affect the outcome.

53. Also called ignorability, or selection on observables, because we can adjust only for the observed individual characteristics.

54. Pearl 2009.

55. Confounding might alternatively take a form in which the unobserved confounder does not directly affect college completion and its effect operates through the precollege characteristics. In this scenario, once we condition on those factors, *U* is no longer a confounder (Abadie and Cattaneo 2018). We block the path from *U* to college completion.

56. Stuart 2010.

57. Rubin 2006.

58. Heckman and Navarro-Lozano 2003, 3.

59. For example, Freedman and Hawley 1949; Greenwood 1945.

60. For example, Berk and Newton 1985; Smith 1997.

61. For example, Brand and Halaby 2006; DiPrete and Engelhardt 2004; Harding 2003.

62. Huber 2021; Stuart 2010.

63. Abadie and Imbens 2016; Heckman and Navarro-Lozano 2003.

64. One approach advocated by Stefano Iacus, Gary King, and Giuseppe Porro (2012) is to use coarsened exact matching: matching on coarse categories of precollege variables, like parental income categories.

65. Rosenbaum and Rubin 1983, 1984.

66. Individuals with dissimilar characteristics may have similar values for their propensity scores. For example, in the NLSY79 data, I observe a matched college and non-college graduate in which both have a propensity score of 0.26. The parents of these individuals had the same level of education and were in the same income category, and both individuals were White. But one individual had high test scores and low self-esteem, while the matched counterpart had average test scores and average self-esteem.

67. I estimate the propensity for college based on the observed characteristics of respondents. The true propensity for college is a latent construct. Alberto Abadie and Guido Imbens (2016) show that matching on the estimated propensity score is more efficient than matching on the true propensity score in large samples. I use adjustments to the large sample variance of matching estimators that correct for first-step estimation of the propensity score. Inverse probability weighting methods are also based on the propensity score and offer an alternative to matching estimators (Abadie and Cattaneo 2019). See the methodological appendix for more details on estimating propensity scores.

68. Stuart 2010, 6. Matching and subclassification approaches rely only on selecting individuals with similar propensity score values. They are less subject to misspecification of the propensity score model than regression adjustment and weighting procedures (Lee, Lessler, and Stuart 2010).

69. Matching is much simpler to explain than adjusting for covariates in standard regression models. Referencing dozens of covariates complicates the exposition of our estimation strategy.

70. In conventional regression analyses, social scientists typically consider modeling the outcome process rather than the treatment selection process.

71. Morgan and Harding 2006, 51.

72. Nevertheless, matching methods have several attractive properties relative to regression methods (Imbens 2015). There is a debate about whether analysts should use propensity scores for matching, with King and Nielsen (2019) arguing against it and others, such as Imbens (2015), arguing for it. Some of King and Nielsen's arguments may apply to one-to-one matching without replacement, a specific form of propensity score matching, while conceding that other matching algorithms perform better.

73. I match with replacement, meaning that I return the non-college graduate to the pool of potential matches after a match. With one nearest neighbor, the non-college graduate gets a weight of 1. With four nearest-neighbors, I use a weight of one-quarter. Matching more non-college graduates per college graduate results in lower variance of the college effect estimate. However, it increases the possible bias as the likelihood of suboptimal matches increases.

74. Imbens and Rubin 2015.

75. The approach excludes terms that would harm precision. The propensity scores generated from the iterative approach correlate highly with those derived from machine learning algorithms.

76. Pearl 2010. We also want to be careful not to include variables that do not directly affect the treatment or the outcome, except insofar as they affect those variables through some other unobserved factors (Caliendo and Kopeinig 2008).

77. Suppose that we are interested in the effect of college completion on unemployment. We know that marital status is also associated with college completion and with unemployment. A researcher may think that marital status should be adjusted for. If the path was {college → marital status → unemployment}, where marital status affected unemployment rather than the reverse, we should not control for marital status. Marital status is along the path we want to estimate, but it does not open a backdoor path. It shuts down the path that we want to estimate. It may appear as if college does not affect unemployment when it does—it just does so via marital status. Suppose instead that unemployment affects marital status. Marital status is a collider variable. The path {college → marital status ← unemployment} has no backdoor path to unemployment because the arrows collide at marital status. Controlling for marital status will open a backdoor. When we condition on a collider variable, we create a correlation between college and unemployment that is not due to the path that we are interested in {college → unemployment} (Elwert and Winship 2014; Pearl 2009). The relationship between college and unemployment may exist only for subgroups of married and single individuals.

78. The estimated college effects throughout my analyses are based on a sample of high school graduates (or GED recipients). To the extent that completing a high school degree improves life outcomes, my estimates are lower than those that would be obtained had I retained individuals who did not complete a high school degree. However, there would be more heterogeneity in the educational credentials of the non-college graduate population.

79. For example, in the NLSY79, I omit college graduates with values higher than the highest estimated propensity score among the non-college graduates (0.923) and non-college graduates with values lower than the lowest propensity score among the college graduates (0.003), where the propensity score ranges from 0 to 1. I also omit college attendees with values higher than the highest estimated propensity score among the non–college attendees (0.976) and non–college attendees with values lower than the lowest propensity score among the college attendees (0.004).

80. When there is possible unobserved confounding, economists often turn to an instrumental variable (IV) estimator. However, we often cannot find valid instruments, or we have weak instruments that give biased estimates. The four instrumental variables I consider have only a minimal effect on whether a student completes college. Even if we were able to estimate a valid effect using an instrumental variable, if we have response variation it only tells us about students who chose to attend college because of that instrument—for example, because a college was nearby. It does not tell us about all the students who do and do not attend college irrespective of having a college nearby. Additionally, we remain in a difficult situation if there are unobserved confounders between the instrument and the outcome. It depends on the context as to whether it is more plausible to accept the assumptions of the IV estimator or the matching estimator.

81. Heckman 2001; Xie 2007; Xie, Brand, and Jann 2012.

82. Heckman and Vytlacil 2001, 107; see also Elwert and Winship 2014; Aronow and Samii 2016.

83. Smith 2003, 460.

84. Carneiro, Hansen, and Heckman 2003; Imbens and Woolridge 2009.

85. Angrist and Pischke 2009; Brand and Simon Thomas 2013; Heckman, Urzua, and Vytlacil 2006; Imai 2017; Morgan and Winship 2014; Smith 2003; Xie 2011; Xie, Brand, and Jann 2012.

86. This method is described in Xie, Brand, and Jann (2012) and Brand and Simon Thomas (2013). I apply the approach in several studies of college effects; for example, Ahearn, Brand, and Zhou 2022; Brand 2010; Brand and Davis 2011; Brand, Pfeffer, and Goldrick-Rab 2014; Brand and Xie 2010; Cheng et al. 2021; Musick, Brand, and Davis 2012.

87. Rosenbaum and Rubin 1984; Rubin 1997.

88. Likewise, an increase in the effect of college with an increase in the propen-

sity for college is like observing TT > ATE—evidence that the effect of college increases as the likelihood of college increases.

89. Xie, Brand, and Jann 2012.

90. Some scholars describe the propensity to college as a summary measure of indicators of socioeconomic background. Although socioeconomic differences are an important component of the story underlying differences in effects by the propensity for college completion, additional factors, such as high school achievement, self-esteem, and the expectation and normativity of college, also elucidate the story behind the estimated effects. Analogously, when we estimate interaction effects by race, we might explain these differences as reflecting differences in socioeconomic conditions. This does not lead us to abandon the use of race as an interaction. Although socioeconomic differences are often an important component of the story underlying differences in effects by race, we know that effects may also differ by race for other reasons, such as racial discrimination.

91. Athey and Imbens 2017; Brand et al. 2019a, 2019b; Brand et al. 2021.

92. Suppose researchers select which subgroup estimates to report based on such analyses and do not draw on cross-validation procedures or multiple-testing adjustments. In that case, they are subject to incorrectly rejecting a correct null hypothesis.

93. Researchers can use several alternative machine learning strategies to study treatment effect heterogeneity; for a discussion, see Brand et al. 2021. However, the tree-based approach is straightforward and yields highly interpretable results.

94. Hainmueller, Mummolo, and Xu 2018.

95. Blau and Duncan 1967, 175.

96. Duncan 1984, 226; quoted in Xie and Wu 2005, 865.

97. Angrist and Pischke 2015, xi.

98. Brand and Xie 2010, 294.

99. Assuming substantial selection bias among low-propensity college-goers will of course affect a negative selection result. I note that, despite some confusion, the model used by Richard Breen, Seongsoo Choi, and Anders Holm (2015) to test the sensitivity of the Brand and Xie (2010) findings presumes a bias that is constant by the propensity score. Their model should thus not actually lead to any change in the pattern or degree of effect heterogeneity.

100. Hainmueller, Mummolo, and Xu 2018.

101. Moreover, a pattern may not be robust for one outcome and quite robust for another. Or a pattern may not be linear and instead require a more flexible specification.

102. Zhou and Xie 2019, 2020.

103. Halaby 2004, 541.

104. Einstein 1921.

105. King et al. 1994, 76.

106. Arah 2017; Gangl 2013; Rosenbaum 2002.

107. I define two parameters that constitute a bias factor. First, λ is the difference in resilience to college between college and non-college-goers. Second, γ is the difference in poverty between those who have such resilience and those who do not. When λ quals 10 percent, I assume that the prevalence of resilience is 10 percent higher among the college-educated relative to the high school–educated. When γ equals −10 percent, I assume that those who are resilient have a 10 percent lower level of poverty than those who are not (all else equal).

108. Cheng et al. 2021. This bias formula implies a larger bias for low- and high-propensity individuals.

109. As relatively few cases in the sample are Black and Hispanic high-propensity college graduates, I select Black and Hispanic high-propensity non-college graduates with the closest propensity score (all within 0.01 of the college graduate), but not the exact value.

110. Iacus, King, and Porro 2012.

111. Angrist, Imbens, and Rubin 1996; Angrist and Pischke 2009; Heckman, Urzua, and Vytlacil 2006; Imbens and Angrist 1994.

112. I am unable to do so, however, for the Black and Hispanic high-propensity cases owing to data sparseness. In this case, cases are all near the bottom of the distribution of high-propensity scores.

113. Of course, an individual treatment effect is not identified, but I nevertheless use this strategy to select individuals who represent a typical case.

114. The vignettes are based on public data from the NLSY79. I do not reveal any identifying information. The BLS staff and the NLSY principal investigator approved the data for these purposes.

Chapter 4: Unequal College Chances

1. At least since the work of the sociologist Pitrim Sorokin (1927) in the 1920s, scholars have noted that education sorts and sieves access to privilege.

2. Blau and Duncan 1967.

3. This approach stands in contrast to the focus in mobility research on how the O-D association varies across levels of E.

4. Michael Dunlop Young (1958, 106–7), an English social critic, did not coin the term "meritocracy" to describe an ideal type but to describe an alarming social order in which competition reigned supreme. He sardonically wrote

that "today the eminent know that success is just reward for their own capacity, for their own efforts, and for their own undeniable achievement."

5. Bell 1973.
6. Delbanco 2012, 126.
7. Ibid., 135.
8. Erzsebet Bukodi and John Goldthorpe (2016, 836) note that Bell continues to impact political and public discourse to this day.
9. Hout and Janus 2011.
10. Hout 2018.
11. Blau and Duncan 1967, 428.
12. Bailey and Dynarski 20111; Voss, Hout, and George 2022.
13. For example, the influential status attainment model, or "Wisconsin model" based on data from a cohort of high school graduates in Wisconsin, expanded the original Blau-Duncan model to include a variety of social origin factors and psychosocial and cognitive attributes (Sewell, Haller, and Ohlendorf 1970; Sewell, Haller, and Portes 1969).
14. Indeed, as good as our models are, including new machine learning algorithms to predict who attains a college degree and who does not, we still fall quite short of being able to predict individual educational trajectories.
15. Hout 1988.
16. Bailey and Dynarski 2011.
17. Ibid.; Bloome, Dyer, and Zhou 2018.
18. In the NLSY79, parental income terciles range from $0 to $40,500 (in 2020 dollars) for low-income households, $40,500 to $74,000 for middle-income households, and $74,000 to $267,000 for high-income households. In the NLSY97, parental income ranged from $0 to $49,200 (in 2020 dollars) for low-income households, $49,200 to $88,900 for middle-income households, and $88,900 to $397,400 for high-income households. Patterns by parental income quartiles and quantiles are similar to patterns by terciles, suggesting a uniform increase in the likelihood of college attendance and completion with an increase in parental income. Here I use terciles for simplicity.
19. Charles Manski (1992), using data on respondents who were high school seniors in 1980, similarly found that about 11 percent of respondents from low-income families graduated from college, as did about 24 percent of respondents from middle-income families and 39 percent from high-income families.
20. Martha Bailey and Sue Dynarski (2011) report the same pattern. Wealth inequality, which is more unequally distributed than income and is increasing, also leads to educational disparities. Pfeffer (2018) shows that only about 10 percent of children born in the 1980s who were from the bottom

quintile of the wealth distribution obtained a college degree relative to 60 percent from the top quintile.

21. Goldrick-Rab 2016.

22. Chetty et al. 2017; Witteveen and Attewell 2017. Differential college attendance rates explain about half of the family income gap in college completion rates, while college persistence explains the remaining gap (Bailey and Dynarski 2011).

23. Chetty et al. (2017) base their findings on administrative data for over 30 million college students. Although highly selective colleges recently enacted substantial tuition reductions and other outreach policies, the fraction of low-income students attending these colleges has not significantly increased. This does not necessarily imply that increases in financial aid did not affect access. In the absence of these positive changes, the fraction of low-income students might have fallen, especially given that low-income families' real income declined over recent decades.

24. Hoxby and Avery 2013; Hoxby and Turner 2015.

25. Nagaoka, Roderick, and Coca 2009.

26. Ibid.

27. DeLuca, Clampet-Lundquist, and Edin 2016, 11.

28. Derek Bok (2015, 162) contends that "the sense of democratic legitimation is undermined" if people believe that the rich attend selective colleges regardless of merit while able and deserving candidates from poor backgrounds do not.

29. Bound, Lovenheim, and Turner 2010.

30. Kornrich and Furstenberg 2013.

31. Duncan and Murnane 2011a; Farkas 2018; Reardon 2011; Schneider, Hastings, and LaBriola 2018.

32. Bloome, Dyer, and Zhou 2018; Kornrich 2016.

33. Schneider, Hastings, and LaBriola 2018.

34. Hough 2021.

35. Goldrick-Rab 2016.

36. Houle 2014.

37. Regan 2020; see also the Hope Center for College, Community, and Justice website at https://hope.temple.edu/. Some estimates suggest that as many as half of community college students are food- and housing-insecure, and that more than 10 percent are homeless.

38. Jack 2019b.

39. Voss, Hout, and George 2022.

40. Far more than it does by constraining credit, Carneiro and Heckman (2002)

argue, family income influences educational attainment for all the reasons I describe that operate throughout childhood.

41. In figures 4.2 and 4.3, the category "Whites and other" includes all those who were not Black or Hispanic, including Asians. Very few respondents were Asian. In the NLSY79, for example, only nineteen respondents were Asian.

42. In 2018, college enrollment rates were 60, 66, and 70 percent for Black, Hispanic, and White students, respectively. The percentages of women ages twenty-five to twenty-nine in 2018 who had completed a bachelor's degree were 25, 22, and 47 percent for Black, Hispanic, and White students, respectively; the corresponding percentages of men were 20, 17, and 39 percent (Ma, Pender, and Welch 2019).

43. Alba 2020; Arum et al. 2018; Riegle-Crumb, Kyte, and Morton 2018; Voss, Hout, and George 2020.

44. Bowen and Bok 1998; Bowen, Chingos, and McPherson 2009; Kurlander and Hibel 2018; Roksa et al. 2007.

45. Carter 2018, 23. Still, broad racial and ethnic categories mask considerable heterogeneity in educational achievement and attainment within these populations.

46. Ciocca Eller and DiPrete 2018.

47. Alba 2020; Reardon and Fahle 2017. Immigrant-origin students experience additional educational hurdles (Telles and Ortiz 2009).

48. DeLuca, Clampet-Lundquist, and Edin 2016, 2. Black males also face unique obstacles. Even after adjusting for academic preparation and family background, they have particularly low college completion rates (Baum, Kurose, and McPherson 2013; see also Badger et al. 2018).

49. Young and DeLuca, forthcoming.

50. Christina Ciocca Eller and Thomas DiPrete (2018) show that if we adjust for academic and socioeconomic resources, Black students are more likely to enroll in four-year colleges than are White students but less likely to complete a degree.

51. Carter 2018, 26.

52. Hout and Janus 2011.

53. Hoxby and Turner 2015; Nagaoka, Roderick, and Coca 2009.

54. Bourdieu 1977.

55. Jaeger and Karlson 2018. Goldthorpe (2007a) is critical of the theory of cultural capital and argues for measures of cultural resources that can be empirically demonstrated to affect educational attainment.

56. Bourdieu 1986; Bowles and Gintis 1976; Jencks et al. 1979; MacLeod 1989; Willis 1981. Although inequality scholars question the measurement of these latent constructs, some work by Mads Meier Jaeger and Kristian

Karlson (2018) shows that the socioeconomic differentials in educational attainment would be smaller if cultural capital were equalized across families.

57. Lareau 2011.
58. Coleman 1988; Lareau 2011.
59. DeLuca, Clampet-Lundquist, and Edin 2016; Kurlander and Hibel 2018; Harding 2010.
60. McLanahan and Percheski 2008.
61. Brand et al. 2019a, 2019b; McLanahan and Percheski 2008; McLanahan and Sandefur 1994; Sweeney 2011. Most single-parent households are headed by women. The absence of a male role model may have a differential impact on boys, who have fallen behind in college completion rates (Bailey and Dynarski 2011).
62. Brand et al. 2019a, 2019b.
63. Park and Burgess 1925; Sampson 2011; Wilson 1987.
64. Chetty and Hendren 2018.
65. Harding 2007.
66. Jack 2019b; see also Alexander, Entwisle, and Olsen 2014.
67. Kozol 1991.
68. Duncan and Murnane 2011a; Reardon 2011.
69. Condron and Roscigno 2003; Crosnoe 2009.
70. Farkas 2018; Lauen and Gaddis 2013; Rothstein 2017. Jesse Rothstein (2017) contends that other out-of-school aspects of communities, like the concentration of poverty and single-parent households, make a larger difference in attainment than school quality. Some work suggests that educational achievement inequalities happen when school is not in session, while the gaps narrow during the school year, indicating an equalizing role of schooling (Alexander 1997; Entwisle, Alexander, and Olson 1997). Douglas Downey, Aimee Yoon, and Elizabeth Martin (2018) contend that school-based solutions to achievement gaps run the risk of distracting us from the broader social reform needed to reduce inequality.
71. I measure school disadvantage by the percentage of students who are disadvantaged according to the Elementary and Secondary Education Act of 1965 (ESEA) guidelines.
72. The ASVAB tests assess knowledge and skill in areas such as mathematics and language. I residualized each of the ASVAB tests on age at the time of the test separately by race and gender, with the residuals standardized to have mean zero and variance one. I then combined the items (with equal loadings, which sum to one) into a composite scale (Cronbach's $\alpha = 0.92$).

73. For example, Dael Wolfe (1954, 163) noted that the probability of enrolling in college decreased more sharply going down the test score distribution for disadvantaged children than it did for more advantaged children.

74. Carnevale et al. 2019.

75. Conley and French 2014; Owens 2018; Reardon 2011.

76. I divide the ASVAB into terciles. In the NLSY79, terciles ranged from −2.48 to −0.24 for low ASVAB, −0.24 to 0.40 for middle ASVAB, and 0.40 to 2.39 for high ASVAB. In the NLSY97, terciles ranged from −3.10 to −0.37 for low ASVAB, −0.37 to 0.06 for middle ASVAB, and 0.06 to 2.46 for high ASVAB.

77. Heckman, Stixrud, and Urzua 2006; see also Borghans et al. 2008. Paula England (2016) argues in her American Sociological Association presidential address that elucidating personal characteristics that lead to behaviors that influence socioeconomic position do not necessarily shift attention away from the importance of social structure. Social structure is what helps determine those dispositions (see also Farkas 2018).

78. Ashworth et al. 2020; Deming 2017.

79. Self-esteem is measured by the Rosenberg (1965) self-esteem scale, a ten-item scale that measures global self-worth by measuring both positive and negative feelings about the self. The scale is a widely used self-report instrument for evaluating individual self-esteem. All items use a four-point Likert scale format ranging from "strongly agree" to "strongly disagree." Examples include "At times I think that I am no good at all" and "I certainly feel useless at times." The Rotter (1966) Locus of Control is a thirteen-item scale to measure social control. It measures generalized expectancies for internal versus external control. People with an internal locus of control believe that their actions determine the rewards that they obtain. Those with an external locus of control believe that their own behavior does not matter much and that rewards in life are generally outside of their control. A low score indicates internal control, while a high score indicates external control.

80. Kurlander and Hibel 2018; MacLeod 1989; Sewell, Haller, and Ohlendorf 1970; Sewell and Shah 1967. Today's high school students are nearly universal in reporting their aspiration to attend college, but their high aspirations are not accompanied by the same level of attainment (Duncan and Murnane 2011a; Kurlander and Hibel 2018).

81. Ciocca Eller and DiPrete 2018.

82. DeLuca, Clampet-Lundquist, and Edin 2016; Kurlander and Hibel 2018; Nagaoka, Roderick, and Coca 2009. James Rosenbaum (2000, 117) argues that the college-for-all ethos is problematic because getting everyone to want to go to college is insufficient when many of those students are ill equipped to succeed there: "Americans are eager to believe that a positive attitude is all that is needed for success, and consequently, those who fail

have only themselves to blame." If we are going to take college-for-all seriously, we must do a great deal more than simply convince students to aspire to attend college. Rosenbaum contends that he is not arguing *against* college-for-all, despite some interpretations of his influential book's title, but instead emphasizing the barriers to enacting college-for-all.

83. Imbens and Rubin 2008.
84. The one-dimensional propensity score can be likened to how college admissions committees reduce applications from hopeful college entrants to a score that leads to admission.
85. With few exceptions, these differences are statistically significant at the $p < .05$ level.
86. Imbens and Rubin 2015. Moore, Brand, and Shinkre (2021) developed a Stata program to implement the procedure (in Stata: ssc install itpscore). I report logistic regression model results in appendix tables 3(a) and 3(b) for the NLSY79 and NLSY97, respectively.
87. In addition to this iterative procedure, I use a machine learning random forest model to predict college attendance and completion. The resulting propensity scores between the iterative procedures and the random forest model are highly correlated.
88. Blau and Duncan 1967, 174. With recent advances in machine learning models, some researchers anticipate that social scientists will predict social behavior more effectively. Yet Matthew Salganik and his colleagues (2020) find that notwithstanding hundreds of researchers attempting to predict a range of life outcomes in a mass scientific challenge, many using machine learning models optimized for prediction, the results suggest practical limits to the predictability of life outcomes. In other words, researchers should not be dismayed that data and models, including machine learning models, cannot perfectly predict social behavior.
89. The approach I use adopts a method derived by Abadie and Imbens (2016) to estimate the standard errors of the estimator that matches on estimated (uncertain, rather than known) college completion probabilities.
90. In the NLSY79, the mean propensity score is 0.20 for those who did not attend college, 0.61 for those who attended college, 0.13 for those who did not complete college, and 0.49 for those who completed college. In the NLSY97, the mean propensity score is 0.25 for those who did not attend college, 0.62 for those who attended college, 0.16 for those who did not complete college, and 0.51 for those who completed college. The propensity score distribution is right-skewed among those who did not attend and complete college. In contrast, the distribution is more equally distributed among college attendees and graduates.
91. For college attendance, low propensity ranges from 0 to less than 0.2, middle propensity from 0.2 to less than 0.6, and high propensity from 0.6 to 1.

For college completion, low propensity ranges from 0 to less than 0.2, middle propensity from 0.2 to less than 0.5, and high propensity from 0.5 to 1 (as a high propensity for college completion is less common than a high propensity for college attendance, yielding different thresholds at the high end).

92. As discussed in chapter 1, "elite college" indicates an institution in the top two *Barron's Profiles of American Colleges* selectivity categories.
93. Appendix tables B.4(a) for the NLSY79 and B.4(b) for the NLSY97 offer a full set of descriptive statistics by propensity for college completion strata.
94. This reasoning could also be extended to consider students who do not complete high school degrees (or the GED). They too may benefit from attending and completing college. I do not consider them in these analyses to match the most comparable college and non—college graduates, yet their characteristics resemble those of some of the low-propensity youth in the sample.
95. The observed propensity for college completion is orthogonal to unobserved selection into college, which also focuses our attention on the (observed and unobserved) selection process more explicitly.

Chapter 5: Cultivating Privilege and Circumventing Precarity

1. Diego and Javier differ with respect to an instrumental variable that may impact Diego's college attainment relative to Javier. I construct the instrumental variables described in chapter 3 using private geocode data from the NLSY merged with data from the Bureau of Labor Statistics, the Bureau of Economic Analysis, the Higher Education General Information Survey, and *Barron's Profiles of American Colleges*. To avoid any disclosure of identifying information, I do not specifically state the difference I observe between vignette cases.
2. Barrow and Malamud 2015.
3. Carnevale, Rose, and Cheah 2013; Cheng et al. 2021.
4. Hout 2012; Oreopoulos and Salvanes 2011.
5. Barrow, Brock, and Rouse 2013; Barrow and Malamud 2015; Ma, Pender, and Welch 2019.
6. Howell and Kalleberg 2019. For example, in 2018 high school graduates had a roughly 6 percent unemployment rate relative to a little over 2 percent among college graduates (Ma, Pender, and Welch 2019).
7. Card 1999, 1802.
8. Attewell et al. 2009.

9. Kalleberg 2009, 2011.
10. Howell and Kalleberg 2019.
11. Dwyer and Wright 2019.
12. Rosenfeld 2014; Western et al. 2012; Western and Rosenfeld 2011.
13. Howell and Kalleberg 2019, 1–2.
14. Brand 2015; Howell and Kalleberg 2019; Kalleberg 2009.
15. Desmond 2018.
16. Semega et al. 2019. The rate of poverty for the less-educated has increased. A Pew Research Center report documents a poverty rate for high school graduates of 12 percent among late boomers and 22 percent among millennials (Caumont 2014).
17. Deming and Dynarski 2009.
18. Ibid., 100–101. Other work examines the role of college in providing welfare recipients with paths out of poverty (London 2006).
19. Glenn 2020. Highlighting the Brand and Xie (2010) findings, NPR's *Marketplace* noted that those results show how important it is to make college more accessible (Scott 2010).
20. Webber 2018.
21. Attewell et al. 2009, 44.
22. The Organization for Economic Cooperation and Development (OECD) defines low-wage work as two-thirds of the median hourly wage in any given year.
23. Caleb and Isaiah differed with respect to an instrument variable, and that difference may have motivated Caleb to attend college while Isaiah instead entered the labor market.
24. On the one hand, if there is ability bias, such that more capable individuals complete college and have better socioeconomic outcomes, then our estimates are upwardly biased. However, suppose we believe that there is comparative advantage. In that case, we may assume that the college-educated would have been worse off than those who did not complete college in the absence of a degree, in which case our estimates would be downwardly biased. See appendix A for a more detailed discussion of the sensitivity analyses.
25. Doubly robust estimation produces the same pattern in results as matching.
26. The propensity score for the most responsive group is about average, probably the result of pulls from both low- and high-propensity individuals.
27. Daniela and Josefina differ with respect to several instrumental variables that may have motivated Daniela to pursue higher education.
28. The pattern of results is roughly the same if I separate the effects by gender.

29. Results differ modestly between matching and doubly robust estimation, with larger effects for the low-propensity using doubly robust methods. However, patterns are generally the same except for unemployment. I report results based on doubly robust estimation for unemployment, which suggest a 2 percent larger effect for low-propensity graduates than matching estimates. When the tails of the distribution exert influence on the results, doubly robust methods parallel findings better that eliminate those cases.
30. DeLuca et al. 2021.
31. See also Cheng et al. 2021.
32. See ibid. for a discussion of this approach. Appendix figure C.5 demonstrates the assumed error correlation for this method. Appendix figure C.6 displays results for log average wage and proportion of time in low-wage work. If some individuals are more able and motivated, then we may have a negative error correlation (for positive outcomes) and a positive error correlation (for negative outcomes). The comparative advantage argument that forms the theory of positive selection predicts that those who completed college would be worse off without college than those who did not complete college. In this case, the pattern I observe would be even more strongly downwardly sloped for low wages.
33. Bloome, Dyer, and Zhou 2018, 1238–39.

Chapter 6: Forming Families and Preventing Poverty

1. Cooper and Pugh 2020; Gibson-Davis, Edin, and McLanahan 2005; Western et al. 2012.
2. Brady 2020; Brady, Finnigan, and Hubgen 2017; Cellini, McKernan, and Ratcliffe 2008.
3. Ellwood and Jencks 2004; Goldstein and Kenney 2001; Hout 2012; Martin 2006; Oreopoulos and Salvanes 2011; Raley and Bumpass 2003; Schwartz 2010.
4. Cooper and Pugh 2020; Martin 2006; McLanahan and Percheski 2008; Raley and Bumpass 2003.
5. Cherlin 2020; Gibson-Davis 2009; Gibson-Davis, Edin, and McLanahan 2005; Oppenheimer 1994; Sweeney 2002; Xie et al. 2003.
6. Gibson-Davis, Edin, and McLanahan 2005; Gibson-Davis, Gassman-Pines, and Lehrman 2018.
7. McCall 2000; Oppenheimer 1994; Rindfuss, Bumpass, and St. John 1980; Rindfuss, Morgan, and Offutt 1996; Upchurch, Lillard, and Panis 2002. Many scholars note that the association between education and reduced fertility is subject to possible selection bias, but studies using methods

that address selection continue to find that more schooling is associated with delayed childbearing and fewer children overall (Amin and Behrman 2014).

8. Edin and Kefalas 2005; Ellwood and Jencks 2004; Kennedy and Bumpass 2008; Lundberg and Pollak 2007; Musick et al. 2009; Smock and Greenland 2010.
9. Bailey and Dynarski 2011; Cooper and Pugh 2020; Ellwood and Jencks 2004; Gibson-Davis 2011; Hout 2012; McLanahan and Percheski 2008; Rackin and Gibson-Davis 2017, 1096; Raley and Bumpass 2003. Advantaged, educated married women with firmly established careers can use their higher incomes to buffer some of the time and energy costs of raising children (Spain and Bianchi 1996). Insofar as employers strive to keep their most valuable employees, highly educated women may also effectively negotiate maternity leaves to lessen the impact on their career trajectories.
10. Cooper and Pugh 2020.
11. Hout 2012. The simultaneity of these strategizing decisions makes separating causal effects of schooling on family formation, or vice versa, very difficult.
12. Settersten and Schneider 2018. Yet economic models sometimes fail to account for the difficulty that young people have in accurately predicting how their lives will unfold, including the timing of fertility (Musick et al. 2009).
13. Becker 1991; Brewster and Rindfuss 2000; Ellwood and Jencks 2004.
14. Edin and Kefalas 2005, 171.
15. Rackin and Gibson-Davis 2017, 1096. Rackin and Gibson-Davis also find that childbearing and marriage often become disconnected for low-income women once they have had children outside of marriage. Prior to childbearing, they express goals and economic prerequisites for fertility and marriage similar to those of higher-income women.
16. Cherlin 2020; Edin and Kefalas 2005; Oppenheimer 1994; Smock and Greenland 2010; Wilson 1987.
17. Gibson-Davis, Edin, and McLanahan 2005.
18. Guzzo and Hayford 2020.
19. McLanahan 2004, 608.
20. Smock and Schwartz 2020.
21. Raley, Sweeney, and Wondra 2015.
22. Goldstein and Kenney 2001; Sweeney 2002.
23. Sweeney 2002.
24. Attewell et al. (2009) focus on a cohort of women who entered CUNY be-

tween 1970 and 1972 when the university increased its representation of poor and minority students.

25. Blackwell 1998; Kalmijn 1991.
26. See the discussion in Carey 2018.
27. King 2021.
28. Musick, Brand, and Davis 2012.
29. For women, graduating from an elite college or university increases the probability of marrying a high-income man; for men, graduating from an elite college or university increases the probability of marrying a woman from a privileged background (Arum, Roksa, and Budig 2008).
30. Oreopoulos and Salvanes 2011.
31. DiPrete and Buchmann 2013; Schwartz and Mare 2005.
32. Kalmijn 1991; Schwartz and Mare 2005.
33. Armstrong and Hamilton 2015. Other research has likewise highlighted working-class students' experiences as they move back and forth between working-class homes and postsecondary institutions and ultimately higher-status jobs (for example, Lee and Kramer 2013).
34. Lee and Kramer 2013.
35. Brand and Davis 2011.
36. Musick et al. 2009; Yang and Morgan 2003.
37. Raley, Sweeney, and Wondra 2015; Sweeney and Phillips 2004; Ventura and Bachrach 2000.
38. I include a precollege measure of marriage and fertility in the propensity score specification. Very few respondents had a child by age eighteen. About 5 percent of college graduates and 35 percent of non-college graduates, however, had a child by age twenty-two. We cannot disentangle whether this difference reflects precollege preferences or the impact of college on reducing fertility. Some individuals may also begin college, have a child, and then not complete a degree. I find that about 10 percent of respondents fell into this category. It may be that the student would not have completed a degree regardless, or that having the child caused the person not to complete a degree. To include an indicator of fertility during the college years is thus potentially endogenous and could increase bias in the effect estimates rather than reduce it. For example, if someone begins college and decides not to have a child at age twenty-one because they are in college, while the non-college-goer has a child because they are not in college, and we adjust for this, then we are overcontrolling and introducing bias. On the other hand, if someone attends college and fails to complete college because of having a child, then we have selection bias. As a robustness check, I remove those cases who were single parents during college.

The patterns remain roughly the same. Likewise, if I remove the cases who were single parents before age twenty, patterns remain the same.

39. They also must be at least twenty-five years old.
40. In results not shown, I stratify by gender and do not observe notable differences in college effects for men and women.
41. I estimate the total effects of college on family-level outcomes. Some of the effects are likely to be indirect effects due to the socioeconomic outcomes considered in chapter 5.
42. Henry and Brian differ with respect to an instrumental variable.
43. Like Henry and Brian, Brenda and Helen differ with respect to an instrumental variable.
44. We can assume that the causal effect of college reaches nonsignificance when an unobserved confounder has a sizable difference between individuals who did and did not complete college (λ) or a substantial effect on the family outcome of interest (γ). Suppose that resilience decreases poverty and is higher among individuals who completed college than among those who did not. When λ equals 10 percent, we assume that resilient individuals are 10 percent more prevalent in the college-educated group than in the non-college-educated group. When γ equals −10 percent, we assume that resilient individuals spent a ten-percentage-point-lower proportion of time in poverty than those who are not resilient (all else equal). I let the values of γ range from 40 to 10 percent (or −40 to −10 for negative outcomes) and fix the value of λ at 10 percent.
45. I report results for having ever been in poverty using doubly robust estimation.
46. I note that 0.2 is the average of the full distribution of propensity scores. The bottom 5 percent (propensity less than 0.005) and the top 5 percent (propensity greater than 0.75) of cases are omitted.
47. McLanahan and Percheski 2008.
48. Attewell et al. 2009, 3.

Chapter 7: Reducing Social Assistance

1. Deming and Dynarski 2009.
2. White House 2010.
3. Major reforms to the AFDC program in the mid-1990s changed how the program was funded and introduced work requirements. In 1996, AFDC was replaced by TANF, which is designed to facilitate and incentivize labor-force participation among the poor, linking antipoverty policy to the low-wage labor market. Since 1996, adults ages eighteen to forty-nine who can work and who have no dependents are limited in the length of time they can access SNAP.

4. The Earned Income Tax Credit (EITC) is a refundable tax credit that provides large cash transfers to low-income families, particularly those near poverty. I do not observe EITC benefits.
5. Tach and Edin 2017.
6. Ibid., 542.
7. Ibid.
8. Baum and Payea 2004.
9. Baum, Ma, and Payea 2013.
10. Several studies show that holding at least a high school degree is associated with shorter welfare spells (Barrett 2000; Blank 1989; Coelli, Green, and Warburton 2007; London 2006; Oreopoulos and Salvanes 2011). For example, Philip Oreopoulos and Kjell Salvanes (2011) find that high school completion decreases social assistance, and Michael Coelli, David Green, and William Warburton (2007) find that high school completion would reduce high school dropouts' probability of welfare receipt by one-half to three-quarters in Canada. They also find that effects are larger for individuals with low parental income.
11. See Freeman 2015.
12. Heckman, Humphries, and Veramendi 2018.
13. Ibid., 283.
14. I do not observe UI benefits, or the cumulative amount received in the NLSY97.
15. Brand 2015.

Chapter 8: Engaging in Civic Society

1. Checkoway 2001.
2. Grubb and Lazerson 2004.
3. See, for example, Facing History & Ourselves 2022.
4. Checkoway 2001.
5. Quoted in Roth 2014, 85.
6. Durkheim 1925, 59.
7. Campbell 2006, 25.
8. Giroux 2009, 253.
9. Delbanco 2012, 175–76.
10. Brand 2010: Dee 2004; Hauser 2000; Putnam 1995, 2000; Verba, Schlozman, and Brady 1995.
11. Almond and Verba 1963/1989, 316.

12. Converse 1972, 324.
13. Wilson 2000.
14. Putnam 1995, 186. Jian Huang, Henriette Maassen van den Brink, and Wim Groot (2009) find, in contrast to wage returns to schooling, a decline in civic returns to schooling over time. They consider, however, many different countries and educational and social contexts. Some analysts argue that new forms of engagement are emerging. For example, Robert Sampson and his colleagues (2005) shift the dominant focus on individual civic engagement to collective action events that bring people together in public to realize a common purpose. They contend that declines described by Putnam (2000) and others in traditional social engagement are not as consequential for civic capacity.
15. Putnam 1995, 672.
16. Baum, Ma, and Payea 2013. Although educational attainment rates have increased, levels of social participation have by some measures decreased. Norman Nie, Jane Junn, and Kenneth Stehlik-Barry (1996) explain this seeming paradox by differentiating between relative and absolute levels of education. As educational attainment has increased, its social significance is devalued and its impact on social capital becomes less significant. John Helliwell and Robert Putnam (2007) counter and conclude that rising levels of education are likely to be accompanied by higher levels of political and social engagement.
17. Ma, Pender, and Welch 2016.
18. Rainie, Keeter, and Perrin 2019.
19. Astin, Sax, and Avalos 1999; Checkoway 2001; Johnson 2004.
20. Brady, Verba, and Schlozman 1995; Hillygus 2005; Oreopoulos and Salvanes 2011; Verba, Schlozman, and Brady 1995.
21. Perrin and Gillis 2019, abstract.
22. McPherson and Rotolo 1996.
23. Ahearn, Brand, and Zhou 2022; Freeman 2003; Leighley and Nagler 2013. Some research suggests that the more politically engaged are overrepresented in surveys ("voter overrepresentation") and that respondents overreport their voting behavior ("vote overreporting") (Ansolabehere and Hersh 2012; Goldberg and Sciarini 2019; Selb and Munzert 2013). Voter overrepresentation and vote overreporting tend to increase with education, potentially upwardly biasing the effects of college attendance and completion on voting. Scholars have noted similar patterns for civic engagement. Indeed, responding to surveys is one form of civic engagement. Conversely, although voter "validation" studies question the accuracy of self-reported voting, Matthew Berent, Jon Krosnick, and Arthur Lupia (2016) question the accuracy of some voter validation studies. They argue that several ap-

parently viable methods of matching survey respondents to government records severely underestimate the proportion of Americans who were registered to vote, and that among respondents whose self-reports can be validated against government records, the accuracy of self-reports is extremely high. It is also unclear whether the bias differentially impacts college graduates across social origins.

24. Hauser 2000.

25. Nie and Hillygus 2001. There are exceptions. For example, Cindy Kam and Carl Palmer (2008) find that college attendance does not have an impact on political participation once they match college-goers to non-college-goers, although others have questioned their conclusion (for example, Henderson and Chatfield 2011; see also Gibson 2001). Huang, van den Brink, and Groot (2009), however, drawing on a meta-analysis synthesizing over 280 evaluations, find that education has a strong and robust effect on social participation. The effect is reduced once researchers adjust for selection into higher education.

26. Dee 2004; Doyle and Skinner 2017; Heckman, Humphries, and Veramendi 2018.

27. Dee 2004, 1710.

28. Heckman, Humphries, and Veramendi 2018, 303. They also find larger effects of college completion among "low-skill" than among "high-skill" individuals for depression and self-esteem.

29. Doyle and Skinner 2017, 889.

30. Brand 2010.

31. Skinner and Doyle 2021.

32. Ahearn, Brand, and Zhou 2022.

33. Referring to first-generation Black college students, Delbanco (2012, 180) reports: "I heard them speak about their hopes to return someday to their troubled communities in order to 'give back.'" My motivation for studying this topic similarly originated with the disadvantaged UCLA undergraduate students in my classes who repeatedly emphasized their desire to give back to the communities in which they grew up.

34. The exact question was "Let's talk about volunteering your time through or for religious or not-for-profit organizations such as schools, hospitals, museums, charities, or the United Way. By 'volunteering' I don't mean just belonging to an organization—I mean doing unpaid work or providing unpaid assistance, either on a regular basis or infrequently. In [calendar year prior to survey year], did you do any volunteer activity through or for an organization?" The patterns of college effects are similar if I eliminate religious volunteering.

35. NLSY political questions are based on questions from the American National Election Studies (ANES) and were included in the surveys through a grant received by Jon Krosnick and Arthur Lupia.

36. Stephen Ansolabehere, Bernard Fraga, and Brian Schaffner (2021) suggest that while the CPS is widely used to calibrate surveys for voter turnout, there are discrepancies between CPS estimates and official voter turnout records. Specifically, CPS data overestimate Black and Hispanic turnout relative to non-Hispanic White turnout.

37. Sources of voter turnout bias in survey data include overrepresentation (initial survey and attrition) and overreporting. The NLSY voting measure benefits from four factors. First, misreporting may be lower in reporting turnout for midterm than presidential elections. Second, misreporting may be lower in nonpolitical surveys like the NLSY relative to political surveys like the ANES. Third, accuracy is greater in face-to-face interviews (as in the NLSY) than in phone interviews (DeBell et al. 2020). Fourth, the NLSY question wording is intended to reduce social desirability pressures by allowing nonvoters to express their identity as habitual voters (option 2) and to indicate that they voted only if they were sure.

38. Thus, even if the sample is misleadingly underrepresenting nonvoters, within-sample analyses may still be reasonable. As the NLSY is not a political survey, this also reduces the likelihood of response bias. Still, people who do not vote are disproportionately unlikely to participate in surveys. If I code all those who did not respond and attrite as nonvoters, 53 percent reported voting. This estimate is below the CPS's. It has the same difference (about 20 percent) between college graduates and non-college graduates as when I delete those cases.

39. If I eliminate religious volunteering, effects are larger for low- and mid-propensity graduates and smaller for high-propensity graduates, but the pattern remains the same.

40. There is no evidence to suggest that voter overreporting is greater among low-propensity college graduates than among high-propensity college graduates (see discussion in Ahearn, Brand, and Zhou 2022).

41. Estimates remain significant for the mid-propensity college graduates even when unobserved differences have a substantial impact on voting or volunteering (and the prevalence of the unobserved factor differs between college and non-college graduates by 10 percent).

42. I report results based on doubly robust estimation for voting.

43. As this is a more inclusive measure of volunteering than the "any volunteering" measure for the NLSY79, levels are higher for the NLSY97.

44. The figures delete the bottom and top 5 percent of the propensity distribution, which may correspond better to the doubly robust estimator.

45. For a related discussion, see Allen 2016.

Chapter 9: Inequality and Investment

1. A privileged background, however, does not lead to socioeconomic attainment levels without a college degree in the same way that it did for the older cohort. Nevertheless, social background still plays a larger role in determining life outcomes among non-college graduates than among college graduates.
2. Likewise, individuals with a high likelihood of completing college but who do not are doing so against the odds. They are also selective.
3. Rosenbaum, Ahearn, and Lansing 2018.
4. We can have positive selection among low-income youth, first-generation students, students with low test scores, and low-propensity students, and we can also observe a pattern of negative selection across the whole population (Zhou and Xie 2020).
5. When an educational level becomes universal, selectivity is by definition null (Torche 2011).
6. Torche 2011, 801.
7. Attewell et al. 2009, 5.
8. Among those with a high propensity for college completion based on observed factors, there is probably more variation in unobserved factors for those who do complete college (Zhou and Xie 2019, 2020). Importantly, the theory of positive selection is the very mechanism that causes the observed pattern of negative association between the propensity score and the returns to college completion among students at the margin.
9. Experiences can be weighted differently. An experience that is life-altering for some may be only one of many similar events for others. Outcomes can likewise be differently weighted across social origins.
10. Delbanco 2012, 172, 182.
11. Kozol 1991, 79–80.
12. Grubb 2011.
13. Rauscher and Shen 2022.
14. Morgan 2001, abstract.
15. Feller et al. 2016; Kline and Walters 2016.
16. Aschaffenburg and Maas 1997; DiMaggio 1982; Jaeger and Karlson 2018.
17. Jaeger and Karlson 2018, 790.
18. Bryk, Lee, and Holland 1993; Downey, von Hippel, and Broh 2004; Fischer et al. 1996; Hoffer, Greeley, Coleman 1985.
19. Hout (2012, 10.7–10.8) notes that the most-disadvantaged and lowest-measured-aptitude students may not benefit as much as those who score

nearer to the middle of the test score distribution, and that these latter students are the low-propensity students who attend college.

20. Rauscher 2016.
21. Conlin and Thompson 2017; Martorell, Stange, and McFarlin 2016.
22. Long, Conger, and Iatarola 2012.
23. Angrist et al. 2012.
24. Walters 2018, 2179.
25. Ibid., 2219. Walters speculates that disadvantaged families may lack knowledge about school quality, consistent with evidence that such students are less likely to choose high-quality schools in various settings (see, for example, Hoxby and Avery 2013).
26. Walters 2018, 2219.
27. Shi 2020, abstract.
28. Jackson et al. 2020.
29. Coelli, Green, and Warburton 2007.
30. Heckman, Humphries, and Veramendi 2018.
31. Dynarski et al. 2018.
32. Patterns of negative selection also extend beyond educational resources. For example, better neighborhood conditions are likely to yield greater benefits to people who are unlikely to live in them than to their typical residents (see, for example, Burdick-Will et al. 2011).
33. Hout 2012, 10.17.
34. Quoted in Freire 1974, 35.
35. Eckel and King 2004; Grubb and Lazerson 2004; Hanson and Zogby 2010. Some 90 percent of college graduates report that college is worth the investment (Pew Research Center 2014).
36. Potts 2022.
37. Goldrick-Rab 2016.
38. The factors that influence degree completion include social background and structural inequalities (Voss, Hout, and George 2022).
39. Webber 2016.
40. Average student loan debt is about $30,000 (Kerr and Wood 2022).
41. Baum et al. 2009.
42. Hout 2012, 10.9–10.10.
43. Oreopoulos and Petronijevic 2013.
44. Hout 2012.
45. Delbanco 2012.

46. U.S. Department of Education 2018.

47. Some youth who do not complete high school have characteristics resembling those of youth with a low propensity for college completion, and thus an argument could be made that there are students within that population who would also benefit from attending and completing a college degree.

48. Since the COVID-19 pandemic, inequality in educational experiences has become even starker. The pandemic and the associated economic crisis impacted low-income students' likelihood of college enrollment. In 2020, about 22 percent fewer high school graduates went straight to college than in 2019 (National Association of Colleges and Employers 2020). The evidence suggests that the pandemic has hit low-income students hardest, especially those from urban high schools (Hoover 2000).

49. Student loan debt stokes fear among new entrants (Fernandes 2017).

50. Roth 2014, 147–48.

51. Ibid., 149.

52. Moreover, when we train students for vocations, we tend to train them for the vocations of today (or yesterday). When we train students to think critically, we train them for the vocations of tomorrow.

53. Giroux 2009, 257–58.

54. Excerpt from a collective 2019 letter in response to Brazil's President Jair Bolsonaro and Minister of Education Abraham Weintraub regarding the government's intention to decentralize investments in philosophy and sociology within public universities (see "Open Letter" 2019).

55. Delbanco 2012, 28, 177.

56. Baum and Payea 2004; Baum, Ma, and Payea 2010; Ma, Pender, and Welch 2019.

57. Cunningham 2006, 1. Cunningham notes that the standard rate-of-return projections used to measure the benefits of increased learning may capture only three-fifths of the full value of education.

58. Hout 2012, 10.14.

59. As Enrico Moretti (2004) documents, workers earn more in cities with higher proportions of college graduates, suggesting that more-educated workers generate positive "spillovers" to other workers. He argues that cities with more highly educated populations are hubs of innovation and experience faster economic growth than those with less-educated populations.

60. Roth 2014, 195. Some scholars estimate, for example, that as much as three-quarters of the schooling effect on self-reported life satisfaction is due to nonpecuniary factors (Oreopoulos and Salvanes 2011, 180).

61. Jonathan Marks (2021) argues that conservative visions of liberal indoctrination bear little resemblance to what actually goes on in college classrooms.
62. Dink Stover, in the novel *Stover at Yale*, states that the purpose of college is to educate ourselves by knowing opposite lives (Johnson 1931).
63. McGuire 2021.
64. Crow quoted in Wermund 2017.
65. Bunch 2019.
66. Zimmerman 2014, 742.
67. Biddle quoted in Goldstein 2011.
68. Autor quoted in Leonhardt 2015.
69. Leonhardt 2018.
70. Some low-cost interventions could alleviate some of the information gap; see Barrow, Brock, and Rouse (2013) and Dynarski et al. (2018).
71. Oreopoulos and Petronijevic 2013.
72. Dynarski 2014; Dynarski and Scott-Clayton 2013.
73. Bloome, Dyer, and Zhou 2018.
74. Krueger quoted in Leonhardt 2011.
75. Jack 2019b.
76. Zhou 2021.
77. Thompson 2018.
78. Hout 2009, A8. A large proportion of growth in college enrollment over the last two decades has been in for-profit colleges, which targets low-income and minority youth and does not offer significant returns (Cottom 2017; Dynarski 2019). States whose investments in higher education are declining have rising for-profit enrollment (Dwyer, Houle, and Phillips n.d.). Dynarski (2014) describes the consequences of student demand for college alongside reduction in state support for public colleges: underresourced public colleges with higher tuition as well as record enrollment at high-priced, low-return for-profit colleges. In addition, that student loan payments are due when earnings are lowest and most variable creates a repayment crisis (see also Dynarski 2019).
79. Bound et al. 2019. Private donations from individuals and corporations provide another source of revenue for American colleges and universities, including some public universities that face diminishing state funds.
80. The key sources of revenue for American colleges and universities include tuition and fee payments from students and families (including the government-backed financial aid that students use to pay tuition); appropriations, grants, and contracts from federal, state, and local governments;

private gifts; endowment and other investment earnings; and sales from auxiliary enterprises and services.

81. Public colleges and universities enroll more than three-quarters of all undergraduate students.
82. In the social and economic upheaval of 2020, colleges and universities faced dramatic drops in revenue and steep declines in undergraduate enrollment (National Association of Colleges and Employers 2020).
83. Jason Houle and Fenaba Addo (2022) argue that first-generation college students, low-income students, and students of color are disadvantaged in both debt accumulation and debt repayment. These processes perpetuate the racial wealth gap and intergenerational inequality.
84. Tuition has risen at twice the inflation rate over the past twenty years, outstripping increases in both family income and financial aid resources. Universities and colleges have three options in the face of increased costs and reduced revenue from states and other sources. They can reduce spending, improve efficiencies, and generate additional revenue. For the most part, institutions engage in a combination of all three. Some institutions pursue efficiencies in academic areas, such as using technology to reach more students, increasing class size, and hiring adjunct instructors.
85. Quoted in Gunn 2019.
86. Middle-class families may feel an obligation to cover (to the extent that they can) the high costs of college for their children and significantly strain their finances to do so (Zaloom 2019).
87. Quoted in Williams 2019.
88. Greenwald 2018.
89. Leonhardt 2017.
90. Carnevale, Smith, and Strohl 2013.
91. For example, if current trends continue, by 2030 California will be short of economic demand by over one million workers with bachelor's degrees. Alongside this undersupply of educated workers, tuition at the California state universities and in the University of California system has more than tripled over the last twenty years (Public Policy Institute of California 2016).
92. Council of Economic Advisers 2023.
93. Bound et al. 2019, 44; Ehrenberg 2006.
94. Goldrick-Rab et al. 2016.
95. Hout and Janus 2011, 168–69, 183.
96. Zimmerman 2014, 712–13. Dynarski et al. (2018) show that encouragement to apply to selective schools and a promise of aid can substantially close income gaps in college choice.
97. Jencks 2009.

98. Hanson and Zogby 2010; Eckel and King 2004.
99. Grubb and Lazerson 2004; Quadlin and Powell 2022; see also Russell Sage Foundation 2018; Leonhardt 2018.
100. Harvard Kennedy School, "5 Big Ideas in Inequality Series" Videos," https://inequality.hks.harvard.edu/5-big-ideas-inequality-series-2020-2021.
101. Deming 2019; see also Kim 2019.
102. Leonhardt 2015.
103. Bartik and Hershbein 2018b.
104. Bloome, Dyer, and Zhou 2018.
105. Delbanco 2012, 172.
106. Roth 2014, 131.
107. Duncan and Murnane 2011b.
108. Goldin and Katz 2008, 353. There has been historical resistance to educational expansion in the United States. Many states, particularly those in the South, lagged the rest of the country in providing public secondary education. That lag reflected efforts to restrict the access of Southern Blacks to education. The concept of public goods was threatening in the South, where discrimination was used to uphold racial hierarchy at all levels of government and throughout the Southern economy. W.E.B. Du Bois (2014, 19) wrote that the South feared educated Blacks, observing that the "South was not wholly wrong: for education among all kinds of men always has had, and always will have, an element of danger and revolution, of dissatisfaction and discontent. Nevertheless, men strive to know."
109. Carter 2018, 27.

References

Abadie, Alberto, and Matias D. Cattaneo. 2018. "Econometric Methods for Program Evaluation." *Annual Review of Economics* 10: 465–503.

Abadie, Alberto, and Guido W. Imbens. 2016. "Matching on the Estimated Propensity Score." *Econometrica* 84(2): 781–807.

Ahearn, Caitlin, Jennie E. Brand, and Xiang Zhou. 2022. "How, and for Whom, Does Higher Education Increase Voting?" *Research in Higher Education* (September).

Alba, Richard. 2020. *The Great Demographic Illusion: Majority, Minority, and the Expanding American Mainstream.* Princeton, N.J.: Princeton University Press.

Alexander, Karl L. 1997. "Public Schools and the Public Good." *Social Forces* 76(1): 1–30.

Alexander, Karl L., Doris Entwisle, and Linda Olson. 2014. *The Long Shadow: Family Background, Disadvantaged Urban Youth, and the Transition to Adulthood.* New York: Russell Sage Foundation.

Alexander, F. King. 2019. "The Reality of State Disinvestment of Higher Education." *Inside Higher Education*, November 26.

Allen, Danielle. 2016. *Education and Equality.* Chicago: University of Chicago Press.

Almond, Gabriel, and Sidney Verba. 1989. *The Civic Culture: Political Attitudes and Democracy in Five Nations.* Newbury Park, Calif.: Sage Publications. Originally published in 1963.

Altonji, Joseph G., and Ling Zhong. 2021. "The Labor Market Returns to Advanced Degrees." *Journal of Labor Economics* 39(2): 303–60.

Amin, Vikesh, and Jere R. Behrman. 2014. "Do More-Schooled Women Have Fewer Children and Delay Childbearing? Evidence from a Sample of U.S. Twins." *Journal of Population Economics* 27(1): 1–31.

Angrist, Joshua D., Susan M. Dynarski, Thomas J. Kane, Parag A. Pathak, and Christopher R. Walters. 2012. "Who Benefits from Kipp?" *Journal of Policy Analysis and Management* 31(4): 837–60.

Angrist, Joshua D., Guido W. Imbens, and Donald B. Rubin. 1996. "Identification of Causal Effects Using Instrumental Variables." *Journal of the American Statistical Association* 91(434): 444–55.

Angrist, Joshua D., and Jörn-Steffen Pischke. 2009. *Mostly Harmless Econometrics: An Empiricist's Companion.* Princeton, N.J.: Princeton University Press.

Ansolabehere, Stephen, Bernard Fraga, and Brian Schaffner. 2021. "The CPS Voting and Registration Supplement Overstates Minority Turnout." *Journal of Politics* 84(3).

Ansolabehere, Stephen, and Eitan Hersh. 2012. "Validation: What Big Data Reveal about Survey Misreporting and the Real Electorate." *Political Analysis* 20(4): 437–59.

Arah, Onyebuchi. 2017. "Bias Analysis for Uncontrolled Confounding in the Health Sciences." *Annual Review of Public Health* 38(March): 12.1–16.

Arcidiacono, Peter, Patrick Bayer, and Aurel Hizmo. 2010. "Beyond Signaling and Human Capital: Education and the Revelation of Ability." *American Economic Journal: Applied Economics* 2(4): 76–104.

Armstrong, Elizabeth, and Laura Hamilton. 2015. *Paying for the Party: How College Maintains Inequality.* Cambridge, Mass.: Harvard University Press.

Aronow, Peter, and Cyrus Samii. 2016. "Does Regression Produce Representative Estimates of Causal Effects?" *American Journal of Political Science* 60(1): 250–67.

Arum, Richard, and Josipa Roksa. 2011. *Academically Adrift: Limited Learning on College Campuses.* Chicago: University of Chicago Press.

Arum, Richard, Josipa Roksa, and Michelle Budig. 2008. "The Romance of College Attendance: Higher Education Stratification and Mate Selection." *Research in Social Stratification and Mobility* 26(2): 107–21.

Arum, Richard, Josipa Roksa, Jacqueline Cruz, and Blake Silver. 2018. "Student Experiences in College." In *Handbook of the Sociology of Education in the 21st Century*, edited by Barbara Schneider. Cham: Springer International.

Aschaffenburg, Karen, and Ineke Maas. 1997. "Cultural and Educational Careers: The Dynamics of Social Reproduction." *American Sociological Review* 62(4): 573–87.

Ashenfelter, Orley, and Cecilia Rouse. 1998. "Income, Schooling, and Ability: Evidence from a New Sample of Identical Twins." *Quarterly Journal of Economics* 113(1): 253–84.

Ashworth, Jared, V. Joseph Hotz, Arnaud Maurel, and Tyler Ransom. 2020. "Changes across Cohorts in Wage Returns to Schooling and Early Work Experiences." Working paper.

Ashworth, Jared, and Tyler Ransom. 2019. "Has the College Wage Premium Continued to Rise? Evidence from Multiple U.S. Surveys." *Economics of Education Review* 69(C): 149–54.

Astin, Alexander W., Linda J. Sax, and Juan Avalos. 1999. "Long-Term Effects of

Volunteerism during the Undergraduate Years." *Review of Higher Education* 22(2): 187–202.

Athey, Susan, and Guido Imbens. 2017. "The State of Applied Econometrics: Causality and Policy Evaluation." *Journal of Economic Perspectives* 31(2): 3–32.

Attewell, Paul, and David Lavin. 2007. *Passing the Torch: Does Higher Education for the Disadvantaged Pay Off across the Generations?* New York: Russell Sage Foundation.

Attewell, Paul, David Lavin, Thurston Domina, and Tania Levey. 2009. *Passing the Torch: Does Higher Education for the Disadvantaged Pay Off across the Generations?* New York: Russell Sage Foundation.

Autor, David. 2010. "The Polarization of Job Opportunities in the U.S. Labor Market: Implications for Employment and Earnings." Washington, D.C.: Center for Economic Progress and the Hamilton Project.

———. 2014. "Skills, Education, and the Rise of Earnings Inequality among the 'Other 99 Percent.'" *Science* 344(6186): 843–51.

Autor, David, Claudia Goldin, and Lawrence F. Katz. 2020. "Extending the Race between Education and Technology." Working Paper 26705. National Bureau of Economic Research, January.

Autor, David H., Lawrence F. Katz, and Melissa S. Kearney. 2008. "Trends in U.S. Wage Inequality: Revising the Revisionists." *Review of Economics and Statistics* 90(2): 300–323.

Backes, Benjamin, Harry Holzer, and Erin Dunlop Velez. 2014. "Is It Worth It? Postsecondary and Employment Outcomes of Disadvantaged Students." IZA discussion paper 8474. Bonn: Institute of Labor Economics (September).

Badger, Emily, Claire Cain Miller, Adam Pearce, and Kevin Quealy. 2018. "Extensive Data Shows Punishing Reach of Racism for Black Boys." *New York Times*, March 19.

Bailey, Martha, and Sue Dynarski. 2011. "Inequality in Postsecondary Education." In *Wither Opportunity: Rising Inequalities, Schools, and Children's Life Chances*, edited by Greg J. Duncan and Richard J. Murnane. New York: Russell Sage Foundation.

Barrett, Garry F. 2000. "The Effect of Educational Attainment on Welfare Dependence: Evidence from Canada." *Journal of Public Economics* 77(2): 209–32.

Barrow, Lisa, Thomas Brock, and Cecilia Elena Rouse. 2013. "Postsecondary Education in the United States: Introducing the Issue." *The Future of Children* 23(1): 3–16.

Barrow, Lisa, and Ofer Malamud. 2015. "Is College a Worthwhile Investment?" *Annual Review of Economics* 7: 519–55.

Bartik, Timothy J., and Brad J. Hershbein. 2018a. "Degrees of Poverty: The Relationship between Family Income Background and the Returns to Education." Working paper. W. E. Upjohn Institute, March 1.

———. 2018b. "College Is Worth It for Persons from Low-Income Backgrounds." W. E. Upjohn Institute, May 18.

Baum, Sandy. 2014. "Higher Education Earnings Premium: Value, Variation, and Trends." Urban Institute, February. https://www.urban.org/sites/default/files/publication/22316/413033-higher-education-earnings-premium-value-variation-and-trends_1.pdf.

Baum, Sandy, Bryan Caplan, W. Norton Grubb, Charles Murray, Marty Nemko, Richard K. Vedder, Marcus A. Winters, and Alison Wolf. 2009. "Are Too Many Students Going to College?" *Chronicle of Higher Education*, November 8. https://www.chronicle.com/article/are-too-many-students-going-to-college-49039/.

Baum, Sandy, Charles Kurose, and Michael McPherson. 2013. "An Overview of Higher Education." *The Future of Children* 23(1): 17–39.

Baum, Sandy, Jennifer Ma, and Kathleen Payea. 2010. "Education Pays Update 2005: The Benefits of Higher Education for Individuals and Society." New York: College Board.

———. 2013. "Education Pays 2010: The Benefits of Higher Education for Individuals and Society." New York: College Board.

Baum, Sandy, and Kathleen Payea. 2004. "Education Pays 2004: The Benefits of Higher Education for Individuals and Society." Washington, D.C.: College Board.

Becker, Gary S. 1964. *Human Capital: A Theoretical and Empirical Analysis, with Special Reference to Education*. New York: Columbia University Press.

———. 1991. *A Treatise on the Family*. Cambridge, Mass.: Harvard University Press.

Bell, Daniel. 1973. *The Coming of Post-Industrial Society*. New York: Basic Books.

Berent, Matthew K., Jon Krosnick, and Arthur Lupia. 2016. "Measuring Voter Registration and Turnout in Surveys: Do Official Government Records Yield More Accurate Assessments?" *Public Opinion Quarterly* 80(3): 597–621.

Berk, Richard A., and Phyllis J. Newton. 1985. "Does Arrest Really Deter Wife Battery? An Effort to Replicate the Findings of the Minneapolis Spouse Abuse Experiment." *American Sociological Review* 50(2): 253–62.

Bernard, Tara Siegel, and Karl Russell. 2018. "The New Toll of Student Debt in 3 Charts." *New York Times*, July 11.

Bernardi, Fabrizio, and Gabrielle Ballarino, eds. 2016. *Education, Occupation, and Social Origin: A Comparative Analysis of the Transmission of Socio-Economic Inequalities*. Northampton, Mass.: Edward Elgar Publishing.

Bialik, Carl. 2011. "College Does Pay Off, but It's No Free Ride." *Wall Street Journal*, November 19.

Bind, Marie-Abele C., and Donald B. Rubin. 2019. "Bridging Observational Studies and Randomized Experiments by Embedding the Former in the Latter." *Statistical Methods in Medical Research* 28(7): 1958–78.

Binder, Amy, Daniel B. Davis, and Nick Bloom. 2016. "Career Funneling: How

Elite Students Learn to Define and Desire 'Prestigious' Jobs." *Sociology of Education* 89(1): 20–39.

Bjerk, David. 2007. "The Differing Nature of Black-White Wage Inequality across Occupational Sectors." *Journal of Human Resources* 42(2): 398–434.

Black, Sandra, Jeffrey T. Denning, and Jesse Rothstein. 2020. "Winners and Losers? The Effect of Gaining and Losing Access to Selective Colleges on Education and Labor Market Outcomes." Working Paper 26821. National Bureau of Economic Research, March.

Blackwell, Debra L. 1998. "Marital Homogamy in the United States: The Influence of Individual and Paternal Education." *Social Science Research* 27(2): 159–88.

Blair, Peter Q., and David J. Deming. 2020. "Structural Increases in Demand for Skill after the Great Recession." *AEA Papers and Proceedings* 110(May): 362–65.

Blank, Rebecca M. 1989. "Analyzing the Length of Welfare Spells." *Journal of Public Economics* 39(3): 245–73.

Blau, Peter M., and Otis Dudley Duncan. 1967. *The American Occupational Structure.* New York: John Wiley & Sons.

Blinkley, Collin. 2023. "Jaded with Education, More Americans Are Skipping College." *AP News*, March 9.

Bloome, Deidre, Shauna Dyer, and Xiang Zhou. 2018. "Educational Inequality, Educational Expansion, and Intergenerational Income Persistence in the United States." *American Sociological Review* 83(6): 1215–53.

Bok, Derek. 2015. *Higher Education in America.* Rev. ed. Princeton, N.J.: Princeton University Press.

Borghans, Lex, Angela L. Duckworth, James J. Heckman, and Bas ter Weel. 2008. "The Economics and Psychology of Personality Traits." *Journal of Human Resources* 63(4): 972–1059.

Boudon, Raymond. 2003. "Beyond Rational Choice Theory." *Annual Review of Sociology* 29: 1–21.

Bound, John, Breno Braga, Gaurav Khanna, and Sarah Turner. 2019. "Public Universities: The Supply Side of Building a Skilled Workforce." *RSF: The Russell Sage Foundation Journal of the Social Sciences* 5(5): 43–66. DOI: https://doi.org/10.7758/rsf.2019.5.5.03.

Bound, John, Michael F. Lovenheim, and Sarah Turner. 2010. "Why Have College Completion Rates Declined? An Analysis of Student Preparation and Collegiate Resources." *American Economic Journal: Applied Economics* 2(3): 129–57.

Bourdieu, Pierre. 1977. "Cultural Reproduction and Social Reproduction." In *Power and Ideology in Education*, edited by Jerome Karabel and A. H. Halsey. New York: Oxford University Press.

———. 1984. *Distinction: A Social Critique of the Judgement of Taste.* Cambridge, Mass.: Harvard University Press.

———. 1986. "The Forms of Capital." In *Handbook of Theory and Research for the Sociology of Education*, edited by J. Richardson, translated by Richard Nice. New York: Greenwood, 1986.

Bowen, William, and Derek Bok. 1998. *The Shape of the River: Long-Term Consequences of Considering Race in College and University Admissions*. Princeton, N.J.: Princeton University Press.

Bowen, William G., Matthew M. Chingos, and Michael S. McPherson. 2009. *Crossing the Finish Line: Completing College at America's Public Universities*. Princeton, N.J.: Princeton University Press.

Bowles, Samuel, and Herbert Gintis. 1976. *Schooling in Capitalist America: Educational Reform and the Contradictions of Economic Life*. New York: Basic Books.

Brady, David. 2020. "Theories of the Causes of Poverty." *Annual Review of Sociology* 45: 155–75.

Brady, David, Ryan M. Finnigan, and Sabine Hubgen. 2017. "Rethinking the Risks of Poverty: A Framework for Analyzing Prevalence and Penalties." *American Journal of Sociology* 123(3): 740–86.

Brady, Henry E., Sidney Verba, and Kay L. Schlozman. 1995. "Beyond SES: A Resource Model of Political Participation." *American Political Science Review* 89(2): 271–94.

Brand, Jennie E. 2010. "Civic Returns to Higher Education: A Note on Heterogeneous Effects." *Social Forces* 89(2): 417–34.

———. 2015. "The Far-Reaching Impact of Job Loss and Unemployment." *Annual Review of Sociology* 41: 359–75.

Brand, Jennie E., and Dwight Davis. 2011. "The Impact of College Education on Fertility: Evidence for Heterogeneous Effects." *Demography* 48(3): 863–87.

Brand, Jennie E., and Charles N. Halaby. 2006. "Regression and Matching Estimates of the Effects of Elite College Attendance on Education and Career Achievement." *Social Science Research* 35(3): 749–70.

Brand, Jennie E., Ravaris Moore, Xi Song, and Yu Xie. 2019a. "Why Does Parental Divorce Lower Children's Educational Attainment? A Causal Mediation Analysis." *Sociological Science* 6(April): 264–92.

———. 2019b. "Parental Divorce Is Not Uniformly Disruptive to Children's Educational Attainment." *Proceedings of the National Academy of Sciences* 116(15): 7266–71.

Brand, Jennie E., Fabian Pfeffer, and Sara Goldrick-Rab. 2014. "The Community College Effect Revisited: The Importance of Attending to Heterogeneity and Complex Counterfactuals." *Sociological Science* 1(October 27): 448–65.

Brand, Jennie E., and Juli Simon Thomas. 2013. "Causal Effect Heterogeneity." In *Handbook of Causal Analysis for Social Research*, edited by Stephen L. Morgan. Dordrecht: Springer.

Brand, Jennie E., Jiahui Wu, Bernard Koch, and Pablo Geraldo. 2021. "Uncovering Sociological Effect Heterogeneity Using Machine Learning." *Sociological Methodology* 51(2): 189–223.

Brand, Jennie E., and Yu Xie. 2010. "Who Benefits Most from College? Evidence for Negative Selection in Heterogeneous Economic Returns to Higher Education." *American Sociological Review* 75(2): 273–302.

Brand, Jennie E., Xiang Zhou, and Yu Xie. 2023. "Recent Developments in Causal Inference and Machine Learning." *Annual Review of Sociology* 49. DOI: https://doi.org/10.1146/annurev-soc-030420-015345.

Breen, Richard. 2010. "Educational Expansion and Social Mobility in the 20th Century." *Social Forces* 89(2): 365–88.

Breen, Richard, Seongsoo Choi, and Anders Holm. 2015. "Heterogenous Causal Effects and Sample Selection Bias." *Sociological Science*, June 8. https://sociologicalscience.com/download/volume-2/july/SocSci_v2_351to369.pdf.

Breen, Richard, and John H. Goldthorpe. 1997. "Explaining Educational Differentials: Towards a Formal Rational Action Theory." *Rationality and Society* 9(3): 275–305.

Breen, Richard, and Jan O. Jonsson. 2007. "Explaining Change in Social Fluidity: Educational Equalization and Educational Expansion in Twentieth-Century Sweden." *American Journal of Sociology* 112(6): 1775–1810.

Breen, Richard, and Ruud Luijkx. 2007. "Social Mobility and Education: A Comparative Analysis of Period and Cohort Trends in Britain and Germany." In *From Origin to Destination: Trends and Mechanisms in Social Stratification Research*, edited by Stefani Scherer, Reinhard Pollak, Gunnar Otte, and Markus Gangl. New York: Campus Verlag.

Brewer, Dominic, and Ronald Ehrenberg. 1996. "Does It Pay to Attend an Elite Private College? Evidence from the Senior High School Class of 1980." *Research in Labor Economics* 15: 239–71.

Brewster, Karin, and Ronald Rindfuss. 2000. "Fertility and Women's Employment in Industrialized Nations." *Annual Review of Sociology* 26: 271–96.

Bruch, Elizabeth, Fred Feinberg, and Kee Yeun Lee. 2016. "Extracting Multistage Screening Rules from Online Dating Activity Data." *Proceedings of the National Academy of Sciences* 113(38): 10530–35.

Bryk, Anthony, Valerie Lee, and Peter Holland. 1993. *Catholic Schools and the Common Good*. Cambridge, Mass.: Harvard University Press.

Bukodi, Erzsebet and John H. Goldthorpe. 2016. "Is Education Now Class Destiny? Class Histories across Three British Cohorts." *European Sociological Review* 32(6): 835–49.

Bunch, Will. 2019. "What Pete Buttigieg Doesn't Get about How College Has Ripped America in Two." *Philadelphia Inquirer*, December 5.

Burdick-Will, Julia, Jens Ludwig, Stephen W. Raudenbush, Robert J. Sampson, Lisa Sonbanmatsu, and Patrick Sharkey. 2011. "Converging Evidence for Neighborhood Effects on Children's Test Scores: An Experimental, Quasi-Experimental, and Observational Comparison." In *Whither Opportunity? Rising Inequality, Schools, and Children's Life Chances*, edited by Greg J. Duncan and Richard J. Murnane. New York: Russell Sage Foundation.

Bureau of Labor Statistics. 2015. "National Longitudinal Surveys (NLS) 50th Anniversary." 50th Anniversary Conference, Washington, D.C., September 17. https://www.bls.gov/nls/nls-50th-anniversary.htm.

Caliendo, Marco, and Sabine Kopeinig. 2008. "Some Practical Guidance for the Implementation of Propensity Score Matching." *Journal of Economic Surveys* 22(1): 31–72.

Campbell, David E. 2006. "What Is Education's Impact on Civic Society?" In Organization for Economic Cooperation and Development, *Measuring the Effects of Education on Health and Civic Engagement: Proceedings of the Copenhagen Symposium.*

Caplan, Bryan. 2018a. *The Case against Education: Why the Education System Is a Waste of Time and Money.* Princeton, N.J.: Princeton University Press.

———. 2018b. "The World Might Be Better Off without College for Everyone." *Atlantic*, January/February.

Cappon, Lester, ed. 1971. *The Adams-Jefferson Letters: The Complete Correspondences between Thomas Jefferson and Abigail and John Adams.* New York: Simon & Schuster.

Card, David. 1995. "Using Geographic Variation in College Proximity to Estimate the Return to Schooling." In *Aspects of Labour Market Behaviour: Essays in Honor of John Vanderkamp*, edited by Louis N. Christofides, E. Kenneth Grant, and Robert Swidinsky. Toronto: University of Toronto Press.

———. 1999. "The Causal Effect of Education on Earnings." In *Handbook of Labor Economics*, vol. 3A, edited by Orley Ashenfelter and David Card. Amsterdam: Elsevier.

———. 2001. "Estimating the Return to Schooling: Progress on Some Persistent Econometric Problems." *Econometrica* 69(5): 1127–60.

Carey, Kevin. 2018. "The Ivy League Students Least Likely to Get Married." *New York Times*, March 29.

———. 2019. "How Much Does Getting into an Elite College Actually Matter?" *New York Times*, March 15.

Carlson, Scott. 2016. "Should Everyone Go to College?" *Chronicle of Higher Education*, May 1.

Carneiro, Pedro, Karsen T. Hansen, and James J. Heckman. 2003. "Estimating Distributions of Treatment Effects with an Application to the Returns to Schooling and Measurement of the Effects of Uncertainty on College Choice." *International Economic Review* 44(2): 361–422.

Carneiro, Pedro, and James J. Heckman. 2002. "The Evidence on Credit Constraints in Post-Secondary Schooling." *Economic Journal* 112(482): 705–34.

Carneiro, Pedro, James J. Heckman, and Edward J. Vytlacil. 2010. "Estimating Marginal Returns to Education." Working Paper 16474. National Bureau of Economic Research, October.

———. 2011. "Estimating Marginal Returns to Education." *American Economic Review* 101(6): 2754–81.

Carnevale, Anthony P., Megan L. Fasules, Michael Quinn, and Kathryn Peltier Campbell. 2019. "Born to Win, Schooled to Lose: Why Equally Talented Students Don't Get Equal Chances to Be All They Can Be." Georgetown University Center on Education and the Workforce.

Carnevale, Anthony P., and Stephen J. Rose. 2011. "The Undereducated American." Georgetown University Center on Education and the Workforce, November 1. http://hdl.handle.net/10919/83052.

Carnevale, Anthony P., Stephen J. Rose, and Ban Cheah. 2013. "The College Payoff: Education, Occupations, Lifetime Earnings." Georgetown University Center on Education and the Workforce. https://cewgeorgetown.wpenginepowered.com/wp-content/uploads/collegepayoff-completed.pdf.

Carnevale, Anthony, Nicole Smith, and Jeff Strohl. 2013. "Recovery: Job Growth and Education Requirements through 2020" (executive summary). Georgetown Public Policy Institute, Center on Education and the Workforce, June.

Carter, Prudence. 2018. "Education's Limitations and Its Radial Possibilities." *Contexts* 17(2): 22–27.

Caumont, Andrea. 2014. "6 Key Findings about Going to College." Pew Research Center, February 11. https://www.pewresearch.org/fact-tank/2014/02/11/6-key-findings-about-going-to-college/.

Cellini, Stephanie Riegg, Signe-Mary McKernan, and Caroline Ratcliffe. 2008. "The Dynamics of Poverty in the United States: A Review of Data, Methods, and Findings." *Journal of Policy Analysis and Management* 27(3): 577–605.

Checkoway, Barry. 2001. "Renewing the Civic Mission of the American Research University." *Journal of Higher Education* 72(2): 125–47.

Cheng, Michelle. 2017. "Students at Most Colleges Don't Pick 'Useless' Majors." *FiveThirtyEight*, August 14.

Cheng, Siwei, Jennie E. Brand, Xiang Zhou, Yu Xie, and Michael Hout. 2021. "Heterogeneous Economic Returns to College over the Life Cycle." *Science Advances* 7(51): 1–14.

Cheng, Siwei, Christopher R. Tamborini, ChangHwan Kim, and Arthur Sakamoto. 2019. "Educational Variations in Cohort Trends in the Black-White Earnings Gap among Men: Evidence from Administrative Earnings Data." *Demography* 56(6): 2253–77.

Cherlin, Andrew. 2020. "Degrees of Change: An Assessment of the Deinstitutionalization of Marriage Thesis." *Journal of Marriage and Family* 82(1): 62–80.

Chetty, Raj, John N. Friedman, Emmanuel Saez, Nicholas Turner, and Danny Yagan. 2017. "Mobility Report Cards: The Role of Colleges in Intergenerational Mobility." Working Paper 23618. National Bureau of Economic Research, July.

Chetty, Raj, and Nathanial Hendren. 2018. "The Impacts of Neighborhoods on Intergenerational Mobility I: Childhood Exposure Effects." *Quarterly Journal of Economics* 133(3): 1107–62.

Chetty, Raj, Nathanial Hendren, Patrick Kline, and Emmanuel Saez. 2014. "Where Is the Land of Opportunity? The Geography of Intergenerational Mobility in the United States." Working Paper 19843. National Bureau of Economic Research, January.

Chicago Ideas Week. 2011. "Too Many Kids Go to College." *Chicago Ideas Week,* October 12. https://www.intelligencesquaredus.org/debate/too-many-kids-go-college/#/.

Ciocca Eller, Christina, and Thomas A. DiPrete. 2018. "The Paradox of Persistence: Explaining the Black-White Gap in Bachelor's Degree Completion." *American Sociological Review* 83(6): 1171–1214.

Cochran, William G. 1965. "The Planning of Observational Studies of Human Populations (with Discussion)." *Journal of the Royal Statistical Society, Series A* 128(2): 134–55.

Coelli, Michael, David A. Green, and William P. Warburton. 2007. "Breaking the Cycle? The Effect of Education on Welfare Receipt among Children of Welfare Recipients." *Journal of Public Economics* 91(7/8): 1369–98.

Coleman, James A. 1988. "Social Capital and the Creation of Human Capital." *American Journal of Sociology* 94: S95–S120.

Collins, Randall. 2019. *The Credential Society: An Historical Sociology of Education and Stratification.* New York: Wiley. Originally published in 1979.

Condron, Dennis J., and Vincent J. Roscigno. 2003. "Disparities Within: Unequal Spending and Achievement in an Urban School District." *Sociology of Education* 76(1): 18–36.

Conley, David T., and Elizabeth M. French. 2014. "Student Ownership of Learning as a Key Component of College Readiness." *American Behavioral Scientist* 58(8): 1018–34.

Conlin, Michael, and Paul N. Thompson. 2017. "Impacts of New School Facility Construction: An Analysis of a State-Financed Capital Subsidy Program in Ohio." *Economics of Education Review* 59(C): 13–28.

Converse, Phillip Ernest. 1972. "Change in the American Electorate." In *The Human Meaning of Social Change,* edited by Angus Campbell and Phillip E. Converse. New York: Russell Sage Foundation.

Conwell, Jordan A., and Natasha Quadlin. 2021. "Race, Gender, Higher Education, and Socioeconomic Attainment: Evidence from Baby Boomers at Midlife." *Social Forces* 100(3): 990–1024.

Cooper, Marianne, and Allison J. Pugh. 2020. "Families across the Income Spectrum: A Decade in Review." *Journal of Marriage and Family* 82(1): 272–99.

Cottom, Tressie McMillam. 2017. *Lower Ed: The Troubling Rise of For-Profit Colleges in the New Economy.* New York: New Press.

Council of Economic Advisers. 2023. *Economic Report of the President* and *Annual Report of the Council of Economic Advisers.* Transmitted to Congress in March 2023.

Crosnoe, Robert. 2009. "Low-Income Students and the Socioeconomic Composition of Public High Schools." *American Sociological Review* 74(5): 709–30.

Cunningham, Alisa. 2006. "The Broader Societal Benefits of Higher Education." Solutions for Our Future Project, January.

Dale, Stacy Berg, and Alan B. Krueger. 2011. "Estimating the Return to College Selectivity over the Life Career Using Administrative Earnings Data." Working Paper 17159. National Bureau of Economic Research, June.

Darity, William A., Jr., Darrick Hamilton, Mark Paul, Alan Aja, Anne Price, Antonio Moore, and Caterina Chiopros. 2018. "What We Get Wrong about Closing the Racial Wealth Gap." Insight Center for Community Economic Development, April.

Davidson, Cathy N. 2017. "The Surprising Thing Google Learned about Its Employees—and What It Means for Today's Students." *Washington Post*, December 20.

Day, Jennifer Cheeseman, and Eric C. Newburger. 2002. "The Big Payoff: Educational Attainment and Synthetic Estimates of Work-Life Earnings." *Current Population Reports* P23-210. U.S. Census Bureau Special Studies, July. https://www.census.gov/content/dam/Census/library/publications/2002/demo/p23-210.pdf.

Deaton, Angus. 2010. "Instruments, Randomization, and Learning about Development." *Journal of Economic Literature* 48(2): 424–55.

DeBell, Matthew, Jon A. Krosnick, Katie Gera, David S. Yeager, and Michael P. McDonald. 2020. "The Turnout Gap in Surveys: Explanations and Solutions." *Sociological Methods and Research* 49(4): 1133–62.

Dee, Thomas S. 2004. "Are There Civic Returns to Education?" *Journal of Public Economics* 88(9/10): 1697–1720.

Delbanco, Andrew. 2012. *College: What It Was, Is, and Should Be.* Princeton, N.J.: Princeton University Press.

DeLuca, Stefanie, Susan Clampet-Lundquist, and Kathryn Edin. 2016. *Coming of Age in the Other America.* New York: Russell Sage Foundation.

DeLuca, Stefanie, Nicholas W. Papageorge, Joseph L. Boselovic, Seth Gershenson, Andrew Gray, Kiara M. Nerenberg, Jasmine Sausedo, and Allison Young. 2021. "'When Anything Can Happen': Anticipated Adversity and Postsecondary Decision-Making." Working Paper 29472. National Bureau of Economic Research, November.

Deming, David J. 2017. "The Growing Importance of Social Skills in the Labor Market." *Quarterly Journal of Economics* 132(4): 1593–1640.

———. 2019. "Tuition-Free College Could Cost Less than You Think." *New York Times*, July 19.

Deming, David, and Sue Dynarski. 2009. "Into College, Out of Poverty? Policies to Increase the Postsecondary Attainment of the Poor." Working Paper 15387. National Bureau of Economic Research, September.

Desmond, Matthew. 2018. "Americans Want to Believe Jobs Are the Solution to Poverty. They're Not." *New York Times*, September 11.

Dewey, John. 1916. "Education vs. Trade Training" [1915]. In John Dewey, *Democracy and Education*. New York: MacMillan.

Dickson, Matt, and Colm Harmon. 2011. "Economic Returns to Education: What We Know, What We Don't Know, and Where We Are Going—Some Brief Pointers." *Economics of Education Review* 30(6): 1118–22.

DiMaggio, Paul. 1982. "Cultural Capital and School Success: The Impact of Status Culture Participation on the Grades of U.S. High School Students." *American Sociological Review* 47(2): 189–201.

DiPrete, Thomas A., and Claudia Buchmann. 2013. *The Rise of Women: The Growing Gender Gap in Education and What It Means for American Schools*. New York: Russell Sage Foundation.

DiPrete, Thomas A., and Henriette Engelhardt. 2004. "Estimating Causal Effects with Matching Methods in the Presence and Absence of Bias Cancellation." *Sociological Methods and Research* 32(4): 501–28.

Downey, Douglas B., Paul T. von Hippel, and Beckett A. Broh. 2004. "Are Schools the Great Equalizer? Cognitive Inequality during the Summer Months and the School Year." *American Sociological Review* 69(5): 613–35.

Downey, Douglas B., Aimee Yoon, and Elizabeth Martin. 2018. "Schools and Inequality: Implications from Seasonal Comparison Research." In *Handbook of the Sociology of Education in the 21st Century*, edited by Barbara Schneider. Cham: Springer International.

Doyle, William R., and Benjamin T. Skinner. 2017. "Does Postsecondary Education Result in Civic Benefits?" *Journal of Higher Education* 88(6): 863–93.

Du Bois, W.E.B. 2014. *The Souls of Black Folk*. New York: Tribeca Books. Originally published in 1903.

Duncan, Greg, and Richard J. Murnane. 2011a. "Introduction: The American Dream, Then and Now." In *Wither Opportunity? Rising Inequality, Schools, and Children's Life Chances*, edited by Greg J. Duncan and Richard J. Murnane. New York: Russell Sage Foundation.

———. 2011b. "Foreword." In *Whither Opportunity: Rising Inequality, Schools, and Children's Life Chances*, edited by Greg J. Duncan and Richard J. Murnane. New York: Russell Sage Foundation

Duncan, Otis Dudley. 1984. *Notes on Social Measurement, Historical and Critical*. New York: Russell Sage Foundation.

Durkheim, Émile. 1925. *L'éducation morale*. Paris: Alcan/Presses universitaires de France.

Dwyer, Rachel, Jason N. Houle, and Erica Phillips. n.d. "Opportunity for Sale: State Disinvestment in Higher Education and the Rise of For-Profit College Enrollments." Working paper.

Dwyer, Rachel, and Erik Olin Wright. 2019. "Low-Wage Job Growth, Polarization, and the Limits and Opportunities of the Service Economy." *RSF: Russell Sage Foundation Journal of the Social Sciences* 5(4): 56–76. DOI: https://doi.org/10.7758/RSF.2019.5.4.02.

Dynarski, Susan. 2014. "An Economist's Perspective on Student Loans in the United States." Economic Studies Working Paper, Brookings Institution, September.

———. 2019. "Student Debt." In "State of the Union: Millennial Dilemma" (special issue of *Pathways: A Magazine on Poverty, Inequality, and Social Policy*). Stanford University, Stanford Center on Poverty and Inequality.

Dynarski, Susan, C. J. Libassi, Katherine Michelmore, and Stephanie Owen. 2018. "Closing the Gap: The Effect of a Targeted, Tuition-Free Promise on College Choices of High-Achieving, Low-Income Students." *American Economic Review* 111(6): 1721–56.

Dynarski, Susan, and Judith Scott-Clayton. 2013. "'Financial Aid Policy': Lessons from Research." Working Paper 18710. National Bureau of Economic Research, January.

Eckel, Peter D., and Jacqueline E. King. 2004. "An Overview of Higher Education in the United States: Diversity, Access, and the Role of the Marketplace." In *The International Handbook of High Education, Part 2: Regions and Countries*, edited by James J. F. Forest and Philip G. Altbach. Dordrecht: Springer.

Edin, Kathryn, and Maria J. Kefalas. 2005. *Promises I Can Keep: Why Poor Women Put Motherhood before Marriage.* Berkeley: University of California Press.

Edsall, Thomas B. 2021. "Is Education No Longer the 'Great Equalizer'?" *New York Times*, June 23.

Ehrenberg, Ronald G. 2006. "The Perfect Storm and the Privatization of Public Higher Education." *Change* 38(1): 45–53.

Eide, Eric, and Mark Showalter. 1999. "Factors Affecting the Transmission of Earnings across Generations." *Journal of Human Resources* 34(2): 253–67.

Einstein, Albert. 1921. "Geometry and Experience." Lecture before the Prussian Academy of Sciences, January 27, 1921.

Ellwood, David, and Christopher Jencks. 2004. "The Uneven Spread of Single-Parent Families: What Do We Know? Where Do We Look for Answers?" In *Social Inequality*, edited by Kathryn Neckerman. New York: Russell Sage Foundation.

Elwert, Felix, and Christopher Winship. 2014. "Endogenous Selection Bias: The Problem of Conditioning on a Collider Variable." *Annual Review of Sociology* 40: 31–53.

England, Paula. 2016. "Sometimes the Social Becomes Personal: Gender, Class, and Sexualities." *American Sociological Review* 81(1): 4–28.

Entwisle, Doris R., Karl L. Alexander, and Linda Steffel Olson. 1997. *Children, Schools, and Inequality.* Boulder, Colo.: Westview Press.

Facing History & Ourselves. 2022. *As American as Public School: 1900–1950* (video). April 7. https://www.facinghistory.org/resource-library/american-public-school-1900-1950.

Falcon, Julie, and Pierre Bataille. 2018. "Equalization or Reproduction? Long-

Term Trends in the Intergenerational Transmission of Advantages in Higher Education in France." *European Sociological Review* 34(4): 335–47.

Farkas, George. 2018. "Family, Schooling, and Cultural Capital." In *Handbook of the Sociology of Education in the 21st Century*, edited by Barbara Schneider. Cham: Springer International.

Feller, Avi, Togg Grindal, Luke Miratrix, and Lindsay C. Page. 2016. "Compared to What? Variation in the Impacts of Early Childhood Education by Alternative Care Type." *Annals of Applied Statistics* 10(3): 1245–85.

Fernandes, Deirdre. 2017. "For Black Students, a College Degree Means Long-Term Debt." *Boston Globe*, November 26.

Fischer, Claude S., and Michael Hout 2006. *Century of Difference: How America Changed in the Last One Hundred Years.* New York: Russell Sage Foundation.

Fischer, Claude S., Michael Hout, Martin Sanchez Jankowski, Samuel R. Lucas, Ann Swidler, and Kim Voss. 1996. *Inequality by Design: Cracking the Bell Curve Myth.* Princeton, N.J.: Princeton University Press.

Fisher, Irving. 1930. *The Theory of Interest.* New York: Macmillan.

Fisher, Ronald A. 1925. *The Design of Experiments.* London: Oliver and Boyd.

Flaherty, Colleen. 2018. "Higher Ed and the American Dream." *Inside Higher Ed*, January 30.

Forster, Andrea G., Herman G. van de Werfhorst, and Thomas Leopold. 2021. "Who Benefits Most from College? Dimensions of Selection and Heterogeneous Returns to Higher Education in the United States and the Netherlands." *Research in Social Stratification and Mobility* 73(June): 100607.

Freedman, Ronald, and Amos H. Hawley. 1949. "Unemployment and Migration in the Depression." *Journal of the American Statistical Association* 44(246): 260–72.

Freeman, Amanda. 2015. "Why Welfare Reform Is Keeping Poor, Single Moms from Getting College Degrees." *Atlantic*, August 18.

Freeman, Richard B. 2003. "What, Me Vote?" Working Paper 9896. National Bureau of Economic Research, August.

Freire, Paulo. 1974. *Education for Critical Consciousness.* London: Bloomsbury Press.

Gaddis, S. Michael. 2015. "Discrimination in the Credential Society: An Audit Study of Race and College Selectivity in the Labor Market." *Social Forces* 93(4): 1451–79.

Gallup. 2014. "Great Jobs, Great Lives: The 2014 Gallup-Purdue Index Report." Gallup and Purdue University.

Gangl, Markus. 2013. "Partial Identification and Sensitivity Analysis." In *Handbook of Causal Analysis for Social Research*, edited by Stephen L. Morgan. Dordrecht: Springer.

Gelman, Andrew and Aki Vehtari. 2020. "What Are the Most Important Statistical Ideas of the Past 50 Years?" Working paper. December 8.

Giani, Matt S., Paul Attewell, and David Walling. 2020. "The Value of an Incomplete Degree: Heterogeneity in the Labor Market Benefits of College Non-Completion." *Journal of Higher Education* 91(4): 514–39.

Gibson, John. 2001. "Unobservable Family Effects and the Apparent External Benefits of Education." *Economics of Education Review* 20(3): 225–33.

Gibson-Davis, Christina M. 2009. "Money, Marriage, and Children: Testing the Financial Expectations and Family Formation Theory." *Journal of Marriage and Family* 71(1): 146–60.

———. 2011. "Mothers but Not Wives: The Increasing Lag between Nonmartial Births and Marriage." *Journal of Marriage and Family* 73(1): 264–78.

Gibson-Davis, Christina M., Kathryn Edin, and Sara McLanahan. 2005. "High Hopes but Even Higher Expectations: The Retreat from Marriage among Low-Income Couples." *Journal of Marriage and Family* 67(5): 1301–12.

Gibson-Davis, Christina, Anna Gassman-Pines, and Rebecca Lehrman. 2018. "'His' and 'Hers': Meeting the Economic Bar to Marriage." *Demography* 55(6): 2321–43.

Giroux, Henry. 2002. "The Corporate War against Higher Education." *Workplace* 9(October): 103–17.

———. 2009. "Obama's Dilemma: Postpartisan Politics and the Crisis of American Education." *Harvard Educational Review* 79(2): 250–66.

Glenn, David. 2020. "Disadvantaged Students May Benefit Most from Attending College." *Chronicle of Higher Education*, April 1.

Goldberg, Andreas, and Pascal Sciarini. 2019. "Who Gets Lost, and What Difference Does It Make? Mixed Modes, Nonresponse Follow-up Surveys, and the Estimation of Turnout." *Journal of Survey Statistics and Methodology* 7(4): 520–44.

Goldin, Claudia, and Lawrence Katz. 2008. *The Race between Education and Technology.* Cambridge, Mass.: Harvard University Press.

Goldrick-Rab, Sara. 2016. *Paying the Price: College Costs, Financial Aid, and the Betrayal of the American Dream.* Chicago: University of Chicago Press.

Goldrick-Rab, Sara, Robert Kelchen, Douglas N. Harris, and James Benson. 2016. "Reducing Income Inequality in Educational Attainment: Experimental Evidence on the Impact of Financial Aid on College Completion." *American Journal of Sociology* 121(6): 1762–1817.

Goldstein, Dana. 2011. "Should All Kids Go to College?" *The Nation*, June 15.

Goldstein, Joshua R., and Catherine T. Kenney. 2001. "Marriage Delayed or Marriage Forgone? New Cohort Forecasts of First Marriage for U.S. Women." *American Sociological Review* 66(4): 506–19.

Goldthorpe, John H. 2007a. "'Cultural Capital': Some Critical Observations." *Sociologica* 2: 1–22.

———. 2007b. *On Sociology*, 2nd ed., 2 vols. Stanford, Calif.: Stanford University Press.

Goldthorpe, John, and Michelle Jackson. 2008. "Education-Based Meritocracy: The Barriers to Its Realization." In *Social Class: How Does It Work?*, edited by Dalton Conley and Annette Lareau. New York: Russell Sage Foundation.

Goyette, Kimberly, and Ann Mullen. 2006. "Who Studies the Arts and Sciences? Social Background and the Choice and Consequences of Undergraduate Field of Study." *Journal of Higher Education* 77(3): 497–538.

Granovetter, Mark, and Charles Tilly. 1988. "Inequality and Labor Processes." In *Handbook of Sociology*, edited by Neil Smelser. Newbury Park, CA: Sage Publications.

Grasgreen, Allie. 2014. "Liberal Arts Grads Win Long-Term." *Inside Higher Education*, January 22.

Greenwald, Richard. 2018. "Just as More Minorities Access Higher Education, Public Support Recedes." *Daily Beast*, March 13.

Greenwood, Ernest. 1945. *Experimental Sociology: A Study in Method*. New York: King's Crown Press.

Gregg, Paul, Jan O. Jonsson, Lindsey Macmillan, and Carina Mood. 2017. "The Role of Education for Intergenerational Income Mobility: A Comparison of the United States, Great Britain, and Sweden." *Social Forces* 96(1): 121–52.

Griliches, Zvi. 1977. "Estimating the Returns to Schooling: Some Econometric Problems." *Econometrica* 45(1): 1–22.

Grossman, Michael. 2006. "Education and Nonmarket Outcomes." In *Handbook of the Economics of Education*, vol. 1, edited by Eric Hanushek and Finis Welch. Amsterdam: Elsevier/North-Holland.

Grubb, W. Norton. 2011. *The Money Myth: School Resources, Outcomes, and Equity*. New York: Russell Sage Foundation.

Grubb, W. Norton, and Marvin Lazerson. 2004. *The Education Gospel: The Economic Power of Schooling*. Cambridge, Mass.: Harvard University Press.

Gunn, Dwyer. 2019. "America Needs to Rethink Higher Education." *Pacific Standard*, March 9.

Guthrie, Lori C., Stephen C. Butler, and Michael M. Ward. 2009. "Time Perspective and Socioeconomic Status: A Link to Socioeconomic Disparities in Health?" *Social Science and Medicine* 68(12): 2145–51.

Guzzo, Karen Benjamin, and Sarah R. Hayford. 2020. "Pathways to Parenthood in Social and Family Contexts: Decade in Review, 2020." *Journal of Marriage and Family* 82(1): 117–44.

Haavelmo, Trygve. 1943. "The Statistical Implications of a System for Randomized Experiments." *Econometrica* 11(1): 1–12.

Habibi, Nader. 2015. "America Has an Overeducation Problem." *The New Republic*, December 2.

Hainmueller, Jens, Jonathan Mummolo, and Yiqing Xu. 2018. "How Much Should We Trust Estimates from Multiplicative Interaction Models? Simple Tools to Improve Empirical Practice." *Political Analysis* 27(2): 163–92.

Halaby, Charles N. 2004. "Panel Models in Sociological Research: Theory into Practice." *Annual Review of Sociology* 30: 507–44.

Hamilton, Darrick, William Darity Jr., Anne Price, Vishnu Sridharan, and Rebecca Tippett. 2015. "Umbrellas Don't Make It Rain: Why Studying and Working Hard Isn't Enough for Black Americans." Samuel DuBois Cook Center on Social Equity at Duke University, the New School, and Insight Center for Community Economic Development, April.

Hamilton, Laura, and Kelly Nielsen. 2021. *Broke: The Racial Consequences of Underfunding Public Universities.* Chicago: University of Chicago Press.

Hanson, Sandra L., and John Zogby. 2010. "The Polls—Trends: Attitudes about the American Dream." *Public Opinion Quarterly* 74(3): 570–84.

Harding, David J. 2003. "Counterfactual Models of Neighborhood Effects: The Effect of Neighborhood Poverty on Dropping Out and Teenage Pregnancy." *American Journal of Sociology* 109(3): 676–719.

———. 2007. "Cultural Context, Sexual Behavior, and Romantic Relationships in Disadvantaged Neighborhoods." *American Sociological Review* 72(3): 341–64.

———. 2010. *Living the Drama: Community, Conflict, and Culture among Inner-City Boys.* Chicago: University of Chicago Press.

Harris, Adam. 2018. "The University of California Stands Out among Top Schools When It Comes to Serving Poor Students." *Atlantic,* May 1.

Hauser, Robert M., and Min-Hsiung Huang. 1997. "Verbal Ability and Socioeconomic Success: A Trend Analysis." *Social Science Research* 26(3): 331–76.

Hauser, Robert, and John Allen Logan. 1992. "How Not to Measure Intergenerational Occupational Persistence." *American Journal of Sociology* 97(6): 1689–1711.

Hauser, Seth. 2000. "Education, Ability, and Civic Engagement in the Contemporary United States." *Social Science Research* 29(4): 556–82.

Heckman, James J. 1998. "Detecting Discrimination." *Journal of Economic Perspectives* 12(2): 101–16.

———. 2001. "Micro Data, Heterogeneity, and the Evaluation of Public Policy: Nobel Lecture." *Journal of Political Economics* 109(4): 673–748.

Heckman, James J., John Eric Humphries, and Gregory Veramendi. 2018. "The Nonmarket Benefits of Education and Ability." *Journal of Human Capital* 12(2): 282–304.

Heckman, James J., and Salvador Navarro-Lozano. 2003. "Using Matching, Instrumental Variables, and Control Functions to Estimate Economic Choice Models." Working Paper 9497. National Bureau of Economic Research, February.

Heckman, James J., Jora Stixrud, and Sergio Urzua. 2006. "The Effects of Cognitive and Noncognitive Abilities on Labor Market Outcomes and Social Behavior." *Journal of Labor Economics* 24(3): 411–82.

Heckman, James J., Sergio Urzua, and Edward Vytlacil. 2006. "Understanding Instrumental Variables in Models with Essential Heterogeneity." *Review of Economics and Statistics* 88(3): 389–432.

Heckman, James J. and Edward J. Vytlacil. 2001. "Policy-Relevant Treatment Effects." *American Economic Review* 91(2): 107–11.

Helliwell, John F., and Robert D. Putnam. 2007. "Education and Social Capital." *Eastern Economic Journal* 33(1): 1–20.

Henderson, Daniel J., Solomon W. Polachek, and Le Wang. 2011. "Heterogeneity in Schooling Rates of Return." *Economics of Education Review* 30(6): 1202–14.

Henderson, John, and Sara Chatfield. 2011. "Who Matches? Propensity Scores and Bias in the Causal Effects of Education on Participation." *Journal of Politics* 73(3): 646–58.

Hillygus, D. Sunshine. 2005. "The Missing Link: Exploring the Relationship between Higher Education and Political Engagement." *Political Behavior* 27(1): 25–47.

Hoffer, Thomas, Andrew Greeley, and James Coleman. 1985. "Achievement Growth in Public and Catholic Schools." *Sociology of Education* 58(2): 74–97.

Holland, Paul W. 1986. "Statistics and Causal Inference." *Journal of the American Statistical Association* 81(396): 945–70.

Hoover, Eric. 2020. "The Real COVID-19 Enrollment Crisis: Fewer Low-Income Students Went Straight to College." *Chronicle of Higher Education*, December 10.

Horowitz, Jonathon. 2018. "Relative Education and the Advantage of a College Degree." *American Sociological Review* 83(4): 771–801.

Horrigan, Michael. 2015. "Understanding 50 Years of Contributions from the NLS and Envisioning Its Future." Bureau of Labor Statistics 50th Anniversary Conference, Washington, D.C., September 17. https://www.bls.gov/nls/50th-anniversary/contributions-from-nls-data-horrigan.pdf.

Hough, Heather. 2021. "COVID-19, the Education Equity Crisis, and the Opportunity Ahead." Brookings Institution, April 29.

Houle, Jason N. 2014. "A Generation Indebted: Young Adult Debt across Three Cohorts." *Social Problems* 61(3): 448–65.

Houle, Jason N., and Fenaba R. Addo. 2022. *A Dream Defaulted: The Student Loan Crisis among Black Borrowers.* Cambridge, Mass.: Harvard Education Press.

Hout, Michael. 1984. "Status, Anatomy, and Training in Occupational Mobility." *American Journal of Sociology* 89(6). DOI: https://doi.org/10.1086/228020.

———. 1988. "More Universalism, Less Structural Mobility: The American Occupational Structure in the 1980s." *American Journal of Sociology* 93(6): 1358–1400.

———. 2009. "Rationing College Opportunity." *The American Prospect*, October 22.

———. 2012. "Social and Economic Returns to College Education in the United States." *Annual Review of Sociology* 38: 379–400.

———. 2018. "Occupational Changes in a Generation in the United States, 1994–

2016: Medians Show Strong Persistence from Origins to Destinations." Working paper. New York University Population Center, January.

———. Forthcoming. "Rob Mare's Research Trajectory as a Model of Cumulative Science." *Research in Social Stratification and Mobility*.

Hout, Michael, and Alexander Janus. 2011. "Educational Mobility in the United States since the 1930s." In *Whither Opportunity? Rising Inequality, Schools, and Children's Life Chances*, edited by Greg J. Duncan and Richard J. Murnane. New York: Russell Sage Foundation.

Howell, David R., and Arne L. Kalleberg. 2019. "Declining Job Quality in the United States: Explanations and Evidence." *RSF: The Russell Sage Foundation Journal of the Social Sciences* 5(4): 1–53. DOI: https://doi.org/10.7758/RSF.2019.5.4.01.

Hoxby, Caroline M., and Christopher Avery. 2013. "The Missing 'One-Offs': The Hidden Supply of High-Achieving, Low-Income Students." *Brookings Papers on Economic Activity* (Spring).

Hoxby, Caroline, and Sarah Turner. 2015. "What High-Achieving Low-Income Students Know about College." *American Economics Review* 105(5): 514–17.

Huang, Jian, Henriette Maassen van den Brink, and Wim Groot. 2009. "A Meta-analysis of the Effect of Education on Social Capital." *Economics of Education Review* 28(4): 454–64.

Huber, Martin. 2021. *Causal Analysis: Impact Evaluation and Causal Machine Learning with Applications in R*. Cambridge, Mass.: MIT Press.

Hufford, Austin. 2019. "American Factories Demand White-Collar Education for Blue-Collar Work." *Wall Street Journal*, December 9.

Iacus, Stefano, Gary King, and Giuseppe Porro. 2012. "Causal Inference without Balance Checking: Coarsened Exact Matching." *Political Analysis* 20(1): 1–24.

Illing, Sean. 2008. "Why This Economist Thinks Public Education Is Mostly Pointless: Spoiler Alert, We Disagree." *Vox*, September 20.

Imai, Kosuke. 2017. *Quantitative Social Science: An Introduction*. Princeton, N.J.: Princeton University Press.

Imbens, Guido. 2008. "Rubin Causal Model." In *The New Palgrave Dictionary of Economics*, edited by Steven N. Durlauf and Lawrence E. Blume. London: Palgrave Macmillan.

———. 2015. "Matching Methods in Practice." *Journal of Human Resources* 50(2): 373–419.

Imbens, Guido W., and Joshua D. Angrist. 1994. "Identification and Estimation of Local Average Treatment Effects." *Econometrica* 62(2): 467–75.

Imbens, Guido, and Donald Rubin. 2008. "Rubin Causal Model." In *The New Palgrave Dictionary of Economics*, 2nd ed., edited by Steven Durlauf and Lawrence E. Blume. London: Palgrave Macmillan.

———. 2015. *Causal Inference for Statistics, Social, and Biomedical Sciences*. Cambridge: Cambridge University Press.

Imbens, Guido, and Jeffrey M. Woolridge. 2009. "Recent Developments in the Econometrics of Program Evaluation." *Journal of Economic Literature* 47(1): 5–86.

Jack, Anthony. 2019a. *The Privileged Poor: How Elite Colleges Are Failing Disadvantaged Students.* Cambridge, Mass.: Harvard University Press.

———. 2019b. "I Was a Low-Income College Student. Classes Weren't the Hard Part." *New York Times*, September 10.

Jackson, C. Kirabo, Shanette C. Porter, John Q. Easton, and Sebastián Kiguel. 2020. "Who Benefits from Attending Effective Schools? Examining Heterogeneity in High School Impacts." Working Paper 28194. National Bureau of Economic Research, August.

Jaeger, Mads Meier, and Kristian Karlson. 2018. "Cultural Capital and Educational Inequality: A Counterfactual Analysis." *Sociological Science* 5(33): 775–95.

James, Jonathan. 2012. "The College Wage Premium." *Economic Commentary* (Federal Reserve Bank of Cleveland), no. 2012-10, August 8.

Jefferson, Thomas. 2017. "Thomas Jefferson 1743–1826 America Democratic Republic Statesman, 3rd President 1801–9." *Oxford Essential Quotations*. 5th ed. New York: Oxford University Press. https://www.oxfordreference.com/display/10.1093/acref/9780191843730.001.0001/q-oro-ed5-00005878;jsessionid=34B0A78D15575749B02C8F2B59FD5D1A.

Jencks, Christopher. 2009. "The Graduation Gap." *American Prospect*, November 18.

Jencks, Christopher, Susan Bartlett, Mary Corcoran, James Crouse, David Eaglesfield, et al. 1979. *Who Gets Ahead? The Determinants of Economic Success in America.* New York: Basic Books.

Jimenez, Kayla. 2023. "Fewer Students of Color from Underserved Backgrounds Want to Go to College. Here's Why." *USA Today*, March 10.

Johnson, Danette Ifert. 2004. "Relationships between College Experiences and Alumni Participation in the Community." *Review of Higher Education* 27(2): 169–85.

Johnson, Owen. 1931. *Stover at Yale* [1911]. Boston: Little, Brown and Co.

Johnson, Sarah R. Lindstrom, Robert W. Blum, and Tina L. Cheng. 2014. "Future Orientation: A Construct with Implications for Adolescent Health and Wellbeing." *International Journal of Adolescent Medical Health* 26(4): 459–68.

Johnson, William R., and Derek A. Neal. 1998. "Basic Skills and the Black-White Earnings Gap." In *The Black-White Test Score Gap*, edited by Christopher Jencks and Meredith Philips. Washington, D.C.: Brookings Institution Press.

Kahneman, Daniel, and Amos Tversky. 1979. "Prospect Theory: An Analysis of Decision under Risk." *Econometrica* 47(2): 263–91.

———. 1984. "Choices, Values, and Frames." *American Psychologist* 39(4): 341–50.

Kalleberg, Arne L. 2009. "Precarious Work, Insecure Workers: Employment Relations in Transition." *American Sociological Review* 74(1): 1–22.

———. 2011. *Good Jobs, Bad Jobs: The Rise of Polarized and Precarious Employment Systems in the United States, 1970s to 2000s*. New York: Russell Sage Foundation.

Kalleberg, Arne, and David Howell. 2019. "There's an Under-the-Radar Job Crisis Hurting Millions of Americans." *Business Insider*, November 3.

Kalmijn, Matthijs. 1991. "Shifting Boundaries: Trends in Religious and Educational Homogamy." *American Sociological Review* 56(6): 786–800.

Kam, Cindy D., and Carl L. Palmer. 2008. "Reconsidering the Effects of Education on Political Participation." *Journal of Politics* 70(3): 612–31.

Kane, Thomas. 2004. "College-Going and Inequality." In *Social Inequality*, edited by Kathryn M. Neckerman. New York: Russell Sage Foundation.

Karabel, Jerome. 2006. *The Chosen: The Hidden History of Admission and Exclusion at Harvard, Yale, and Princeton*. Boston: Mariner Books.

Karlson, Kristian Bernt. 2019. "College as Equalizer? Testing the Selectivity Hypothesis." *Social Science Research* 80(May): 216–29.

Kejriwal, Mohitosh, Xiaoxiao Li, and Evan Totty. 2020. "Multidimensional Skills and the Returns to Schooling: Evidence from an Interactive Fixed Effects Approach and a Linked Survey-Administrative Dataset." *Journal of Applied Econometrics* 35(5): 548–66.

Kennedy, Sheela, and Larry Bumpass. 2008. "Cohabitation and Children's Living Arrangements: New Estimates from the United States." *Demographic Research* 19: 1663–92.

Kent, Mary Mederios. 2010. "College Education Benefits Some More than Others." Population Reference Bureau, September 13. https://www.prb.org/resources/college-education-benefits-some-more-than-others/.

Kerr, Emma, and Sarah Wood. 2022. "See How Average Student Loan Debt Has Changed." *U.S. News & World Report*, September 13.

Killewald, Alexandra, Fabian T. Pfeffer, and Jared Schachner. 2017. "Wealth Inequality and Accumulation." *Annual Review of Sociology* 43: 379–404.

Kim, Tammy. 2019. "What Free College Really Means." *New York Times*, June 30.

King, Gary, Robert O. Keohane, and Sidney Verba. 1994. *Designing Social Inquiry: Scientific Inference in Qualitative Research*. Princeton, N.J.: Princeton University Press.

King, Gary, and Richard Nielsen 2019. "Why Propensity Scores Should Not Be Used for Matching." *Political Analysis* 27(4): 435–54.

King, Michael D. 2021. "College as a Great Equalizer? Marriage and Assortative Mating among First- and Continuing-Generation College Students." *Demography* 58(6): 2265–89.

Kline, Patrick, and Christopher R. Walters. 2016. "Evaluating Public Programs with Close Substitutes: The Case of Head Start." *Quarterly Journal of Economics* 131(4): 1795–1848.

Koenig, Fredrick, William Swanson, and Carl Harter. 1980. "Future Orientation and Social Status." *Perceptual and Motor Skills* 51(3): 927–30.

Kornrich, Sabino. 2016. "Inequalities in Parental Spending on Young Children: 1972 to 2010." *Demography* 2(2): 1–12.

Kornrich, Sabino, and Frank Furstenberg. 2013. "Investing in Children: Changes in Parental Spending on Children, 1972–2007." *Demography* 50(1): 1–23.

Kozol, Jonathan. 1991. *Savage Inequalities.* New York: Harper Perennial.

Kurlander, Michal, and Jacob Hibel. 2018. "Students' Educational Pathways: Aspirations, Decisions, and Constrained Choices along the Educational Life Course." In *Handbook of the Sociology of Education in the 21st Century*, edited by Barbara Schneider. Cham: Springer International.

Lang, Kevin, and Michael Manove. 2011. "Education and Labor Market Discrimination." *American Economic Review* 101(4): 1467–96.

Lareau, Annette. 2011. *Unequal Childhoods: Class, Race, and Family Life.* Berkeley: University of California Press.

Lauen, Douglas Lee, and S. Michael Gaddis. 2013. "Exposure to Classroom Poverty and Test Score Achievement: Contextual Effects or Selection." *American Journal of Sociology* 118(4): 943–79.

Laurison, Daniel, and Sam Friedman. 2016. "The Class Pay Gap in Higher Professional and Managerial Occupations." *American Sociological Review* 81(4): 668–95.

Lawrance, Emily C. 1991. "Poverty and the Rate of Time Preference: Evidence from Panel Data." *Journal of Political Economy* 99(1): 54–77.

Lee, Brian K., Justin Lessler, and Elizabeth A. Stuart. 2009. "Improving Propensity Score Weighting Using Machine Learning." *Statistics in Medicine* 29(3): 337–46.

Lee, Elizabeth M., and Rory Kramer. 2013. "Out with the Old, In with the New? Habitus and Social Mobility at Selective Colleges." *Sociology of Education* 86(1): 18–35.

Leef, George. 2014. "College Degrees Aren't Becoming More Valuable—Their Glut Confines People without Them to a Shrinking, Low-Pay Sector of the Market." *Forbes*, April 21.

Leighley, Jan E., and Jonathan Nagler. 2013. *Who Votes Now? Demographics, Issues, Inequality, and Turnout in the United States.* Princeton, N.J.: Princeton University Press.

Leonhardt, David. 2011. "Revisiting the Value of Elite College." *New York Times*, February 21.

———. 2015. "College for the Masses." *New York Times*, April 24.

———. 2017. "The Assault on Colleges—and the American Dream." *New York Times*, May 25.

———. 2018. "A Winning Political Issue Hiding in Plain Sight." *New York Times*, March 18.

Levitt, Steven. 2010. "Who Gains the Most from a College Education?" *New York Times*, April 8.

Lewis, David. 2001. *Counterfactuals.* Oxford: Blackwell. Originally published in 1973.

London, Rebecca A. 2006. "The Role of Postsecondary Education in Welfare Recipients' Paths to Self-Sufficiency." *Journal of Higher Education* 77(3): 472–96.

Long, Mark C., Dylan Conger, and Patrice Iatarola. 2012. "Effects of High School Course-Taking on Secondary and Postsecondary Success." *American Educational Research Journal* 49(2): 285–322.

Lubrano, Alfred. 2019. "First-Generation College Graduates Lack the Affluent's Connections to Find Their First Job." *Inquirer*, April 24.

Lundberg, Shelly, and Robert A. Pollak. 2007. "The American Family and Family Economics." *Journal of Economic Perspectives* 21(2): 3–26.

Ma, Jennifer, Matea Pender, and Meredith Welch. 2016. "Education Pays 2016: The Benefits of Higher Education for Individuals and Society." Trends in Higher Education Series, College Board. https://ia800604.us.archive.org/28/items/ERIC_ED572548/ERIC_ED572548.pdf.

———. 2019. "Education Pays: The Benefits of Higher Education for Individuals and Society." Trends in Higher Education Series, College Board. https://research.collegeboard.org/media/pdf/education-pays-2019-full-report.pdf.

Ma, Yingyi. 2009. "Family Socioeconomic Status, Parental Involvement, and College Major Choices." *Sociological Perspectives* 52(2): 211–34.

MacLeod, Jay. 1989. *Ain't No Makin' It: Aspirations and Attainment in a Low-Income Neighborhood.* Boulder, Colo.: Westview Press.

Manski, Charles F. 1992. "Parental Income and College Opportunity: Democratic Study Center Report." Washington, D.C.: Democratic Study Center (August 26).

Mare, Robert D. 1980. "Social Background and School Continuation Decisions." *Journal of the American Statistical Association* 75(370): 295–305.

Marks, Jonathan. 2021. *Let's Be Reasonable: A Conservative Case for Liberal Education.* Princeton, N.J.: Princeton University Press.

Martin, Steven P. 2006. "Trends in Marital Dissolution by Women's Education in the United States." *Demographic Research* 15(20): 537–60.

Martorell, Paco, Kevin Stange, and Isaac McFarlin Jr. 2016. "Investing in Schools: Capital Spending, Facility Conditions, and Student Achievement." *Journal of Public Economics* 140(August): 13–29.

McCall, Leslie. 2000. "Gender and the New Inequality: Explaining the College/Non-College Wage Gap." *American Sociological Review* 65(2): 234–55.

McFarland, Joel, et al. 2017. *The Condition of Education 2017.* NCES 2017-144. U.S. Department of Education, National Center for Education Statistics, Institute of Education Sciences. May 25. https://nces.ed.gov/pubsearch/pubsinfo.asp?pubid=2017144.

McGuire, Patricia. 2021. "Colleges Share the Blame for Assault on Democracy." *Chronicle of Higher Education*, January 8.

McLanahan, Sara. 2004. "Diverging Destinies: How Children Are Faring under the Second Demographic Transition." *Demography* 41(4): 607–27.

McLanahan, Sara, and Christine Percheski. 2008. "Family Structure and Reproduction of Inequalities." *Annual Review of Sociology* 34: 257–76.

McLanahan, Sara, and Gary Sandefur. 1994. *Growing Up with a Single Parent: What Hurts, What Helps.* Cambridge, Mass.: Harvard University Press.

McPherson, J. Miller, and Thomas Rotolo. 1996. "Testing a Dynamic Model of Social Composition." *American Sociological Review* 61(2): 179–202.

Mill, John Stuart. 1843. "A System of Logic." In *Collected Works of John Stuart Mill*, vol. 7, edited by John M. Robson. Toronto: University of Toronto Press.

———. 1867. Inaugural address delivered to the University of St. Andrews, February 1. *Wikisource.* Updated June 15, 2021. https://en.wikisource.org/wiki/Inaugural_address_delivered_to_the_University_of_St._Andrews,_Feb._1st_1867.

Mincer, Jacob. 1974. *Schooling, Experience, and Earnings.* New York: National Bureau of Economic Research.

Mitnik, Pablo A., Erin Cumberworth, and David B. Grusky. 2016. "Social Mobility in a High-Inequality Regime." *ANNALS of the American Academy of Political and Social Science 663*(1): 140–84. DOI: https://doi.org/10.1177/0002716215596971.

Moore, Ravaris L., Jennie E. Brand, and Tanvi Shinkre. 2021. "ITPSCORE: Stata Module to Perform Iterative Propensity Score Logistic Regression Model Search Procedure." *IDEAS*. Statistical Software Components, Boston College Department of Economics. http://ideas.repec.org/c/boc/bocode/s459018.html.

Moretti, Enrico. 2004. "Estimating the Social Return to Higher Education: Evidence from Longitudinal and Repeated Cross-Sectional Data," *Journal of Econometrics* 121(1/2): 175–212.

Morgan, Stephen. 2001. "Counterfactuals, Causal Effect Heterogeneity, and the Catholic School Effect on Learning." *Sociology of Education* 74(4): 341–74.

Morgan, Stephen, and David Harding. 2006. "Matching Estimators of Causal Effects: Prospects and Pitfalls in Theory and Practice." *Sociological Methods and Research* 35(1): 3–60.

Morgan, Stephen, and Christopher Winship. 2014. *Counterfactuals and Causal Inference: Methods and Principles for Social Research.* Cambridge: Cambridge University Press.

Murray, Charles. 2008. "Are Too Many People Going to College?" *The American*, September 8.

Musick, Kelly, Jennie E. Brand, and Dwight Davis. 2012. "Variation in the Relationship between Education and Marriage: Marriage Market Mismatch?" *Journal of Marriage and Family* 74(1): 53–69.

Musick, Kelly, Paula England, Sarah Edgington, and Nicole Kangas. 2009. "Education Differences in Intended and Unintended Fertility." *Social Forces* 88(2): 543–72.

Musk, Elon. 2018. "I Don't Give a Damn about Your Degree." https://www.youtube.com/watch?v=CQbKctnnA-Y.

Nagaoka, Jenny, Melissa Roderick, and Vanessa Coca. 2009. "Barriers to College Attainment: Lessons from Chicago." Center for American Progress, January.

National Association of Colleges and Employers. 2020. "The Significant Impact of COVID-19 on College Enrollments." September 4. https://www.naceweb.org/career-development/trends-and-predictions/the-significant-impact-of-covid-19-on-college-enrollments/.

New York Times. 2017. "Even College Doesn't Bridge the Racial Income Gap" (editorial). *New York Times*, September 20.

Neyman, Jerzy. 1923. "On the Application of Probability Theory to Agricultural Experiments." *Statistical Science* 5(1990): 465–80.

Nie, Norman, and D. Sunshine Hillygus. 2001. "Education and Democratic Citizenship." In *Making Good Citizens: Education and Civil Society*, edited by Diane Ravitch, and Joseph P. Viteritti. New Haven, Conn.: Yale University Press.

Nie, Norman H., Jane Junn, and Kenneth Stehlik-Barry. 1996. *Education and Democratic Citizenship in America.* Chicago: University of Chicago Press.

Nurmi, Jari-Erik. 1991. "How Do Adolescents See Their Future? A Review of the Development of Future Orientation and Planning." *Developmental Review* 11(1): 1–59.

"Open Letter from 17,000 U.S. and Global Sociologists in Support of Brazilian Sociology Departments." 2019. April 26. https://sites.google.com/g.harvard.edu/brazil-solidarity.

Oppenheimer, Valerie. 1994. "Women's Rising Employment and the Future of the Family in Industrial Societies." *Population and Development Review* 20(2): 293–342.

O'Rand, Angela, and Robert A. Ellis. 1974. "Social Class and Social Time Perspective." *Social Forces* 53(1): 53–62.

Oreopoulos, Philip, and Uros Petronijevic. 2013. "Making College Worth It: A Review of the Returns to Higher Education." *The Future of Children* 23(1): 41–65.

Oreopoulos, Philip, and Kjell G. Salvanes. 2011. "Priceless: The Nonpecuniary Benefits of Schooling." *Journal of Economic Perspectives* 25(1): 159–84.

Ost, Ben, Weixiang Pan, and Douglas Webber. 2018. "The Returns to College Persistence for Marginal Students: Regression Discontinuity Evidence from University Dismissal Policies." *Journal of Labor Economics* 36(3): 779–805.

Ovink, Sarah M. 2017. "'In Today's Society, It's a Necessity': Latino/a Postsecondary Plans in the College-for-All Era." *Social Currents* 4(2): 128–45.

Owens, Ann. 2018. "Income Segregation between School Districts and Inequality in Students' Achievement." *Sociology of Education* 91(1): 1–27.

Pager, Devah. 2003. "Mark of a Criminal Record." *American Journal of Sociology* 108(5): 937–75.

Park, Robert E., and Ernest W. Burgess. 1925. *The City*. Chicago: University of Chicago Press.

PBS News Hour. 2016. "If You Grew Up Poor, Your College Degree May Be Worth Less." *PBS News Hour*, March 30.

Pearl, Judea. 2009. *Causality: Models, Reasoning, and Inference*. Cambridge: Cambridge University Press.

———. 2010. "On a Class of Bias-Amplifying Variables That Endanger Effect Estimates." In *Proceedings of the Twenty-Sixth Conference of Uncertainty in Artificial Intelligence (UAI)*, edited by Peter Grunwald and Peter Spirtes. Arlington, Va.: AUAI Press.

Pearl, Judea, Madelyn Glymour, and Nicholas P. Jewell. 2016. *Causal Inference in Statistics*. West Sussex: John Wiley & Sons Ltd.

Perrin, Andrew, and Alanna Gillis. 2019. "How College Makes Citizens: Higher Education Experiences and Political Engagement." *Socius* 5(3): 1–16.

Persell, Caroline, Sofia Catsambis, and Peter Cookson. 1992. "Differential Asset Conversion: Class and Gendered Pathways to Selective Colleges." *Sociology of Education* 65(3): 208–25.

Pew Research Center. 2011. "Is College Worth It?" May 15. https://www.pewresearch.org/social-trends/2011/05/15/is-college-worth-it/.

———. 2014. "The Rising Cost of Not Going to College." February 11. https://www.pewresearch.org/social-trends/2014/02/11/the-rising-cost-of-not-going-to-college/.

———. 2016. "The Value of a College Education." October 6. https://www.pewresearch.org/social-trends/2016/10/06/5-the-value-of-a-college-education/.

Pfeffer, Fabian T. 2018. "Growing Wealth Gaps in Education." *Demography* 55(3): 1033–68.

Pfeffer, Fabian T., and Florian R. Hertel. 2015. "How Has Educational Expansion Shaped Social Mobility Trends in the United States?" *Social Forces* 94(1): 143–80.

Picchi, Aimee. 2016. "The American Dream Is Failing College Grads." *CBS News*, "Moneywatch," February 24.

Posselt, Julie R., and Eric Grodsky. 2017. "Graduate Education and Social Stratification." *Annual Review of Sociology* 43(July): 353–78.

Potts, Monica. 2022. "Is College Worth It? Voters Are Split." *FiveThirtyEight*, October 24.

Public Agenda. 2016. "New Survey Suggests Public Confidence in Higher Ed Waning." September 13. https://www.publicagenda.org/wp-content/uploads/2016/09/PublicOpinionHigherEducation2016_FullTopline_PublicAgenda.pdf.

Public Policy Institute of California. 2016. "Higher Education in California." April 20.

Putnam, Robert D. 1995. "Tuning In, Tuning Out: The Strange Disappearance of Social Capital in America." *Political Science and Politics* 28(4): 664–83.

——. 2000. *Bowling Alone: The Collapse and Revival of American Community.* New York: Simon & Schuster.

Quadlin, Natasha. 2017. "Funding Sources, Family Income, and Fields of Study in College." *Social Forces* 96(1): 91–120.

Quadlin, Natasha, and Brian Powell. 2022. *Who Should Pay? Higher Education, Responsibility, and the Public.* New York: Russell Sage Foundation.

Quintana, Chris. 2019. "Can This Man Change How Elite Colleges Treat Low-Income Students?" *Chronicle of Higher Education*, February 15.

Rackin, Health M., and Christina M. Gibson-Davis. 2017. "Low-Income Childless Young Adults' Marriage and Fertility Frameworks." *Demography* 79(4): 1096–1110.

Rainie, Lee, Scott Keeter, and Andrew Perrin. 2019. "Trust and Distrust in America." Pew Research Center, July 22. https://www.pewresearch.org/politics/2019/07/22/trust-and-distrust-in-america/.

Raley, R. Kelly, and Lawrence L. Bumpass. 2003. "The Topography of the Divorce Plateau: Levels and Trends in Union Stability in the United States after 1980." *Demographic Research* 8(8): 245–60.

Raley, R. Kelly, Megan M. Sweeney, and Danielle Wondra. 2015. "The Growing Racial and Ethnic Divide in U.S. Marriage Patterns." *The Future of Children* 25(2): 89–109.

Rauscher, Emily. 2016. "Does Educational Equality Increase Mobility? Exploiting Nineteenth-Century U.S. Compulsory Schooling Laws." *American Journal of Sociology* 121(6): 1679–1761.

Rauscher, Emily, and Yifen Shen. 2022. "Variation in the Relationship between School Spending and Achievement: Progressive Spending Is Efficient." *American Journal of Sociology* 128(1): 189–223.

Rawlings, Hunter. 2015. "College Is Not a Commodity. Stop Treating It Like One." *Washington Post*, June 9.

Reardon, Sean. 2011. "The Widening Academic Achievement Gap between the Rich and the Poor: New Evidence and Possible Explanations." In *Whither Opportunity? Rising Inequality, Schools, and Children's Life Chances*, edited by Greg J. Duncan and Richard J. Murnane. New York: Russell Sage Foundation.

Reardon, Sean F., and Erin M. Fahle. 2017. "State of the Union 2017: Education." Stanford Center on Poverty and Inequality.

Regan, Erica P. 2020. "Food Insecurity among College Students." *Sociology Compass* 14(6): 1–14.

Riegle-Crumb, Catherine, Sarah Blanchard Kyte, and Karisma Morton. 2018. "Gender and Racial/Ethnic Differences in Educational Outcomes: Examining

Patterns, Explanations, and New Directions for Research." In *Handbook of the Sociology of Education in the 21st Century*, edited by Barbara Schneider. Cham: Springer International.

Rindfuss, Ronald R., Larry Bumpass, and Craig St. John. 1980. "Education and Fertility: Implications for the Roles Women Occupy." *American Sociological Review* 45(3): 431–47.

Rindfuss, Ronald R., S. Philip Morgan, and Kate Offutt. 1996. "Education and the Changing Age Pattern of American Fertility: 1963–1989." *Demography* 33(3): 277–90.

Ripley, Manda. 2018. "Why Is College in America So Expensive?" *Atlantic*, September 11.

Rivera, Lauren A. 2015. *Pedigree: How Elite Students Get Elite Jobs*. Princeton, N.J.: Princeton University Press.

Roese, Neal J. 1997. "Counterfactual Thinking." *Psychological Bulletin* 121(1): 133–48.

Roksa, Josipa. 2011. "Differentiation and Work: Inequality in Degree Attainment in U.S. Higher Education." *Higher Education* 61(3): 293–308.

Roksa, Josipa, Eric Grodsky, Richard Arum, and Adam Gamoran. 2007. "United States: Changes in Higher Education and Social Stratification." In *Stratification in Higher Education: A Comparative Study*, edited by Yossi Shavit, Richard Arum, and Adam Gamoran. Stanford, Calif.: Stanford University Press.

Rose, Mike. 2010. "More than a Paycheck." *Inside Higher Education*, August 6.

———. 2023. *When the Light Goes On: The Life-Changing Wonder of Learning in an Age of Metrics, Screens, and Diminished Human Connection*. Boston: Beacon Press.

Rosenbaum, James. 2000. *Beyond College for All: Career Paths for the Forgotten Half.* New York: Russell Sage Foundation.

Rosenbaum, James E., Caitlin Ahearn, and Jennifer Lansing. 2018. "College-for-All: Alternative Options and Procedures." In *Handbook of the Sociology of Education in the 21st Century*, edited by Barbara Schneider. Cham: Springer International.

Rosenbaum, Paul R. 2002. *Observational Studies*. New York: Springer.

Rosenbaum, Paul R., and Donald B. Rubin. 1983. "The Central Role of the Propensity Score in Observational Studies for Causal Effects." *Biometrika* 70(1): 41–55.

———. 1984. "Reducing Bias in Observational Studies Using Subclassification on the Propensity Score." *Journal of the American Statistical Association* 79(387): 516–24.

Rosenberg, Morris. 1965. *Society and the Adolescent Self-Image*. Princeton, N.J.: Princeton University Press.

Rosenfeld, Jake. 2014. *What Unions No Longer Do*. Cambridge, Mass.: Harvard University Press.

Ross, Catherine E., and John Mirowsky. 2011. "The Interaction of Personal and Parental Education on Health." *Social Science and Medicine* 72(4): 591–99.

Roth, Michael S. 2013. "Why Liberal Education Matters—A Lecture in Beijing." *HuffPost*, February 26. https://www.huffpost.com/entry/why-liberal-education-matters_b_2769991.

———. 2014. *Beyond the University: Why Liberal Education Matters*. New Haven, Conn.: Yale University Press.

Rothstein, Jesse. 2017. "Inequality of Educational Opportunity? Schools as Mediators of the Intergenerational Transmission of Income." *Journal of Labor Economics* 37(1).

Rotter, Ulian B. 1966. "Generalized Expectancies for Internal versus External Control of Reinforcement." *Psychological Monographs: General and Applied* 80(1): 1–28.

Roy, Andrew D. 1951. "Some Thoughts on the Distribution of Earnings." *Oxford Economic Paper* 3(2): 135–46.

Rubin, Donald B. 1997. "Estimating Causal Effects from Large Data Sets Using Propensity Scores." *Annals of Internal Medicine* 127(8, pt. 2): 757–63.

———. 2006. *Matched Sampling for Causal Effects*. Cambridge: Cambridge University Press.

———. 2017. "The Essential Concepts of Causal Inference: A Remarkable History." 1955 IDSS Distinguished Seminar Series Fall 17, MIT Institute for Data, Systems, and Society, Fall. https://youtu.be/34u2MT2_5hI.

Russell Sage Foundation. 2018. "A Conversation with Brian Powell: Who Should Pay for College?" February 27. https://www.russellsage.org/who-should-pay-college.

Sakamoto, Arthur, Christopher R. Tamborini, and ChangHwan Kim. 2018. "Long-Term Earnings Differentials between African American and White Men by Educational Level." *Population Research and Policy Review* 37(1): 91–116.

Salganik, Matthew J., et al. 2020. "Measuring the Predictability of Life Outcomes Using a Scientific Mass Collaboration." *Proceedings of the National Academy of Sciences* 117(5): 8398–8403.

Sampson, Robert J. 2011. *Great American City: Chicago and the Enduring Neighborhood Effect*. Chicago: University of Chicago Press.

Sampson, Robert J., Doug McAdam, Heather MacIndoe, and Simon Weffer-Elizondo. 2005. "Civil Society Reconsidered: The Durable Nature and Community Structure of Collective Social Action." *American Journal of Sociology* 111(3): 673–714.

Sander, Richard, and Stuart Taylor Jr. 2012. *Mismatch: How Affirmative Action Hurts Students It's Intended to Help, and Why Universities Won't Admit It*. New York: Basic Books.

Schneider, Barbara. 2018. "Foreword." In *Handbook of the Sociology of Education in the 21st Century*, edited by Barbara Schneider. Cham: Springer International.

Schneider, Daniel, Orestes P. Hastings, and Joe LaBriola. 2018. "Income Inequality and Class Divides in Parental Investments." *American Sociological Review* 83(3): 475–507.

Schwartz, Christine R. 2010. "Pathways to Homogamy in Marital and Cohabiting Unions." *Demography* 47(3): 735–53.

Schwartz, Christine R., and Robert D. Mare. 2005. "Trends in Educational Assortative Marriage from 1940 to 2003." *Demography* 42(4): 621–46.

Scott, Amy. 2010. "Low-Income Benefit Most from Degree." *Marketplace*, NPR, April 1.

Selb, Peter, and Simon Munzert. 2013. "Voter Overrepresentation, Vote Misreporting, and Turnout Bias in Postelection Surveys." *Electoral Studies* 32(1): 186–96.

Semega, Jessica, Melissa Kollar, John Creamer, and Abinash Mohanty. 2019. "Income and Poverty in the United States: 2018." *Current Population Report*, P60-266. U.S. Census Bureau, September 10.

Settersten, Richard A., Jr., and Barbara Ray. 2010. "What's Going on with Young People Today? The Long and Twisting Path to Adulthood." *The Future of Children* 20(10): 19–41.

Settersten, Richard A., Jr., and Barbara Schneider. 2018. "The Future of Higher Education: What's the Life Course Got to Do with It?" In *Handbook of the Sociology of Education in the 21st Century*, edited by Barbara Schneider. Cham: Springer International.

Sewell, William, Archibald O. Haller, and G. W. Ohlendorf. 1970. "Educational and Early Occupational Status Attainment Process—Replication and Revision." *American Sociological Review* 35(December): 1014–27.

Sewell, William, Archibald O. Haller, and Alejandro Portes. 1969. "The Educational and Early Occupational Attainment Process." *American Sociological Review* (34)1: 82–92.

Sewell, William, and Vimal P. Shah. 1967. "Socioeconomic Status, Intelligence, and the Attainment of Higher Education." *Sociology of Education* 40(1): 1–23.

Shell, Ellen Ruppel. 2018. "College May Not Be Worth It Anymore: For the Poor, Higher Education May Hurt More than It Helps." *New York Times*, May 16.

Shi, Ying. 2020. "Who Benefits from Selective Education? Evidence from Elite Boarding School Admissions." *Economics of Education Review* 74(February): 101907.

Skinner, Benjamin T., and William R. Doyle. 2021. "Do Civic Returns to Higher Education Differ across Subpopulations? An Analysis Using Propensity Forests." *Journal of Education Finance* 46(4): 519–62.

Small, Mario L., and Christopher Winship. 2007. "Black Students' Graduation from Elite Colleges: Institutional Characteristics and Between-Institution Differences." *Social Science Research* 36(3): 1257–75.

Smith, Herbert L. 1997. "Matching with Multiple Controls to Estimate Treatment Effects in Observational Studies." *Sociological Methodology* 27(1): 325–53.

———. 2003. "Some Thoughts on Causation as It Relates to Demography and Population Studies." *Population and Development Review* 29(3): 459–69.

Smith, Noah. 2017. "College Isn't a Waste of Time: Higher Ed Does More than

Reassure Prospective Employers; It Teaches Skills Used for a Lifetime." *Bloomberg*, December 11.

Smock, Pamela J., and Fiona R. Greenland. 2010. "Diversity in Pathways to Parenthood: Patterns, Implications, and Emerging Research Directions." *Journal of Marriage and Family* 72(3): 576–93.

Smock, Pamela J., and Christine R. Schwartz. 2020. "The Demography of Families: A Review of Patterns and Change." *Journal of Marriage and Family* 82(1): 9–34.

Song, Xi, Jennie E. Brand, Xiuqi Yany, and Michael Lachanski. 2023. "When Occupations Disappear: Inequality in Mobility between Workers in Occupations with Job Expansion and Contraction." Working paper.

Spain, Daphne, and Suzanne Bianchi. 1996. *Balancing Act: Motherhood, Marriage, and Employment among American Women*. New York: Russell Sage Foundation.

Spence, Michael. 1973. "Job Market Signaling." *Quarterly Journal of Economics* 87(3): 355–74.

Sorokin, Pitrim. 1927. *Social Mobility*. New York: Harper Brothers.

Steinbaum, Marshall. 2017. "A Brown v. Board for Higher Ed." *Boston Review*, September 4.

Steinbery, Jacques. 2009. "Are Too Many Students Going to College?" *New York Times*, November 10.

Strauss, Valeria. 2011. "Kozol: I'm Sick of Begging Congress to Do the Right Thing." *Washington Post*, July 19.

Stuart, Elizabeth. 2010. "Matching Methods for Causal Inference: A Review and a Look Forward." *Statistical Science* 25(1): 1–21.

Stuber, Jenny M. 2011. *Inside the College Gates: How Class and Culture Matter in Higher Education*. Lanham, Md.: Lexington Books.

Sweeney, Megan. 2002. "Two Decades of Family Change: The Shifting Economic Foundations of Marriage." *American Sociological Review* 67(1): 132–47.

———. 2011. "Family Structure Instability and Educational Outcomes: A Focus on Families with Stepfathers." In *Whither Opportunity? Rising Inequality, Schools, and Children's Life Chances*, edited by Greg J. Duncan and Richard J. Murnane. New York: Russell Sage Foundation.

Sweeney, Megan M., and Julie A. Phillips. 2004. "Understanding Racial Differences in Marital Disruption: Recent Trends and Explanations." *Journal of Marriage and Family* 66(3): 639–50.

Tach, Laura, and Kathryn Edin. 2017. "The Social Safety Net after Welfare Reform: Recent Developments and Consequences for Household Dynamics." *Annual Review of Sociology* 43: 541–61.

Tamborini, Christopher R., ChangHwan Kim, and Arthur Sakamoto. 2015. "Education and Lifetime Earnings in the United States." *Demography* 52(4): 1383–1407.

Telles, Edward, and Vilma Ortiz. 2009. *Generations of Exclusion: Mexican Americans, Assimilation, and Race*. New York: Russell Sage Foundation.

Thompson, Derek. 2018. "Does It Matter Where you Go to College?" *Atlantic*, December 11.

Tilly, Charles. 1999. *Durable Inequality.* Berkeley: University of California Press.

Tolsma, Jochem, and Maarten H. J. Wolbers. 2014. "Social Origin and Occupational Success at Labour Market Entry in the Netherlands, 1931–80." *Acta Sociologica* 57(3): 253–69.

Tomaskovic-Devey, Donald, Dustin Avent-Holt, Catherine Zimmer, and Sandra Harding. 2009. "The Categorical Generation of Organizational Inequality: A Comparative Test of Tilly's Durable Inequality." *Research in Social Stratification and Mobility* 27(3): 128–42.

Torche, Florencia. 2011. "Is a College Degree Still the Great Equalizer? Intergenerational Mobility across Levels of Schooling in the United States." *American Journal of Sociology* 117(3): 763–807.

———. 2018. "Intergenerational Mobility at the Top of the Educational Distribution." *Sociology of Education* 9(4): 266–89.

Torche, Florencia, and Amy L. Johnson. 2019. "Education." In "State of the Union: Millennial Dilemma" (special issue of *Pathways: A Magazine on Poverty, Inequality, and Social Policy*). Stanford University, Stanford Center on Poverty and Inequality.

Tversky, Amos, and Daniel Kahneman. 1986. "Rational Choice and the Framing of Decisions." *Journal of Business* 59(4, pt. 2): S251–S78.

———. 1992. "Advances in Prospect Theory: Cumulative Representation of Uncertainty." *Journal of Risk and Uncertainty* 5: 297–323.

Upchurch, Dawn M., Lee A. Lillard, and Constantijn W. A. Panis. 2002. "Nonmarital Childbearing: Influences of Education, Marriage, and Fertility." *Demography* 39(2): 311–29.

U.S. Department of Education. 2018. "College Affordability and Completion: Ensuring a Pathway to Opportunity." June 3. https://www.ed.gov/sites/default/files/college-affordability-overview.pdf.

Vallet, Louis-André. 2004. *Change in Intergenerational Class Mobility in France from the 1970s to the 1990s and Its Explanation: An Analysis Following the CASMIN Approach.* New York: Oxford University Press.

Vedder, Richard. 2018. "Benefits of College—By Degrees." *Computer*, June.

Ventura, Stephanie J., and Christine A. Bachrach. 2000. "Nonmarital Childbearing in the United states, 1940–99." *National Vital Statistics Reports* 48(16). https://eric.ed.gov/?id=ed446210.

Verba, Sidney, Kay L. Schlozman, and Henry E. Brady. 1995. *Voice and Equality: Civic Voluntarism in American Politics.* Cambridge, Mass.: Harvard University Press.

Voss, Kim, Michael Hout, and Kristen George. 2022. "Persistent Inequalities in College Completion, 1980–2010." *Social Problems* 00(March): 1–29.

Walters, Christopher R. 2018. "The Demand for Effective Charter Schools." *Journal of Political Economy* 126(6): 2179–2223.

Webber, Douglas. 2016. "Are College Costs Worth It? How Ability, Major, and Debt Affect the Returns to Schooling." *Economics of Education Review* 53(August): 296–310.

———. 2018. "Is College Worth It? Going beyond Averages." *Third Way*, September 18.

———. 2019. "The Advantages of Getting into a Name-Brand College Are Wildly Overblown." *Washington Post*, March 17.

Weeden, Kimberly A. 2002. "Why Do Some Occupations Pay More than Others? Social Closure and Earnings Inequality in the United States." *American Journal of Sociology* 108(1): 55–101.

Weeden, Kimberly A., and David B. Grusky. 2012. "The Three Worlds of Inequality." *American Journal of Sociology* 117(6): 1723–85.

Weiss, Andrew. 1995. "Human Capital vs. Signalling Explanations of Wages." *Journal of Economic Perspectives* 9(4): 133–54.

Wen, Frangqi, Erik H. Wang, and Michael Hout. 2023. "Social Mobility in the Tang Dynasty as the Imperial Examination Rose and Aristocratic Family Pedigree Declined, 618-907 CE." Working paper.

Wermund, Benjamin. 2017. "In Trump Country, a University Confronts Its Skeptics." *Politico*, November 9. https://www.politico.com/story/2017/11/09/university-of-michigan-admissions-low-income-244420.

Western, Bruce, Deirdre Bloome, Benjamin Sosnaud, and Laura Tach. 2012. "Economic Insecurity and Social Stratification." *Annual Review of Sociology* 38(1): 341–59.

Western, Bruce, and Jake Rosenfeld. 2011. "Unions, Norms, and the Rise in U.S. Wage Inequality." *American Sociological Review* 74(4): 513–37.

Whistle, Wesley, and Tamra Hiler. 2018. "The Pell Divide: How Four-Year Institutions Are Failing to Graduate Low- and Moderate-Income Students." *Third Way*, May 3.

White House, The. 2010. "Remarks by the President in State of the Union Address." Office of the Press Secretary, January 27. https://obamawhitehouse.archives.gov/the-press-office/remarks-president-state-union-address.

Will, David. 2014. "Many People Shouldn't Go to College." *Daily Princetonian*, February 6.

Williams, Mary Elizabeth. 2019. "Why College Students Are 'Paying the Price' for Their Education." *Salon*, May 29.

Willis, Paul E. 1981. *Learning to Labor: How Working-Class Kids Get Working Class Jobs*. New York: Columbia University Press.

Willis, Robert J., and Sherwin Rosen. 1979. "Education and Self-Selection." *Journal of Political Economy* 87(5, pt. 2): S7–S36.

Wilson, John. 2000. "Volunteering." *Annual Review of Sociology* 26: 215–40.

Wilson, Michael J. 2010. "Are Too Many People Going to College?" *HuffPost*, March 18. https://www.huffpost.com/entry/are-too-many-people-going_b_384538.

Wilson, Valerie, and William M. Rodgers III. 2016. "Black-White Wage Gaps Expand with Rising Wage Inequality." Economic Policy Institute, September 20.

Wilson, William Julius. 1987. *The Truly Disadvantaged: The Inner City, the Underclass, and Public Policy.* Chicago: University of Chicago Press.

Witteveen, Dirk, and Paul Attewell. 2017. "Family Background and Earnings Inequality among College Graduates." *Social Forces* 95(4): 1539–76.

———. 2020. "Reconsidering 'the Meritocratic Power of a College Degree.'" *Research in Social Stratification and Mobility* 66(April): 100479.

Wolfe, Barbara L., and Robert H. Haveman. 1984. "Schooling and Economic Well-being: The Role of Nonmarket Effects." *Journal of Human Resources* 19(3): 377–407.

Wolfe, Dael. 1954. *America's Resources of Specialized Talent.* New York: Harper and Brothers.

Wright, Richard. 1945. *Black Boy.* New York: Harper Brothers.

Xie, Yu. 2007. "Otis Dudley Duncan's Legacy: The Demographic Approach to Quantitative Reasoning in Social Science." *Research in Social Stratification and Mobility* 25(2): 141–56.

———. 2011. "Causal Inference and Heterogeneity Bias in Social Science." *Information Knowledge Systems Management* 10(1–4): 279–89.

Xie, Yu, Jennie E. Brand, and Ben Jann. 2012. "Estimating Heterogeneous Treatment Effects with Observational Data." *Sociological Methodology* 42(1): 314–47.

Xie, Yu, James M. Raymo, Kimberly Goyette, and Arland Thornton. 2003. "Economic Potential and Entry into Marriage and Cohabitation." *Demography* 40(2): 351–67.

Xie, Yu, and Xiaogang Wu. 2005. "Market Premium, Social Process, and Statisticism." *American Sociological Review* 70(5): 865–70.

Yang, Yang, and S. Philip Morgan. 2003. "How Big Are Educational and Racial Fertility Differentials in the U.S.?" *Social Biology* 50(3/4): 167–87.

Young, Allison, and Stefanie DeLuca. Forthcoming. "'I Don't Want to Rush Everything and End Up Where I Started': Disadvantaged Black Youth and the Decision to Delay College." *Social Forces.*

Young, Michael Dunlop. 1958. *The Rise of Meritocracy, 1877–2033.* London: Penguin Books.

Zajacova, Anna, and Elizabeth M. Lawrence. 2018. "The Relationship between Education and Health: Reducing Disparities through a Contextual Approach." *Annual Review of Public Health* 39: 273–89.

Zaloom, Caitlin. 2019. "How Paying for College Is Changing the Middle Class: When Getting a Degree Is Seen as a Moral Obligation, Families Will Spend Whatever It Takes." *New York Times,* August 30.

Zeglen, Julie. 2019. "College Is Creating Poverty, so Let's Make It Free, Says Temple's Sara Goldrick-Rab." *Technical.ly,* July 15.

Zhou, Xiang. 2019. "Equalization or Selection? Reassessing the 'Meritocratic Power' of Schooling in Intergenerational Income Mobility." *American Sociological Review* 84(3): 459–85.

———. 2021. "Semiparametric Estimation for Causal Mediation Analysis with Multiple Causally Ordered Mediators." *Journal of the Royal Statistical Society Series B: Statistical Methodology* 84(3): 794–821.

Zhou, Xiang, and Guanghui Pan. 2021. "Higher Education and the Black-White Earnings Gap." *American Sociological Review* 88(1): 154–88.

Zhou, Xiang, and Yu Xie. 2019. "Marginal Treatment Effects from a Propensity Score Perspective." *Journal of Political Economy* 127(6): 3070–84.

———. 2020. "Heterogeneous Treatment Effects in the Presence of Self-selection: A Propensity Score Perspective." *Sociological Methodology* 50(1): 350–85.

Zimmerman, Seth D. 2014. "The Returns to College Admission for Academically Marginal Students." *Journal of Labor Economics* 32(4): 711–54.

Zühlke, Anne, Philipp Kugler, and Tim Ruberg. 2022. "Heterogeneity in Long-Term Returns to Education: An Inconvenient Truth." IAW Discussion Paper 141. Tübingen: University of Tübingen, Institute for Applied Economic Research (October).

Index

Tables and figures are listed in **boldface**.

Abadie, Alberto, 228*n*65, 238*n*89
Adams, John, 38–39
Addams, Jane, 36–37, 175
Addo, Fenaba, 253*n*83
Ahearn, Caitlin, 178
Almond, Gabriel, 175–76
American Community Survey (ACS), 15
American Council on Education, 30
American National Election Studies (ANES), 248*n*35
Angrist, Joshua D., 65, 199–200, 227*n*50
Ansolabehere, Stephen, 248*n*36
"Are Too Many Students Going to College?" (Baum), 45–46
Armed Services Vocational Aptitude Battery (ASVAB) scores: civic engagement and, 184; earnings and wage outcomes and, 108–9, 114–15; family-level outcomes and, 140, 144; likelihood of college completion and, 91–93, **95–96**; social assistance and, 165; unequal college chances and, 82–83, 236–37*nn*72–73, 237*n*76
Armstrong, Elizabeth, 49, 51, 134
Arum, Richard, 226*n*22
Attewell, Paul, 26, 33, 100–101, 133, 195
Autor, David, 13, 207

Backes, Benjamin, 26
Bailey, Martha, 233*n*20
Barron's Profiles of American Colleges, 15, 218*n*100
Barrow, Lisa, 28
Bartik, Tim, 28–29, 47–48
Bataille, Pierre, 221*n*57
Baum, Sandy, 10, 12
BEA (Bureau of Economic Analysis), 15, 68
Becker, Gary, 23
Bell, Daniel, 72, 233*n*8
benefits of college completion, 19, 22–40; beyond economic returns, 4–5, 36–40, 203–6, 251*n*57, 251*nn*59–60, 252*n*61, 252*n*62; college completion as an equalizer and, 29–34, **31**, 116–27, **119**, **121–27**, 193; economic returns, 11–15, 25–29, 202; holistic view of, 4–5; increase in, 2, 213*n*6; overview, 19–21, **20**; positive and negative selection theories, 23–25; self-selection and economic motivation, 34–35; surveys used to determine, 5–6
Berent, Matthew, 246*n*23
Bialik, Carl, 28
Biddle, Rishawn, 207
Black Boy (Wright), 32
Blair, Peter, 14
Blau, Peter, 4, 64, 71–73, 86
Bloome, Deidre, 31, 217*n*75
BLS (Bureau of Labor Statistics), 5, 11, 68. *See also headings at* National Longitudinal Survey of Youth
Bourdieu, Pierre, 24, 80
Brand, Jennie E., 238*n*86, 240*n*19
Breen, Richard, 221*n*57, 222*n*73, 231*n*99
Broh, Beckett, 221*n*55
Bruch, Elizabeth, 219*n*14
Bukodi, Erzsebet, 233*n*8
Bunch, Will, 206
Bureau of Economic Analysis (BEA), 15, 68

Bureau of Labor Statistics (BLS), 5, 11, 68. *See also headings at* National Longitudinal Survey of Youth

Caplan, Bryan, 47, 226*n*23
Card, David, 27, 100, 220*n*31
Carneiro, Pedro, 219*n*7, 234–35*n*40
Carter, Prudence, 38, 79–80
causal inference, 41–45, 54, 60, 66–67, 191, 225*n*3, 225*n*9
causal trees, 62–63, 231*n*93
Cheng, Siwei, 28–29
Chetty, Raj, 29, 30–31, 75, 81, 133, 226*n*18, 234*n*23
Choi, Seongsoo, 231*n*99
civic engagement, 20–21, 174–90; college completion effects on, 175–78, 246–47*n*23, 246*n*14, 246*n*16, 247*n*25; disadvantaged students and, 180–84, **181–83**, 248*nn*39–40; education and democracy, 38–39; equalizing effect of college completion, 185–90, **185–89**, 248*nn*41–44; participation measures of, 178–80, 247*n*34, 248*nn*34–38
Civil Rights Act (1964), 8
Clampet-Lundquist, Susan, 78
Cochran, William, 227*n*49
Coelli, Michael, 245*n*10
college admissions, 238*n*84
college completion effects: assessing variation in, 60–63; college as equalizer, 29–34, **31**; distinguishing levels from effects, 51–54, **53**; identifying, 54–57, **56**; interpreting variation in, 63–66; matched vignettes for, 67–69, **69**; methods for estimating, 57–60, **59**; robustness checks and sensitivity analyses, 66–67, 232*n*107
college completion rates: criticism of college and, 3; educational expansion and, 2, 202; family structure and, 81, 236*n*61; over time, 6–8, **7**; socioeconomic status and, 8–9, 18, 203, 251*n*47
college counterfactuals: comparisons vs., 45–51; explained, 41–42; life outcomes for college graduates and, 3–4; potential outcome model and, 42–45, **44**
college enrollment: COVID-19 pandemic and, 9, 251*n*48, 253*n*82; declines in, 9; public colleges and universities, 253*nn*81–82; of racial and ethnic minorities, 235*n*42, 235*n*50, 235*nn*47–48; standardized test scores and, 237*n*73
"College May Not Be Worth It Anymore: For the Poor, Higher Education May Hurt More than It Helps" (Shell), 47
Collins, Randall, 13, 217*n*75
community colleges, 7, 75, 79, 214*n*21, 234*n*37
comparative advantage theory, 23, 200, 240*n*24
Converse, Philip Ernest, 176
Cottom, Tressie McMillam, 214*n*26
COVID-19 pandemic: college enrollment declines and, 9, 251*n*48, 253*n*82; educational inequalities and, 78, 251*n*48
Crow, Michael, 206
cultural capital, 80–81, 199, 235–36*nn*55–56. *See also* elite culture
Cunningham, Alisa, 206, 251*n*57

Dale, Stacy, 29, 32
Davis, Dwight, 133–34
decision trees, 62–63, 231*n*93
Dee, Thomas, 177
Delbanco, Andrew, 36, 175, 197–98, 205, 218*n*94, 247*n*33
DeLuca, Stefanie, 35, 78, 116
Deming, David, 10, 12, 14, 31, 100, 210
democracy, 38–39, 175, 206, 211
Department of Education, U.S., 14
Department of Labor, U.S., 5
Desmond, Matthew, 100
Dewey, John, 37, 39
DiPrete, Thomas, 235*n*50
disadvantaged students: civic engagement and, 180–84, **181–83**, 247*n*33, 248*nn*39–40; college completion as an equalizer for, 29–34, **31**, 52–54, **53**, 100–101, 116–27, **119**, **121–27**, 193, 221–22*n*57, 240*n*16; college completion rates of, 8–9, 18; college experience, inequality in, 49–51, 203, 208–10, 251*n*48; COVID-19 pandemic and, 251*n*48; criticisms of college attendance for, 3, 25, 45–48; economic returns on college completion for, 25–29, 108–13, **111–12**, 128–29, 220*n*31, 221*n*37; educational choice and, 24, 66, 219*n*14; family-level outcomes and, 133–34; food and housing insecurity of, 50, 78, 234*n*37; resource allocation and benefits for, 198–

99; self-selection and economic motivation, 34–35, 194–98, 223*n*88, 224*n*92, 249*nn*8–9; social assistance reductions and, 160–66, **162–64**, 166; social mobility and access to college, 26, 214*n*26, 217*n*75; student loans and inequality, 209, 253*n*83; value of college for, 45–46, 192–93, 226*n*18; vocational schools and, 11, 47. *See also* unequal college chances

discrimination. *See* racism

Downey, Douglas, 221*n*55, 236*n*70

Doyle, William, 177–78

Du Bois, W.E.B., 36, 39–40, 175, 254*n*108

Duncan, Otis Dudley, 4, 64, 71–73, 86

Durkheim, Émile, 175

Dyer, Shauna, 31, 217*n*75

Dynarski, Susan, 100, 200, 208, 233*n*20, 252*n*78, 253*n*96

earnings and wages, 19–20, 98–129; circumventing disadvantage for unlikely graduates, 109–16, **111–15**; college completion and increases in, 11–15, 29–34, **31**, 52–54, **53**, 104–9, **107–8**, 193, 202, 221–22*n*57; college completion effects on, 99–103; equalizing effects of college completion for, 116–27, **119**, **121–27**; of high school vs. college graduates, 2, 11, 14–15, 33, 99, 202, 216*n*61, 218*n*94, 223*n*77; human capital theory and, 28–29; low- vs. high-income college student outcomes, 46–48; as motivation to attend college, 34–35, 223*n*88, 224*n*92; NLSY79, wage levels of high school and college graduates from, 52–54, **53**; racial and ethnic minorities, 26, 48–49, 101, 108–9, 114–16, 223*n*82; unlikely college graduates and benefits of college, 25–29, 220*n*31, 221*n*37. *See also* family-level outcomes

Economic Report of the President (2003), 209

Edin, Kathryn, 78, 132, 159

educational aspirations and expectations, 84, 132, 237–38*n*82, 237*nn*79–80

educational expansion: criticisms of, 2–3, 10–11, 45–48, 204, 207, 213–14*nn*10–11; defined, 6; economic rewards of, 11–15, 202; equalizing effects of college completion and, 31, 100–101, 116–27, **119**, **121–27**, 129, 240*n*19; history of, 6–11, **7**; policy recommendations for, 93–97, 206–10, 239*nn*94–95, 254*n*108; representative data from NLSY cohorts and, 15–18, **17**; social mobility and, 8, 214*n*26, 215*n*31, 217*n*75. *See also* unequal college chances

Einstein, Albert, 67

Elementary and Secondary Education Act (ESEA, 1965), 236*n*71

elite colleges and universities: college experience for disadvantaged students and, 49–50, 208; corporate recruiters, access to, 223*n*82; defined, 218*n*100, 239*n*92; limits on equalizing effect of college completion and, 33–34; socioeconomic status of students and, 29, 75, 78, 87, 234*n*23, 234*n*28

elite culture: civic engagement and, 177; class boundaries and higher education, 25; cultural and social capital from, 80–81, 199, 235–36*nn*55–56; economic motivation differences and, 35, 223*n*89; economic return on college completion, 28–29; educational choice and, 24, 66, 219*n*12, 219*n*14; education as luxury reserved for, 37, 208, 211; employment access and, 13, 33; family-level outcomes and, 133–34, 243*n*29; family resources and future success, 49, 192, 249*n*1; residential environments and, 81; skills and networking attained through, 13–14, 32

Eller, Christina Ciocca, 235*n*50

Emerson, Ralph Waldo, 36

employment: college degree required for, 13–14, 32–33, 51, 209, 217*n*77, 253*n*91; equalizing effect of college for, 32, 222*nn*73–74; job polarization and, 100; low-wage and low-skilled, 33, 111–14, **112**, **114**, 116, 121–24, **122–23**, **126–27**, 241*n*29, 241*n*32; racism and, 34, 222*n*75, 223*n*82; social assistance and, 158–59, 244*n*3; stability of, 111–12, **112**, 114, **115**, 124, **127**. *See also* job skills; unemployment rates

England, Paula, 237*n*77

Equal Opportunity Project, 214*n*26

ethnic minorities. *See* racial and ethnic minorities

Falcon, Julie, 221*n*57
family-level outcomes, 20, 130–56; college completion effects on, 131–34; equalizing effect of college completion, 146–55, **148–49**, **151–55**; high- vs. low-likelihood graduates and, 137–46, **139**, **141**, **145–46**, 244*n*42–46; marriage and household income, 135–37, 243–44*nn*38–41; poverty prevention and, 155–56
family structure, 81, 116, 236*n*61
federal student aid program, 8, 9–10, 75, 208, 214*n*26, 219*n*17
Feinberg, Fred, 219*n*14
Fisher, Irving, 35
Fisher, Ronald A., 225*n*5
for-profit institutions, 75, 214*n*26, 215*n*42, 252*n*78
Forster, Andrea, 220*n*23
Fraga, Bernard, 248*n*36
Friedman, John, 31

Gaddis, Michael, 223*n*86
Gallup, 222*n*74
Gelman, Andrew, 225*n*9
gender: college completion rates and, 236*n*61; college enrollment rates and, 235*n*42; earnings outcomes and, 106; family-level outcomes and income, 132–34, 241–42*n*7, 242*n*9, 242*n*15, 243*n*29; positive and negative selection theories and, 220*n*23
General Social Survey, 30
Gibson-Davis, Christina, 132
Gilman, Daniel, 37
Giroux, Henry, 38, 175, 204–5
Goldin, Claudia, 8, 27, 38
Goldrick-Rab, Sara, 201, 209
Goldthorpe, John, 25, 32, 221–22*n*57, 233*n*8, 235*n*55
government trust. *See* civic engagement
graduate degrees, 29, 87, 107, 222*n*59
Great Recession (2007–2009), 9–10, 12
Green, David, 245*n*10
Greenwald, Richard, 10, 209
Griliches, Zvi, 220*n*31
Groot, Wim, 246*n*14, 247*n*25
Grubb, Norton, 198

Haavelmo, Trygve, 225*n*5
Habibi, Nader, 47
Halaby, Charles, 29, 66
Hamilton, Laura, 49, 51, 134
Hansen, Karsen, 219*n*7
Harding, David, 58
health benefits of education, 218*n*102, 224*n*113
Heckman, James, 23, 26, 38, 57, 84, 159, 177, 200, 219*n*7, 219*n*14, 234–35*n*40
HEGIS (Higher Education General Information Survey), 68
Helliwell, John, 246*n*16
Henderson, Daniel, 26
Hendren, Nathanial, 81
Hershbein, Brad, 28–29, 47–48
Hertel, Florian, 30
Higher Education Act (1965), 8, 10
Higher Education General Information Survey (HEGIS), 15, 68
Hillygus, Sunshine, 177
Historically Black Colleges and Universities (HBCUs), 8
Holland, Paul W., 225*n*5
Holm, Anders, 231*n*99
Holzer, Harry, 26
Houle, Jason, 253*n*83
Hout, Michael, 13, 27, 28, 29–30, 199–202, 206, 209, 249–50*n*19
Hoxby, Caroline, 75
Huang, Jian, 246*n*14, 247*n*25
human capital: defined, 218*n*1; earnings of high school vs. college graduates and, 99; economic benefits of college and, 12–13; increasing through education funding, 210; return on, 23, 219*n*7; theory of, 28–29, 132
Humphries, John Eric, 38, 177, 200

Iacus, Stefano, 228*n*64
Imbens, Guido, 43, 58, 228*n*65, 229*n*72, 238*n*89
inequality. *See* unequal college chances

Jack, Anthony, 32, 49–50, 51, 78, 81
Jackson, Kirabo, 200
Jackson, Michelle, 25, 32, 221–22*n*57
Jaeger, Mads Meier, 199, 235–36*n*56
Janus, Alexander, 209
Jefferson, Thomas, 36, 38–39
job skills: critical thinking and, 14, 217*n*79, 251*n*52; elite culture exposure vs. college attendance, 13–14, 32, 217*n*77; high school vs. college graduates and, 226*n*22; socioemotional and psychosocial, 83–84, 200, 237*n*77

Johnson, Amy, 15
Jonsson, Jan O., 222*n*73
Junn, Jane, 246*n*16

Kahneman, Daniel, 25
Kalleberg, Arne, 14, 100
Kam, Cindy, 247*n*25
Karlson, Kristian, 199, 235–36*n*56
Katz, Lawrence, 8, 27, 38
Kefalas, Maria, 132
Keohane, Robert, 67
Kerr, Clark, 214*n*21
King, Gary, 43, 67, 228*n*64, 229*n*72
Kozol, Jonathan, 39, 198
Krosnick, Jon, 246*n*23
Krueger, Alan, 29, 32, 208

Lareau, Annette, 80
Lee, Kee Yeun, 219*n*14
Leonhardt, David, 28, 209, 210
Leopold, Thomas, 220*n*23
Lipset, Seymour, 201
locus of control, 237*n*79
Lupia, Arthur, 246*n*23

Malamud, Ofer, 28
Manski, Charles, 233*n*19
"Many People Shouldn't Go to College" (Will), 47
Mare, Robert, 34
Marks, Jonathan, 252*n*61
marriage. *See* family-level outcomes
Martin, Elizabeth, 236*n*70
Marx, Karl, 80
matched vignettes, 67–69, **69**, 232*n*109, 232*nn*112–14
matching methods, 57–60, **59**, 86, 228–29*nn*68–70, 228*n*64, 228*n*66, 229*n*75, 229*nn*72–73, 230*nn*78–80
McGuire, Patricia, 206
McLanahan, Sara, 132
meritocracy, 30, 72–73, 201, 222*n*73, 232–33*n*4
Mill, John Stuart, 37, 225*n*3
minorities. *See* gender; racial and ethnic minorities
Moore, Ravaris L., 238*n*86
Moretti, Enrico, 251*n*59
Morgan, Stephen, 58, 199
Morrill Act (1862), 8
mothers' education levels. *See* parents' education levels
Murray, Charles, 45–46, 219*n*10
Musick, Kelly, 133
Musk, Elon, 42

National Center for Education Statistics (NCES), 214*n*20
National Longitudinal Survey of Youth 1979 (NLSY79): civic engagement and, 177–82, **181**, 186–90, **189**; college attendance and completion by characteristics, 75, **76**, 233–34*nn*18–20, 235*n*41; college completion rates and, 7–9; college-prep courses and standardized test scores, 83, 237*n*76; earnings outcomes of, 11, 101–3, 106–7, **107**, 118–23, **119**, **121–23**; family-level outcomes of, 143–44, **145**, 147–51, **148–49**, **151–52**; likelihood of college completion, 86–93, **88–89**, **91**, **93**, **95**, 238–39*nn*90–91; likelihood of college completion, estimating, 84–85; overview, 5–6; parents' education levels, 80; racial and ethnic minorities, educational gaps for, 79, 235*n*41; representative data from, 15–18, **17**; self-esteem and, 84; skills and achievements in school, 82; social assistance for, 159–62, **162–63**, 166–68, **167–70**; summary of results, 195, **196**; wage levels of high school and college graduates, 52–54, **53**, 227*nn*46–47
National Longitudinal Survey of Youth 1997 (NLSY97): civic engagement and, 177–80, **182–83**, 182–84, **185–89**, 185–90; college attendance and completion by characteristics, 75, **77**, 233–34*nn*18–20, 235*n*41; college completion effects and, 113–14, **113–15**, 241*n*29; college completion rates and, 7–9; earnings outcomes of, 11, 101–3, 108, **108**, 124, **125–27**; family-level outcomes of, 144, **146**, 152–55, **153–55**; likelihood of college completion, 86–93, **88**, **90**, **92**, **94**, **96**, 238–39*nn*90–91; likelihood of college completion, estimating, 85–86; overview, 5–6; parents' education levels, 80; racial and ethnic minorities, educational gaps for, 79; representative data from, 15–18, **17**; skills and achievements in school, 82; social assistance for, 160, 162, **164**, 165, 168–70, **171–72**; summary of results, 195, **196**

National Longitudinal Surveys (NLS) program, 5, 214*n*15, 248*n*35, 248*nn*37–38
Navarro-Lozano, Salvador, 57
NCES (National Center for Education Statistics), 214*n*20
negative selection, 22–25, 35, 65, 198–200, 220*n*23, 231*n*99, 249–50*n*19, 249*n*4, 250*n*32
Neyman, Jerzy, 225*n*5
Nie, Norman, 177, 246*n*16
Nielsen, Richard, 229*n*72

Obama, Barack, 158
O-E-D triangle, 71–72, **71**, 232*n*3
Oreopoulos, Philip, 202, 245*n*10

Palmer, Carl, 247*n*25
parental income. *See* socioeconomic status
parents' education levels: children's school success and, 78; civic engagement and, 184; earnings and wage outcomes, 114–16; family-level outcomes and, 140, 144; graduate degrees and, 222*n*59; likelihood of college completion and, 90–91, **91–92**; social assistance and, 165; unequal college chances and, 80–81
Pearl, Judea, 43
Petronijevic, Uros, 202
Pew Research Center, 12, 226*n*22, 240*n*16
Pfeffer, Fabian, 30, 233*n*20
Pischke, Jörn-Steffen, 65, 227*n*50
Polachek, Solomon, 26
policy recommendations, 93–97, 206–10, 239*nn*94–95, 254*n*108
political engagement. *See* civic engagement
Population Reference Bureau, 223*n*77
Porro, Giuseppe, 228*n*64
positive selection, 22–25, 26, 33, 34–35, 66, 220*n*23, 249*n*4, 249*n*8
potential outcome model, 42–45, **44**, 55–56, 225*n*5, 225*n*7
poverty. *See* socioeconomic status
prospect theory, 25
psychosocial skills. *See* socioemotional and psychosocial skills
public colleges and universities: disinvestment in, 9–10, 201, 205, 208–9, 215*n*41, 216*n*51, 251*n*54, 252*n*78; enrollment rates of, 253*nn*81–82; key funding sources for, 252–53*nn*79–80; tuition increases and, 209, 253*n*84, 253*n*91
public school districts, 82, 198–200, 202–3, 236*nn*70–71, 250*n*25
Putnam, Robert, 176, 246*n*14, 246*n*16

racial and ethnic minorities: affirmative action programs for, 8, 29, 46, 216*n*51; civic engagement and, 184, 247*n*33; college experience, inequality for, 49–50, 208; economic return on college completion for, 26, 48–49, 101, 108–9, 114–16, 223*n*82; educational aspirations and expectations, 84; educational choice and, 24; educational gaps and barriers to college completion, 63, 79, 235*n*42, 235*n*45, 235*n*50, 235*nn*47–48; elite college attendance and, 29, 49; family-level outcomes and income, 133–34, 140–41, 144; likelihood of college completion and, 91, **93–94**; networking and employment opportunities through college and, 32; resource allocation and benefits for, 199; skills and achievements in school and college completion, 83; social assistance and, 165–66; student loans and inequality, 253*n*83; wealth gap and, 50, 227*n*38
racism: antidiscrimination policies and, 8; degree credentials and reductions in, 32, 222*n*73; diversity of campuses and disinvestment in state schools, 10, 216*n*51; of employers, 34, 222*n*75, 223*n*82; residential environments and, 81; restricting access to education and, 254*n*108
Rackin, Heather, 132
Rauscher, Emily, 199
Rawlings, Hunter, 37
"The Rising Cost of Not Going to College" (Pew Research Center), 226*n*22
Rivera, Lauren, 34
robustness checks, 66–67, 183, 232*n*107
Roksa, Josipa, 226*n*22
Rose, Mike, 39
Rosen, Sherwin, 23
Rosenbaum, James, 237*n*82
Rosenbaum, Paul, 57–58, 61
Rosenberg self-esteem scale, 237*n*79
Roth, Michael, 37, 204, 206
Rothstein, Jesse, 236*n*70
Rotter Locus of Control scale, 237*n*79
Roy, Andrew, 225*n*5
Rubin, Donald, 42–43, 55, 57–58, 61, 225*n*3, 225*n*8

Salganik, Mathew, 238*n*88
Salvanes, Kjell, 245*n*10
Sampson, Robert, 246*n*14
Sander, Richard, 46
Schaffner, Brian, 248*n*36
Schwartz, Christine, 133
Second Morrill Act (1890), 8
selection bias, 27, 55, 63–66, 227*n*50, 231*n*99, 241–42*n*7
self-esteem, 84, 237*n*79
self-reporting accuracy, 246–47*n*23, 248*n*37, 248*n*40
self-selection, 34–35
sensitivity analyses, 67, 107–8, 140, 144, 195, 232*n*107, 240*n*24
Shen, Yifen, 199, 200
Shinkre, Tanvi, 238*n*86
single-parent households. *See* family-level outcomes
Skinner, Benjamin, 177–78
Small, Mario, 50
Smith, Herbert, 60
Smock, Pamela, 133
social assistance reductions, 20–21, 157–73; college completion effects on, 157–59; equalizing effect of college completion for, 166–70, **167–72**; public education investment and, 210; socioeconomic status and, 200; unlikely graduates and, 160–66, **162–64**
social capital, 12–13, 80–81, 235–36*nn*55–56, 246*n*16
social control, 116, 184, 237*n*79
social mobility: educational expansion and, 8, 214*n*26, 215*n*31, 217*n*75; education and, 26, 29–33, 71–73, 156, 209–10, 232*n*1; elite college access and, 208; family-level outcomes and, 134; meritocracy and, 72–73; residential environments and, 81–82, 236*n*70
social reproduction, 71–73, 80–81, 129, 203, 208, 210–11
socioeconomic status: civic engagement and, 184; college completion rates and, 8–9, 18, 203, 251*n*47; economic return on college completion, 28, 158; educational choice and, 24–25; educational gaps for racial and ethnic minorities, 79; elite college attendance and, 29, 75, 78, 87, 234*n*23, 234*n*28; financial aid and access to higher education, 8, 9; of high school vs. college graduates, 12, 100–101, 240*n*16; labor market trajectories and, 15; outcomes for low- vs. high-income college students, 46–48; parental income and children's school success, 78; propensity to complete college and, 62, 231*n*90; resource allocation and, 198–99; social assistance and, 165, 244*n*3, 245*n*10; student loans and inequality, 209, 253*n*83; unequal access to college and, 4, 7–8, 203. *See also* disadvantaged students; elite culture; family-level outcomes; unequal college chances
socioemotional and psychosocial skills, 83–84, 200, 237*n*77
status attainment model (Blau & Duncan), 4, 71, 73, 233*n*13
Stehlik-Barry, Kenneth, 246*n*16
Stover, Dink, 252*n*62
Stover at Yale (Stover), 252*n*62
Stuart, Elizabeth, 58
student loans: creation of, 10; debt resulting from, 2, 46–47, 78, 201, 215*n*46; disadvantaged students and, 209, 253*n*83; disinvestment in state schools and increase in, 9–10; for-profit institutions and, 215*n*42; long-term economic rewards of, 22, 35, 39; repayment crises, 252*n*78
Sweeney, Megan, 133

Tach, Laura, 159
Taylor, Stuart, 46
Thompson, Derek, 29, 208
Torche, Florencia, 15, 30, 195, 222*n*59, 222*n*73
tuition rates, 9–10, 209, 215*n*42, 253*n*84, 253*n*91
Tversky, Amos, 25

unconfoundedness assumption, 56–57, 227*n*52, 228*n*55
unemployment rates: college completion effects on, 110–11, **111**, **113**, 113–14, 116, 120–21, **121–22**, 124, **125–26**, 241*n*29; of high school vs. college graduates, 2, 11–12, 100, 213*n*2, 216*n*65, 239*n*6; reemployment opportunities, 218*n*89
unequal college chances, 19, 70–97; likelihood of college completion, estimating, 84–87; policy recommendations, 93–97, 206–10; social origins associated with

unequal college chances (*cont.*)
skills and achievements, 82–84; social origins model and, 71–73, **71**; social origins patterns and, 73–82, **74**, **76–77**; socioeconomic status and, 4, 7–8, 203; trajectories and characteristics by likelihood of college completion, 87–93, **88–96**
unlikely college graduates. *See* disadvantaged students
upward mobility. *See* social mobility
U.S. Census Bureau, 26, 100

van den Brink, Henriette Maassen, 246*n*14, 247*n*25
van de Werfhorst, Herman, 220*n*23
Vedder, Richard, 46–47
Vehtari, Aki, 225*n*9
Velez, Erin Dunlop, 26
Veramendi, Gregory, 38, 177, 200
Verba, Sidney, 67, 175–76
vocational schools: college degrees and, 204; critical thinking skills and, 251*n*52; disadvantaged students and, 7, 11, 47; marketization of higher education and, 205; narrow subject matter of, 36–39; sorting students for, 224*n*107
volunteering. *See* civic engagement
von Hippel, Paul, 221*n*55
voting. *See* civic engagement

Walters, Christopher, 200, 250*n*25
Wang, Le, 26
Warburton, William, 245*n*10
Webber, Douglas, 32, 101, 202
Weber, Max, 80
welfare. *See* social assistance reductions
Willis, Robert, 23
Wilson, John, 176
Winship, Christopher, 50
Winters, Marcus, 202
Witteveen, Dirk, 33
Wolfe, Dael, 237*n*73
Wright, Richard, 32

Xie, Yu, 24, 25, 28, 34–35, 65, 231*n*99, 240*n*19

Yankelovich, Daniel, 33
Yoon, Aimee, 236*n*70
Young, Michael Dunlop, 232–33*n*4

Zhou, Xiang, 28, 31, 33, 178, 217*n*75
Zimmerman, Seth, 27–28, 207, 210